AF576703

Soldiers Serving the Nation

Editor
General Gordon R. Sullivan
U.S. Army Chief of Staff

Art Editor
Marylou Gjernes
Army Art Curator

Center of Military History
United States Army
Washington, D.C., 1995

U.S. Army Center of Military History

Brig. Gen. John W. Mountcastle, Chief of Military History

Chief Historian	Jeffrey J. Clarke
Chief, Museum Division	Judson E. Bennett, Jr.
Editor in Chief	John W. Elsberg

Col. Raymond K. Bluhm (USA, Ret.), former chief of the Center's Historical Services Division, drafted the four section introductions and was instrumental in many other ways in the production of this book.

Library of Congress Cataloging-in-Publication Data

Soldiers Serving the Nation / editor, Gordon R. Sullivan ; art editor, Marylou Gjernes.
p. cm.
Companion volume to : Portrait of an army. 1991
1. Soldiers—United States—Pictorial works. 2. United States—Armed Forces—Foreign countries—Pictorial works. 3. United States—History, Military—Pictorial works. 4. United States. Army—Art collections—Catalogs. 5. Soldiers in art—Catalogs.
I. Sullivan, Gordon R., 1937–
UA25 .S67 1995
355' .00973—dc20 94-48597
CIP

First Printing—CMH Pub 70–61

For sale by the U.S. Government Printing Office
Superintendent of Documents, Mail Stop: SSOP, Washington, DC 20402-9328
ISBN 0-16-045496-4

Foreword

SHORTLY AFTER I BECAME CHIEF OF STAFF OF THE ARMY I visited the Civil War cemetery at Sharpsburg, Maryland. The simple monument to the soldier which dominates that site made a lasting impression. It bears a brief but moving inscription: "Not for themselves but for their country." Those words capture for me the essence of the selfless service that I have seen around me every day that I have worn the Army's uniform.

My own studies have confirmed my belief that this level of commitment has characterized our soldiers throughout this nation's history in all the many and distant places where they have served. This book is the result. Using the unique perspective of art, particularly art created in the field by soldier-artists, it depicts the fundamental strength, skills, resilience, and underlying individuality of the American soldier—from militiamen and volunteers through regulars and reserves. Although far from providing a complete picture, the images that follow highlight the human face of America's Army.

The art in this book presents a powerful record of an Army on the move. Indeed, the painting on the dust jacket, entitled "We Move Again," in many ways captures the essence of the soldier's life. Soldiers clearly do not always know what lies around the next bend, but individual courage and confidence in their commanders allow them to keep moving forward. They accept their responsibility and do their duty as well as they can despite the uncertainties—not for themselves, but for their country.

Central to the success of a democratic society is the concept of shared responsibility—between appointed and elected officials and the American people, and between professional military leaders and the individual citizen-soldier. It is challenging and highly instructive to walk a battlefield analyzing the decisions of opposing commanders of the past, but it is more difficult to sense the determination and emotions of the soldiers, in their many different roles, on whom those decisions depended. This book at least begins to fill in that gap, and in so doing it humanizes the patriotic, unconditional commitment that has always been required in the defense of freedom.

In making the final selection of art, I wanted to ensure that we recognized the positive results that America has gained from the values, dedication, and self-sacrifice of our soldiers. None of this art, however, is intended to glorify war. War is a last resort, and our soldiers do not seek glory when they take up arms. Preserving peace by being seen as trained and ready for war is as much of an accomplishment as victory on the battlefield. At the same time, men and women do not somehow become less human when they become soldiers, and art can very effectively explore and distill that human dimension, whether in the midst of battle or in providing humanitarian aid. In the following pages you will see many aspects of the Army working as an "institution," but I encourage you to look for the telling details that capture the personal character and experiences of the individual soldier.

When we look back, we honor the survivors and the fallen who together helped to build and preserve the world we enjoy. For today's soldiers, this book, I hope, will forge a link with the soldiers of the past and reinforce an honorable heritage which will in turn strengthen the soldiers of America tomorrow.

15 December 1994

GORDON R. SULLIVAN
General, United States Army
Chief of Staff

Table of Contents

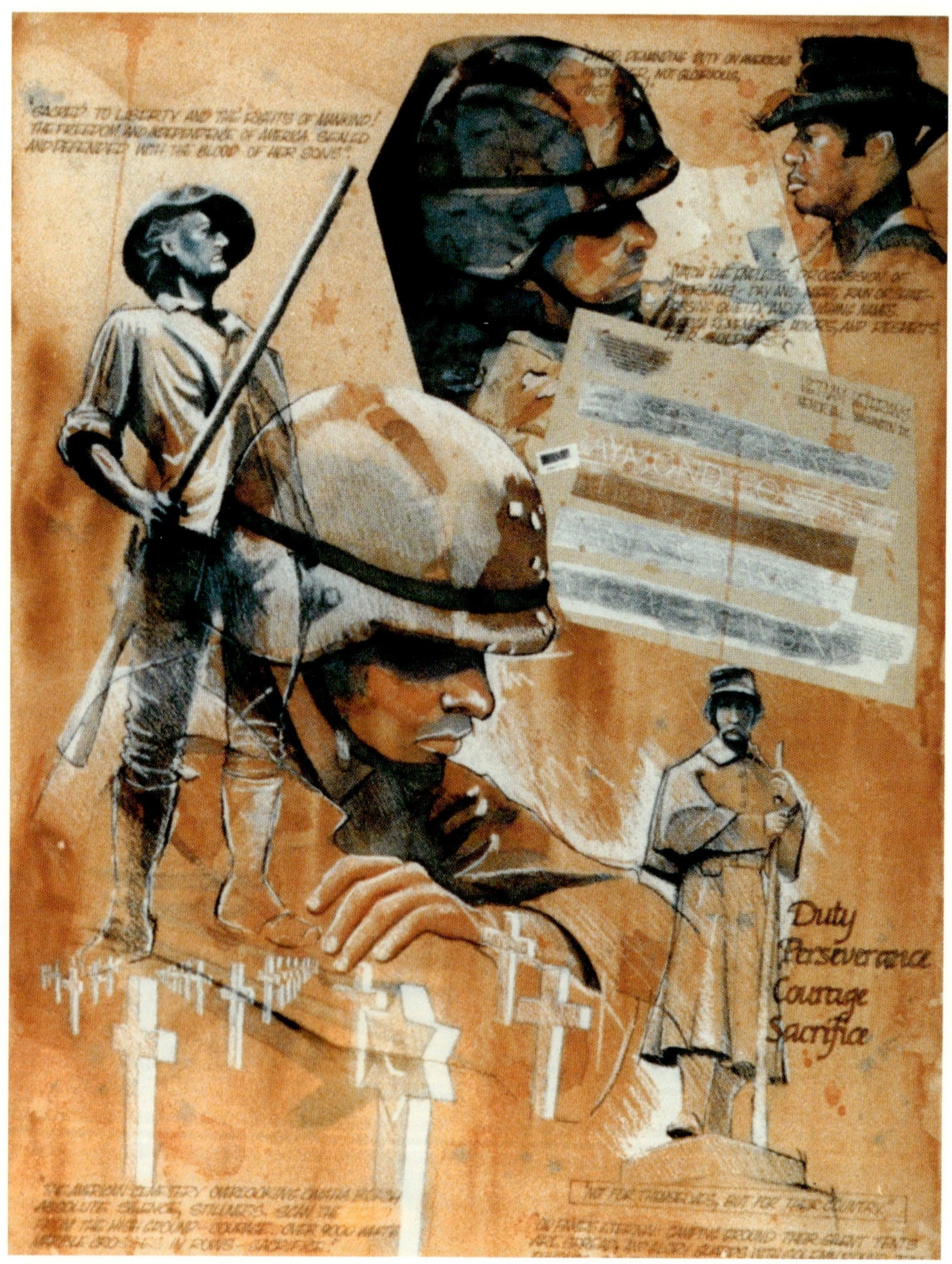

LET'S TAKE A TRIP
Peter G. Varisano, 1991
Watercolor, 29 ½" x 22 ½"

Introduction

The Nation today needs men who think in terms of service to their country and not in terms of their country's debt to them.

Omar N. Bradley

IN 1948 GENERAL BRADLEY EXPRESSED AN IMPERATIVE THAT would be echoed some years later by President John F. Kennedy. Thankfully, for the sake of our national well-being, the need cited by Bradley has been consistently met within the U.S. Army throughout our history. This book portrays men and women who have indeed thought first and foremost about serving the nation through their commitment to the highest levels of military preparedness and combat effectiveness.

Soldiers Serving the Nation, like its earlier companion volume, *Portrait of an Army*, is drawn from the U.S. Army Art Collection. But there is a difference in approach between the two books. *Portrait* contains many images of individual soldiers, but as a first venture in publishing an extensive selection of the Army's art, the book also had a general purpose: to inform the Army about the Art Collection and to show, as one example, how that art could be used to illustrate and record the Army's major functional roles. As indicated by its title, *Soldiers Serving the Nation* has a much more central focus on the American soldier. In the following pages there are many images of individual faces and personalities, but there are also images of the conditions, people, and things that have shaped the soldier's life—from the different landscapes reflecting where the Army has been, to the equipment that has changed so much over time. The intention is thus to present not just a series of portraits of American soldiers but also the experiences reflected in those faces.

This new collection is divided into four geographical sections: "The Americas," "Europe," "The Pacific and Asia," and "Africa and the Middle East." Within each section the coverage is not chronological; instead, the images have been allowed to interact with each other in various ways—to bring out common themes and similar images over time, to show how artists have used various approaches to address the same subjects, and to allow the art *as art* to come together as an effective page-by-page design. The book also contains two appendixes that provide brief biographical sketches of the artists and a short history of the Army Art Collection.

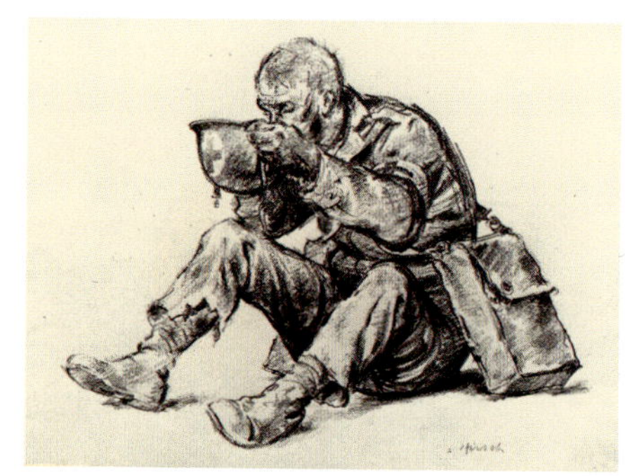

SO WHAT
Italy
Joseph Hirsch, 1944
Crayon, 14" x 19"

The scope of the book is wide-ranging, touching on the entire span of the Army's and the nation's history. The time frame of "The Americas" section stretches from the American Revolution to the aftermath of Hurricane Andrew in Florida in 1993, with settings as diverse as Civil War battlefields, the American West, Alaska, and Latin America. "Europe" captures the American soldier from World War I in France to the Berlin Wall, with scenes from Iceland and England through Germany and Italy to Yugoslavia. Images in "The Pacific and Asia" section range from the island of Rendova off New Guinea in 1943 to the demilitarized zone (DMZ) in Korea in 1991. "Africa and the Middle East" shows logistical support activities in Persia in 1943, as well as soldiers in Somalia in 1994.

Most of the artists represented, whether military or civilian, experienced firsthand the events they painted, sketched, or drew. An artist in the field is able to absorb a much more immediate sense of the climate, the terrain, and the morale and concerns of the soldiers. Although their products were usually completed in a

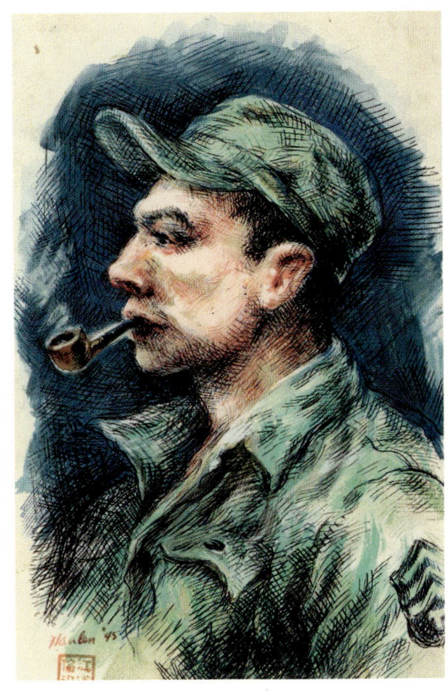

REST PERIOD
China
John G. Hanlen, 1945
Watercolor, 9 ¾" x 6 ¼"

studio, their own participation in the event is often clearly reflected in the vitality and exactness of the result. The artists were free to choose both their subjects and the style and medium that they felt would best capture the moment, particularly in its more transcending or universal aspects.

The Army Art Collection has two major components, the Army Art Central Collection and the Army Museum Art Collection. The Chief of Military History has overall responsibility for the Army's art and immediate control over the central collection. The selections that follow are mainly from that central collection. Other pieces are from the art collections of the West Point Museum at the U.S. Military Academy, West Point, New York, and of the U.S. Army Cavalry Museum at Fort Riley, Kansas.

The caption under each picture provides the title of the work, the geographical area (ranging from the general to the specific) of the subject matter, and the name of the artist and date, if known, of the work's completion. Place names are authentic to the time and have not been updated. Information on the medium and size of the original work is also provided.

The Americas

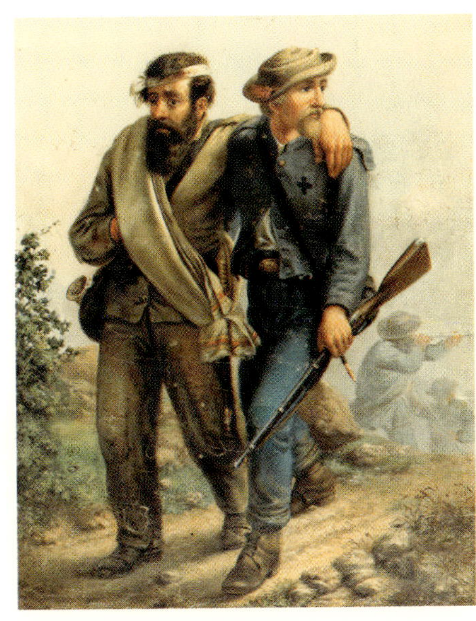

WOUNDED CIVIL WAR SOLDIER
Allen C. Redwood, 1868
Oil, 10" x 8"

ALTHOUGH AMERICA'S MILITARY TRADITION GOES BACK TO the colonial period, the U.S. Army traces its creation to 14 June 1775, when the Second Continental Congress created a national army to put the British in Boston under siege. This was thirteen months before the Declaration of Independence and thirteen years before the ratification of the Constitution, but when Pennsylvania, Maryland, and Virginia riflemen left their homes to march north to join New England troops, they were already united by their willingness to defend American rights. Thus began the Army's unbroken tradition of national service.

Hardened by experience and the rigorous drills of Maj. Gen. Friedrich Wilhelm von Steuben, the citizen-soldiers of the Continental Army developed into a force equal to the best professional armies of the day. During the Revolution, these continentals fought in every corner of the new nation and beyond its borders into Canada. In the process, they set an example of dedication and effectiveness despite adversity that remains the bedrock of the U.S. Army today.

Unlike so many European armies, the Continental Army from its inception was an instrument of service for the people. After the successful conclusion of the Revolutionary War, most of its soldiers went home, but the small regular Army that remained quickly made a consistent transition into a new role as a partner in the development of the country. Soldiers were now as likely to be found carrying surveying transits, maps, and shovels as they were muskets and swords. After the way to the Mississippi was opened, the Army's Corps of Discovery and Corps of Topographical Engineers pushed west over the Great Plains. Soldiers explored the Santa Fe and Oregon Trails, mapped the western rivers, escorted settlers, surveyed railroad routes, and built new outposts, many of which became towns and cities. In

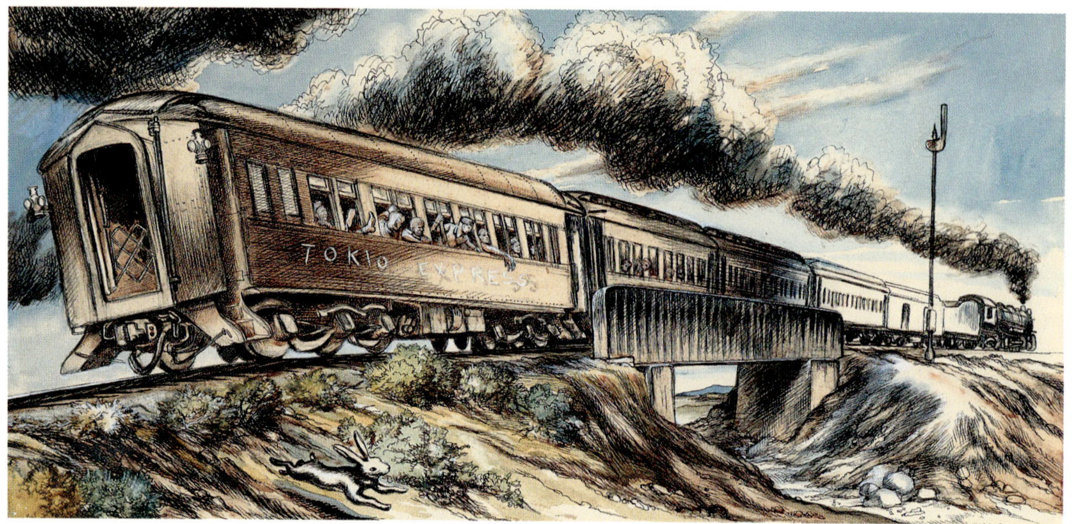

TOKIO EXPRESS
Edward R. Laning, 1942
Watercolor, 22" x 31 ½"

the east, graduates of the young Military Academy at West Point helped to create the infrastructure of the new nation by building a system of canals and improving roads, ports, and harbors.

When the Army was called upon in 1846 to fight its first full-scale war on foreign soil, it proved equal to the task. Striking deep into Mexico and west into California, American soldiers won a string of victories, culminating with the seizure of Mexico City. The peace treaty brought huge new tracts of land under the country's control. These territories had to be secured, and a growing number of settlers then had to be protected. In an era of "manifest destiny," when the expansion of the United States was considered both inevitable and appropriate, this mission inevitably led to frequent clashes with the local Native Americans.

Frontier duty in small and primitive forts was austere and difficult, but it was small preparation for the tremendous sacrifices required in the Civil War. Soldiers by the thousands on both sides gave their lives to resolve the great issues that racked the country. City tradesmen and country boys, former slaves and newly

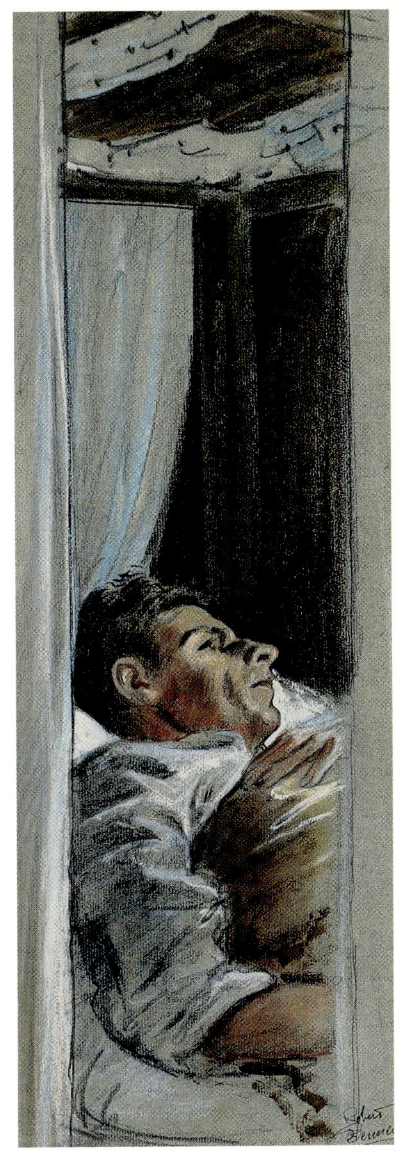

CLIMATIC CASUALTY
Hospital Train, World War II
Robert Benney
Pastel, 20 ½" x 7 ¼"

arrived immigrants, New England Yankees and young farmers from beyond the Tidewater—all found themselves fighting in places far from their homes. Antietam, Shiloh, Gettysburg, and Vicksburg: the names still echo in the American national memory as testimonies to the highest levels of individual courage and commitment.

International events at the turn of the century put American soldiers into new and unfamiliar places. In 1898 the Army found itself engaged against Spain in the Caribbean. American soldiers landed on the islands of Cuba and Puerto Rico, where they encountered disease and tropical heat more deadly than Spanish bullets. As a result of experiences there, the Army's Medical Department began innovative programs to study yellow fever and other tropical health problems. Within a few years that knowledge paid off when Army engineers were given the task of building an ocean-to-ocean canal through the mountains and fever-ridden jungles of Panama, an awesome and dangerous feat. The subsequent responsibility for maintaining and defending the Panama Canal also fell on the Army. Through two world wars and innumerable international crises, successive generations of American soldiers quietly and professionally ensured the security of the canal, so vital to America's commercial and strategic interests.

The post-World War I years saw the Army reduced to a relatively small force. Yet the country, struggling with domestic problems and economic depression, frequently turned to the Army for assistance. Given the recognized discipline, fitness, and responsiveness of its soldiers, they were often the first called to help in the wake of floods, hurricanes, blizzards, or other natural disasters. Soldiers were also called upon to help restore civil order and, during the Great Depression, to organize and run the Civilian Conservation Corps, a broad public works project.

While Europe and Asia slipped into World War II, the Army planned, prepared, and waited. Camps were built, coastal defenses were improved, and training continued, but it took the attack on Pearl Harbor to fully arouse the nation. For the first time in decades there was real fear of invasion. The islands of Alaska lay close to Japan, Hawaii had already been attacked, and the Caribbean and the Panama Canal were vulnerable. As the Army spread a defensive shield in the Americas from the far north to the distant south, soldiers found themselves on the foggy coast of Alaska with Eskimo Scouts, manning radar stations outside

America's largest cities, guarding mountain passes through the Rockies, and conducting coastal gunnery drills beside the locks of the Panama Canal. At the same time, troop trains and long convoys continually moved across the countryside, and scenes of tearful farewells were repeated thousands of times as the nation mobilized for total war.

Victory came in 1945, and with it a return to civilian life for most of the soldiers of World War II. As a world power with many alliances, however, the United States soon faced new foreign challenges and the threat of nuclear attack. At defensive radar and missile sites largely unseen by the average citizen, American soldiers stood protective watch over the country's cities. The Army conducted a highly successful program of civic development and assistance to the countries of Latin America, and efforts to promote and protect democratic governments led to the American soldier's involvement in operations in Grenada, Panama, and Haiti. At home, the Army continued to promote racial equality within its ranks. Together soldiers of all races filled sandbags for Mississippi levees and provided food, shelter, and medical aid for the victims of hurricanes and tornadoes.

The events recounted above clearly represent only a very limited sketch of a complicated history, but the intention—both here and in the other section introductions—is to provide a general background for the art. This section covers over two hundred years. The danger of foreign invasion is past, and America's geographical frontiers have been long settled, but the nation's relationships with its neighbors in the Americas remain an important concern. In addition, providing assistance in domestic disasters and other emergencies continues as a major Army responsibility. But what also remains is a living heritage, for today's soldier still echoes, every day, those first companies of riflemen in 1775 when they replied, "We are ready."

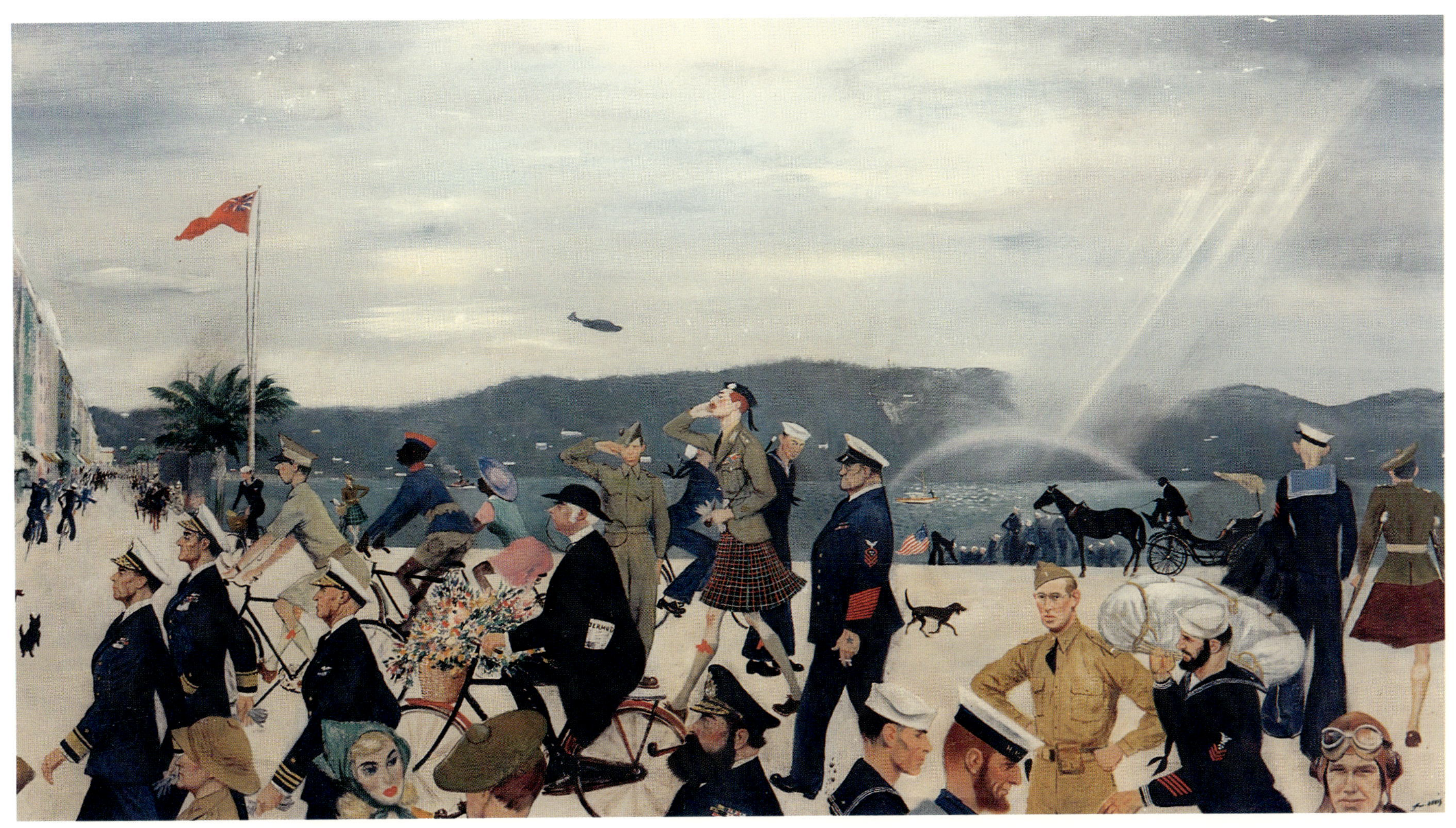

FRONT STREET
Hamilton, Bermuda
Floyd Davis, 1942
Oil, 30" x 53 ½"

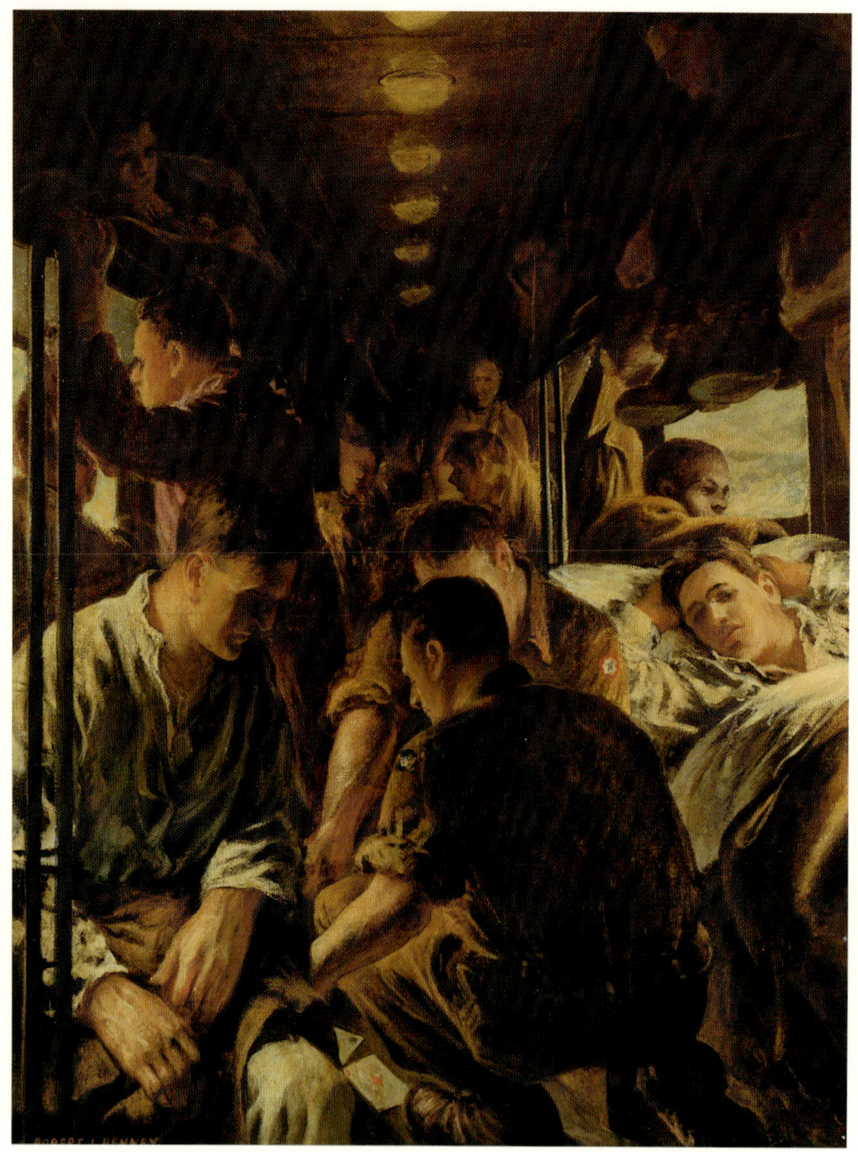

DOUBLE DECK OF ACES
Hospital Train, USA
Robert Benney, 1944
Oil, 41 ½" x 43 ½"

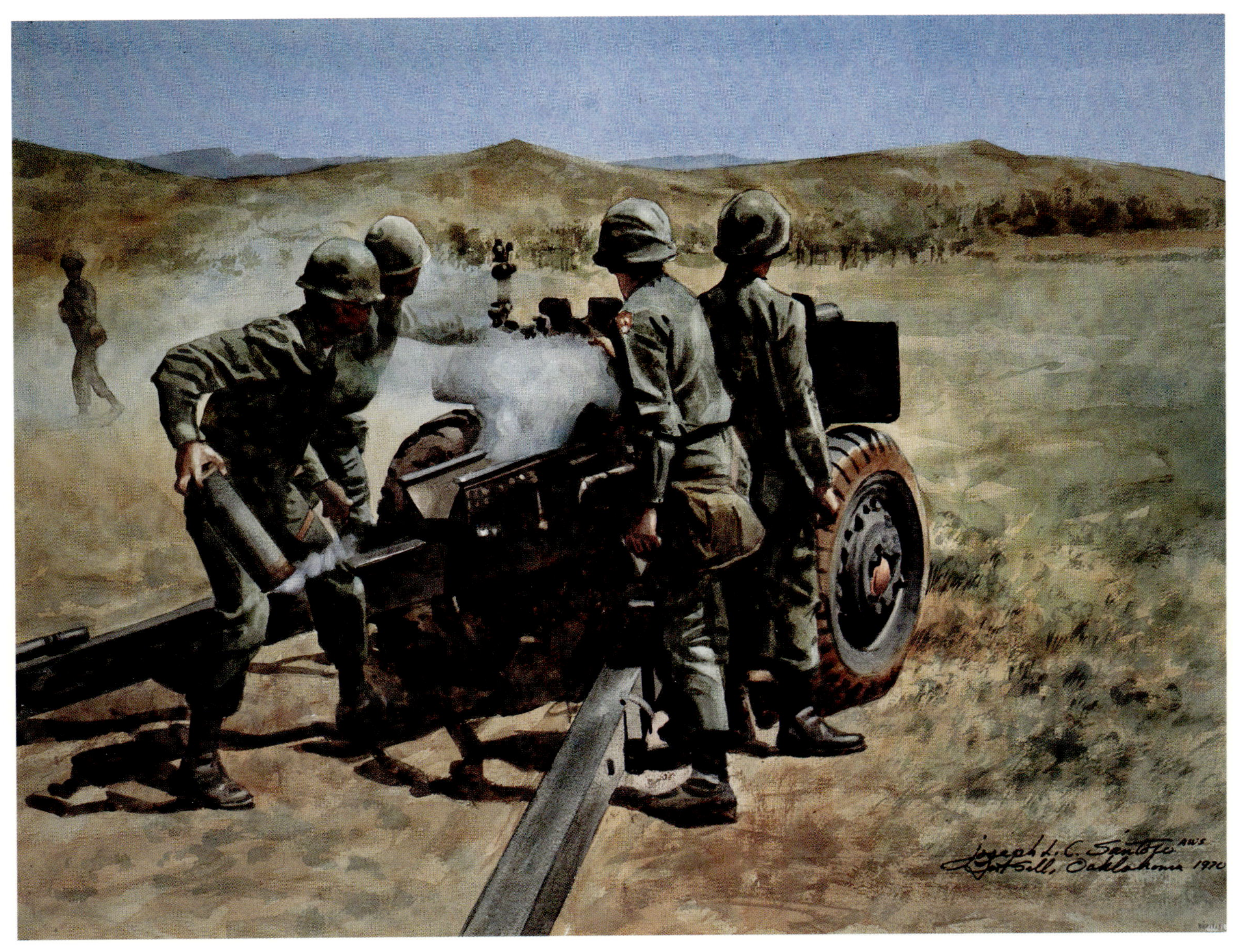

TARGET PRACTICE
Fort Sill, Oklahoma
Joseph Santoro, 1970
Watercolor, 22" x 30"

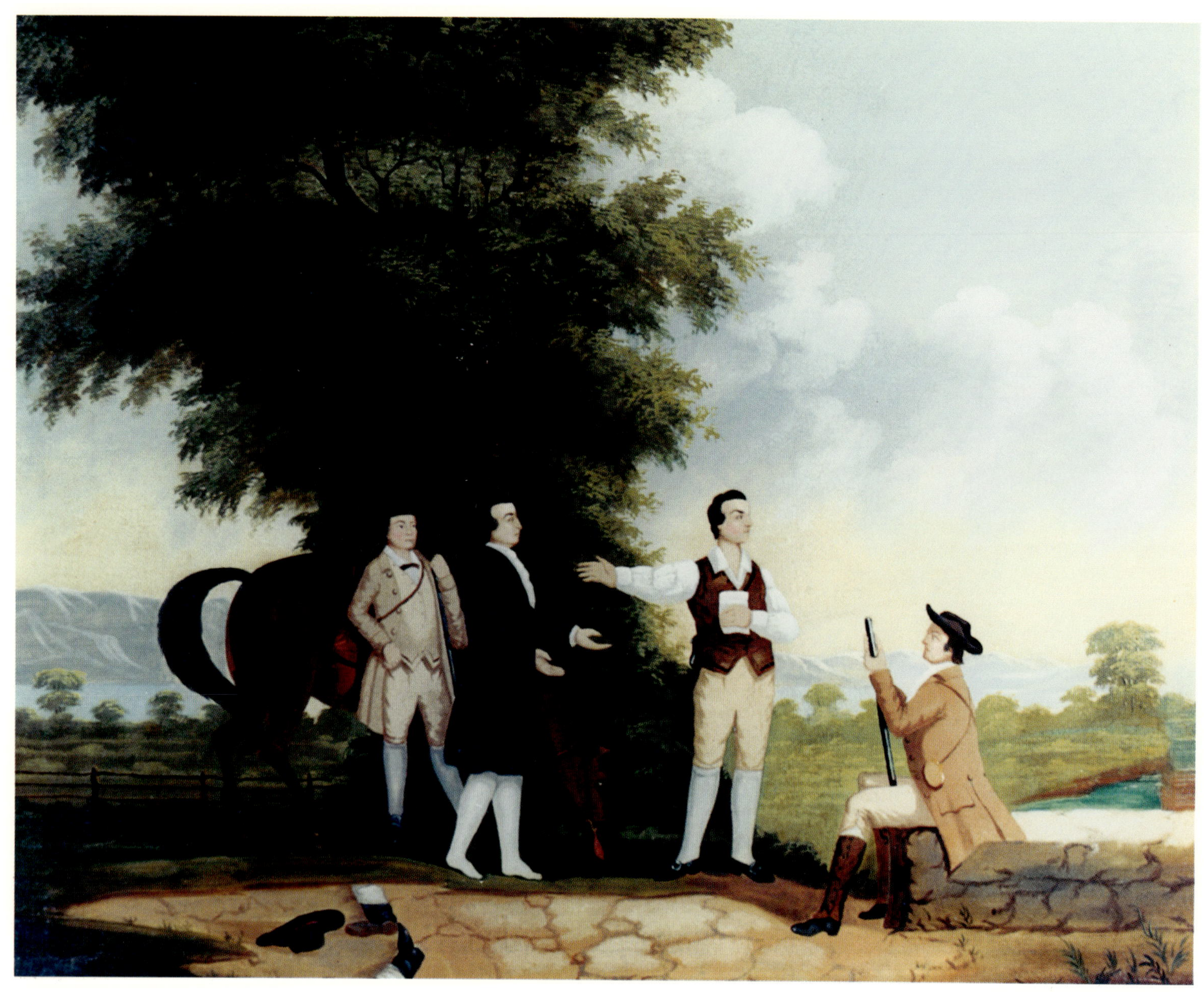

ARREST OF MAJOR ANDRE
Revolutionary War
Artist Unknown (after Asher B. Durand), c. 1880
Oil, 24" x 32"

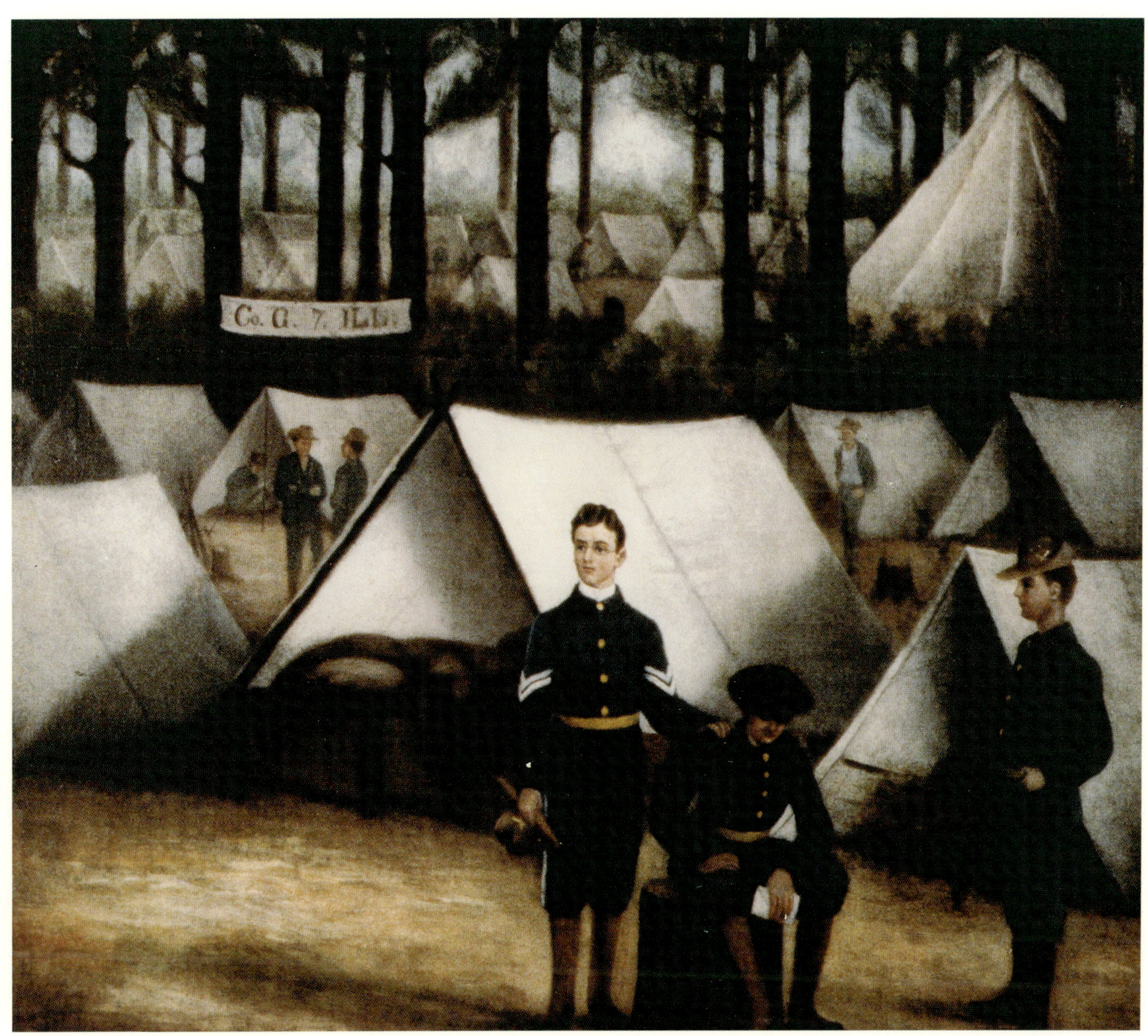

CO. A 7TH ILL. (N.G.)
Spanish-America Camp, Cuba
Artist Unknown, 1898
Oil on masonite, 23 ⅛" x 20 ⅞"

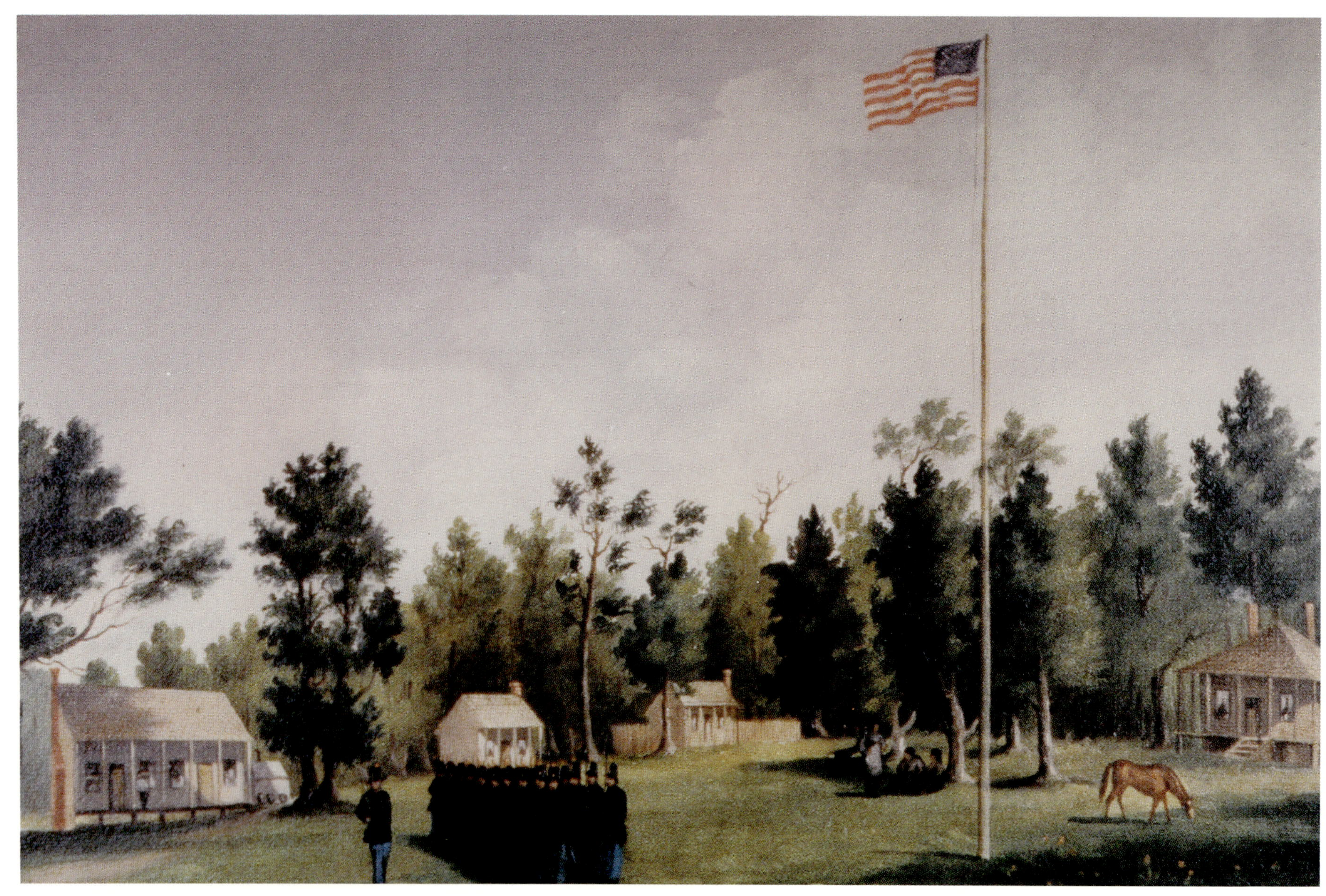

FORT BRAGG
Mendocino County, California
Alexander Edouart, 1858
Oil, 18 ¼" x 26 ¼"

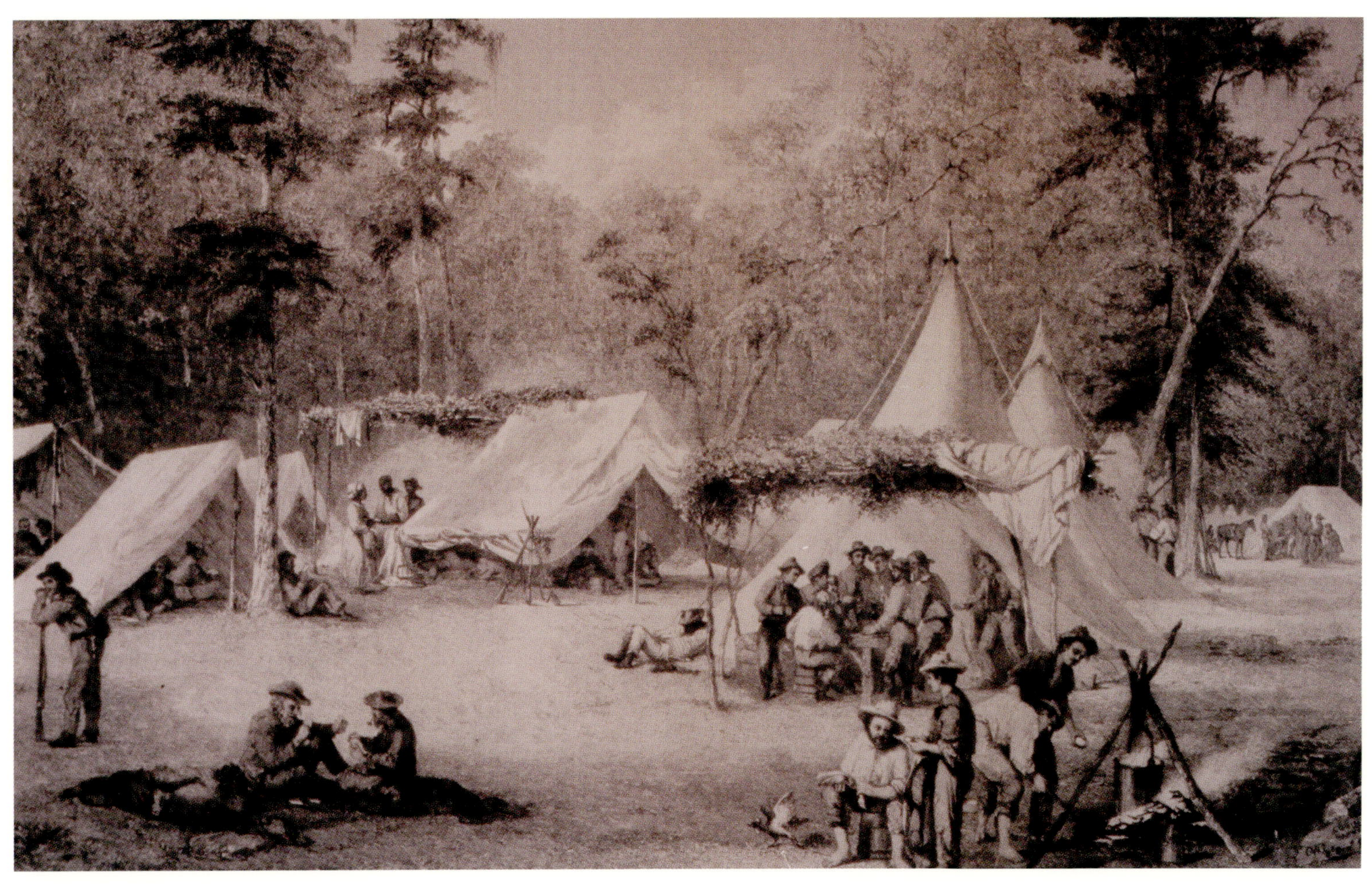

CONFEDERATE CAMP SCENE
Corinth, Mississippi, 1862
Conrad Wise Chapman
Etching, 8 ½"x 13 ½"

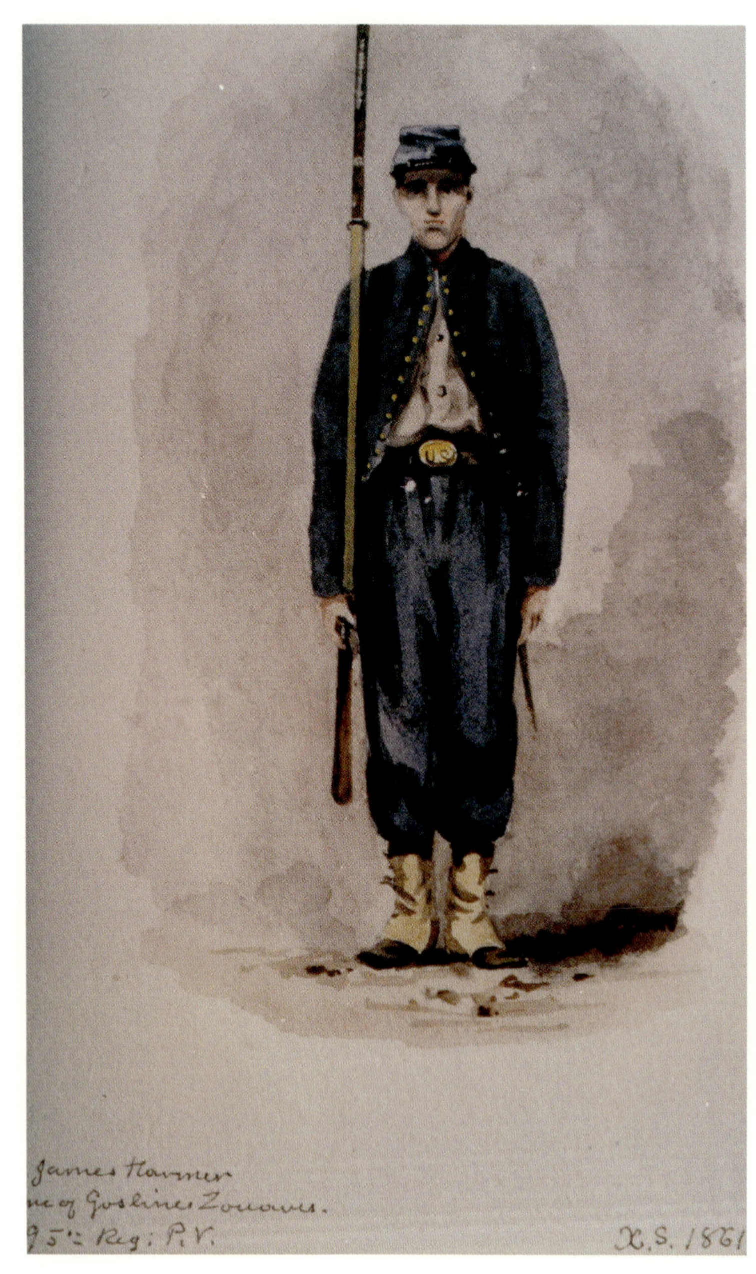

GOSLIN ZOUAVE, 95TH REGT, PV
Xanthus Smith, 1861
Watercolor, 5 ½" x 3 ½"

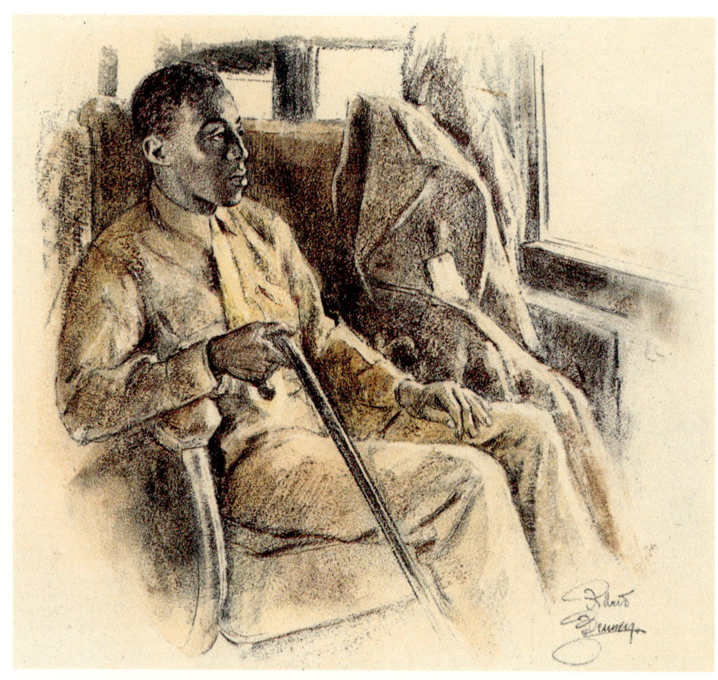

1ST CLASS PASSENGER
Hospital Train, World War II
Robert Benney
Watercolor, 10" x 10 ¼"

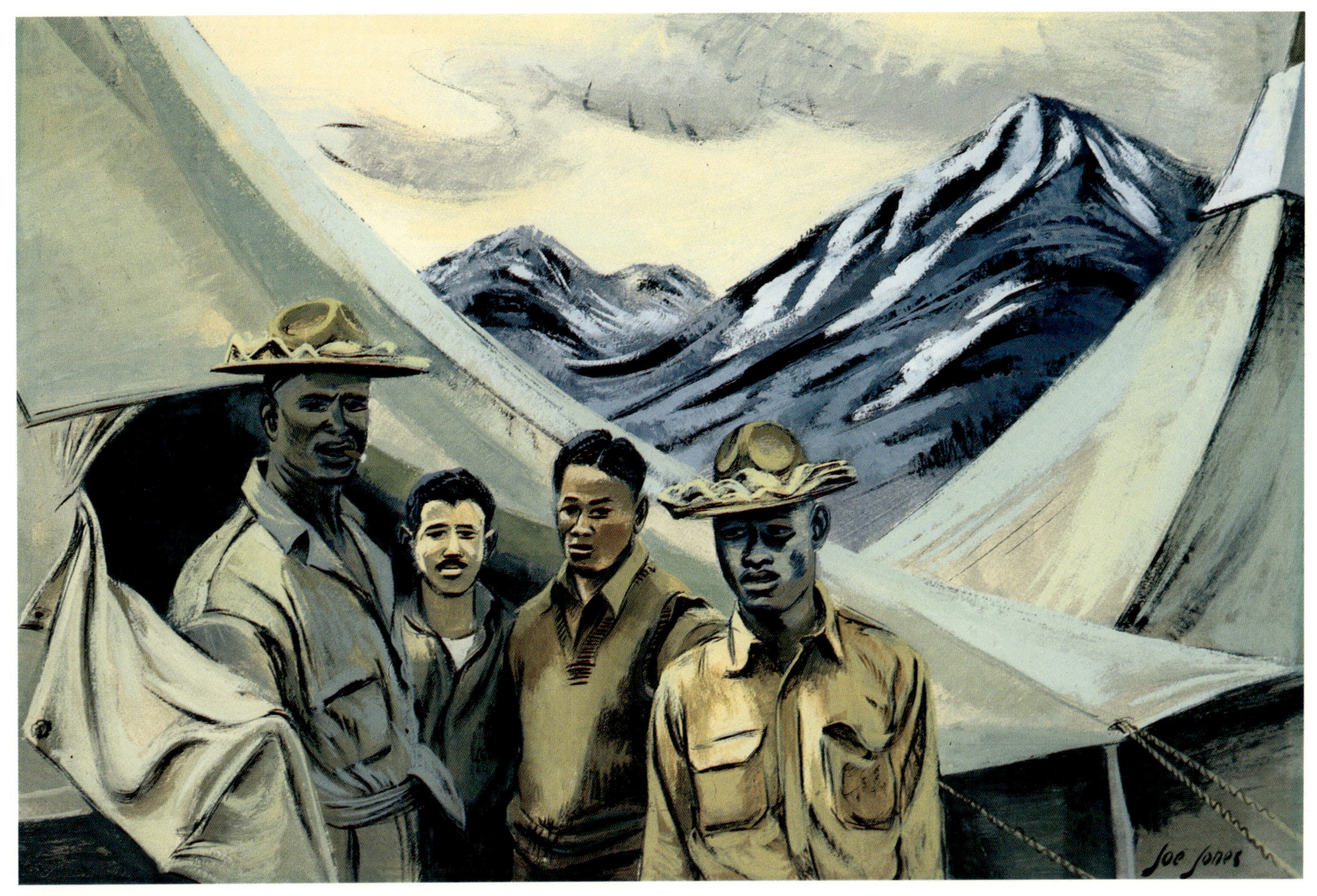

FOUR SOLDIERS
Alaska
Joe Jones, 1943
Watercolor, 14 ½" x 21 ½"

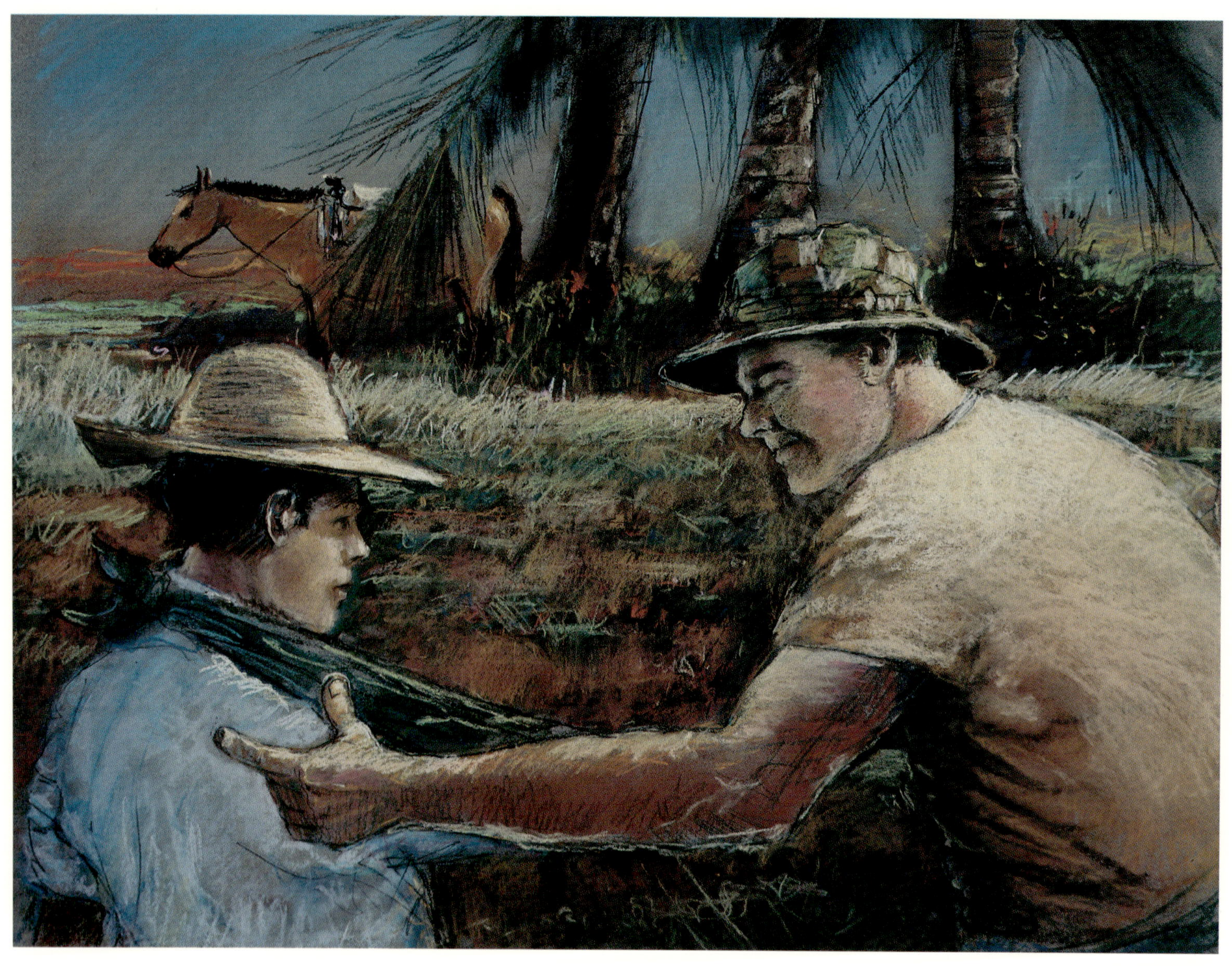

INTERACTION
Panama
Robert Sankner, 1993
Pastel, 19 ½" x 25 ½"

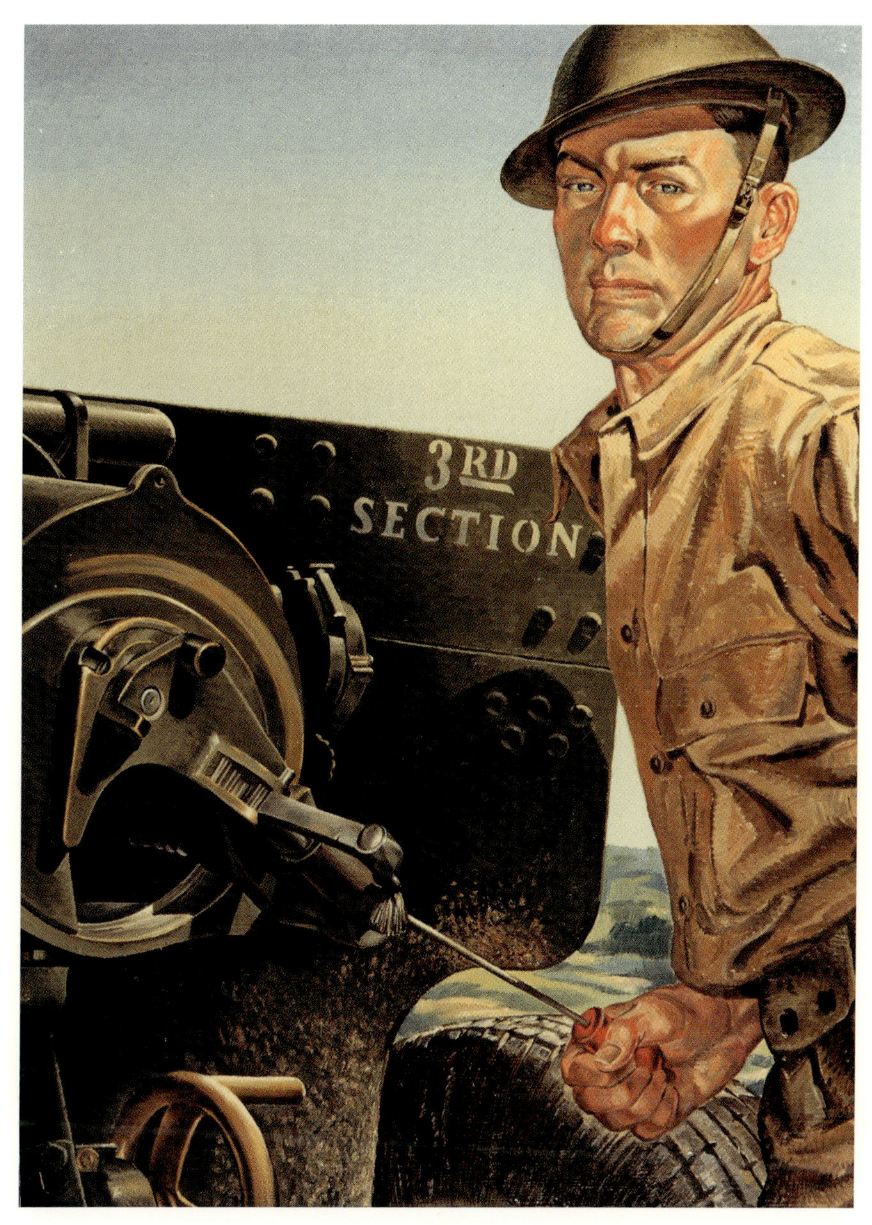

PORTRAIT OF PVT. WYLIE POTTER, B BATTERY
Fort Sam Houston, Texas
Tom Lea, 1941
Oil, 22" x 18"

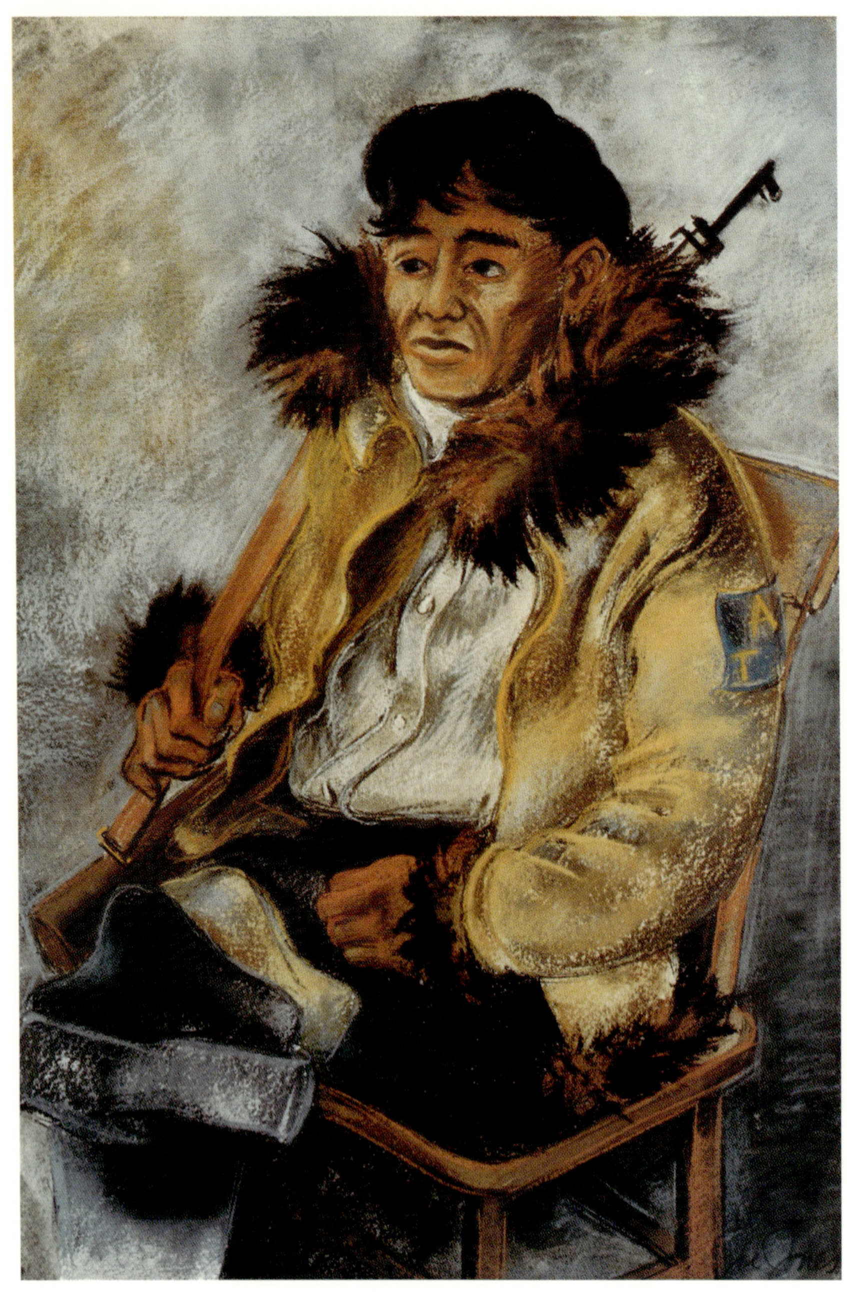

MEMBER OF THE ALASKA TERRITORIAL GUARD
Alaska
Joe Jones, 1943
Pastel, 13 ½" x 19"

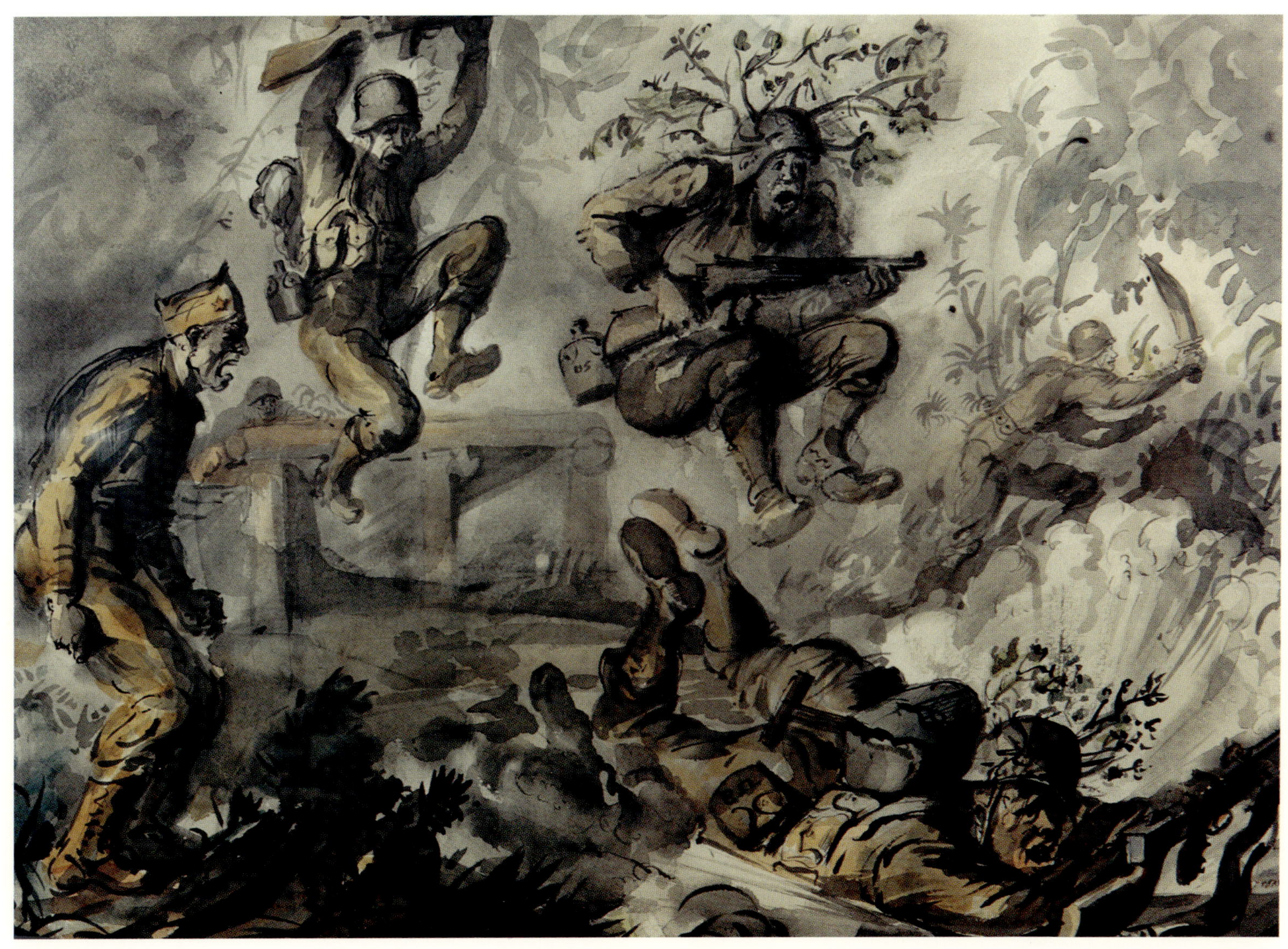

JUNGLE TRAINING
Brazil
Reginald Marsh, 1943
Watercolor, 14" x 20"

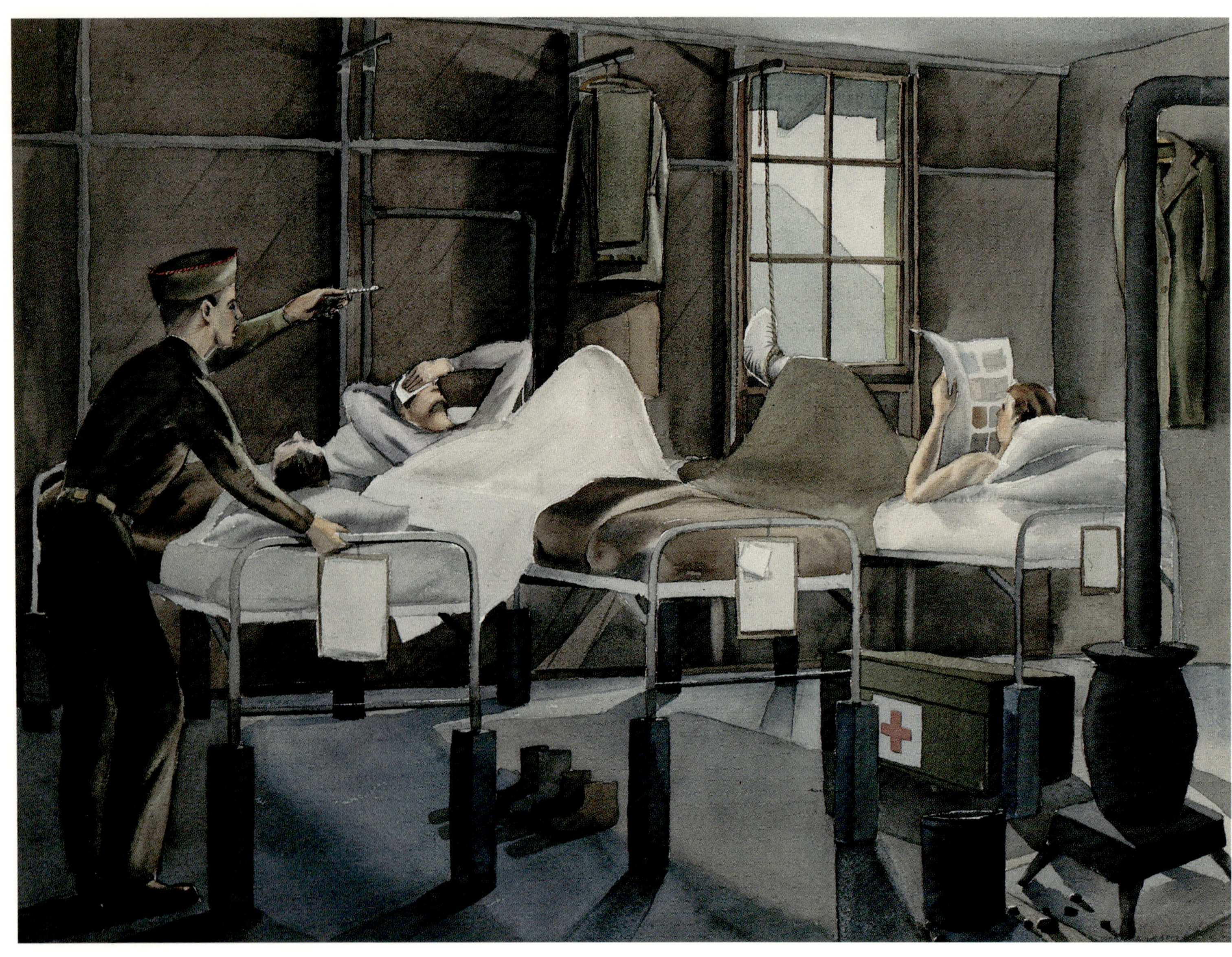

TAKING TEMPERATURES
Warren Leopold, 1943
Watercolor, 21 ½" x 28"

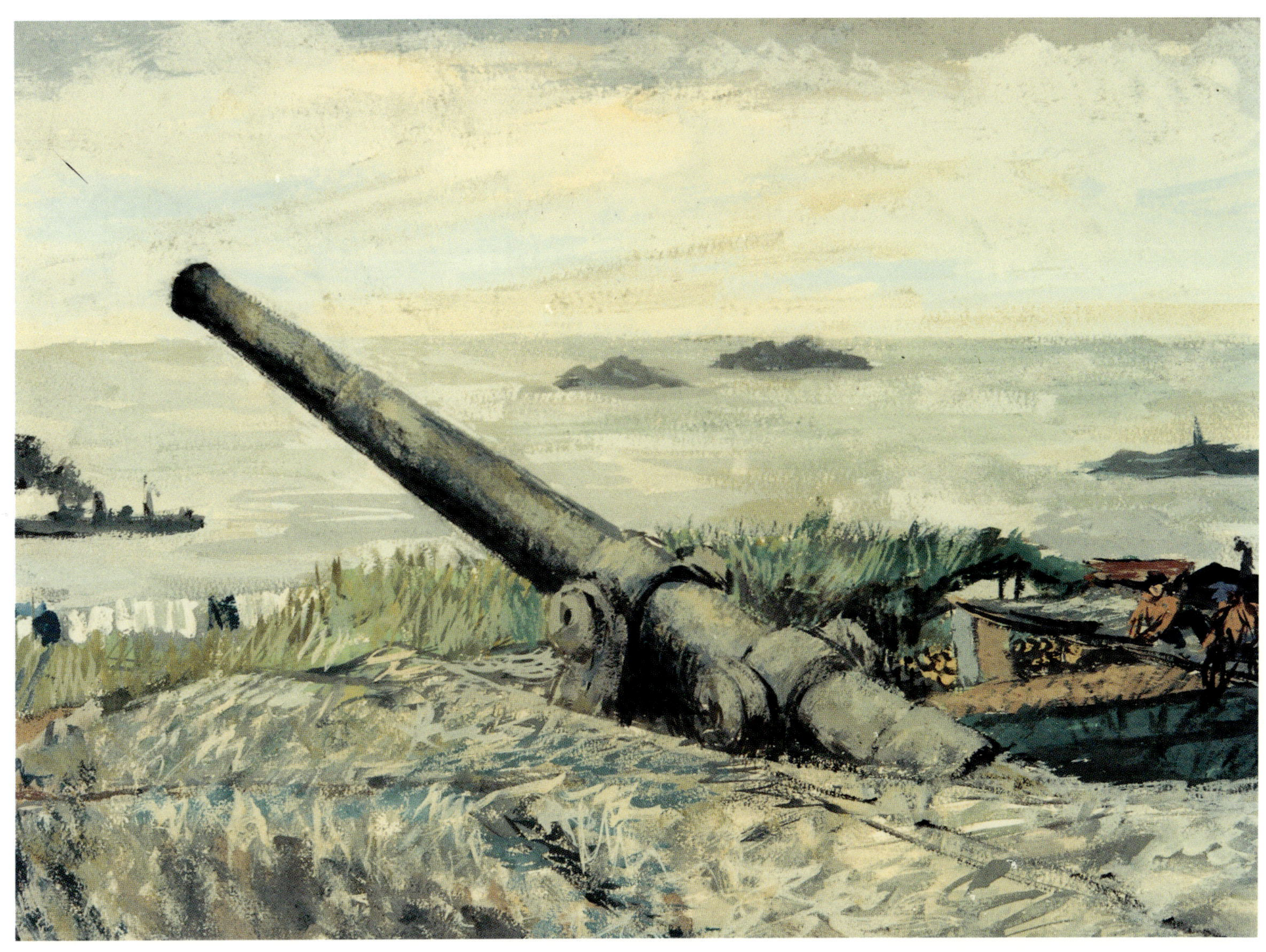

COASTAL GUN
Panama
Alexander Brook, 1943
Gouache, 14″ x 20″

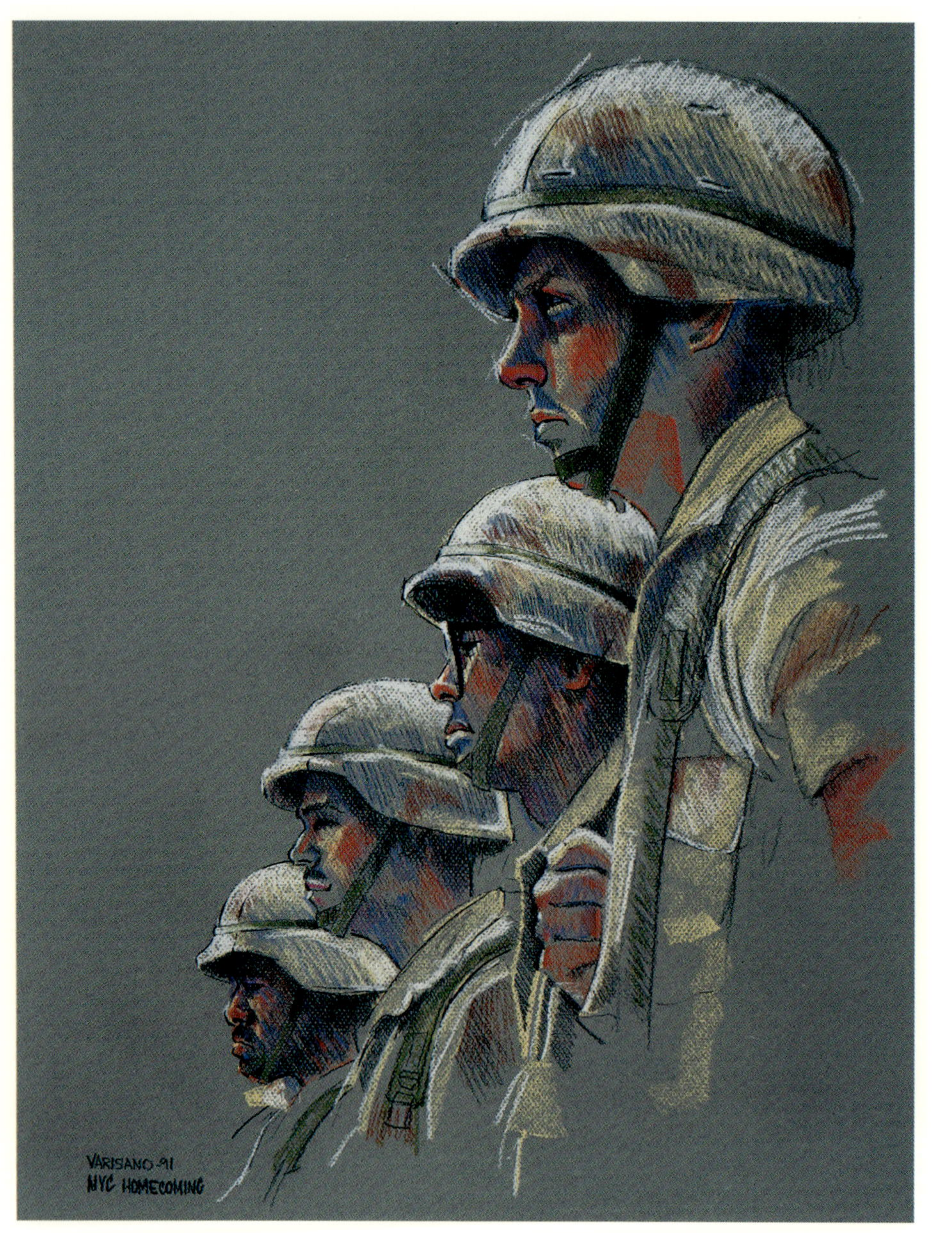

NYC PARADE
New York
Peter G. Varisano, 1992
Pastel, 25 ½" x 19 ½"

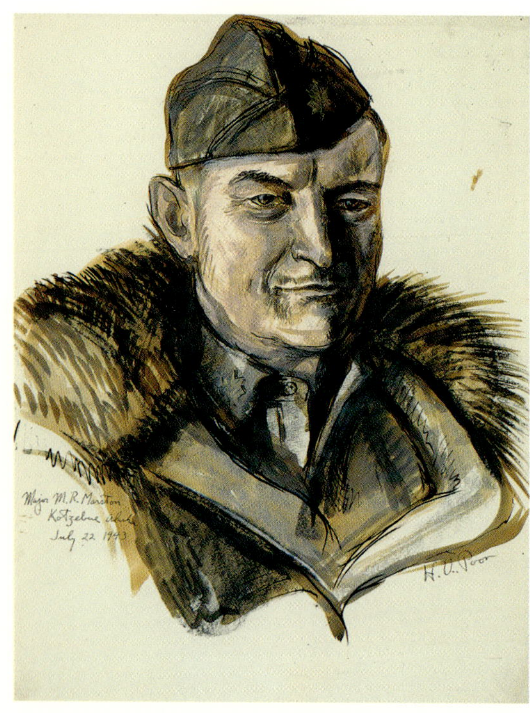

PORTRAIT OF MAJOR M. R. MARSTON
Alaska
Henry Varnum Poor, 1943
Wash, 13 ½" x 17"

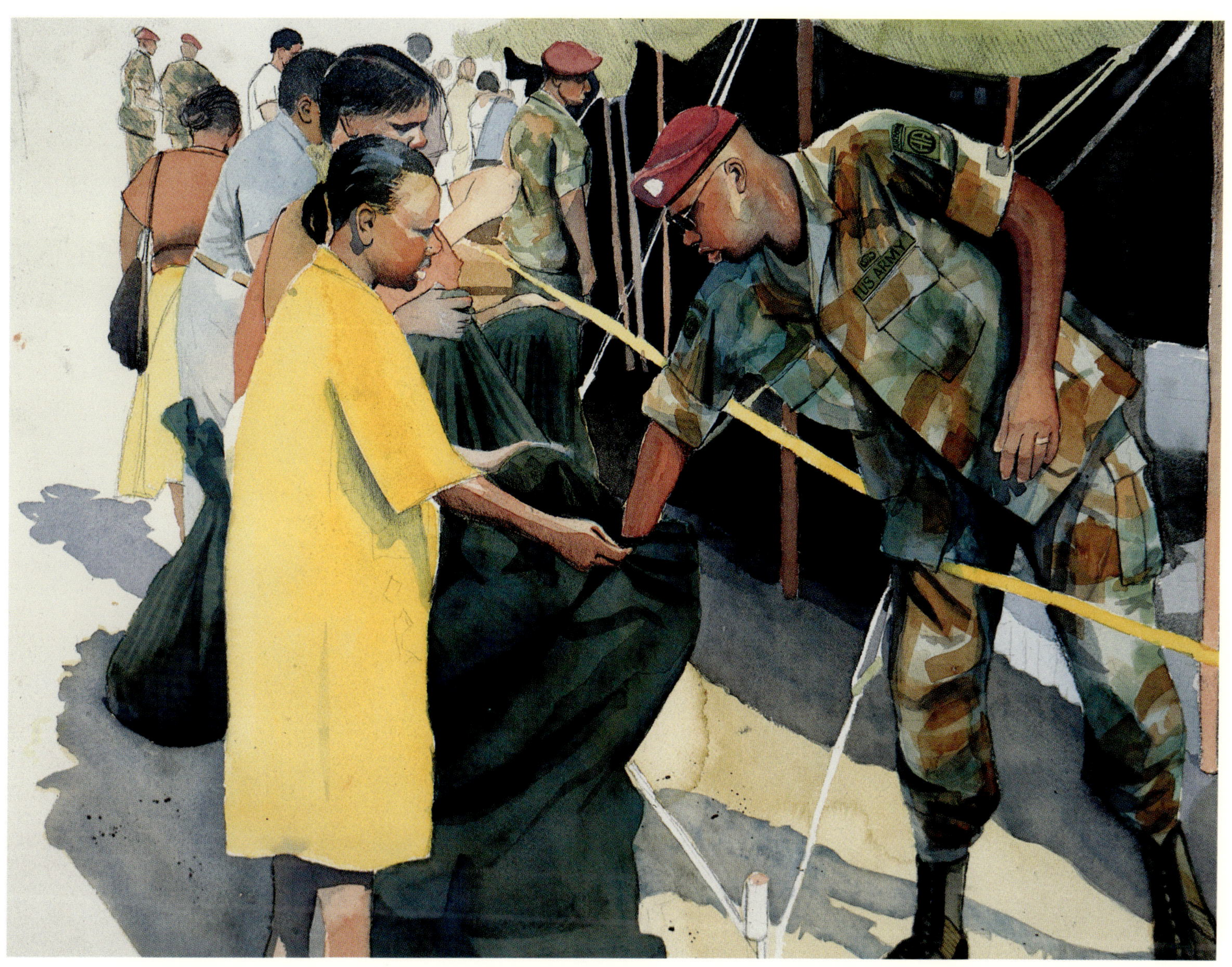

PROVIDING FOOD
Florida
Peter G. Varisano, 1993
Watercolor, 18" x 24"

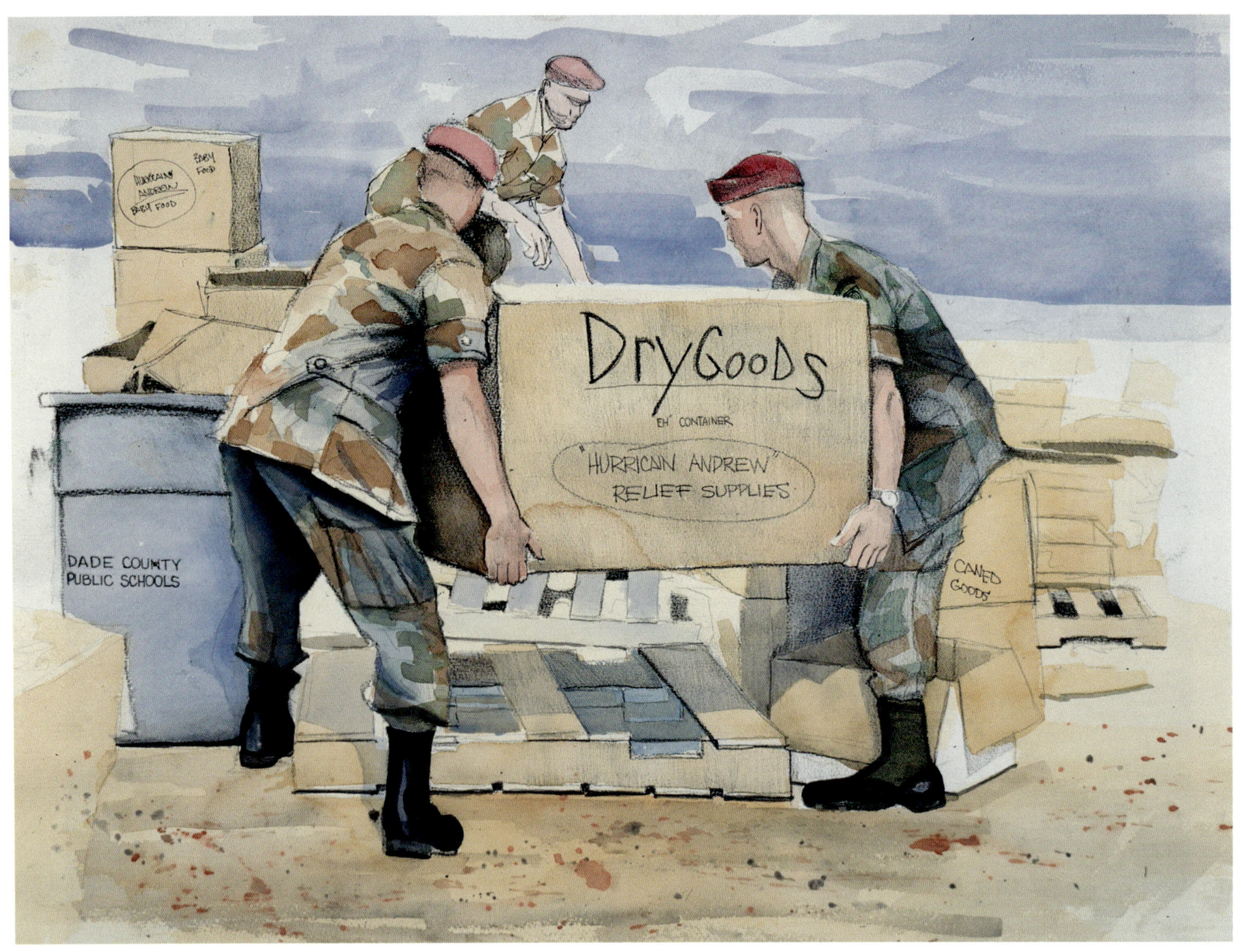

DRY GOODS
Florida
Peter G. Varisano, 1993
Watercolor, 22" x 29 ½"

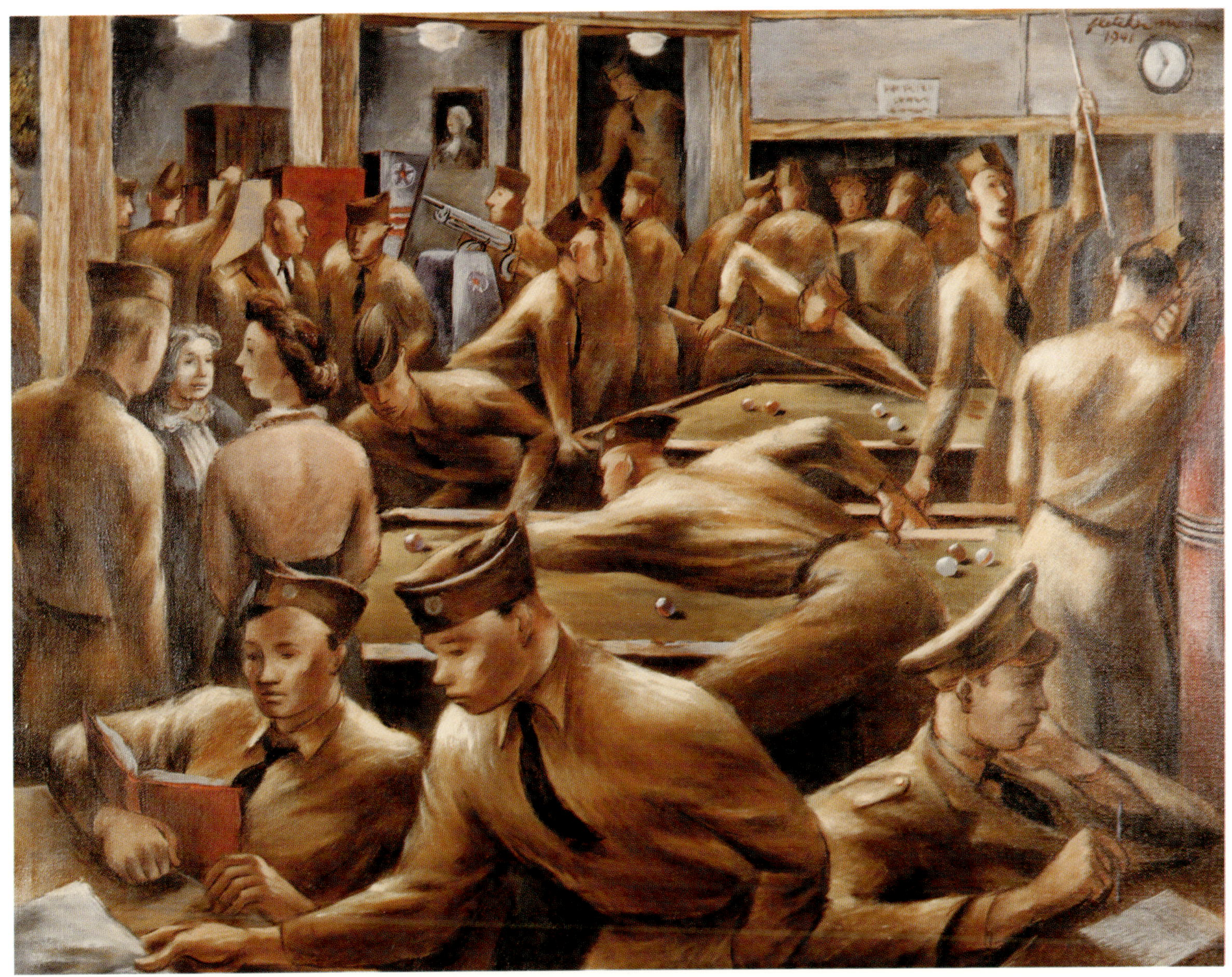

SERVICE CLUB
Camp Shelby, Mississippi
Fletcher Martin, 1941
Oil, 23″ x 40″

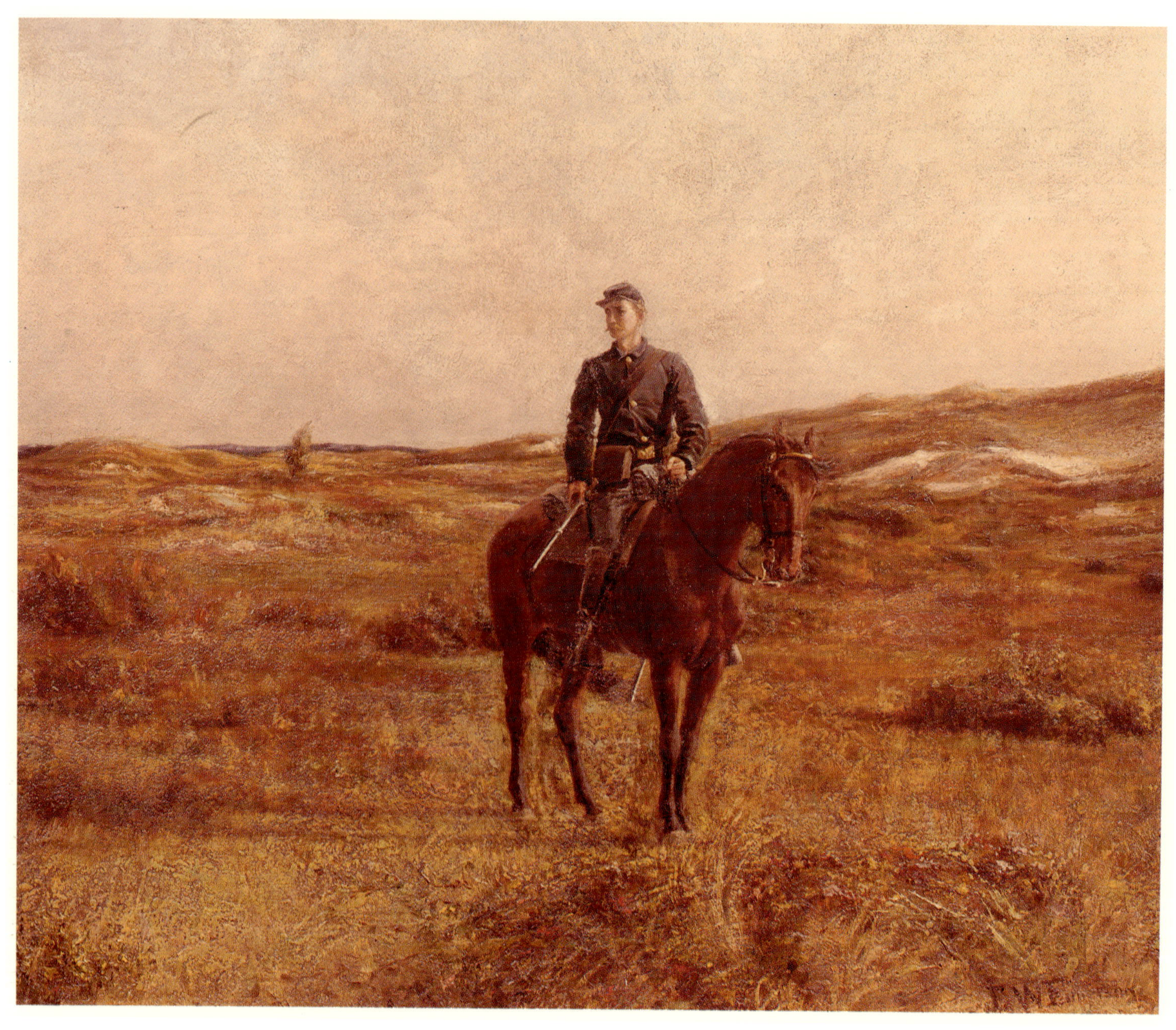

U.S. CAVALRYMAN ON THE PLAINS
E. W. Emerson, 1866–70
Oil, 20" x 24"

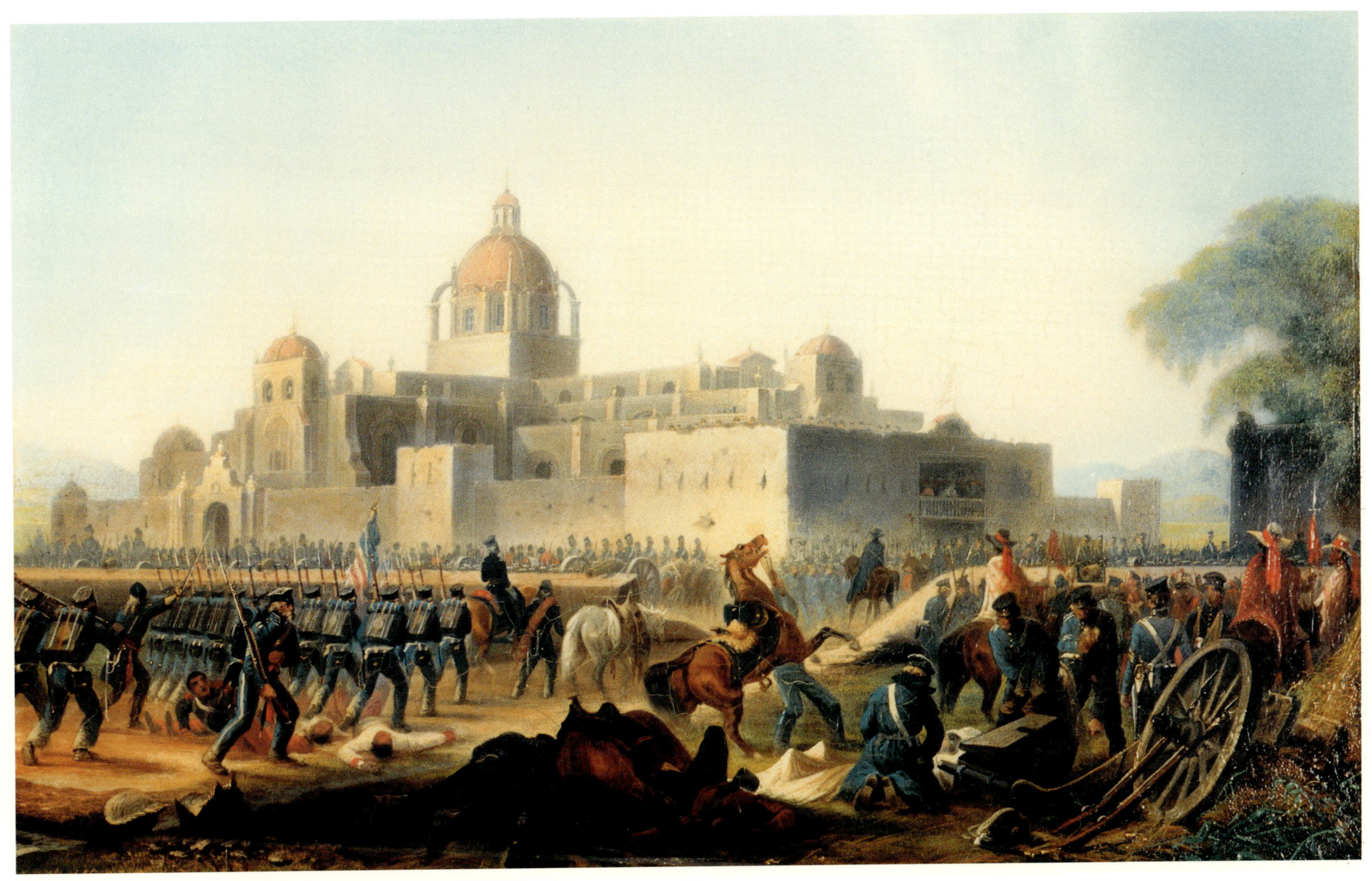

CHURUBUSCO
Mexico
James Walker, 1848
Oil, 8" x 10"

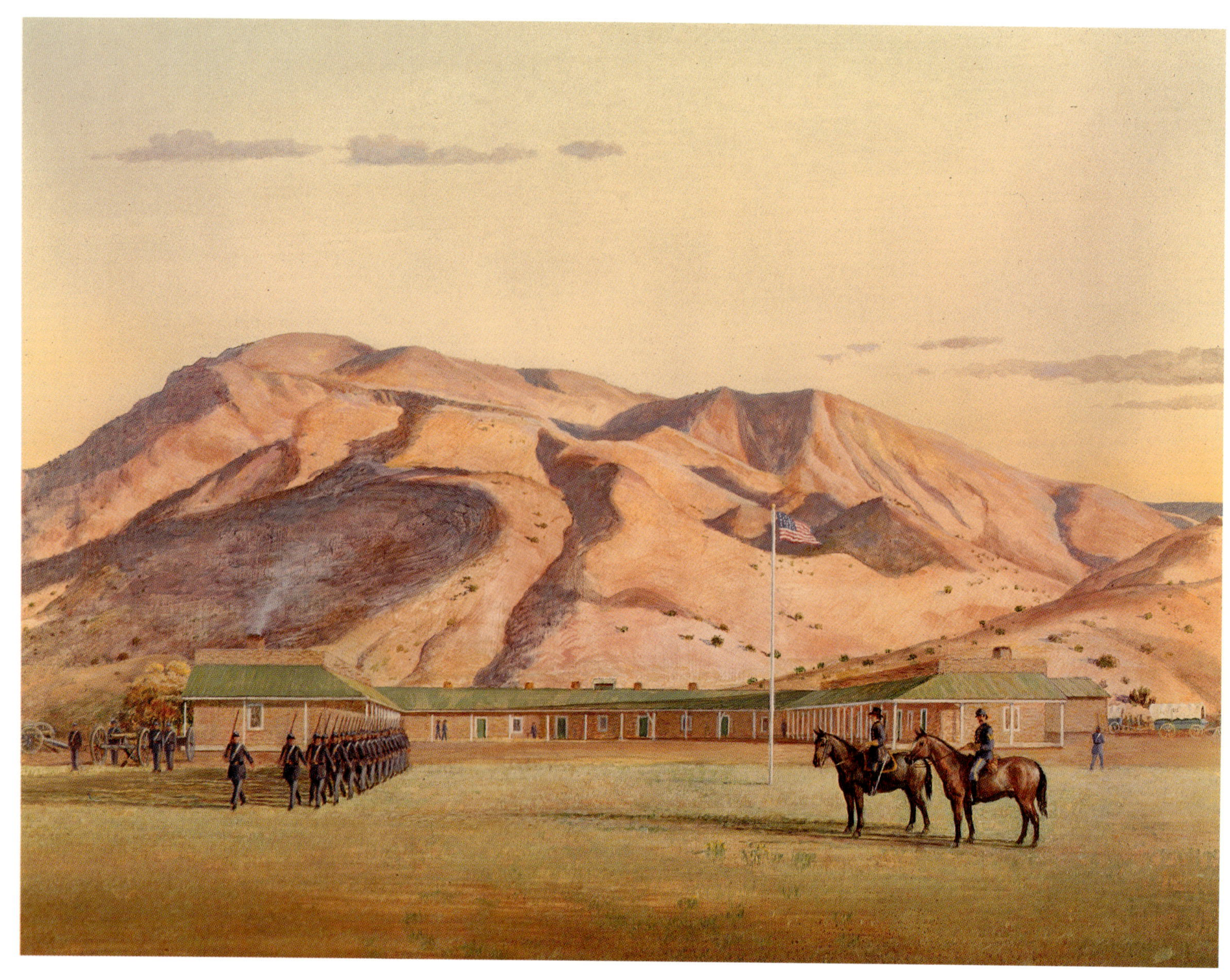

FORT SELDON, TERRITORY OF NEW MEXICO
New Mexico
Peter Hurd
Tempera, 27½" x 36"

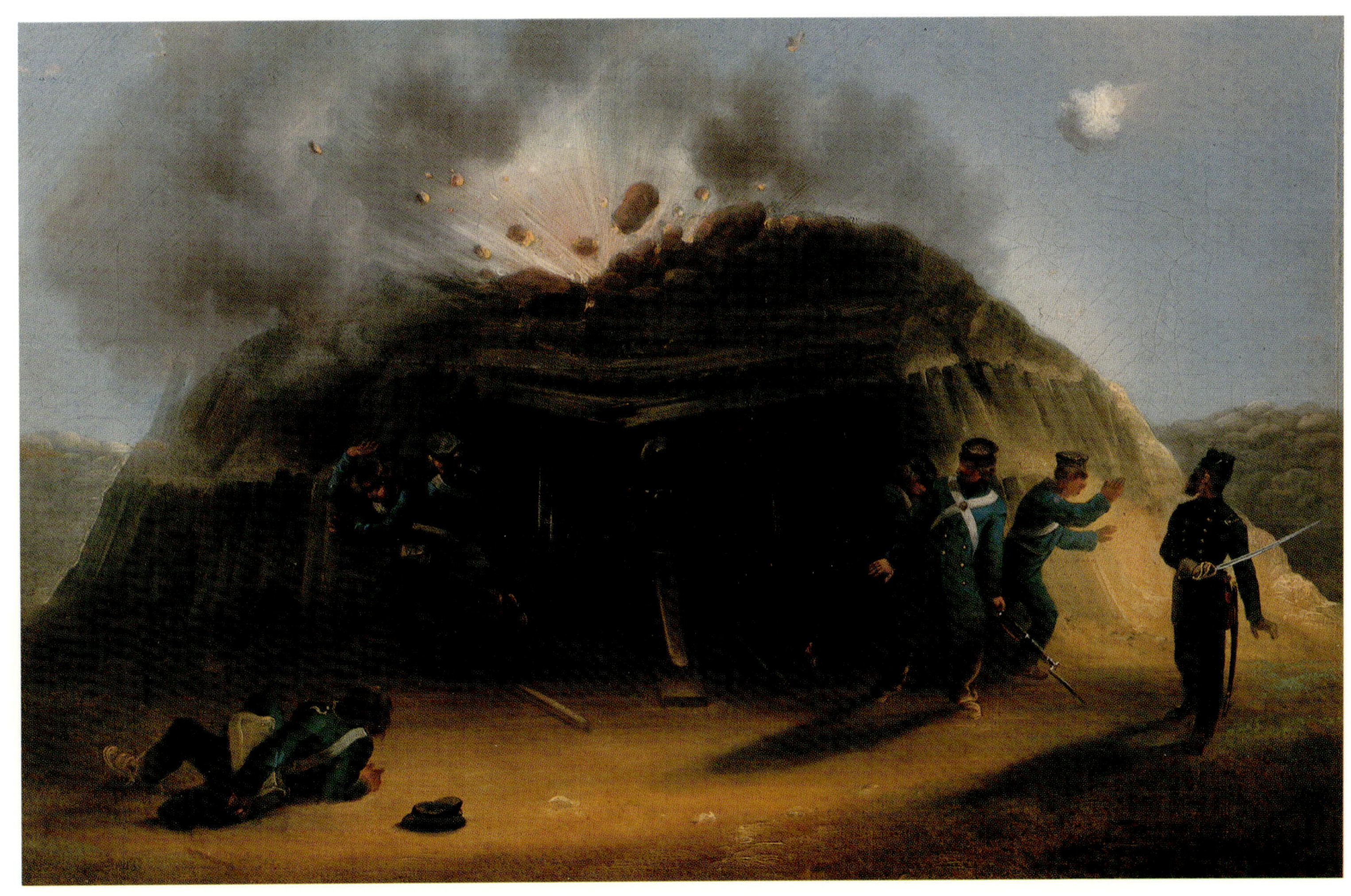

A SIEGE GUN UNDER FIRE
Mexico
James Walker, 1848
Oil, 12" x 18"

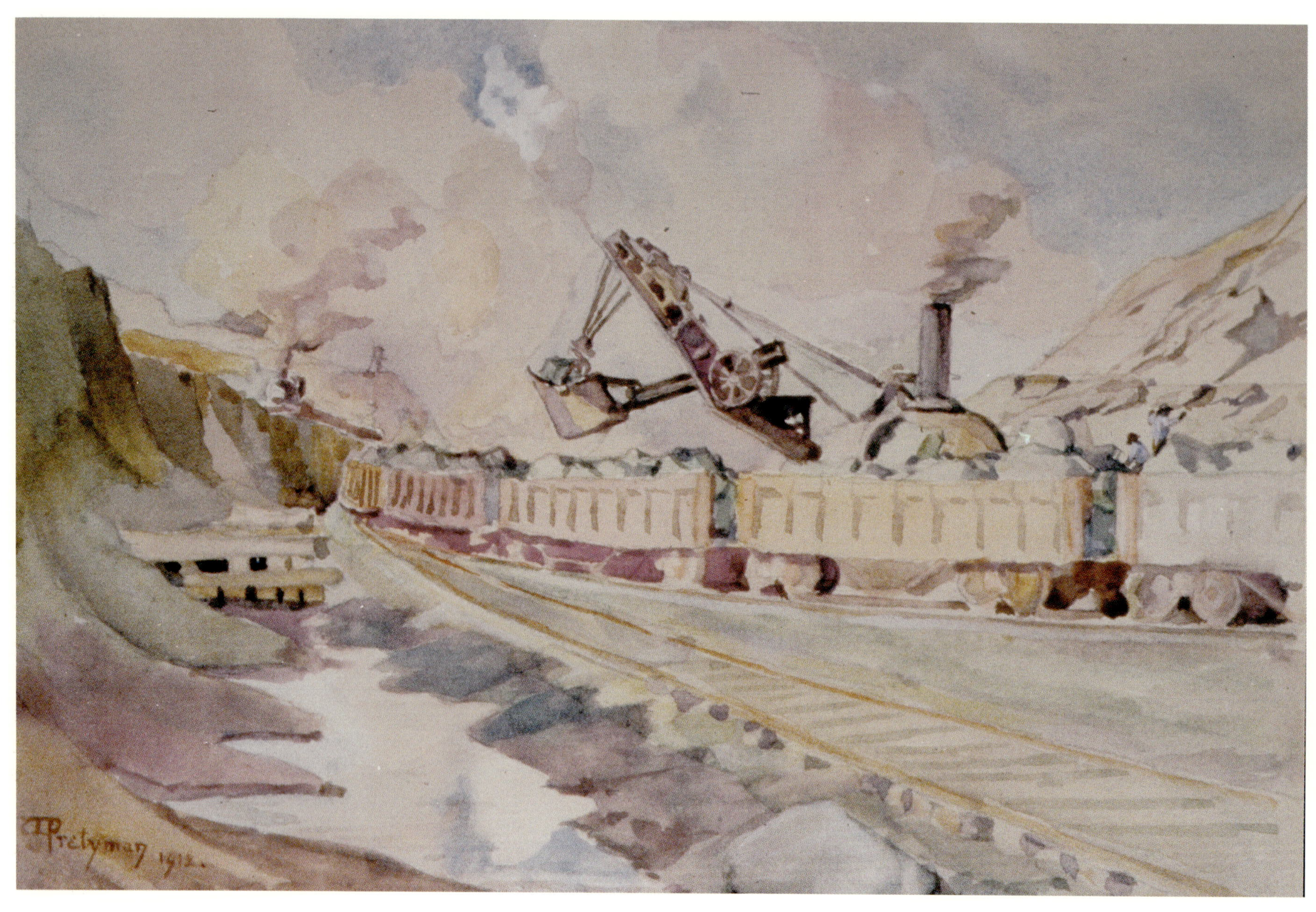

STEAM SHOVEL IN THE CULEBRA CUT
Panama
William Pretyman, 1912
Watercolor, 10 ½" x 7 ½"

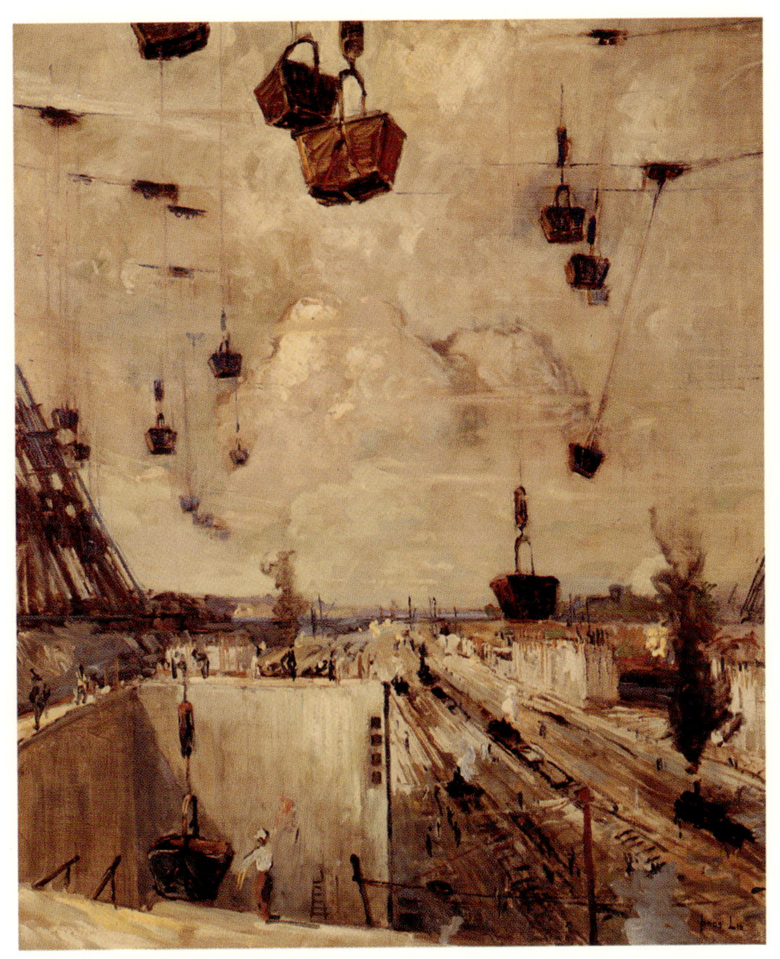

THE HEAVENLY HOIST
Panama
Jonas Lie, 1913
Oil, 50" x 60"

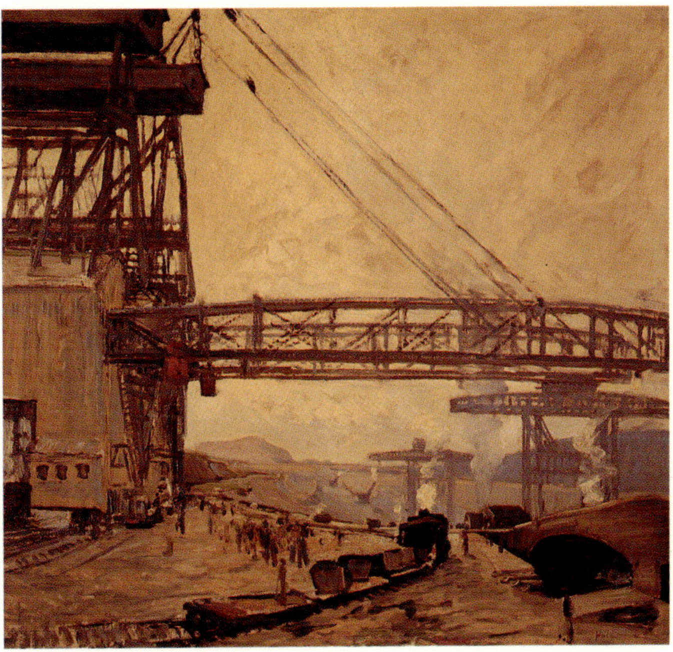

CRANE AT MIRAFLORES
Panama
Jonas Lie, 1913
Oil, 34" x 36"

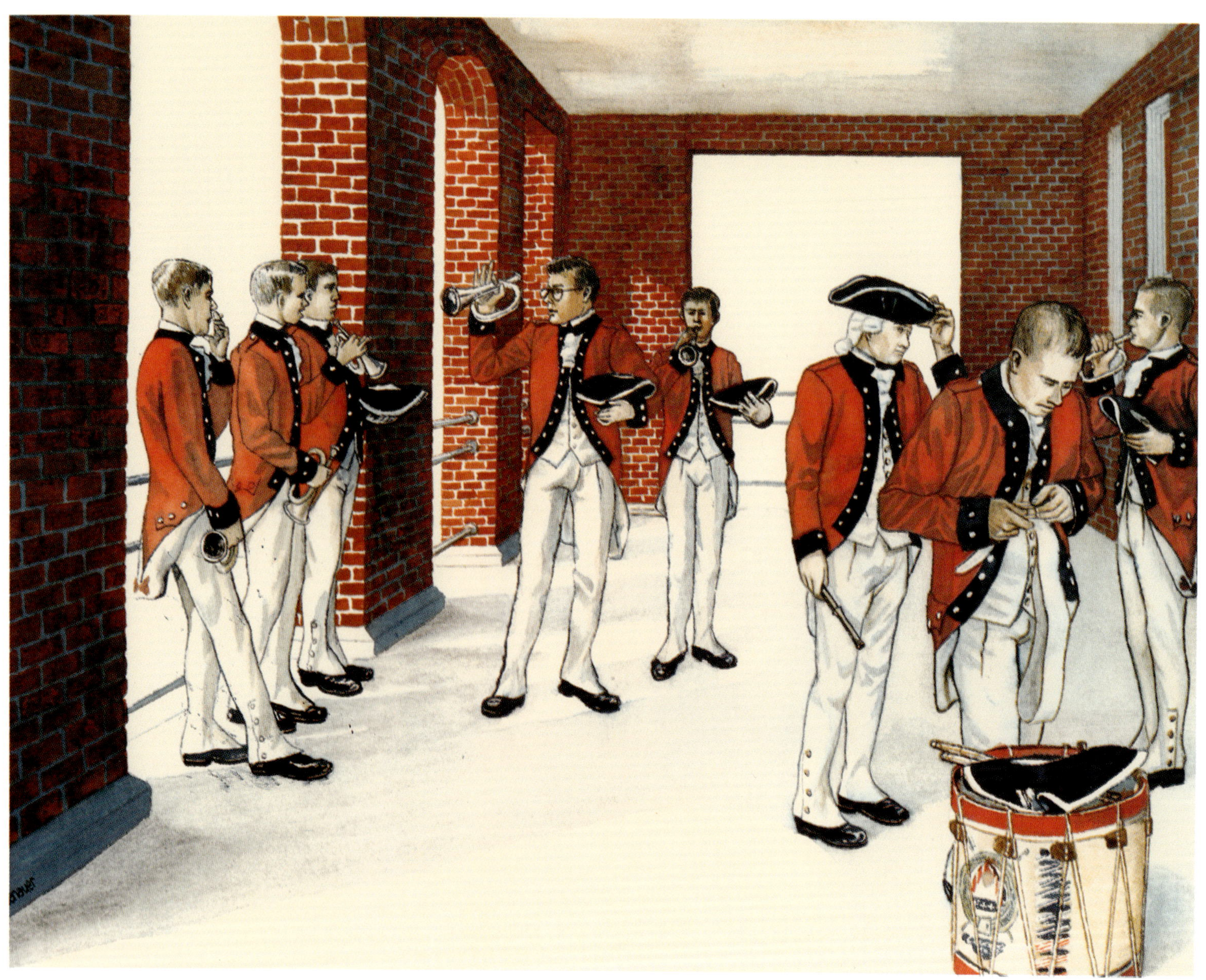

ASSEMBLY POINT
Fort Myer, Virginia
Richard Hasenauer, 1976
Ink, 11" x 14"

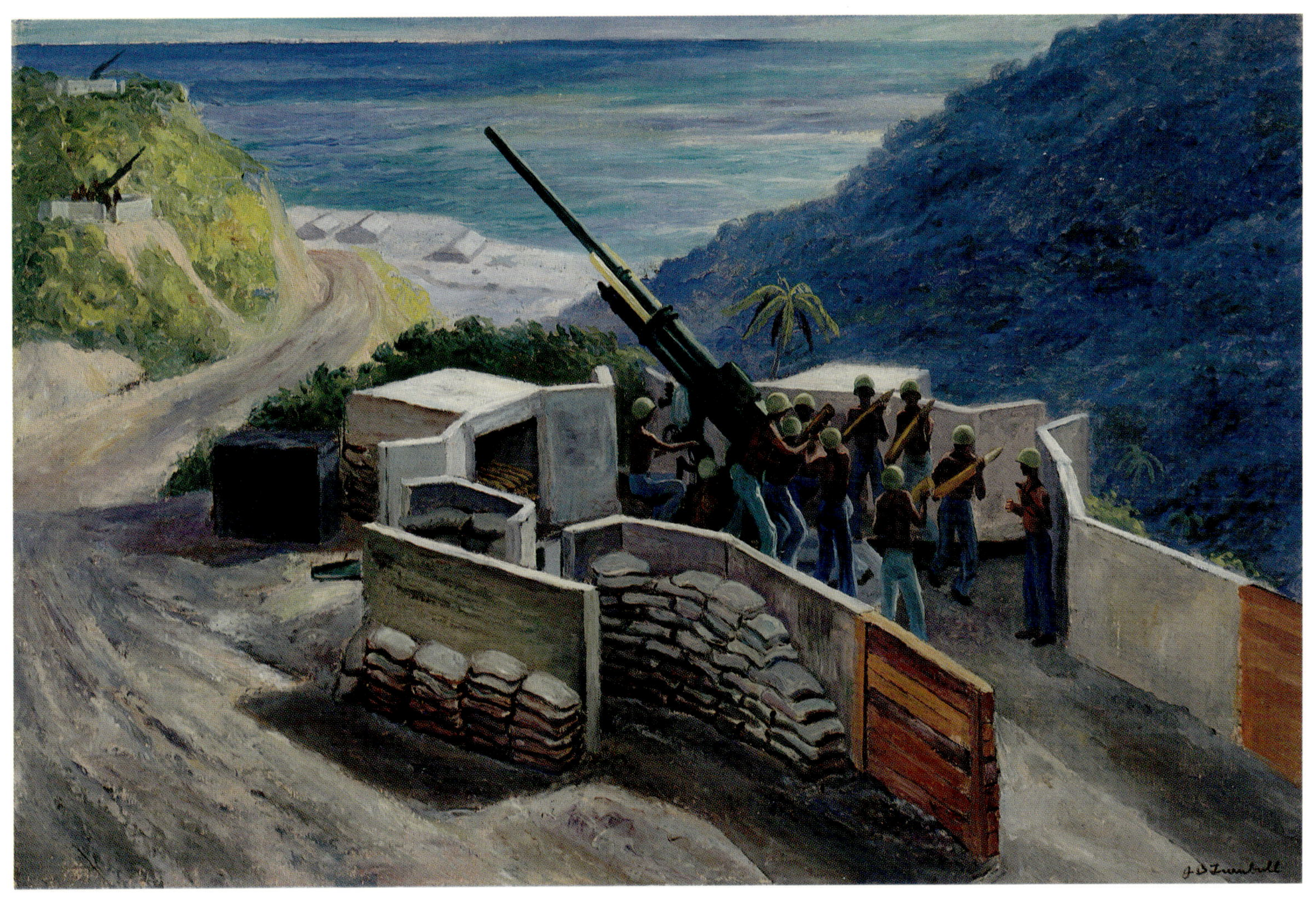

ANTI-AIRCRAFT CREW TRAINING
Trinidad
James Barre Turnbull, 1943
Oil, 15 ¾" x 23 ½"

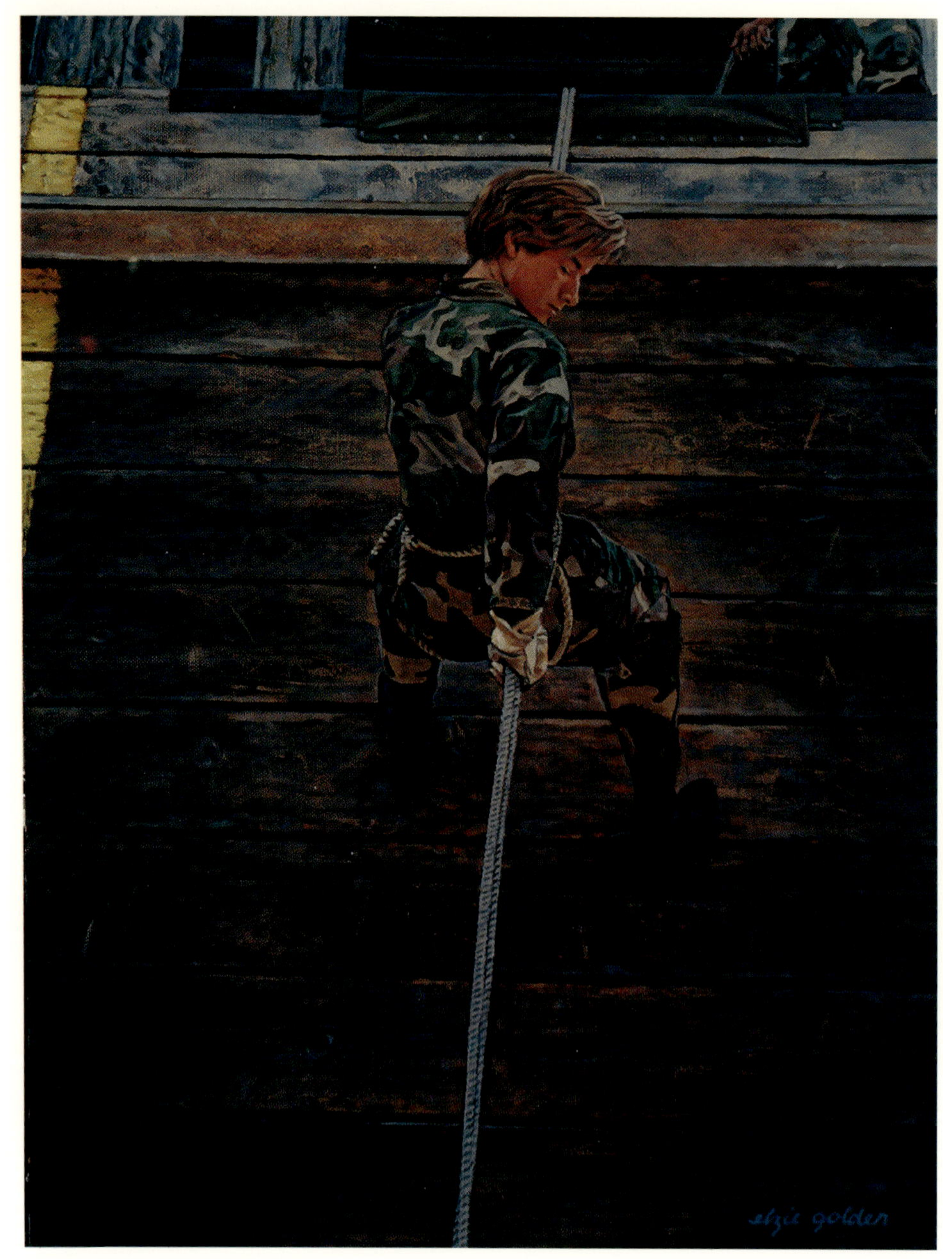

RECONDO
Fort Lewis, Washington
Elzie Golden, 1990
Oil, 24" x 18"

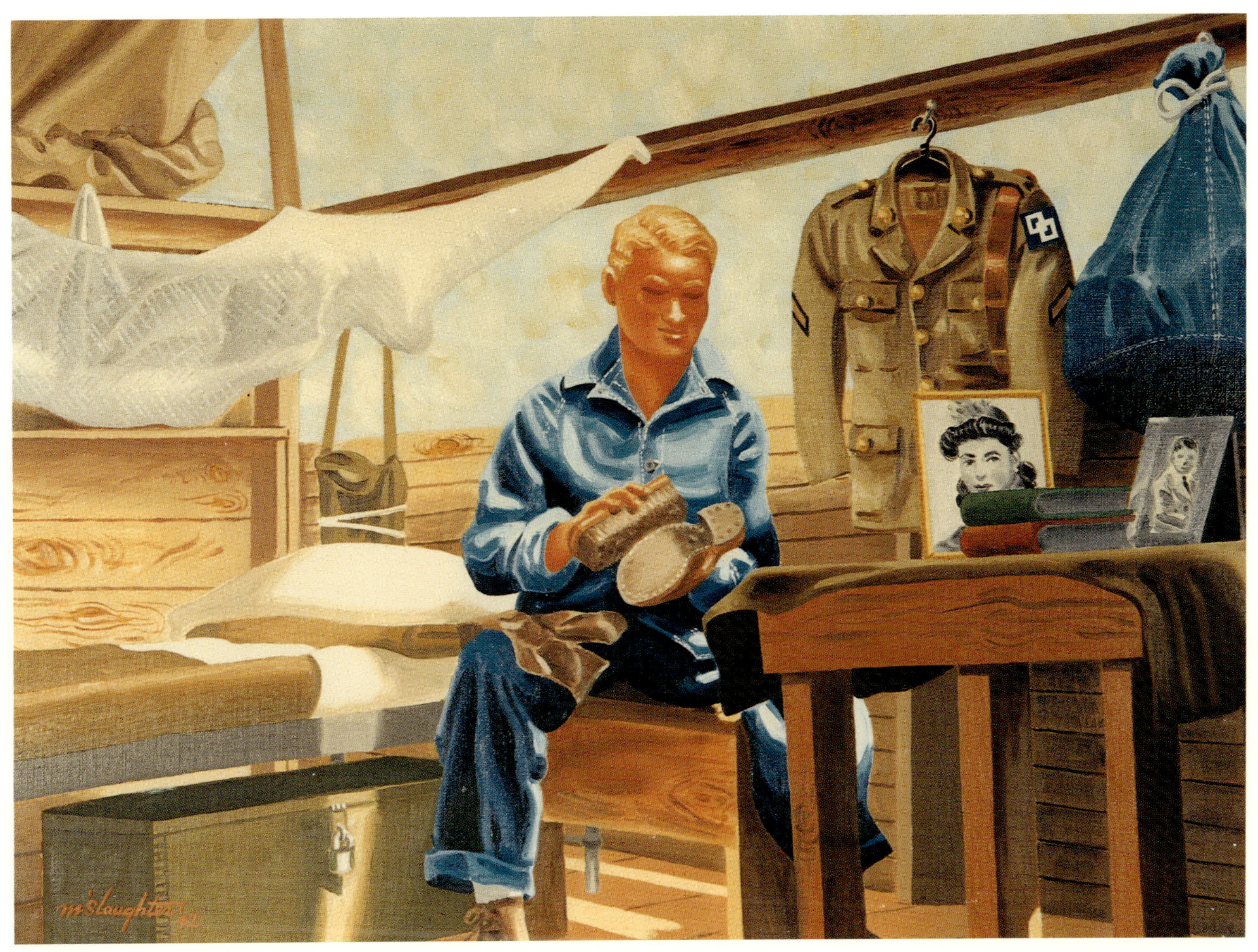

BARRACKS SCENE
Fort Dix, New Jersey
M. W. *Slaughter, 1942*
Oil, 16" x 22"

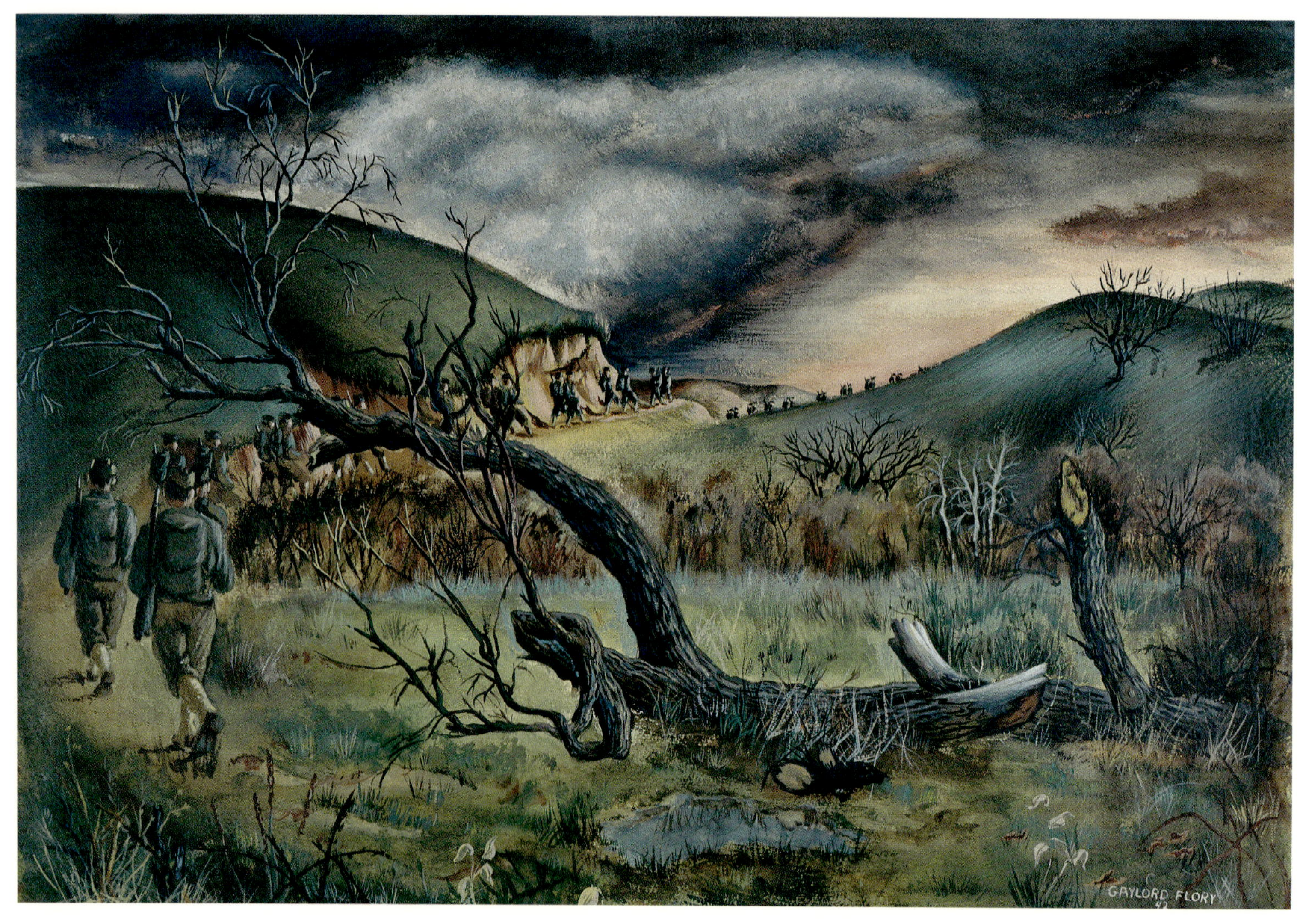

7:00AM
Gaylord Flory, 1942
Gouache, 14 ½" x 21 ½"

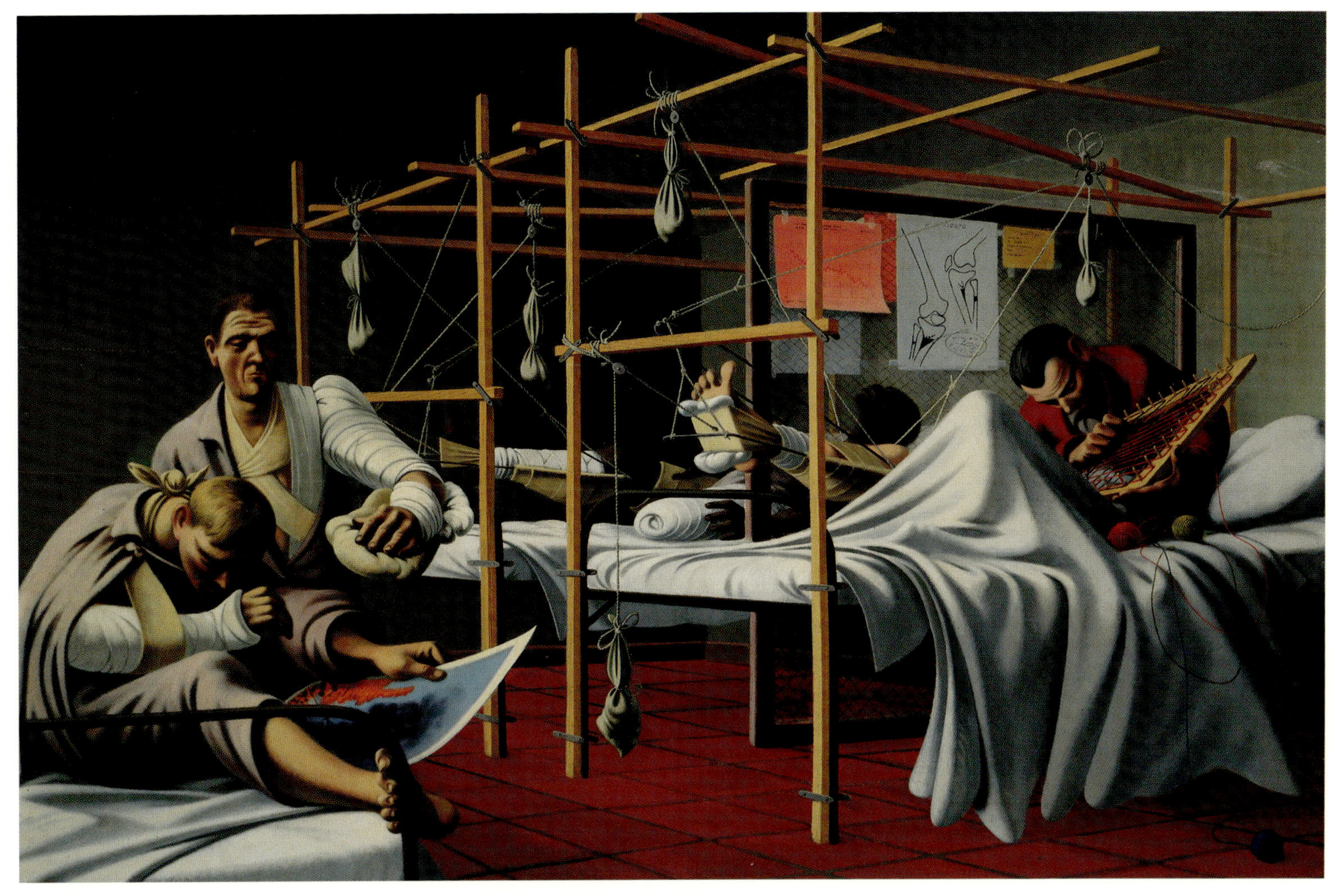

FRACTURE WARD
New York
Peter Blume, 1944
Oil, 24 ⅛" x 36 ¼"

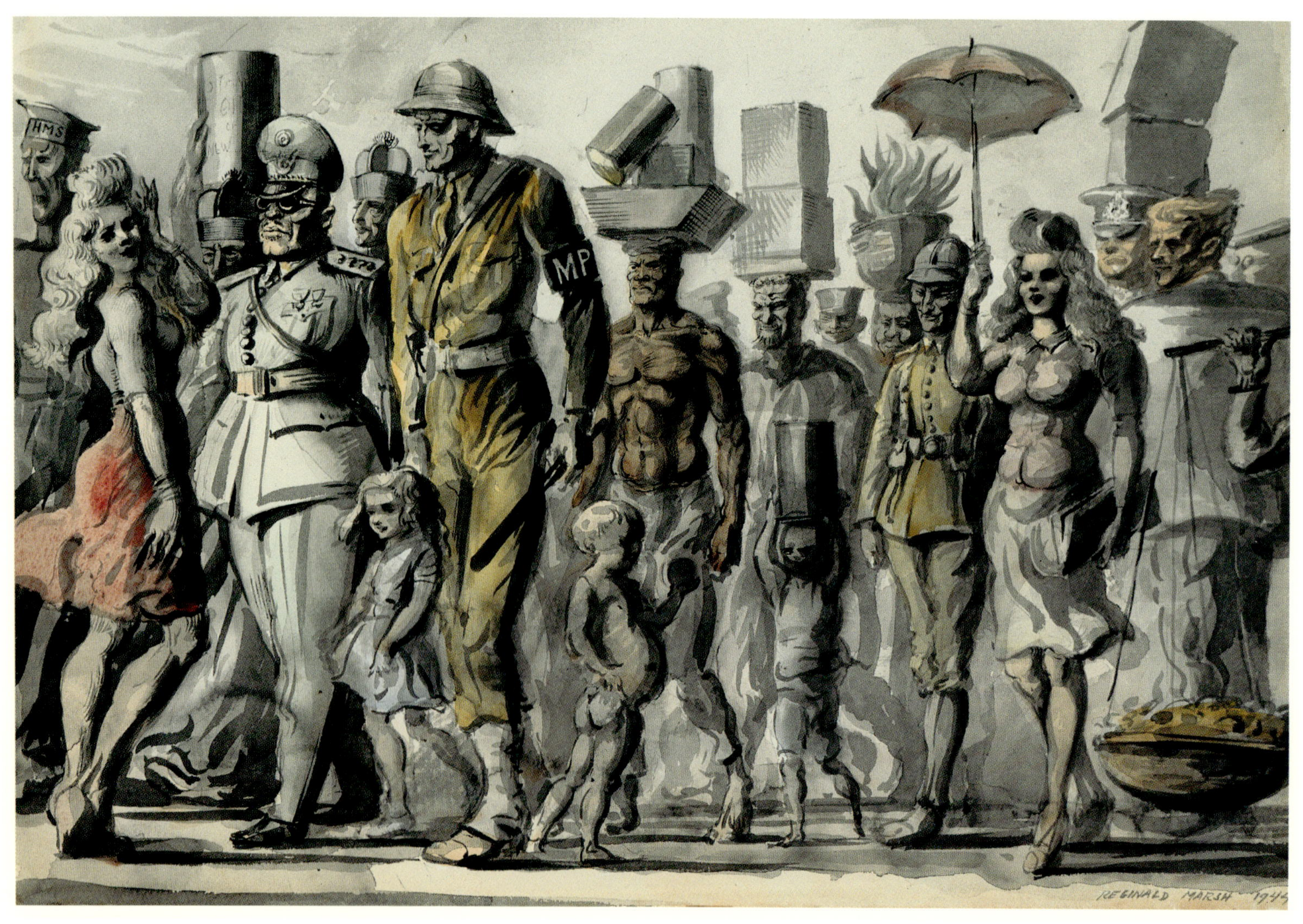

PEOPLE OF ALL NATIONS IN BRAZIL
Brazil
Reginald Marsh, 1943
Watercolor, 13" x 19"

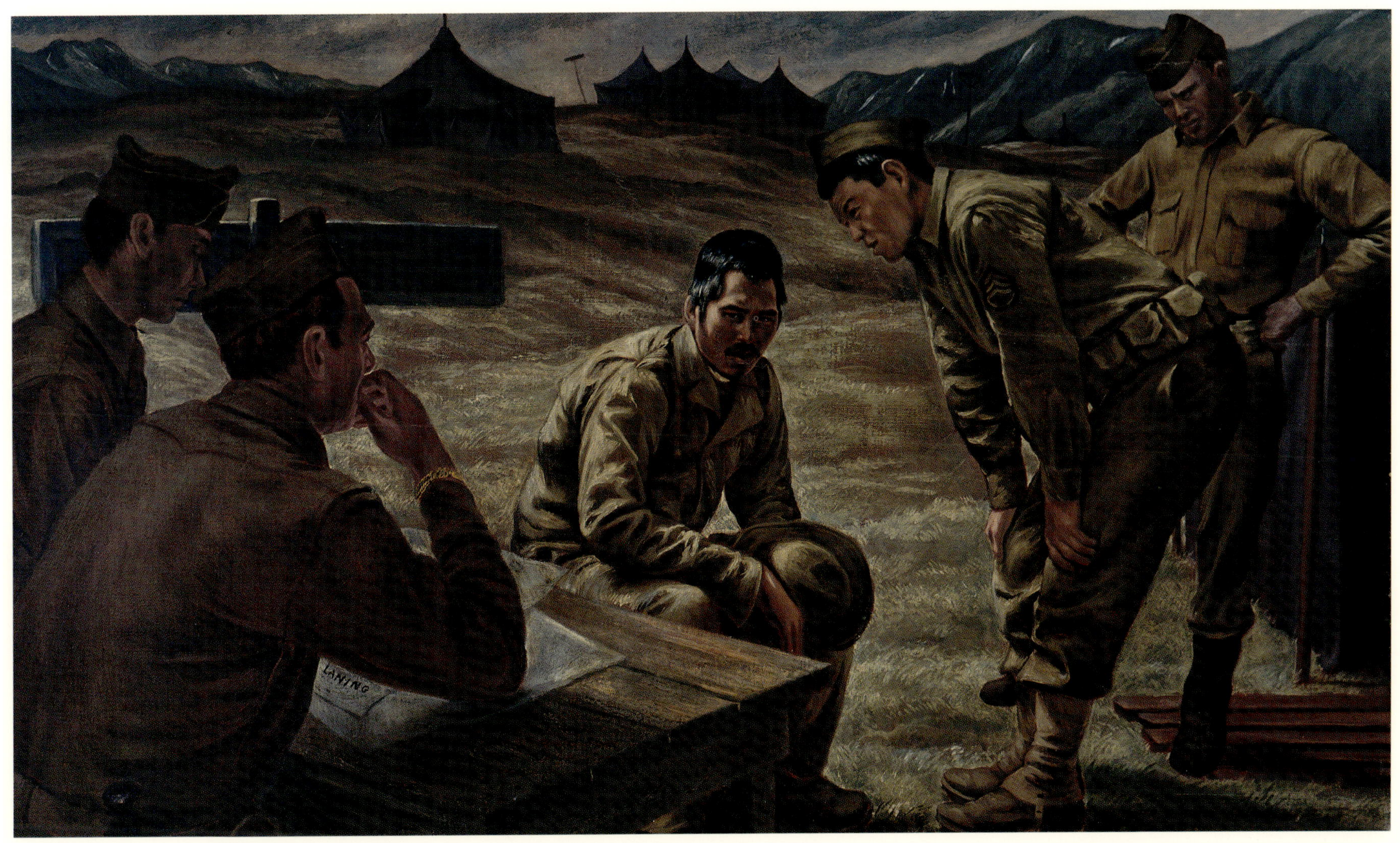

INTERROGATION
Aleutians
Edward R. Laning, 1943
Oil, 24" x 40"

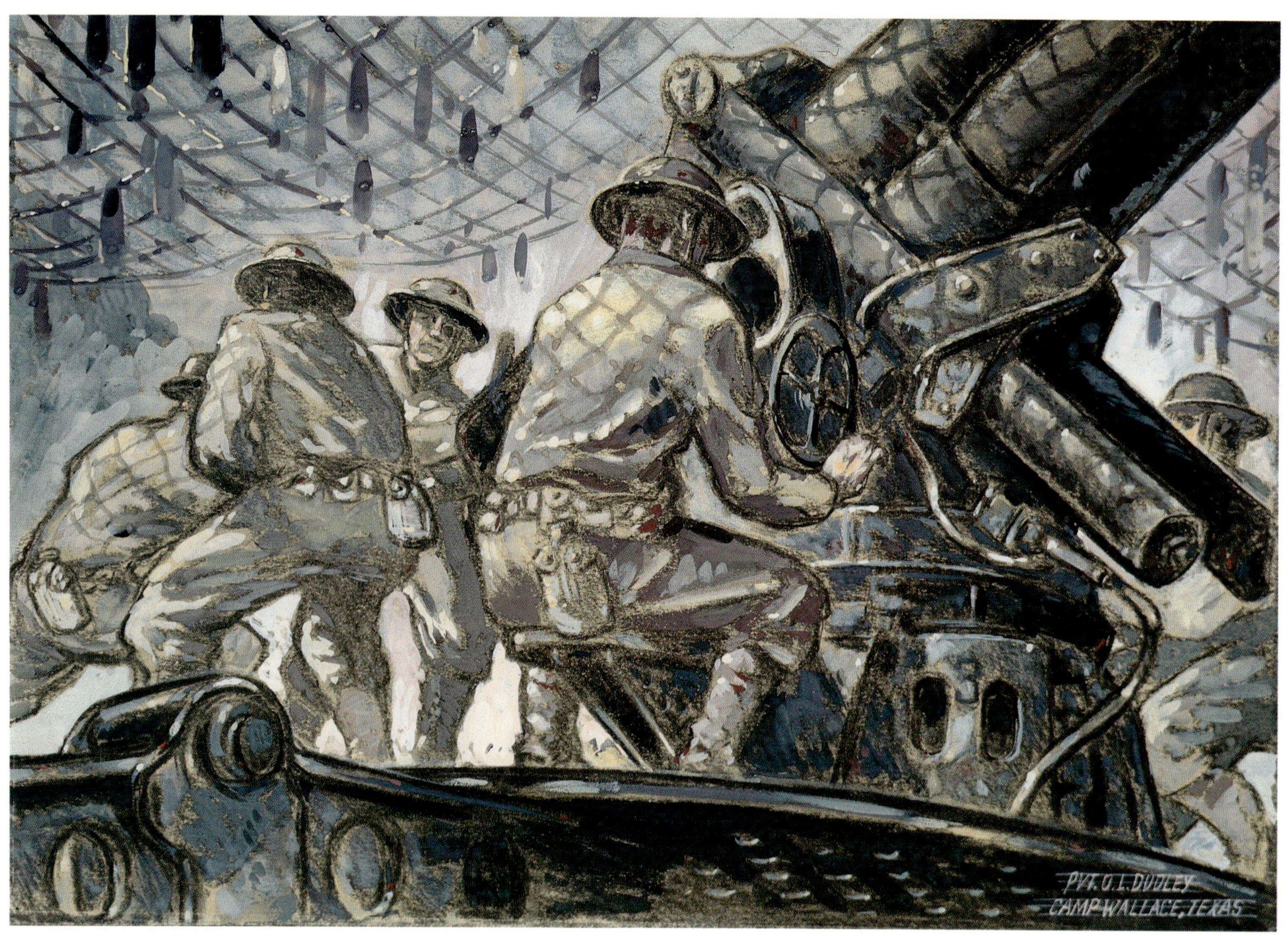

UNDER THE WIRE
Camp Wallace, Texas
O. I. Dudley, 1942
Watercolor, 12 ½" x 18"

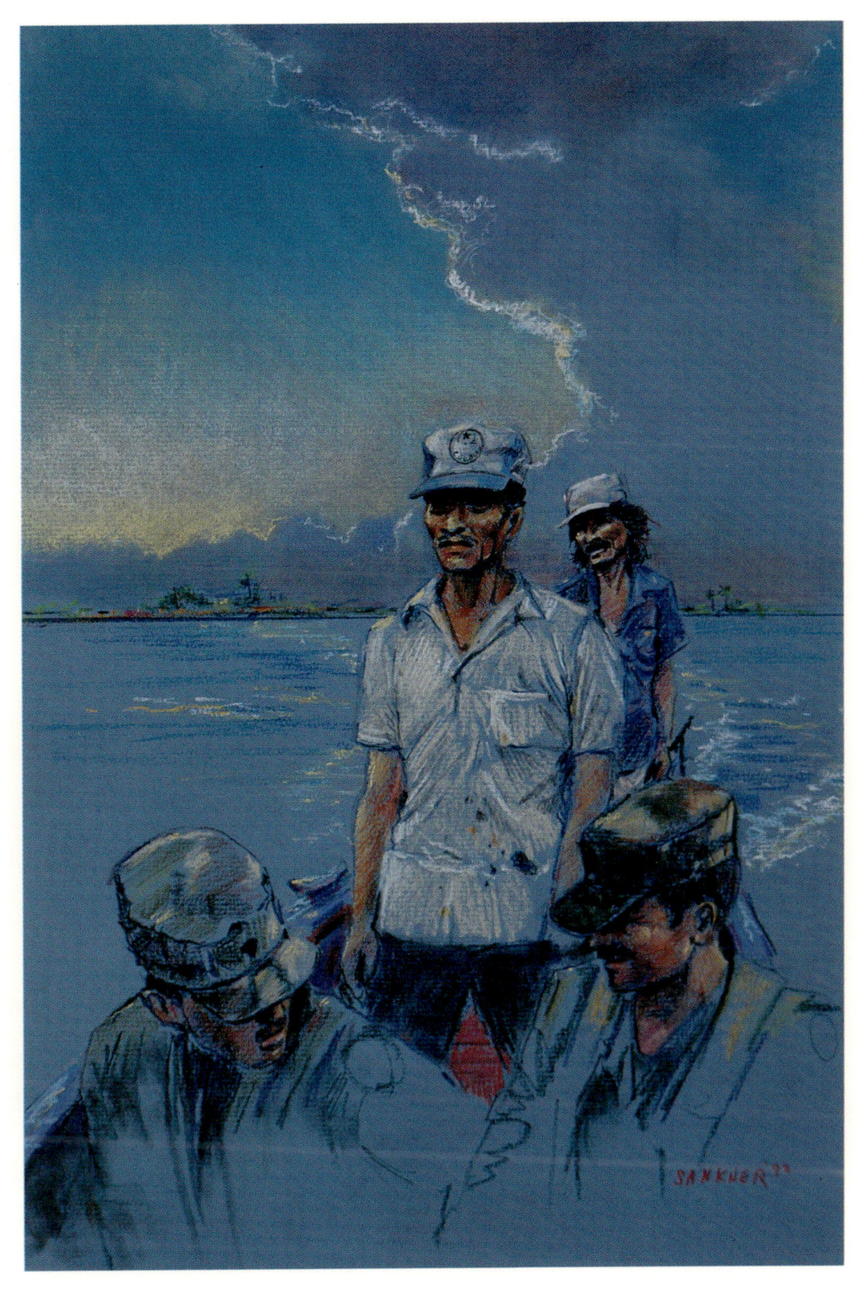

ON THE RIVER
Panama
Robert Sankner, 1993
Pastel, 17 ½" x 12"

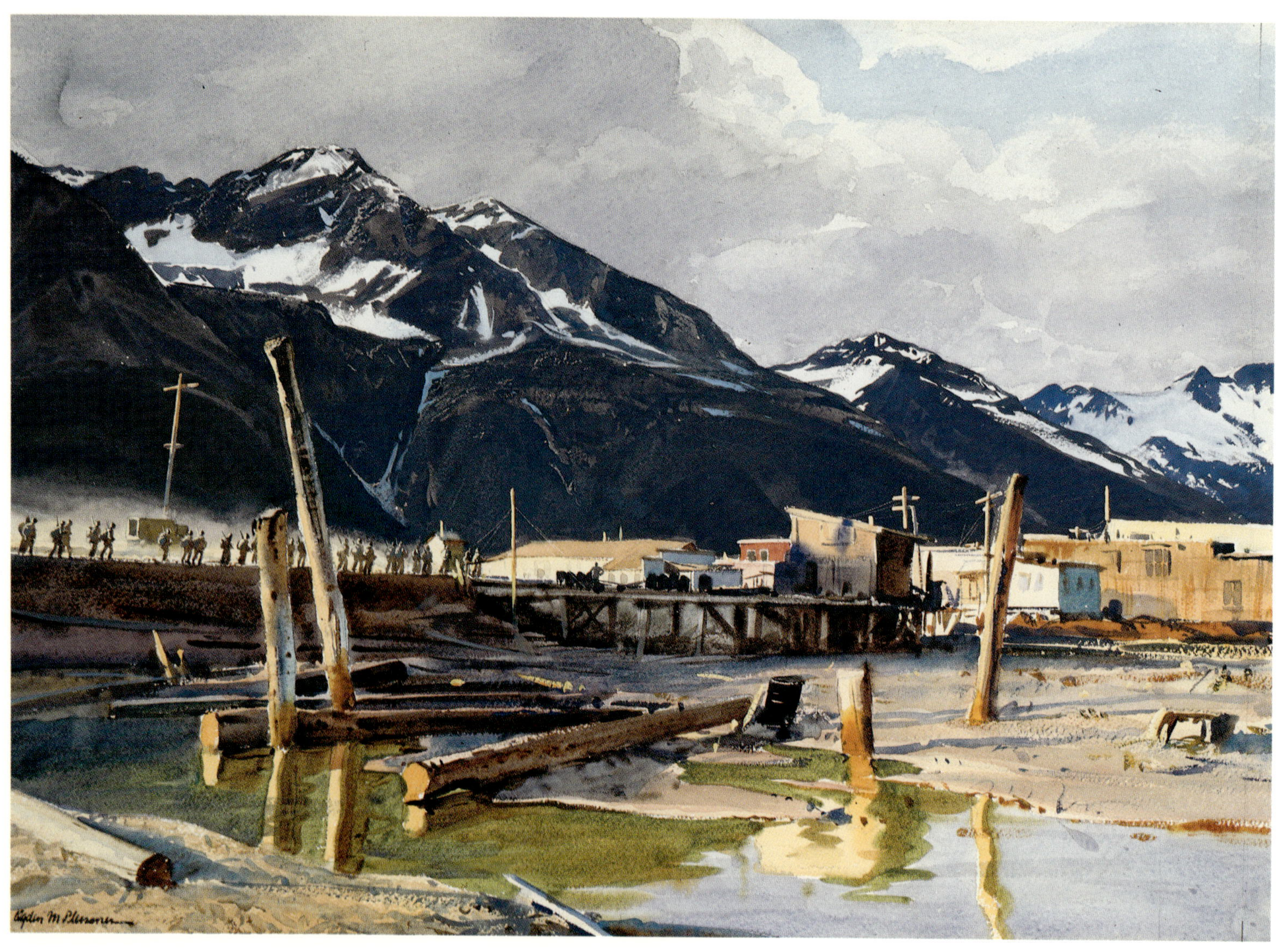

NEW ARRIVALS
Valdez, Aleutians
Ogden Pleissner, 1943
Watercolor, 18 ½" x 25 ½"

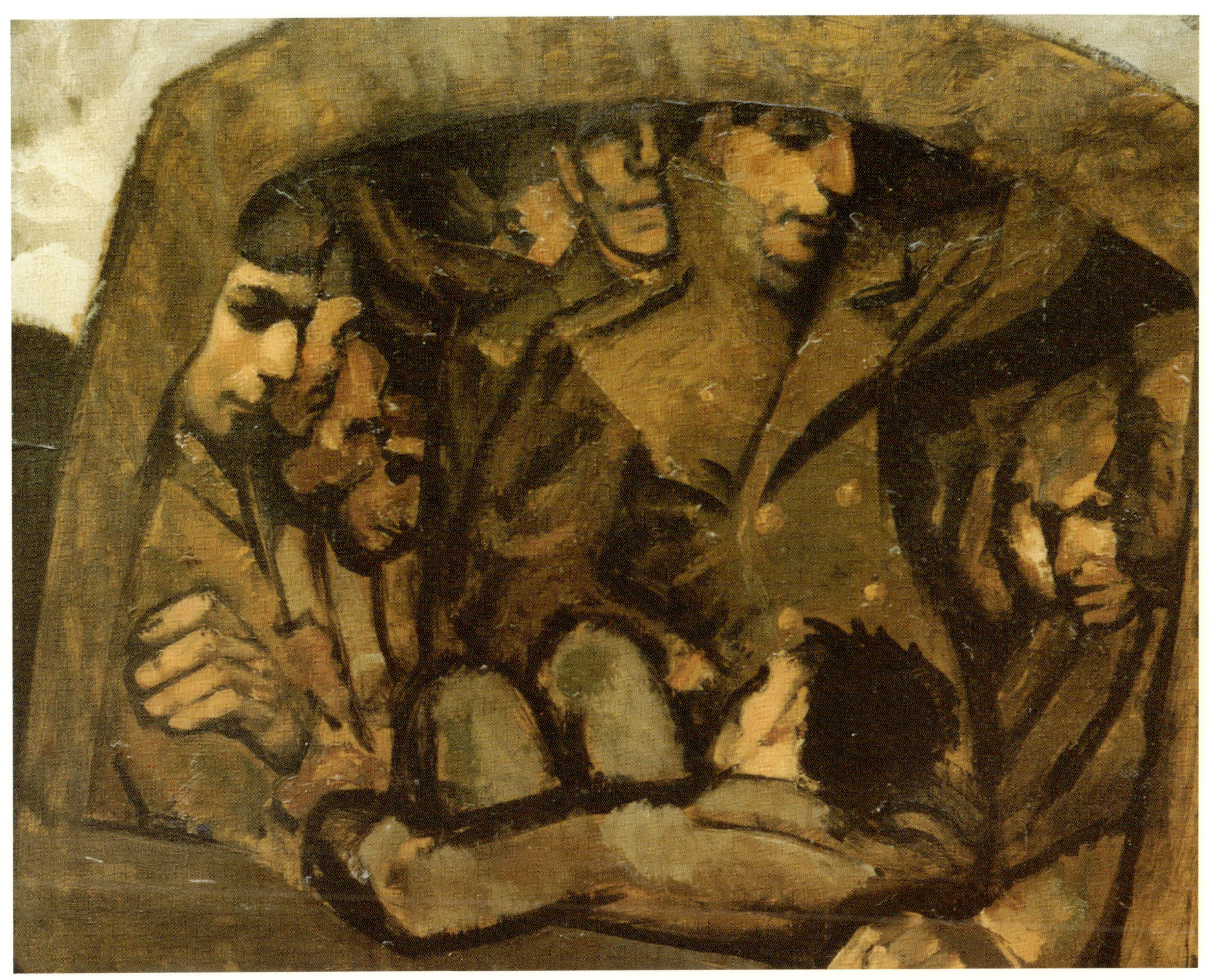

TROOP MOVEMENT
Fort Belvoir, Virginia
Robert C. Burns, 1942
Oil, 29 ½" x 33 ½"

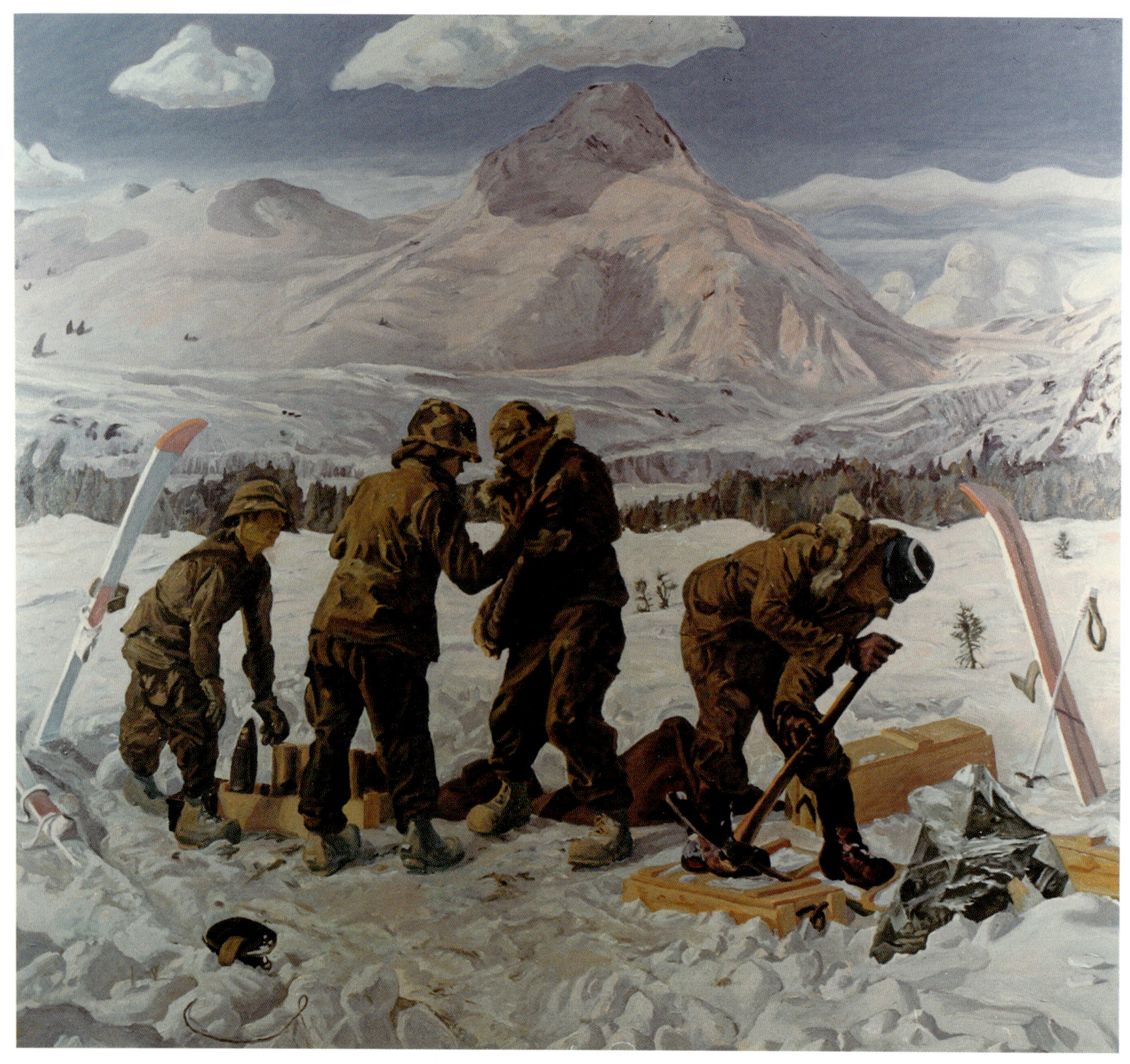

CAPTAIN FREDIA RESURRECTS
Alaska
Richard J. Peterson, 1974
Oil, 58" x 63 ½"

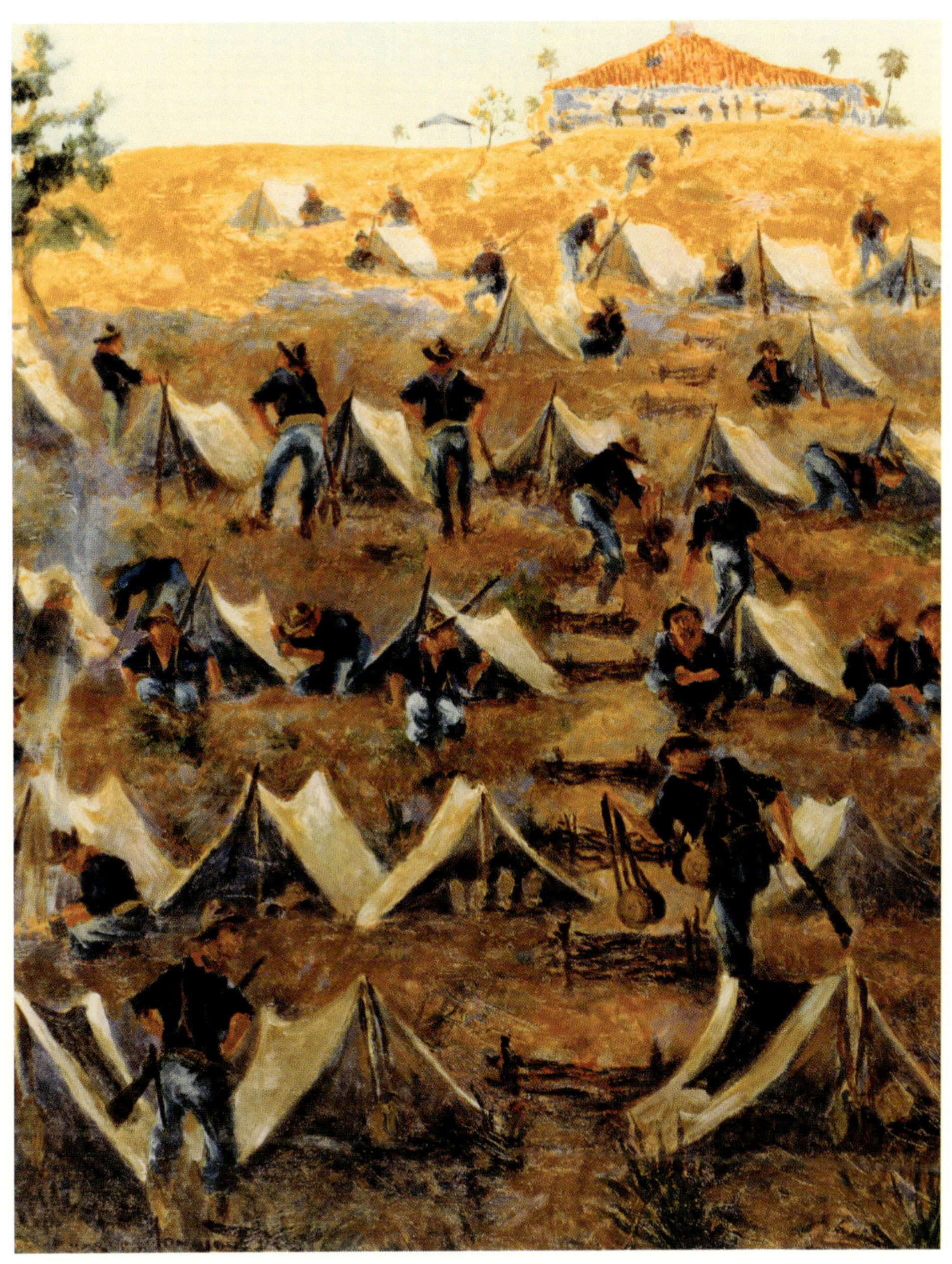

SAN JUAN HILL
Cuba, Spanish-American War
Charles Johnson Post
Oil, 25" x 30"

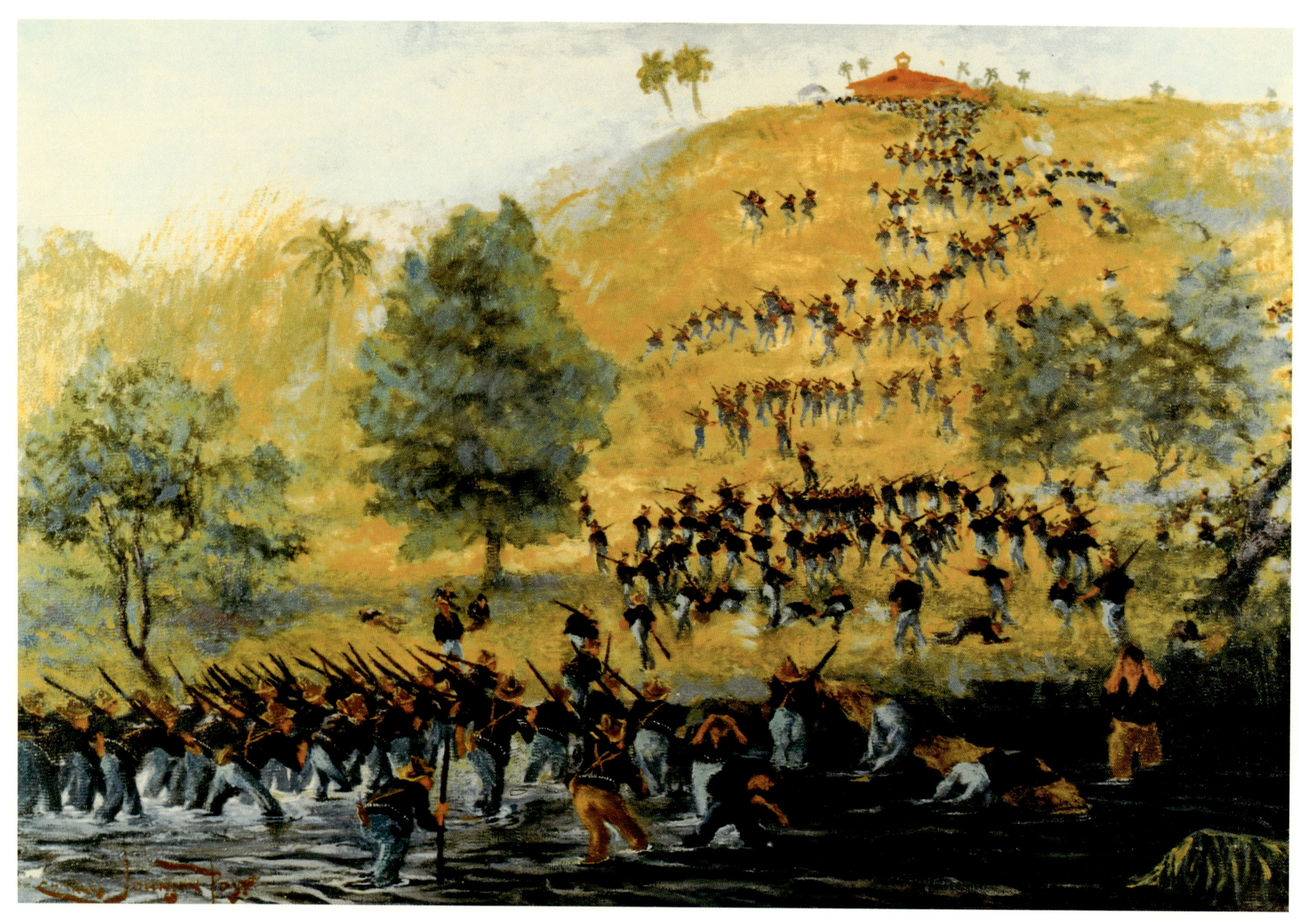

BLOODY FORD, JULY 1ST
Cuba, Spanish-American War
Charles Johnson Post
Oil, 24" x 36"

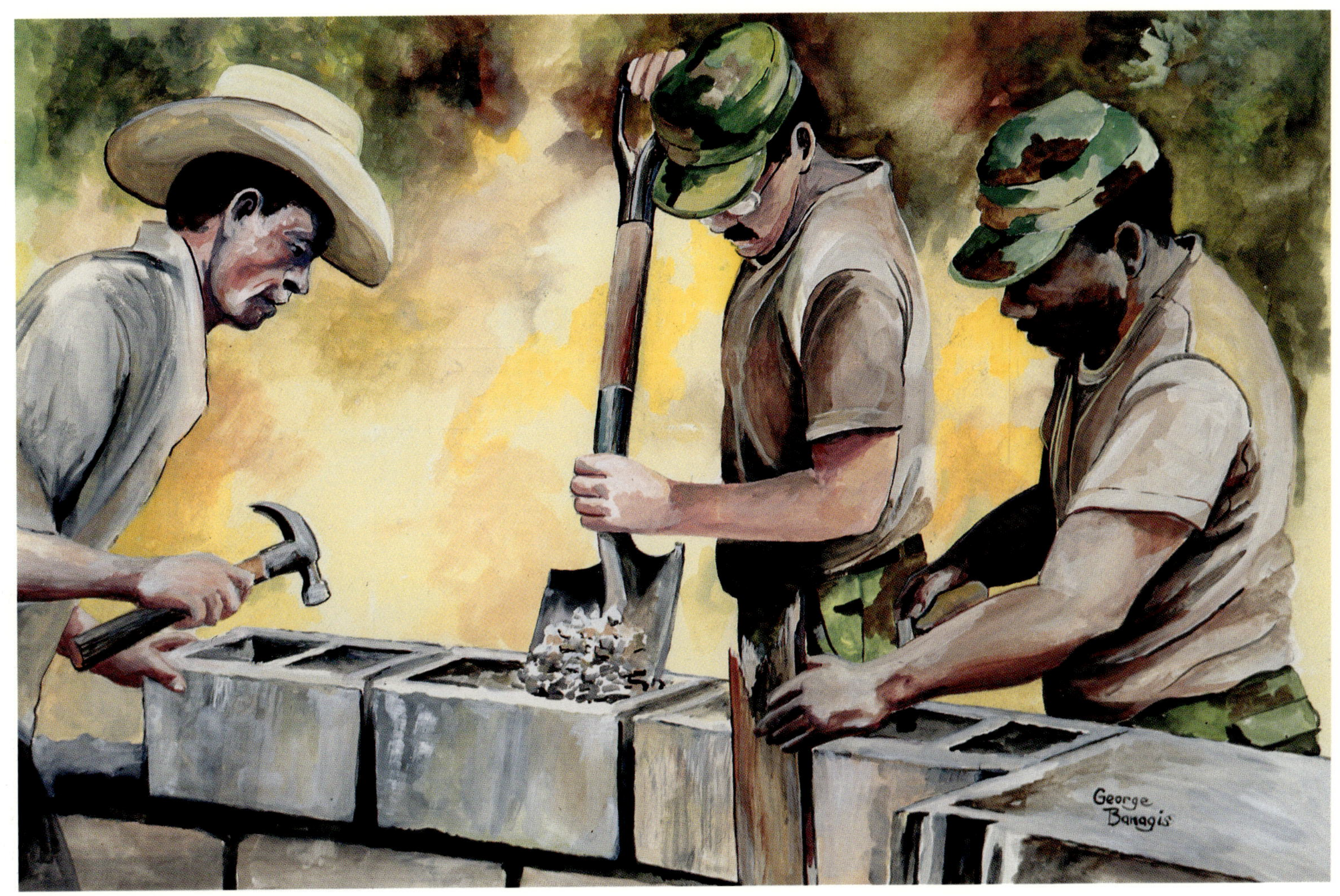

BUILDING COOPERATION
Honduras
George Banagis, 1993
Watercolor, 17″ x 25″

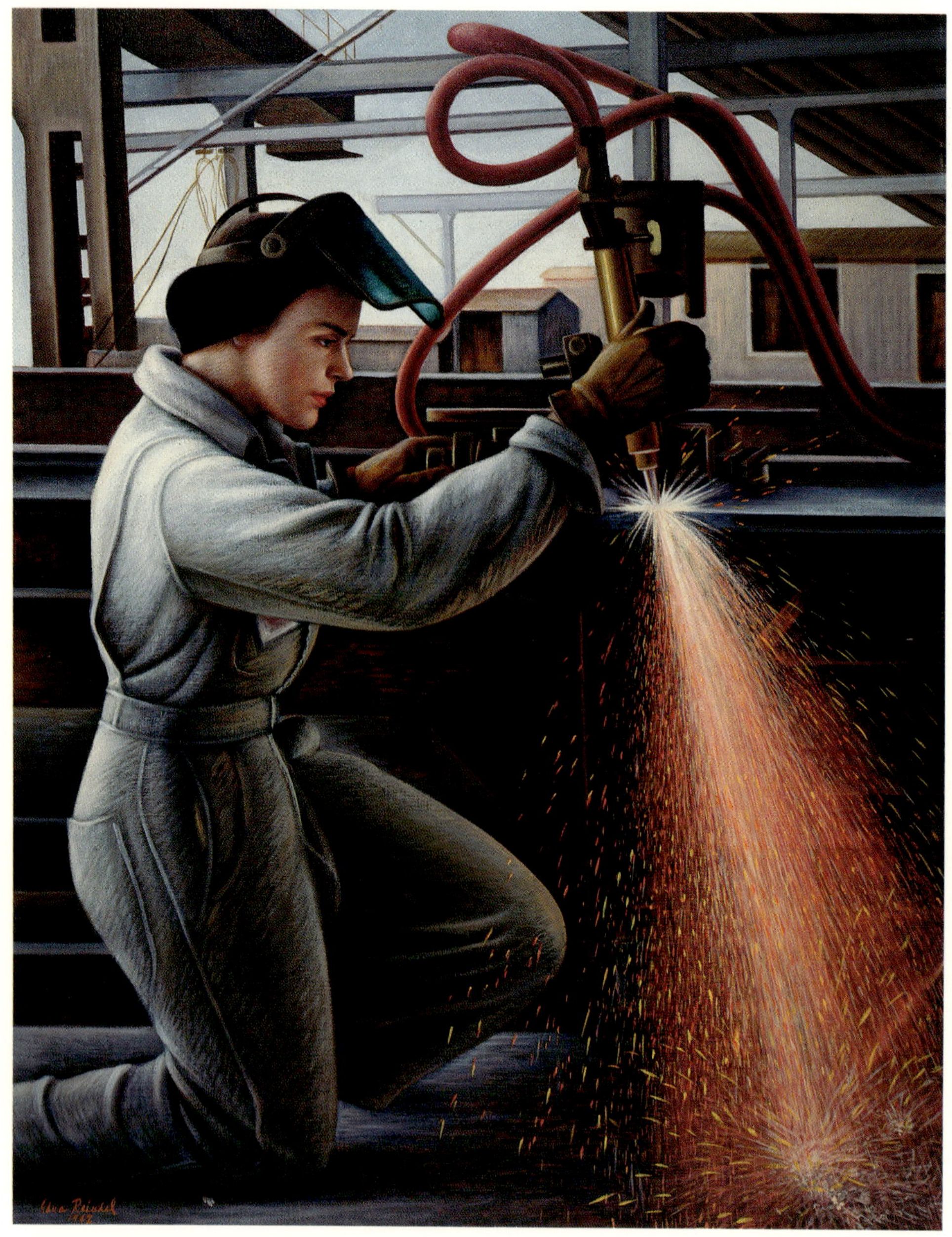

CALSHIP BURNER
Wilmington, California
Edna Reindel, 1943
Oil, 37" x 30"

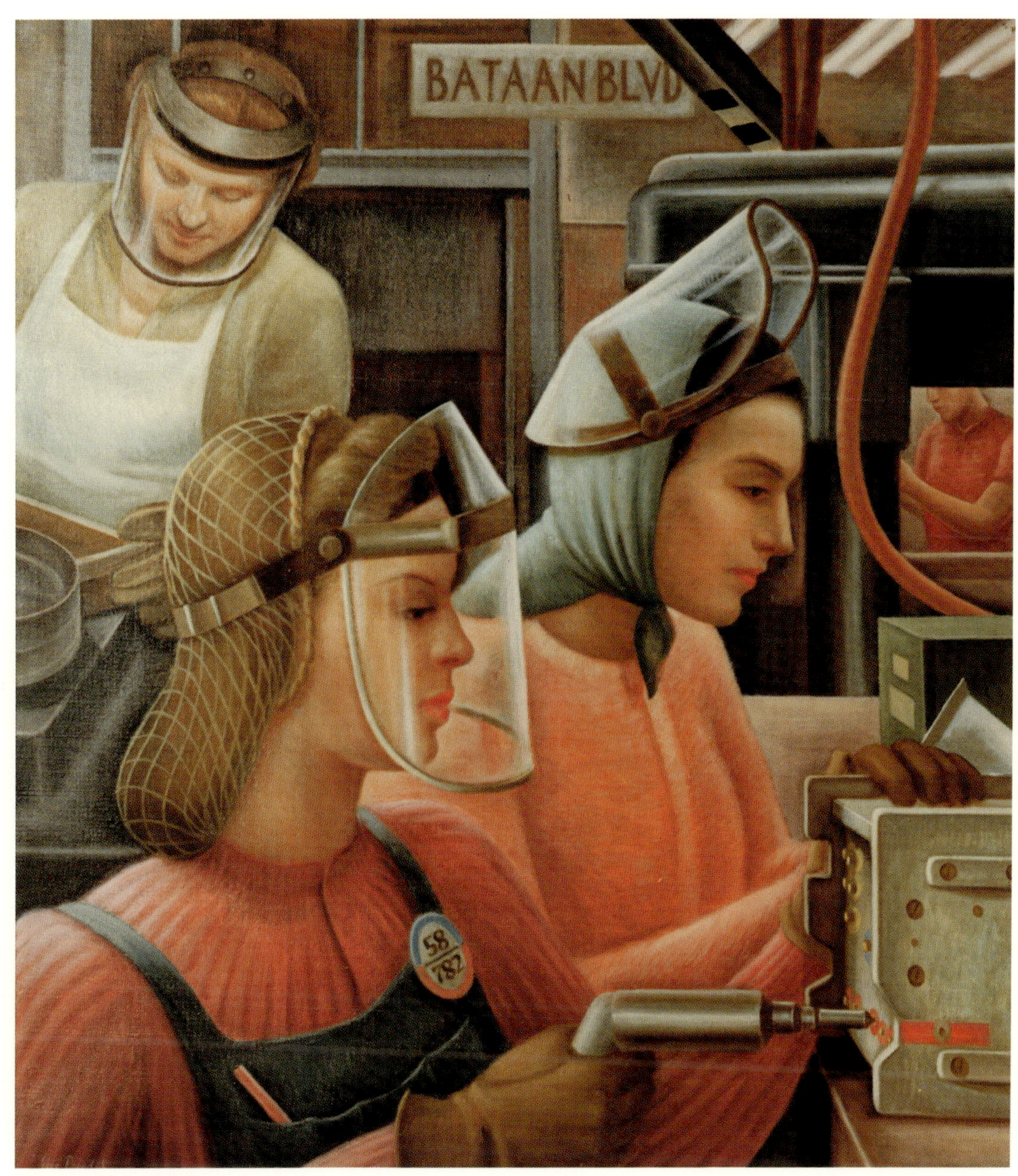

WOMEN WITH MASKS
Burbank, California
Edna Reindel, 1943
Oil, 28" x 32"

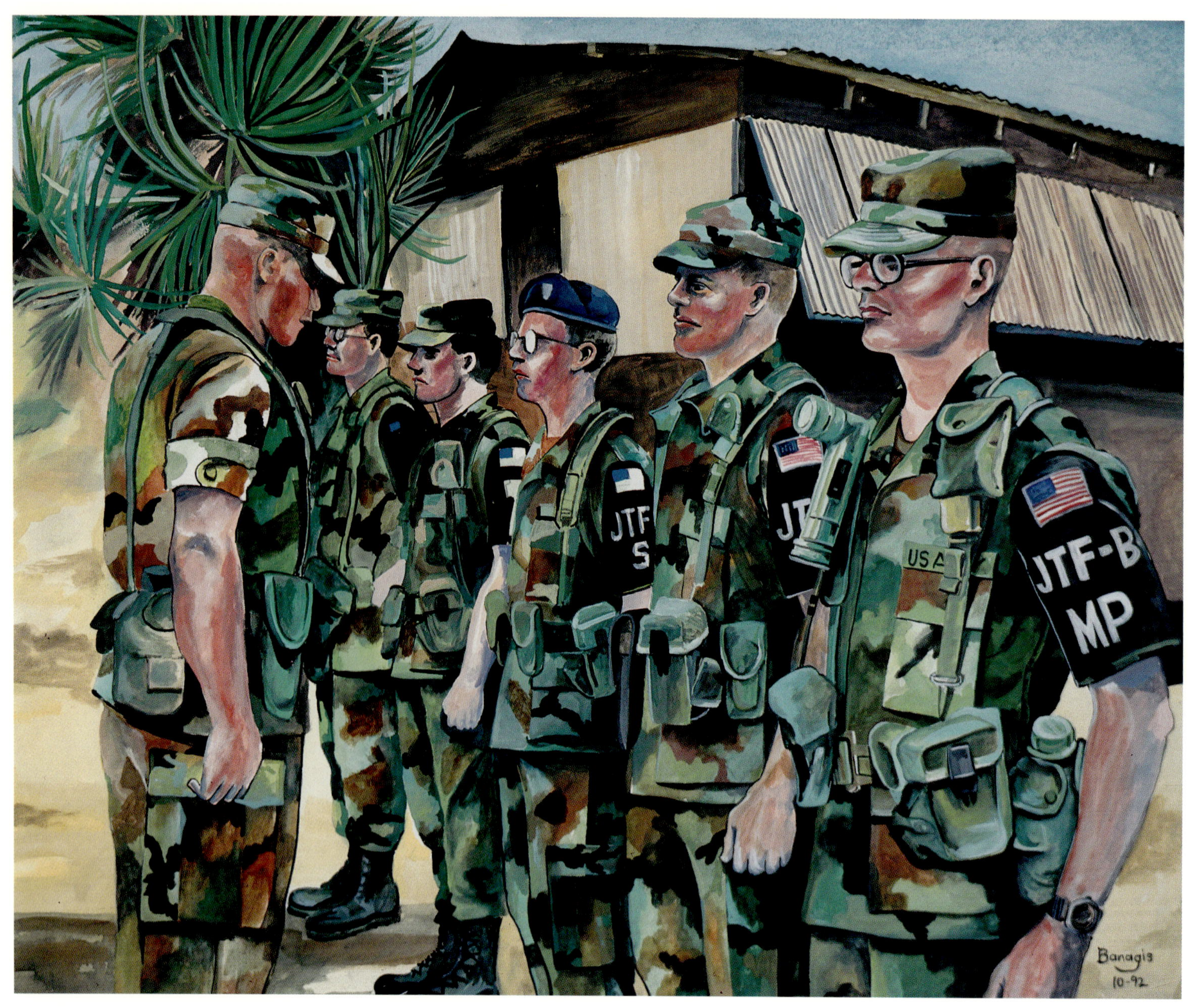

MP FORMATION JTFB
Honduras
George Banagis, 1992
Watercolor, 20" x 24"

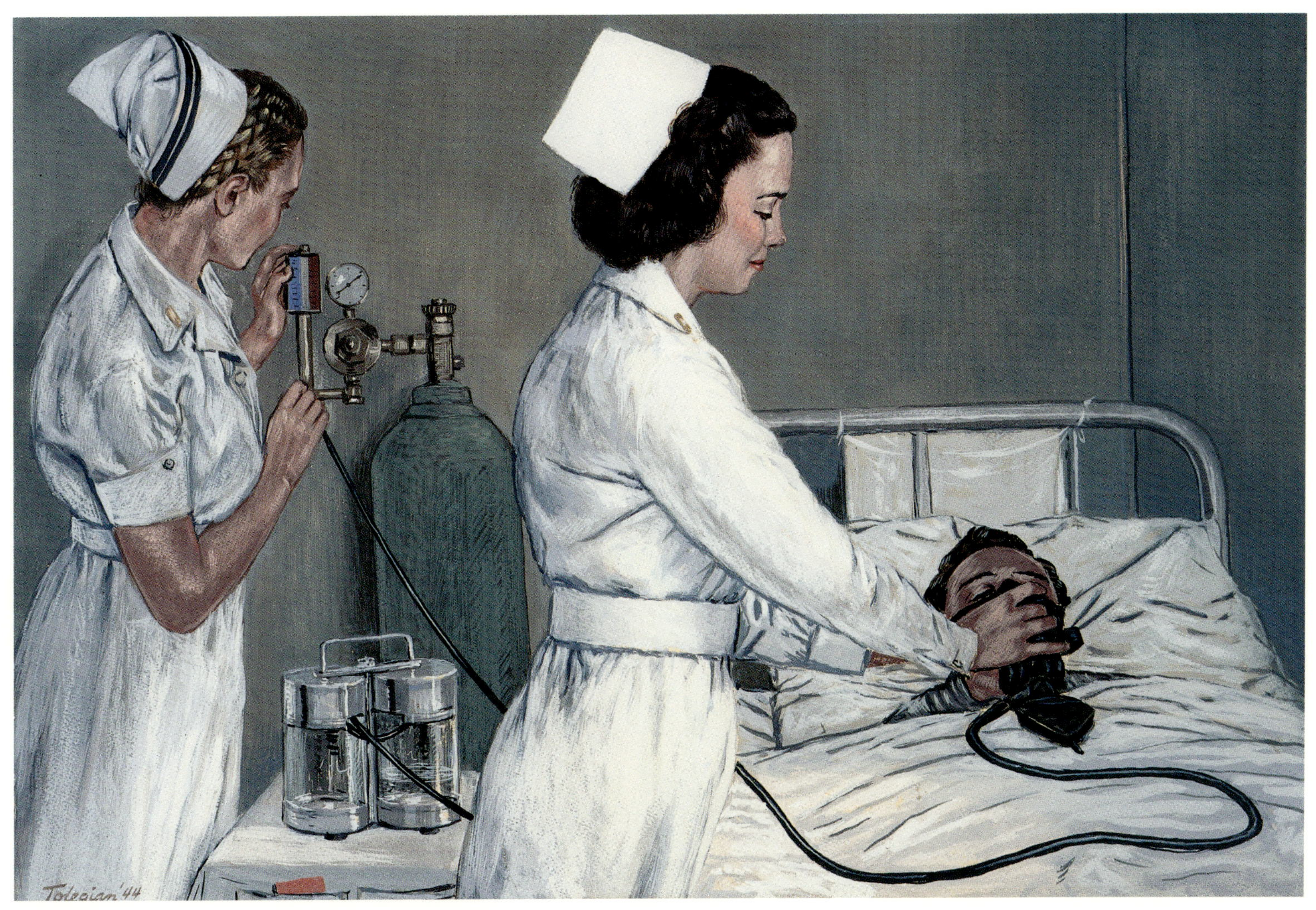

COMBAT TEAM
Camp White, Oregon
Manuel Tolegian, 1944
Watercolor, 13 ⅞" x 18 ⅜"

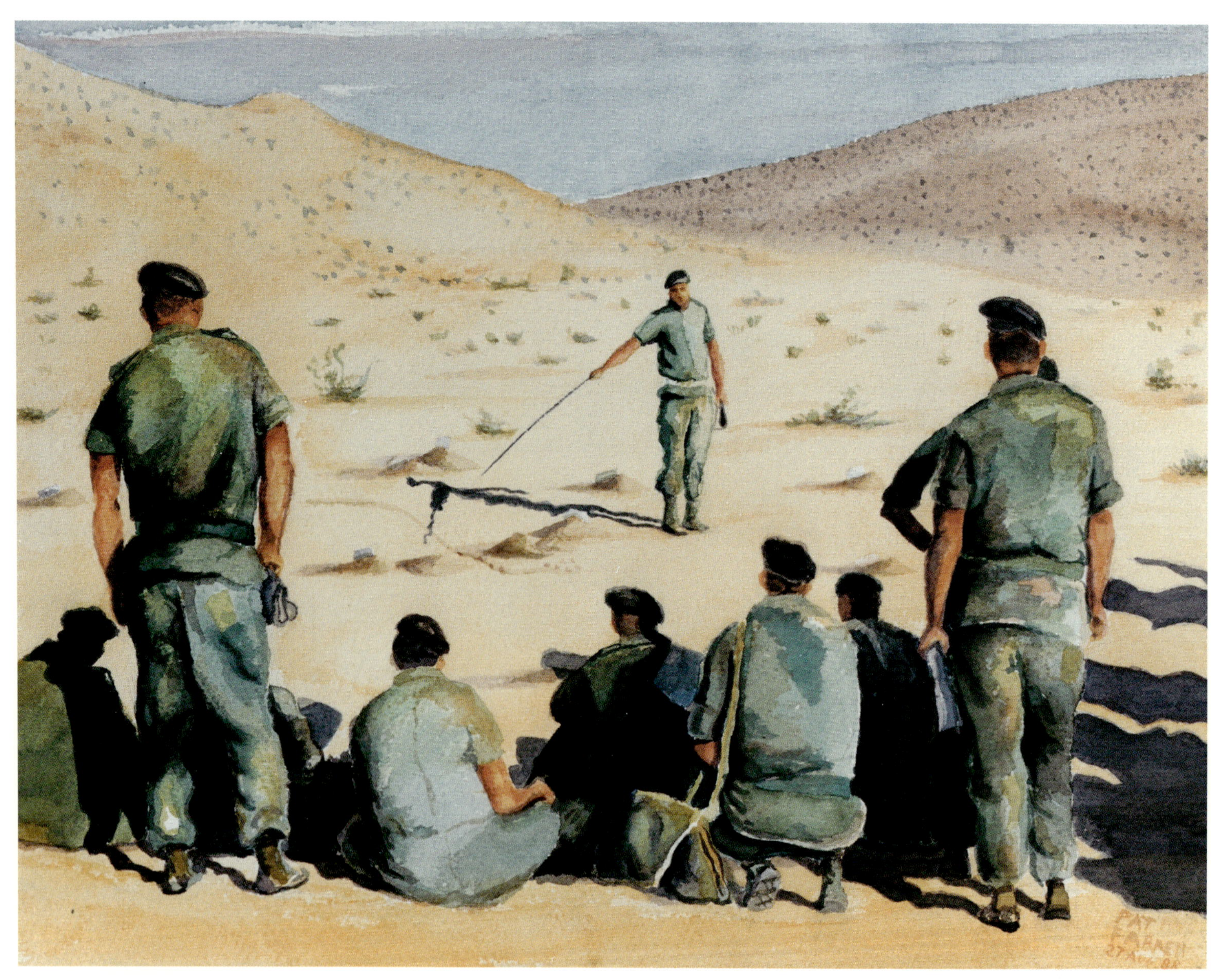

OPFOR BRIEFING
Fort Irwin, California
Patrick Farrell, 1988
Watercolor, 10 ¾" x 15 ⅛"

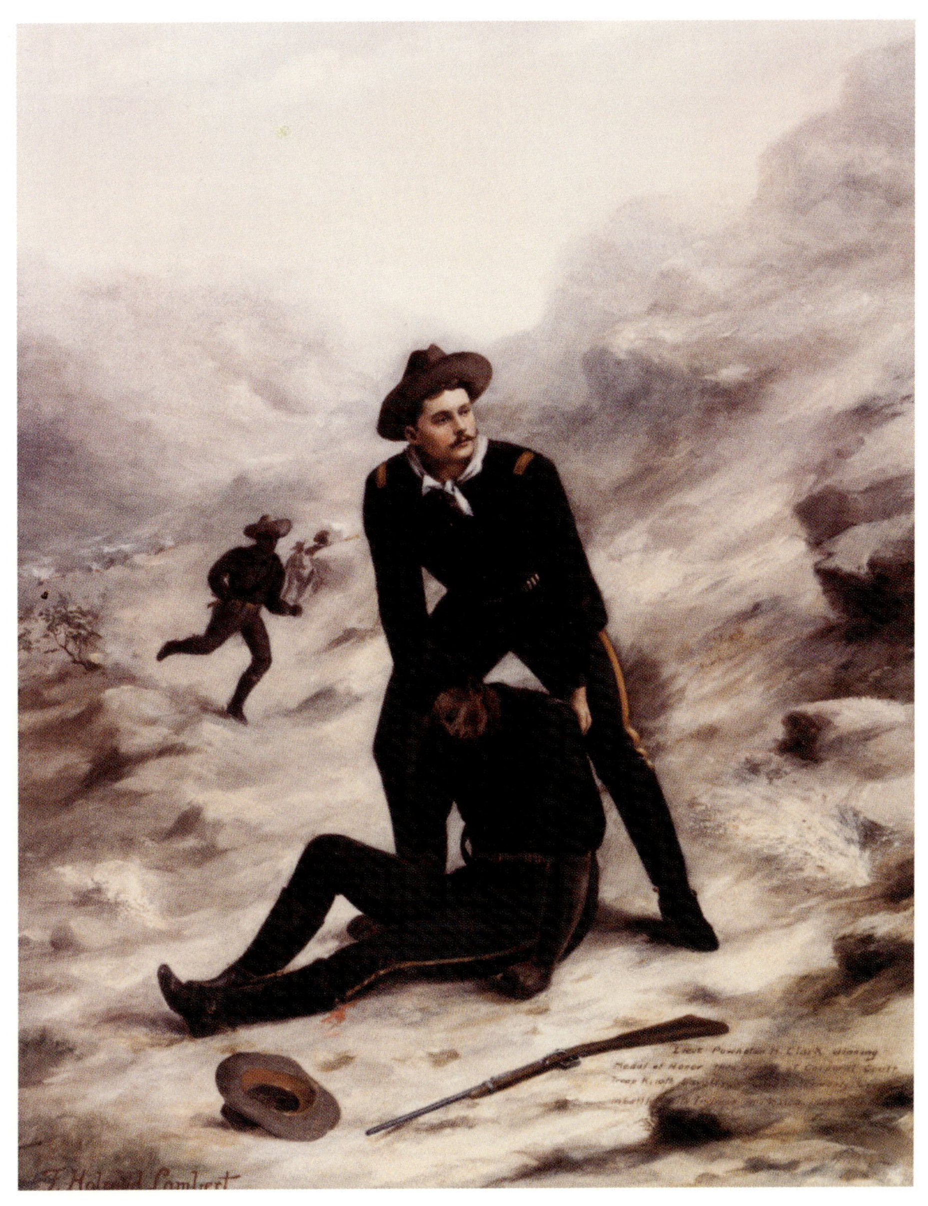

LT. CLARK
Mexico, 1886
F. Holroyd Lambert, 1895
Oil, 44 ⅞" x 35 15/16"

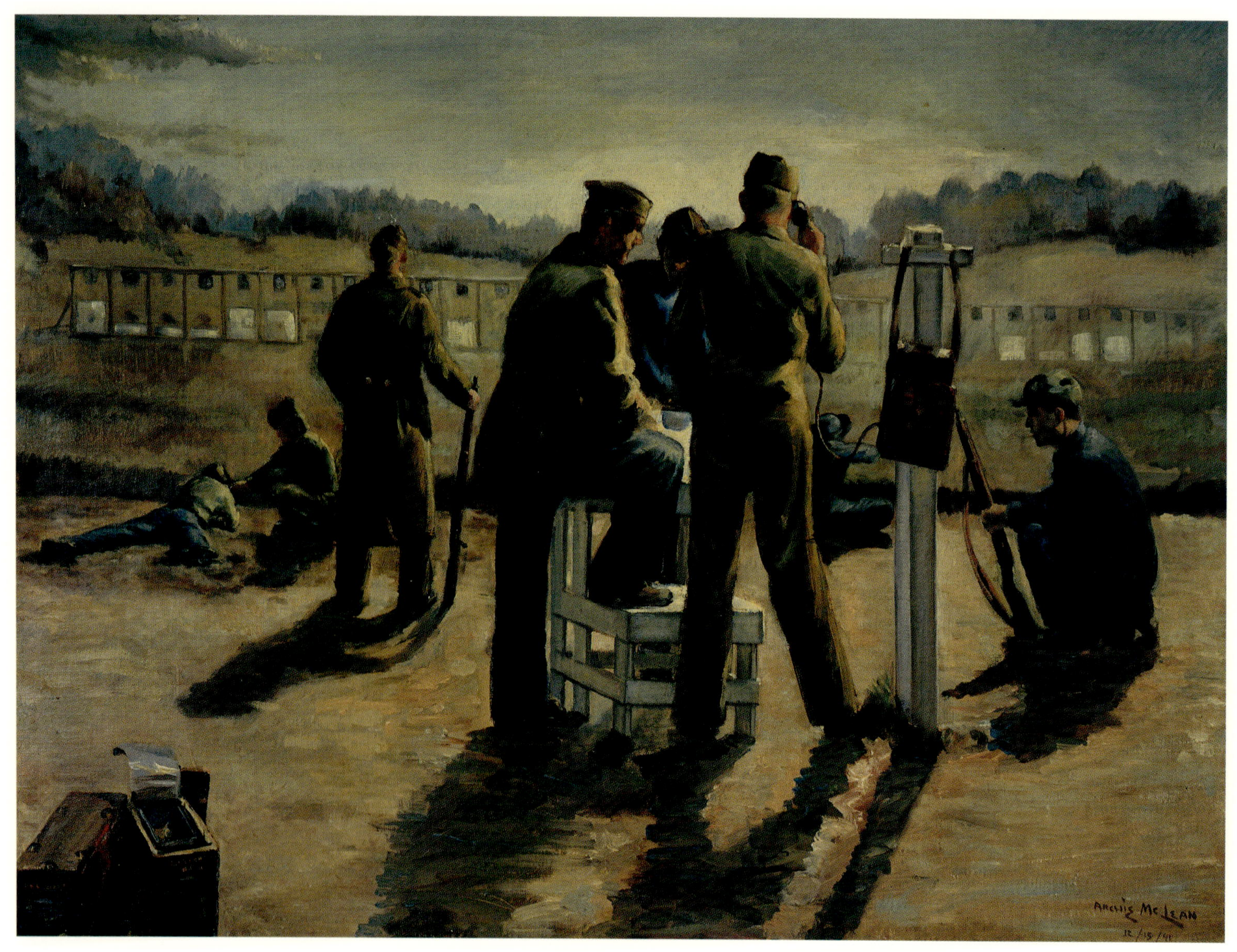

ON THE RANGE
Fort Custer, Michigan
Archie McLean, 1941
Oil, 29 ½" x 39 ½"

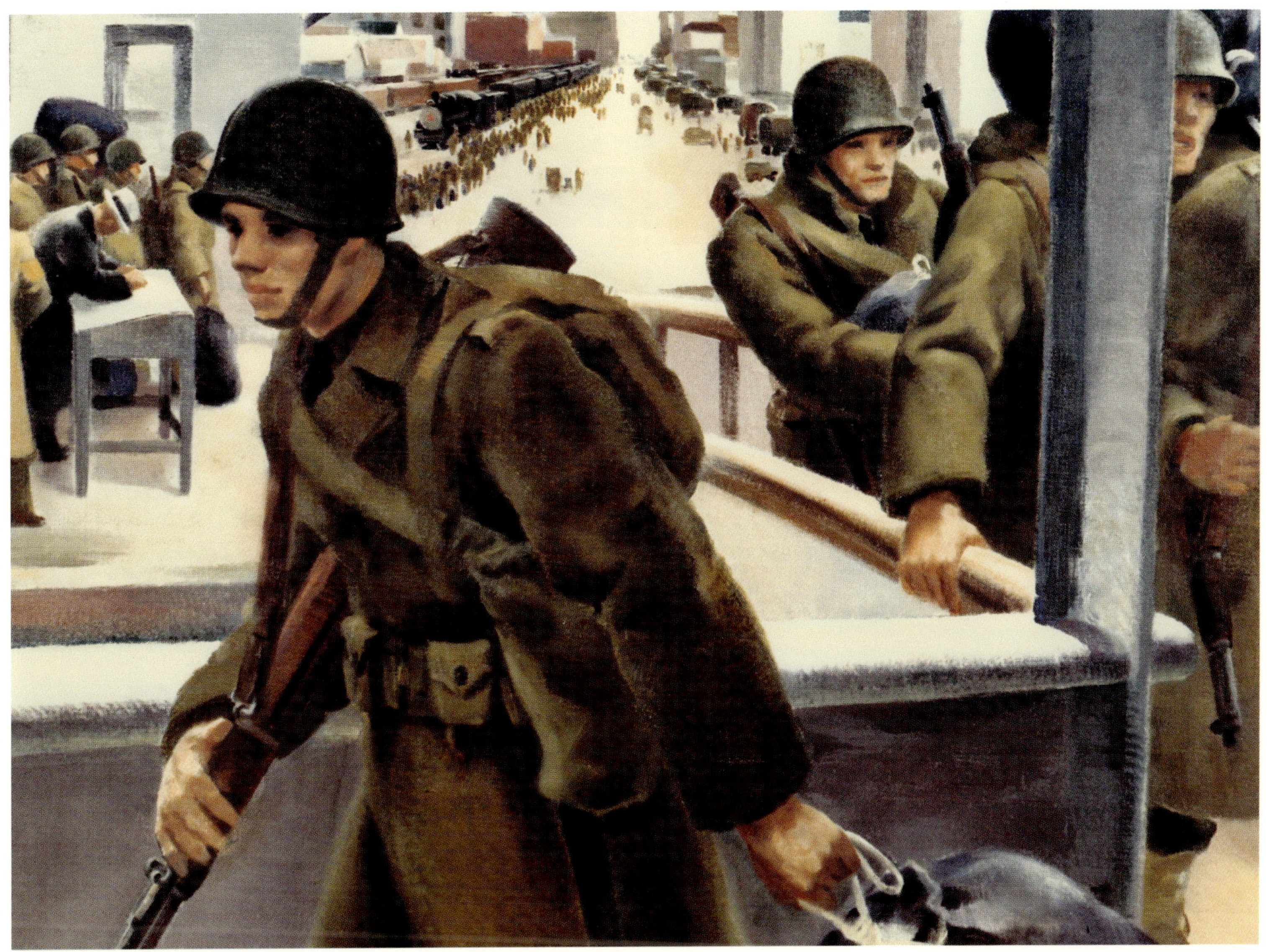

EMBARKATION
San Francisco, California
Barse Miller, 1942
Oil, 26" x 36"

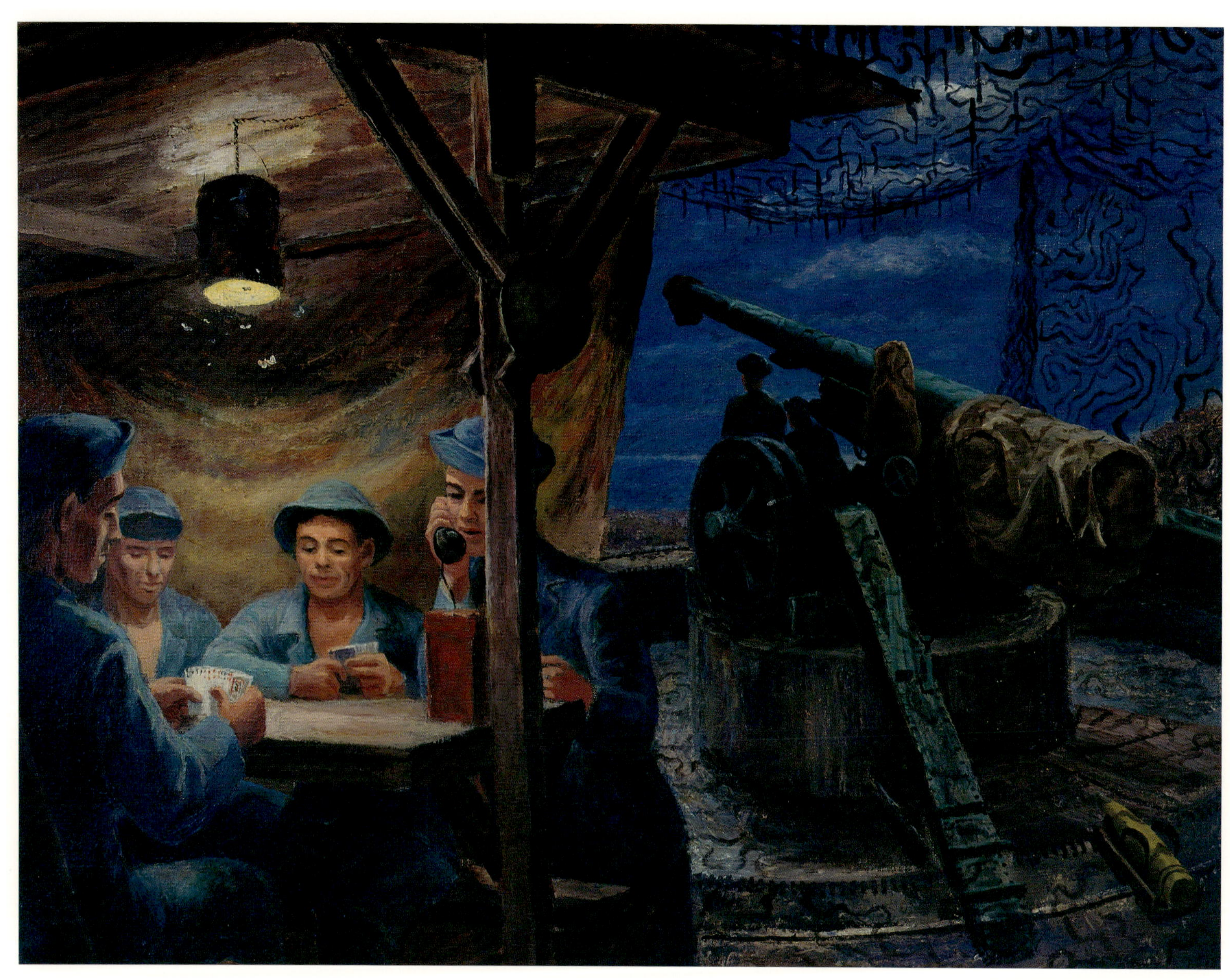

COAST ARTILLERY
Trinidad
James Barre Turnbull, 1943
Oil, 22" x 28"

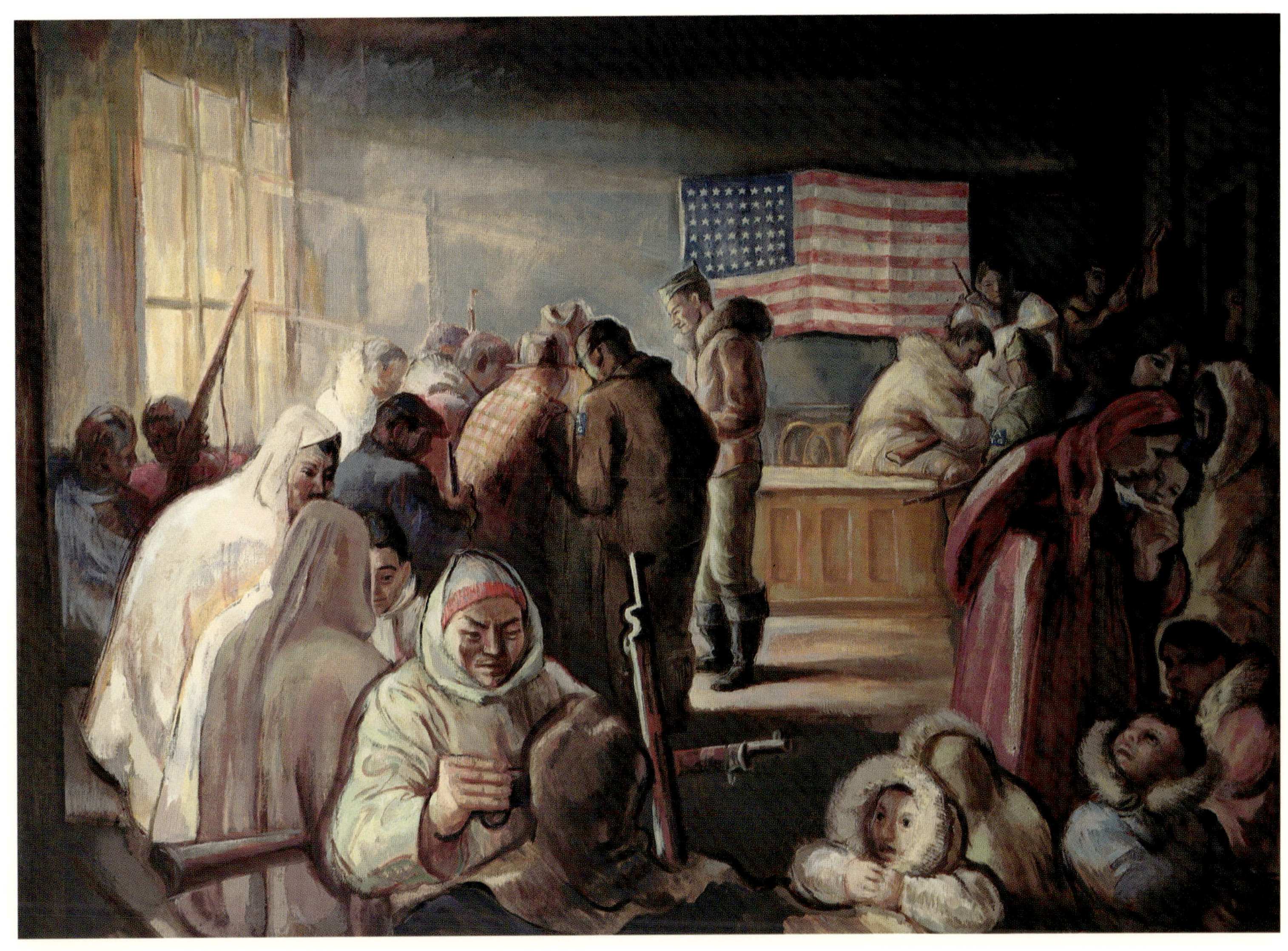

MAJOR MARSTON ARMS THE ESKIMOS
Alaska
Henry Varnum Poor, 1943
Oil, 42" x 58"

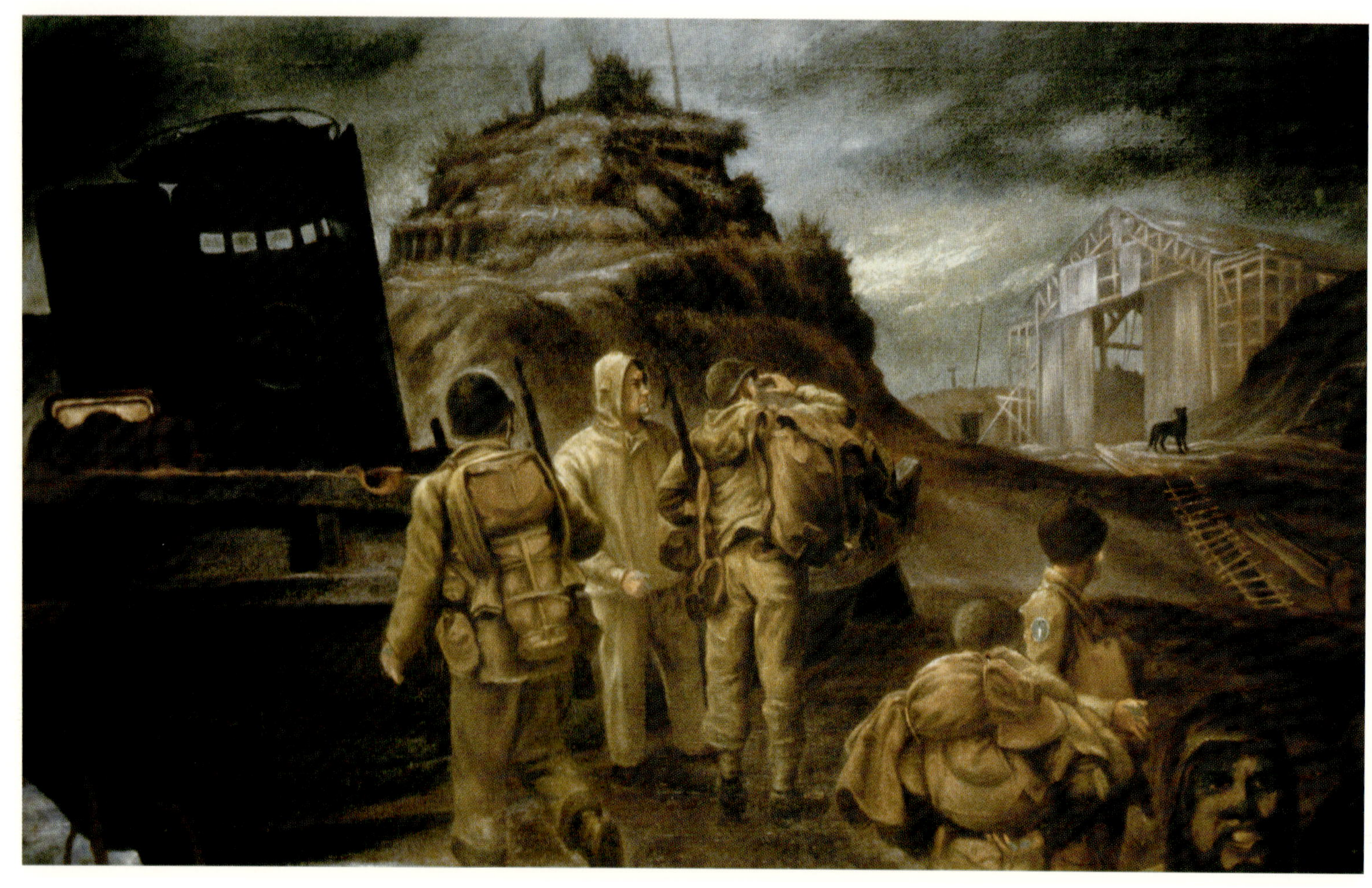

KISKA RAID
Aleutians
Edward R. Laning, 1943
Oil, 24" x 40"

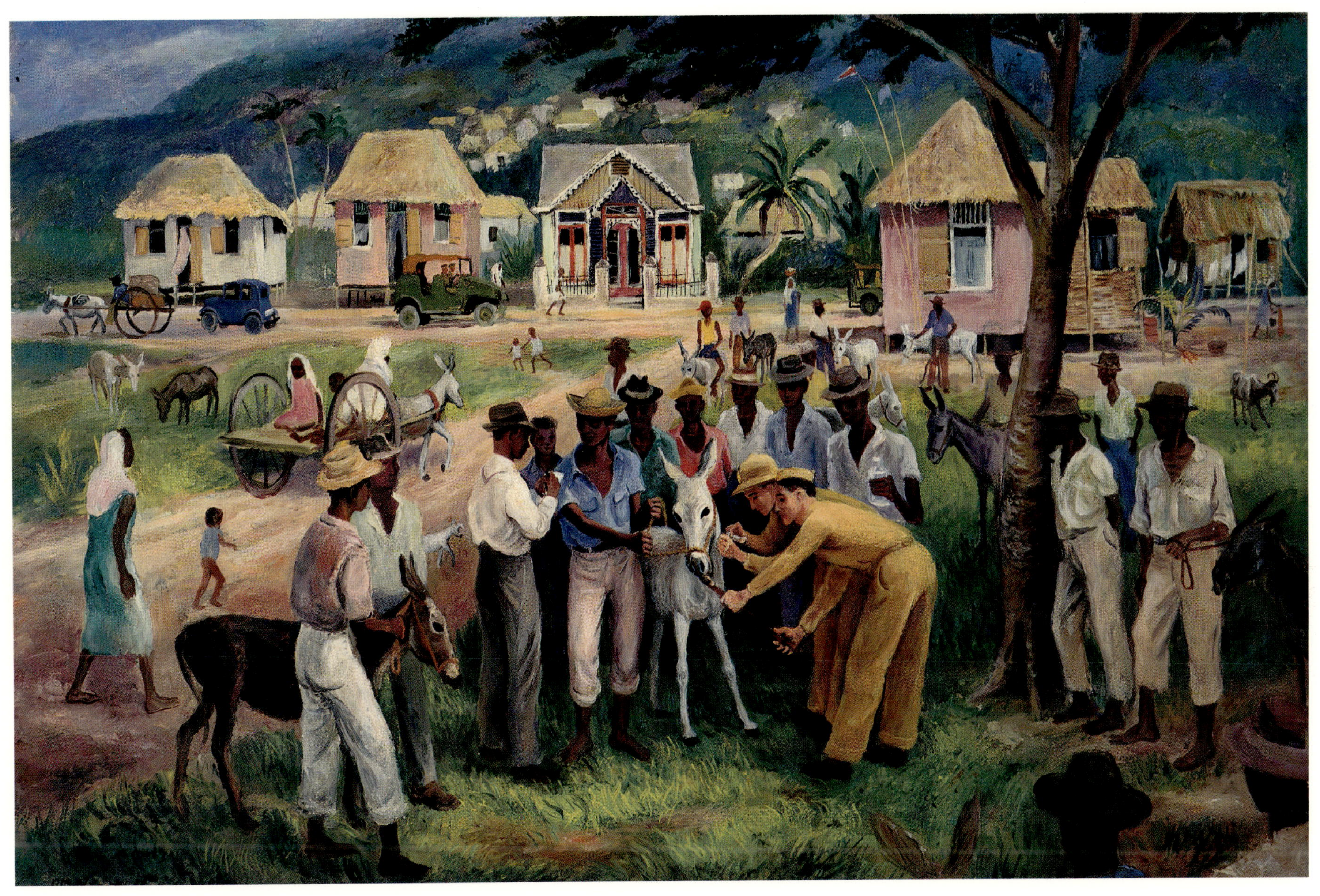

INOCULATING THE DONKEY
Trinidad
James Barre Turnbull, 1943
Oil, 20" x 30"

Europe

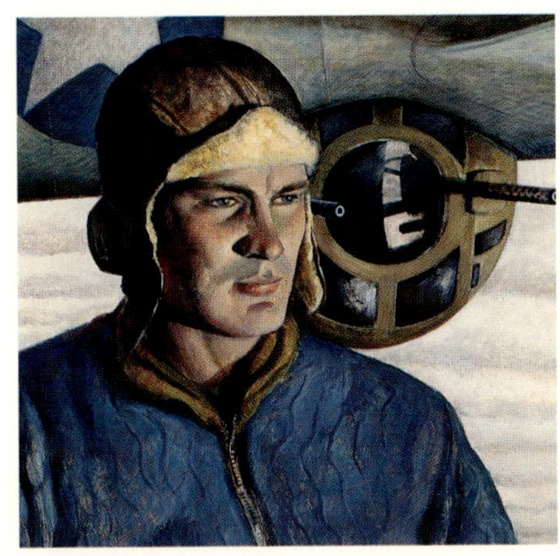

AERIAL GUNNER
England
Peter Hurd, 1942
Tempera, 17 ½" x 18"

TWICE IN THIS CENTURY AMERICAN SOLDIERS HAVE BEEN called to serve their nation in world wars on battlefields in Europe. The twenty American cemeteries and countless other memorials, large and small, that dot the European countryside are enduring testimony to the dedication and sacrifice of those soldiers. For those who had European family roots, service in Europe may have had a special personal meaning. But for most American soldiers, it was simply a call to service, a dangerous duty to perform in defense of the country's interests and in support of a national consensus on what was right to do.

The first U.S. Army units ever to serve in Europe began arriving at French ports in late June 1917. By the armistice seventeen months later, over a million American soldiers were in Europe. Spread across the Continent, they served with traditional and new allies in places from France and Italy to northern Russia, bringing to American headlines names like Flanders, Cantigny, Blanc Mont, Archangel, and Chateau-Thierry. In France the soldiers of the American Expeditionary Forces experienced the drawn-out rigors of trench warfare and fought through poison gas, holding their position on the Marne and piercing the Hindenburg Line. They also sang about the "Mademoiselle from Armentiers" and maybe even saw a little bit of Paris. They belonged to America's first truly modern Army, the product of an unprecedented mobilization and training effort, and after surviving the severe final testing of the Meuse-Argonne offensive, they went on to occupy Germany once an armistice was signed in November 1918. The last of the Yanks "over there" finally came home in 1923.

On another June day, in 1944, American soldiers once again arrived in France, this time landing on the beaches of Normandy, as the U.S. Army and the nation's Allies began the main offensive for the liberation of Europe. Eleven months before, the Allies had gained their first toeholds on the Continent with the capture of Sicily and the invasions of the Italian mainland. Places like Anzio, Cassino, the Liri Valley, and the Rapido River joined more famous names such as Naples and Rome as part of the history of the Army. Pushing out from the Normandy beachhead, American soldiers found themselves fighting over some of the same ground that their fathers had moved across, but new places were added too—the hedgerows, Cherbourg, and Avranches among them. As the march toward victory gathered momentum, American troops reached Luxembourg, the Huertgen Forest, Bastogne, Remagen, the Siegfried Line, and finally Berlin.

The capture of the German capital, however, wasn't the end of the Army's role in Europe. Occupation duty followed, as well as relief and rebuilding programs on a huge scale. This time also marked the beginning of an even longer and potentially more deadly period of service for the American soldier—the Cold War. For fifty years American soldiers, male and female, stood watch on the frontier between Communist and free Europe. German towns that had been enemy strongholds in World War II became garrison homes to three generations of American soldiers and their families. The ranges at Grafenwoehr and Hohenfels were their backyards. Alerts, lonely duty in sentry towers on the Czech border or in weapons storage areas, fence patrols along the Iron Curtain, and riot control drills at the Berlin Wall were all routine. Checkpoint Charlie, the Fulda Gap, the autobahns, and the Military Airlift Command terminal at Rhein-Main all became part of the American soldier's experience.

The commemoration of the fiftieth anniversary of World War II has provided much material that recalls the Army's central role in Europe during that war, and the Army continues to maintain a very real and strategically important presence in Europe today. But ensuring an ongoing clear and vivid memory of the past is a challenge. The art in this section, covering more than seventy-five years of the American soldier's presence in Europe, was selected to provide meaningful images to help support that memory. At a time when the American soldier continues to meet the nation's call to service in support of its European commitments, those generations of soldiers who went before—in their humanity, sacrifices, and successes—provide an invaluable role model for the present and the future.

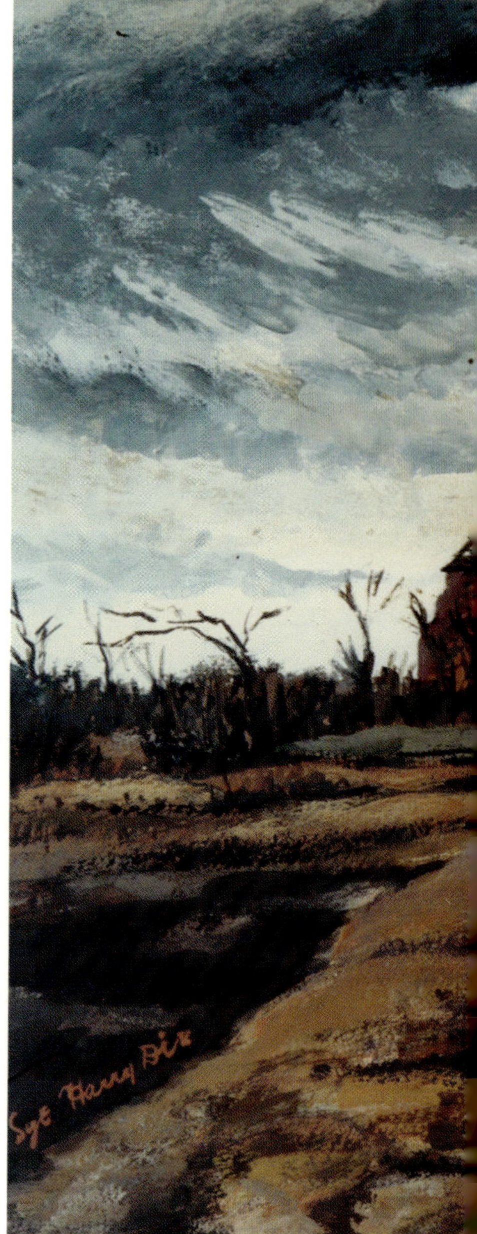

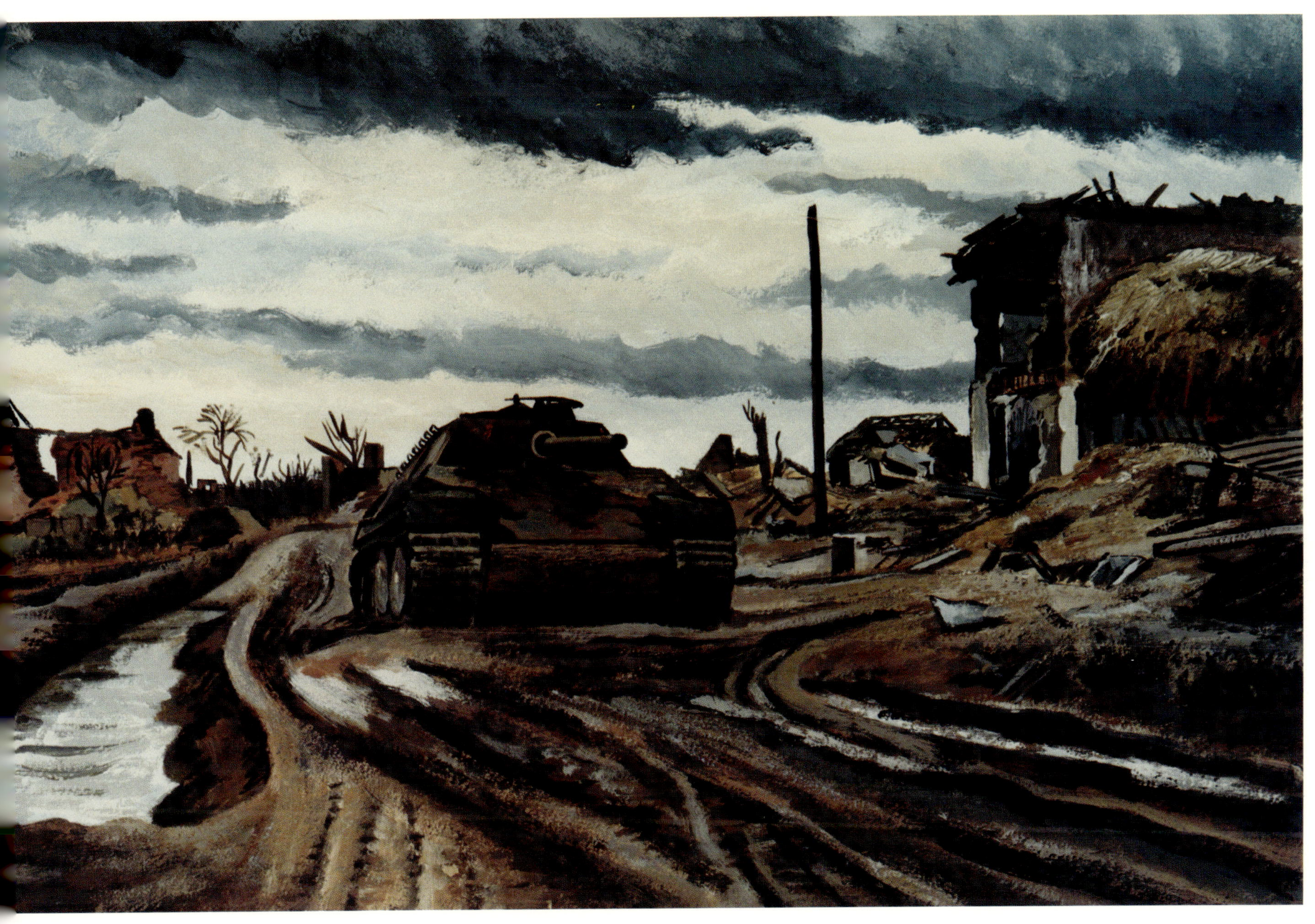

KNOCKED OUT TANK AT SCHMIDT
Germany
Harry Dix, 1945
Gouache, 14" x 22"

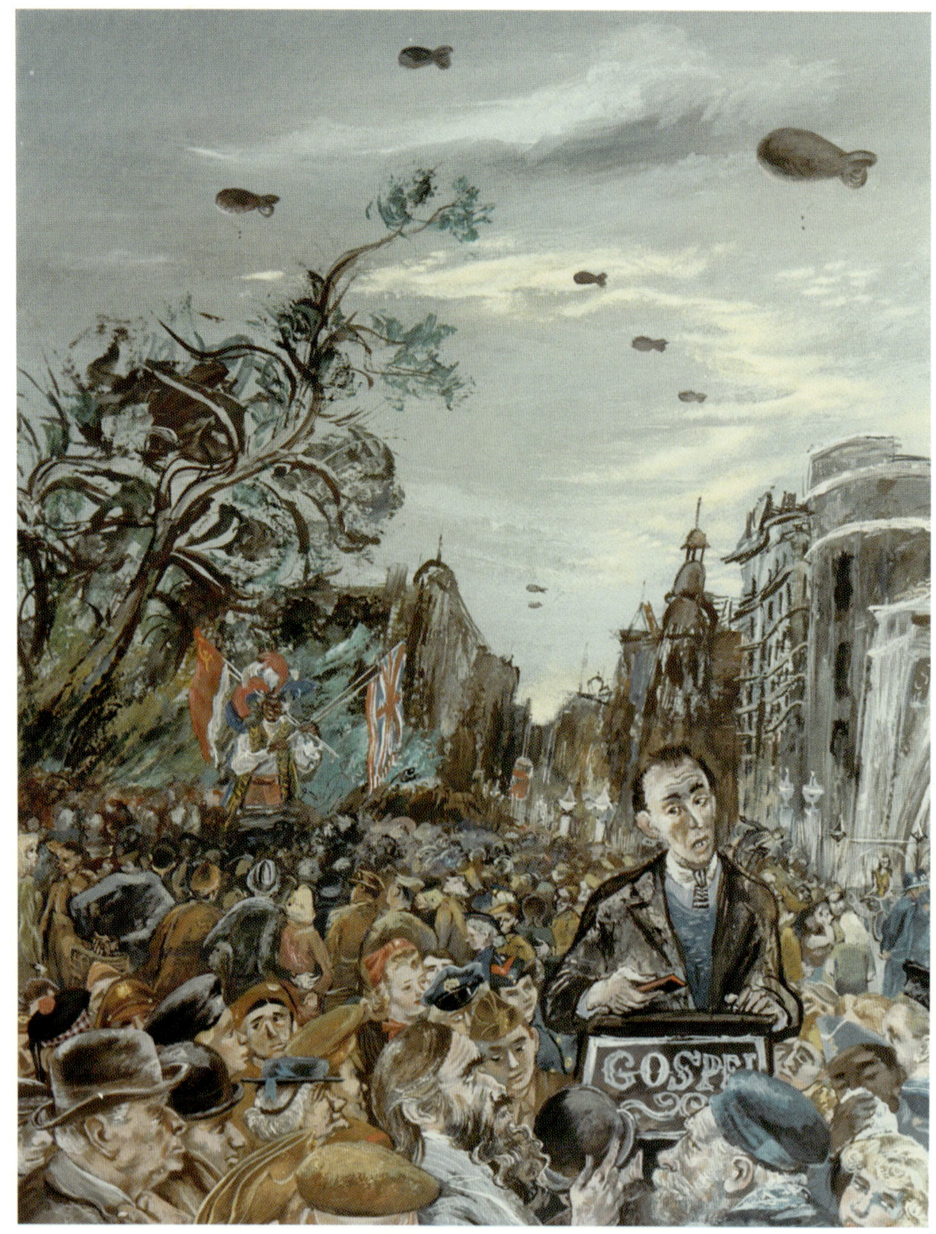

HYDE PARK
England
Aaron Bohrod, 1944
Gouache, 18″ x 14″

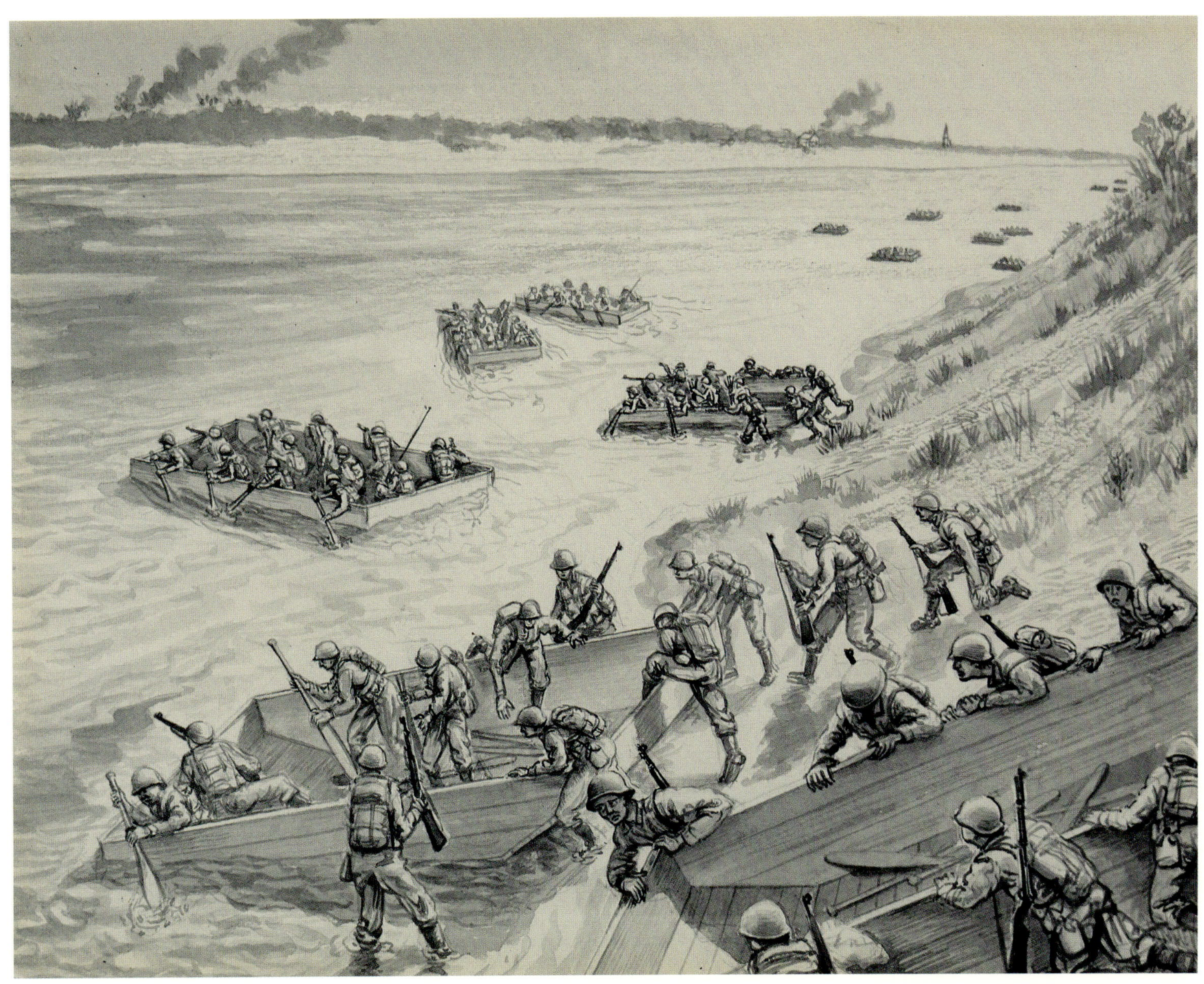

FIRST WAVE AT THE PO
Italy
William V. Caldwell, 1945
Wash, 11" x 17 ½"

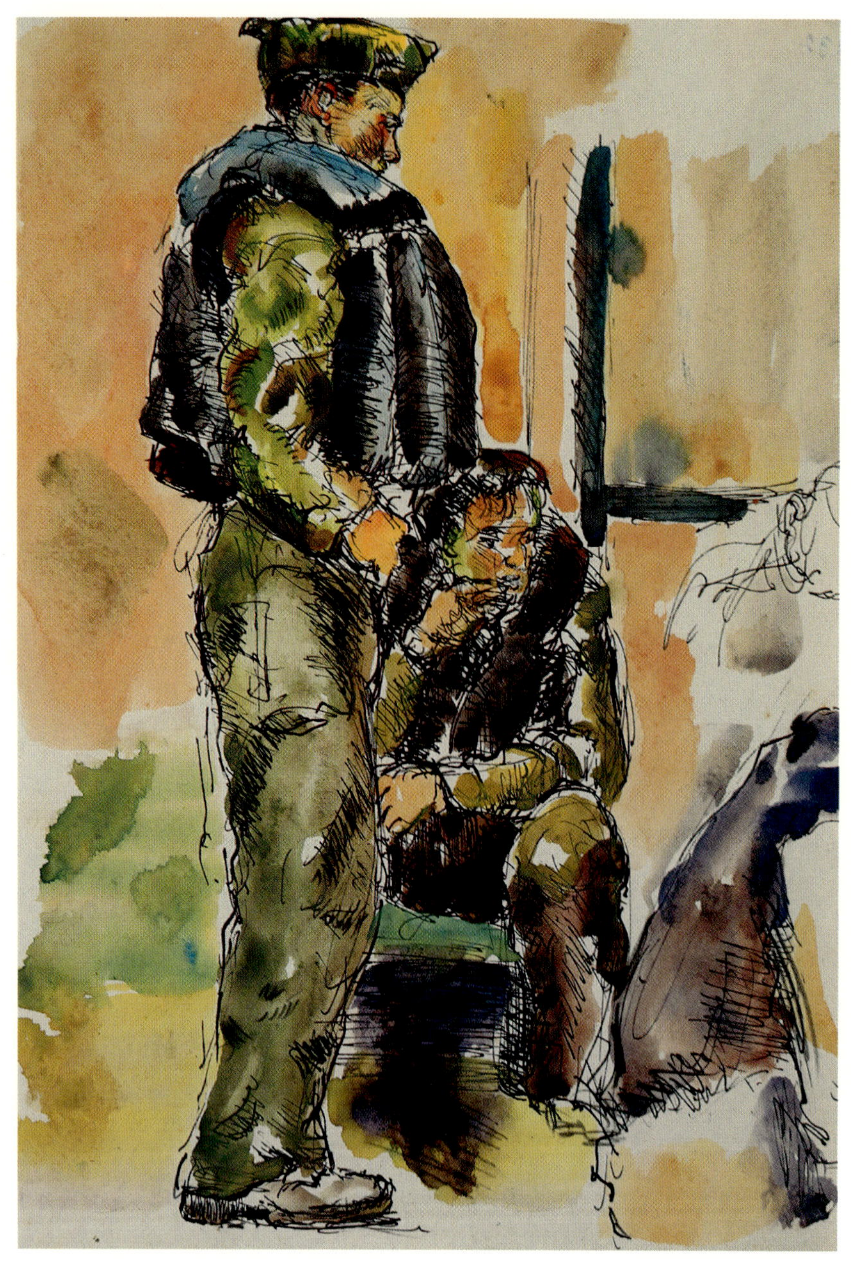

QUEEN MARY CROSSING #5
Atlantic Ocean
H. Robert Bizinsky, 1942
Watercolor and ink, 10 ½" x 8"

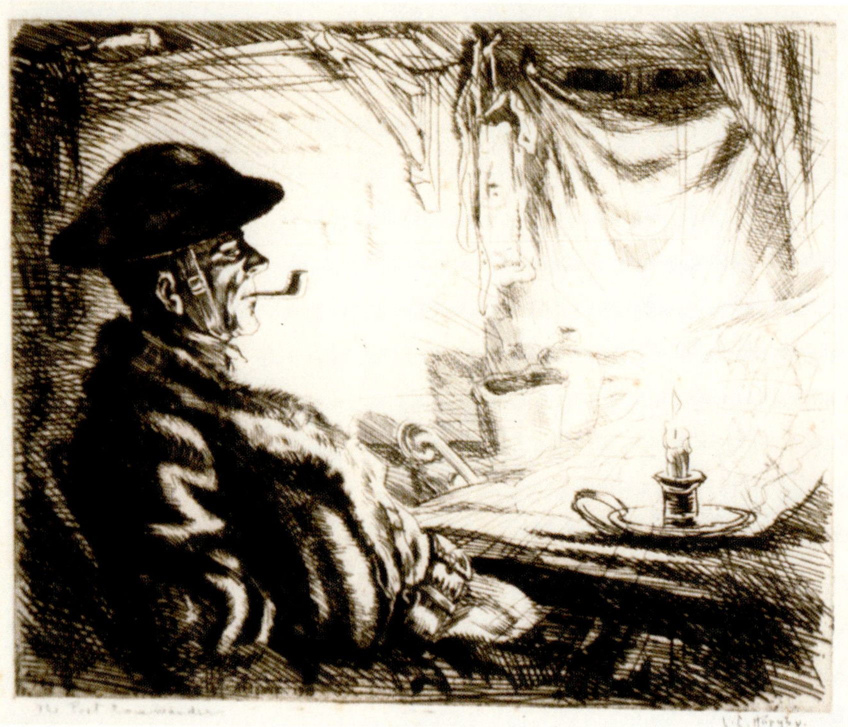

POST COMMANDER
France, World War I
Lester G. Hornby
Etching, 10" x 12 ¾"

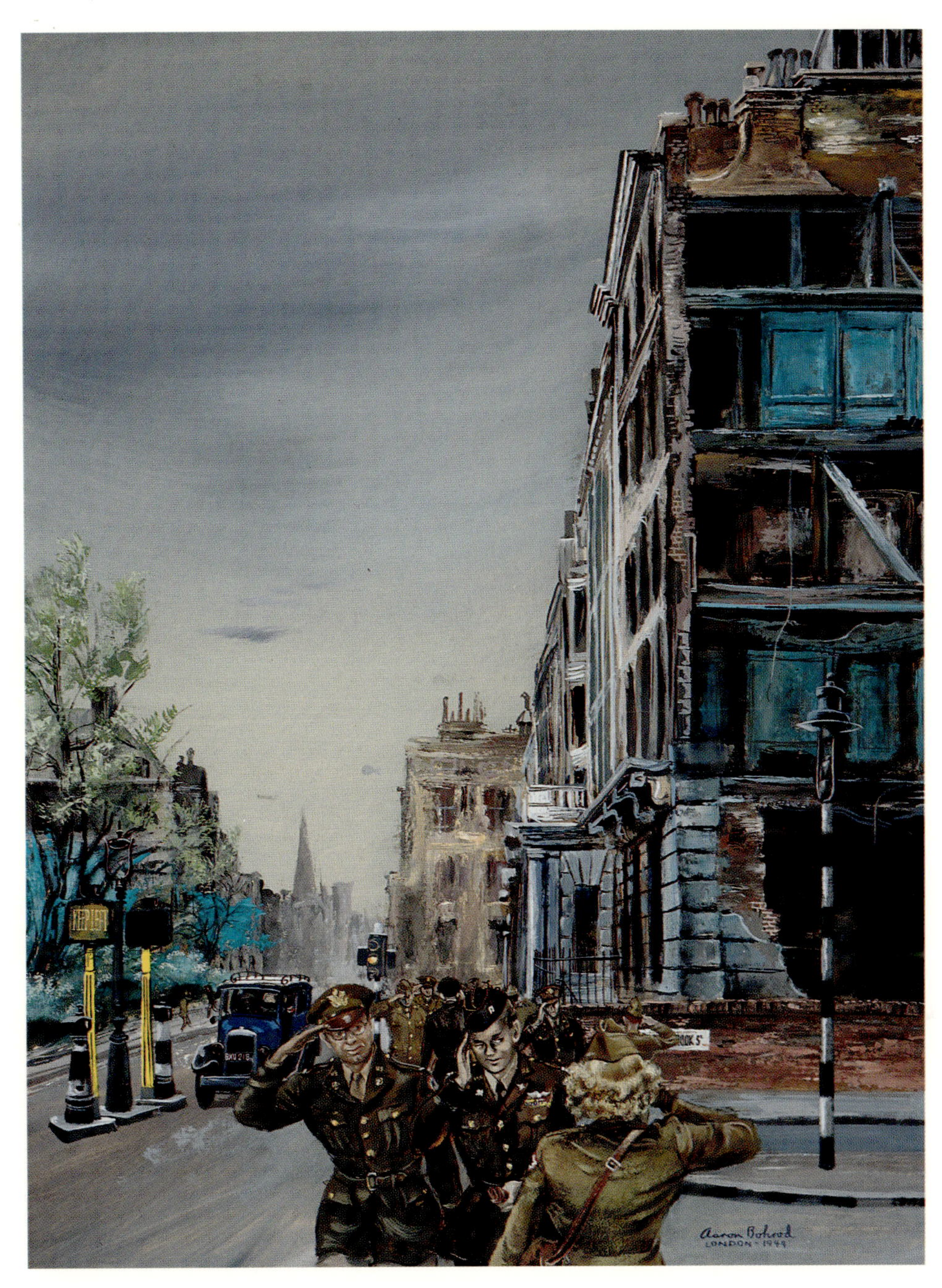

LONDON, ENGLAND
England
Aaron Bohrod, 1944
Gouache, 18" x 13 ½"

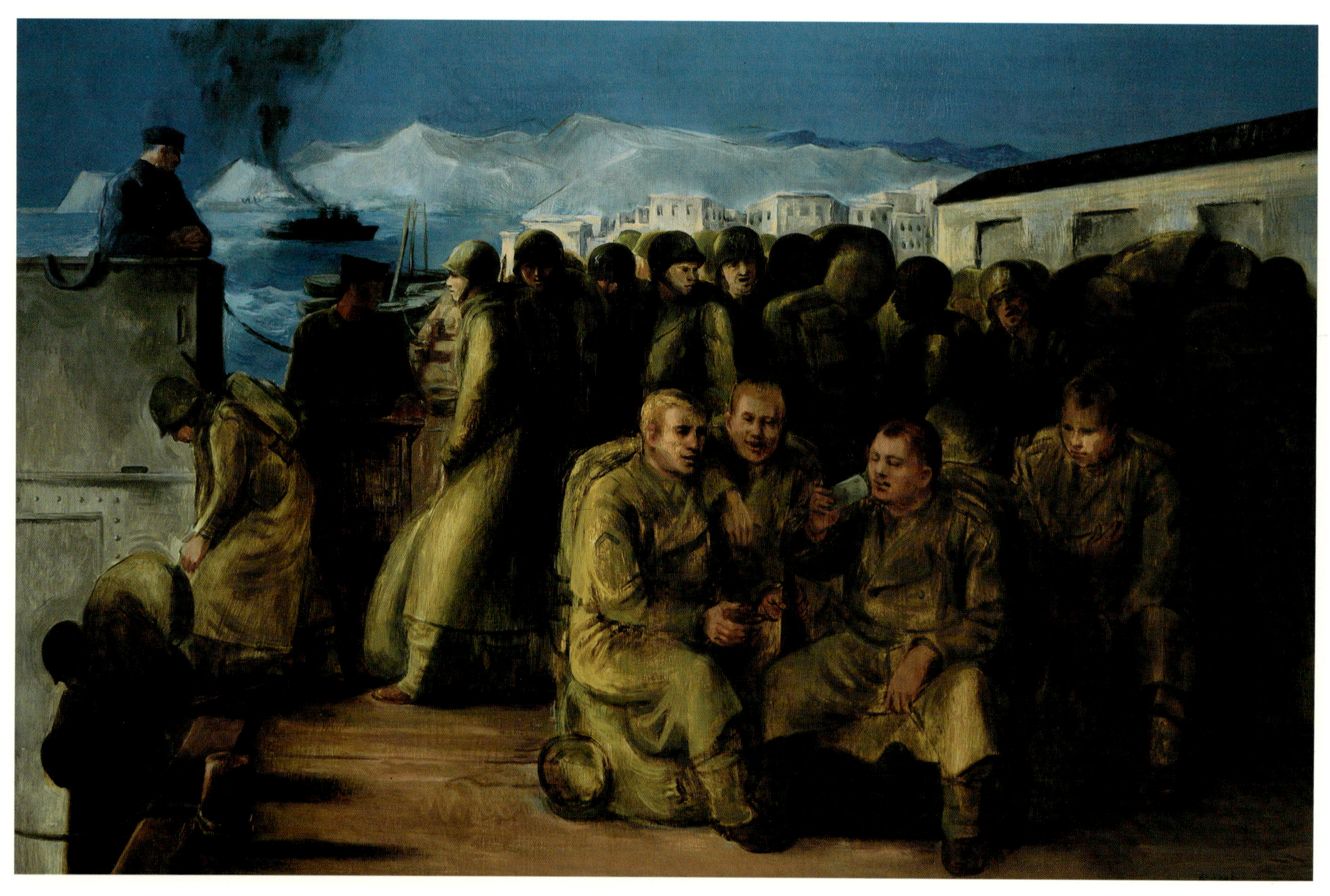

SOLDIERS EMBARKING ON LANDING CRAFT
Iceland
Bernard Arnest, 1944
Oil, 32" x 48"

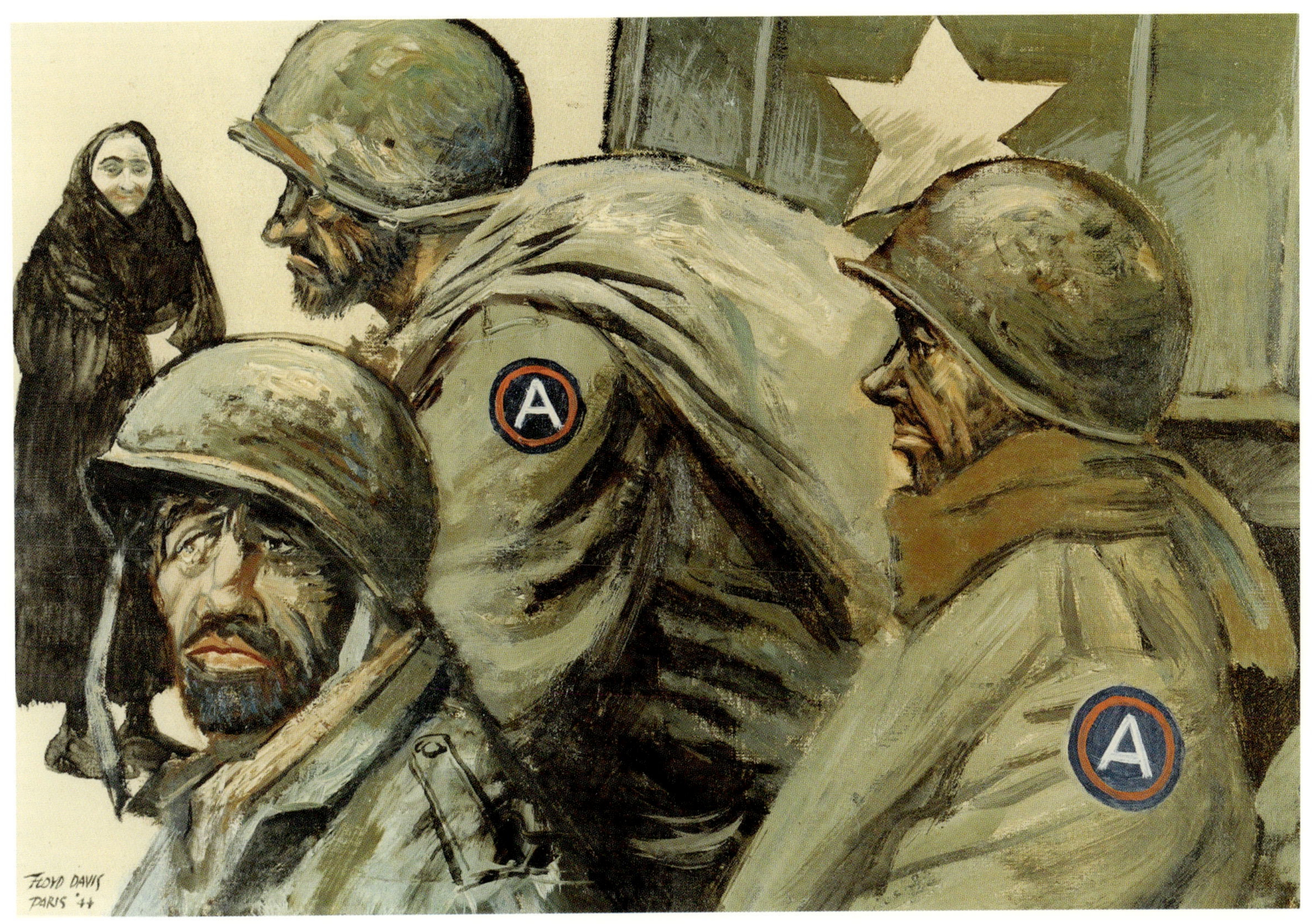

GI'S IN PARIS
France
Floyd Davis, 1944
Oil, 11" x 16"

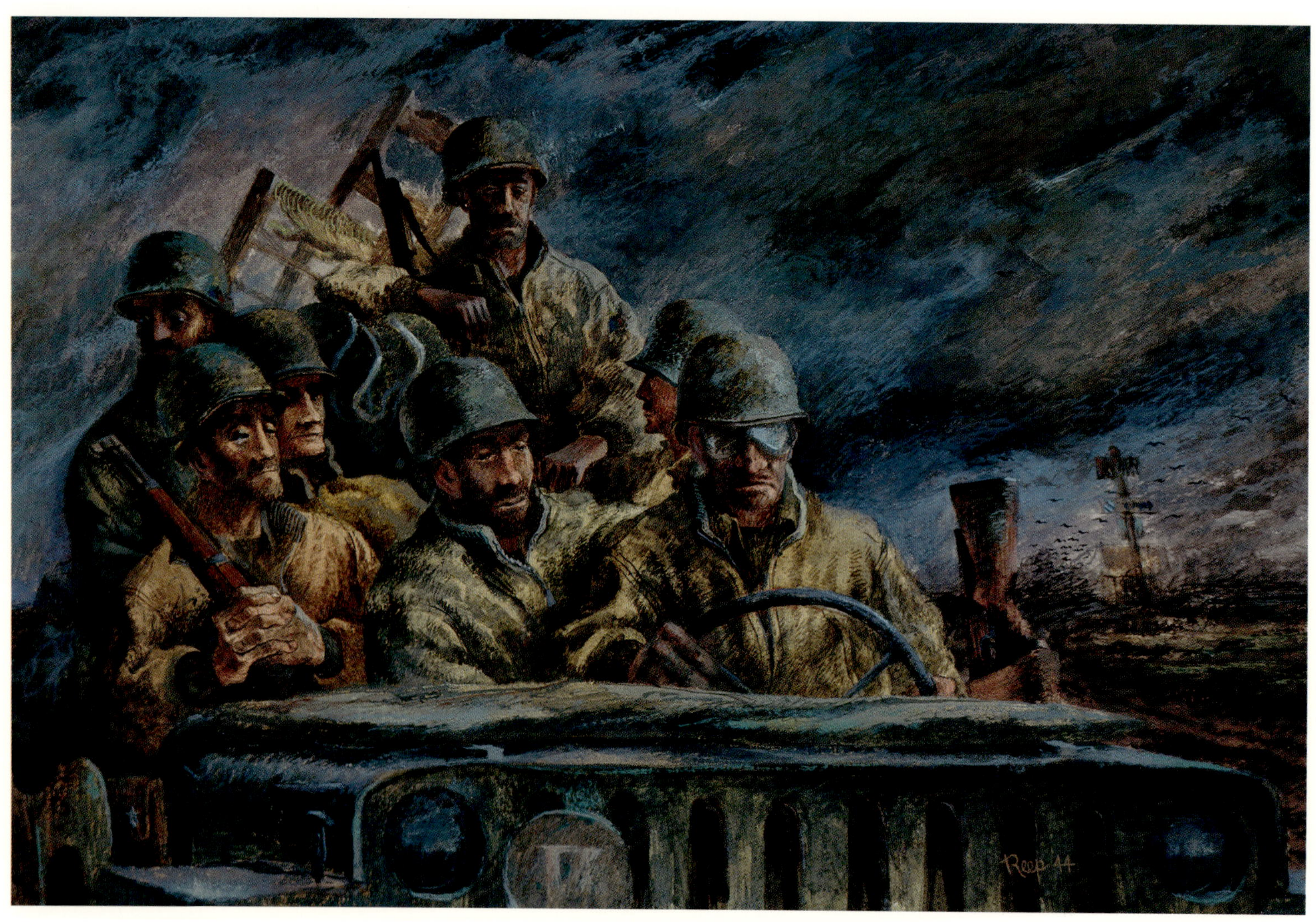

WE MOVE AGAIN
Anzio, Italy
Edward A. Reep, 1944
Gouache, 14" x 19 ⅞"

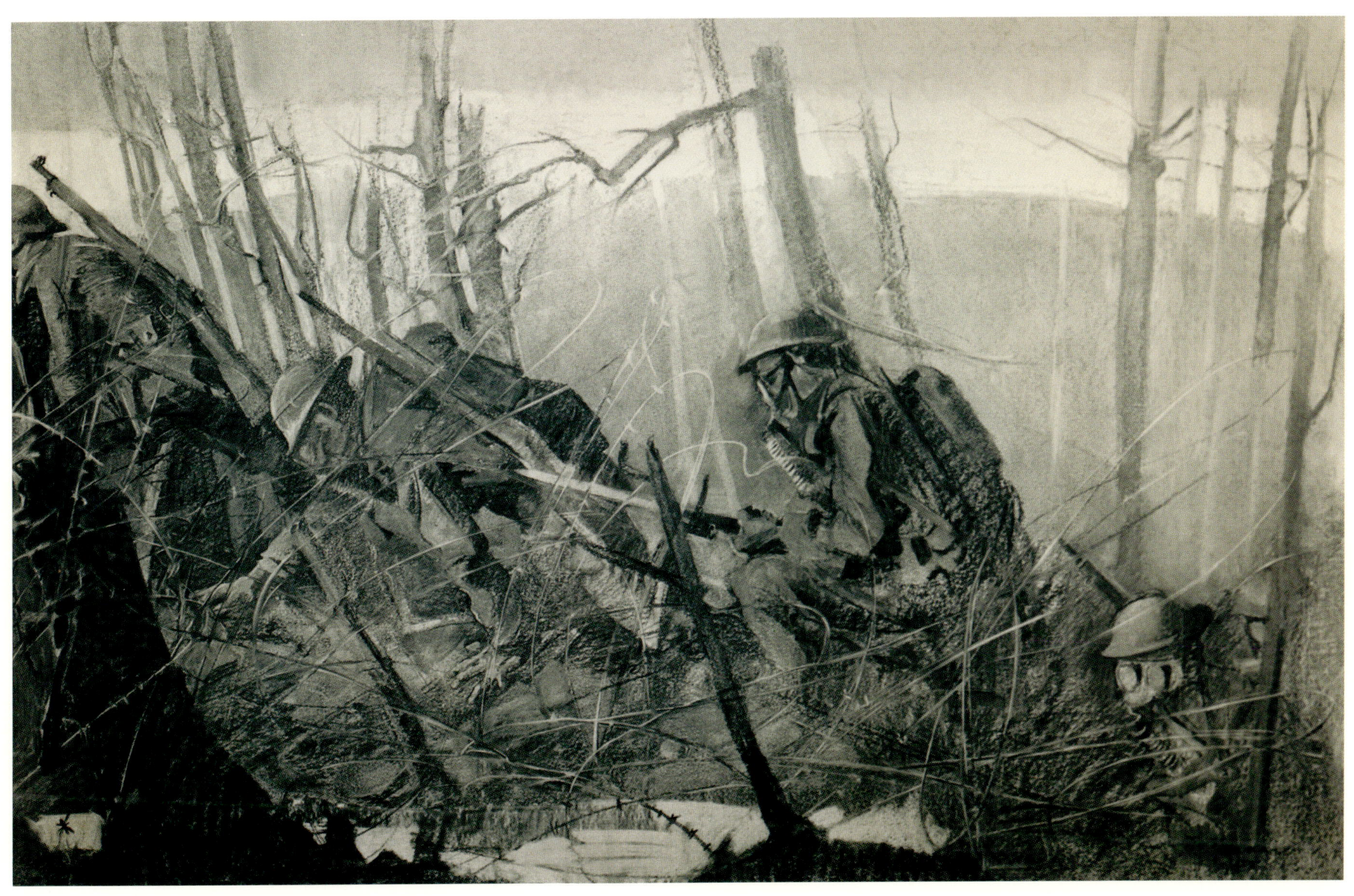

GOING THRU GAS
France
George Harding, 1918
Charcoal, 24 ¼" x 37 ¾"

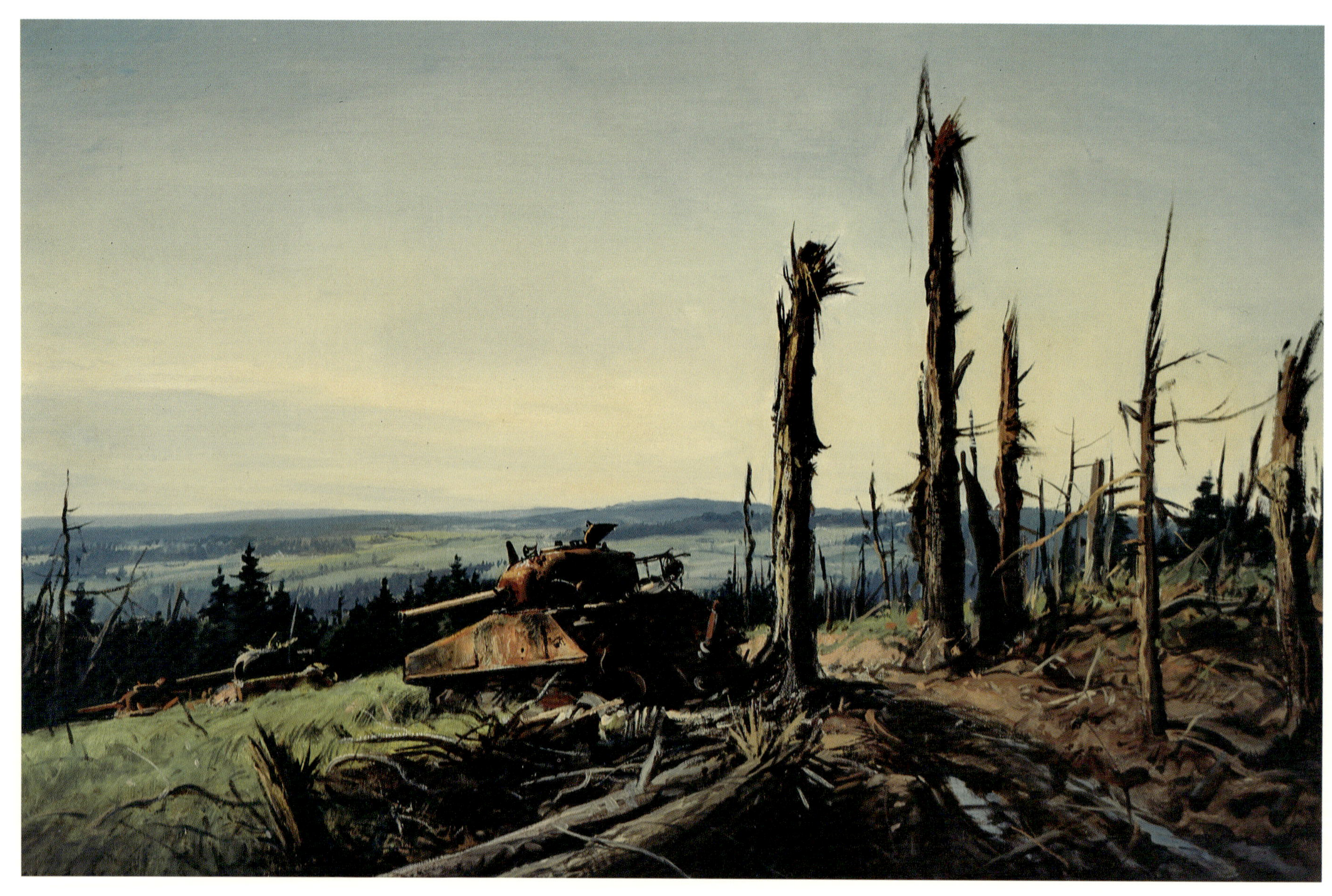

TANKS IN THE HÜRTGEN FOREST
Germany
Ogden Pleissner, 1945
Oil, 20" x 30"

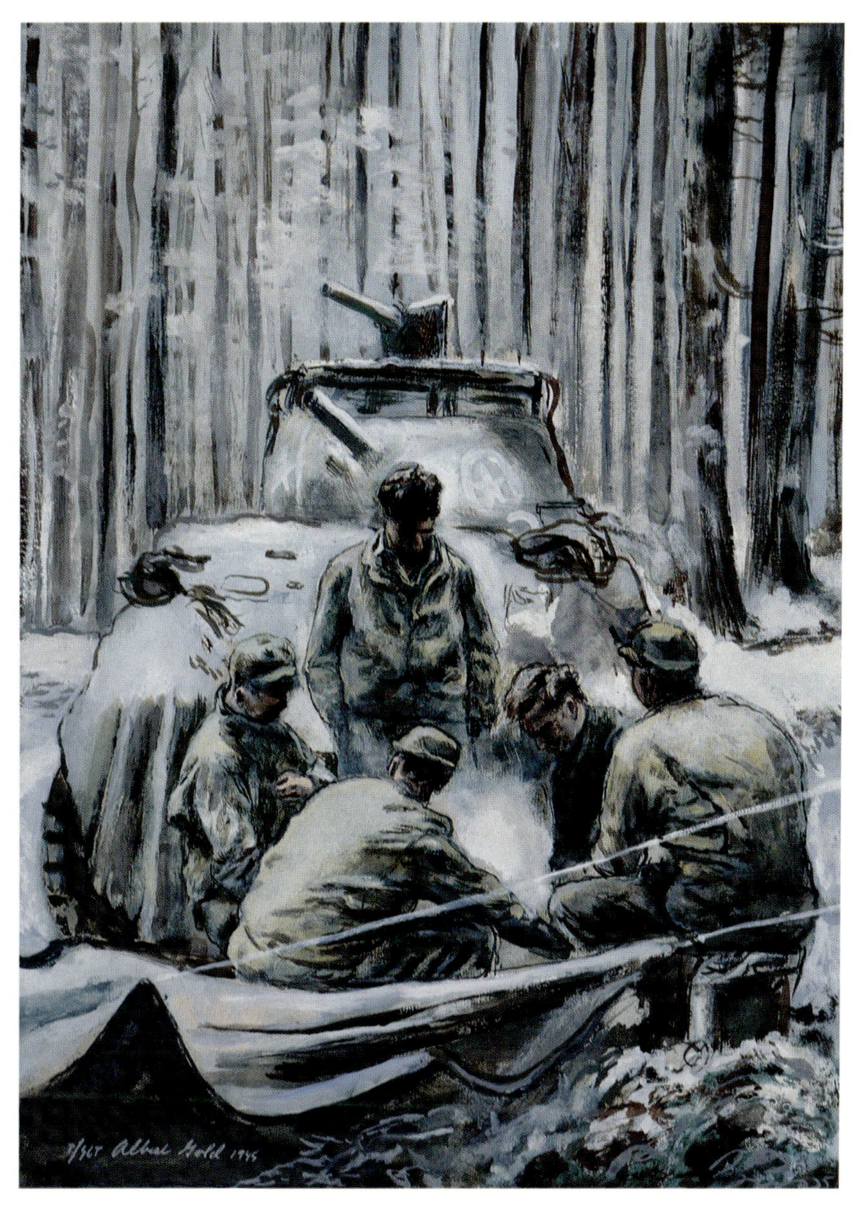

WINTER IN THE VOSGES MOUNTAINS
France
Albert Gold, 1945
Gouache, 19 ½" x 14 ¾"

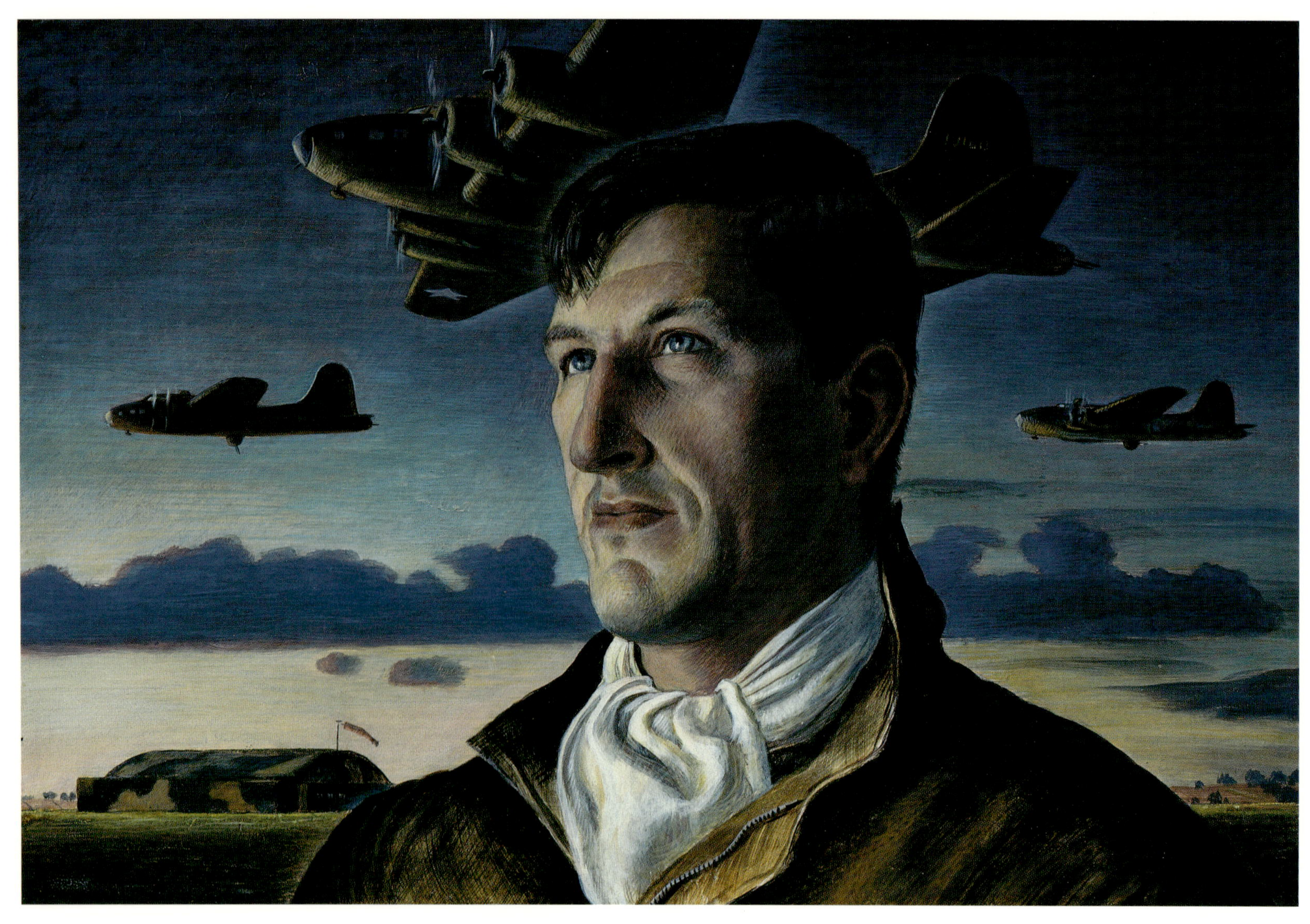

LT. THOMAS BORDERS, PILOT, U.S. AIR FORCE
England
Peter Hurd, 1942
Tempera, 16" x 23 ½"

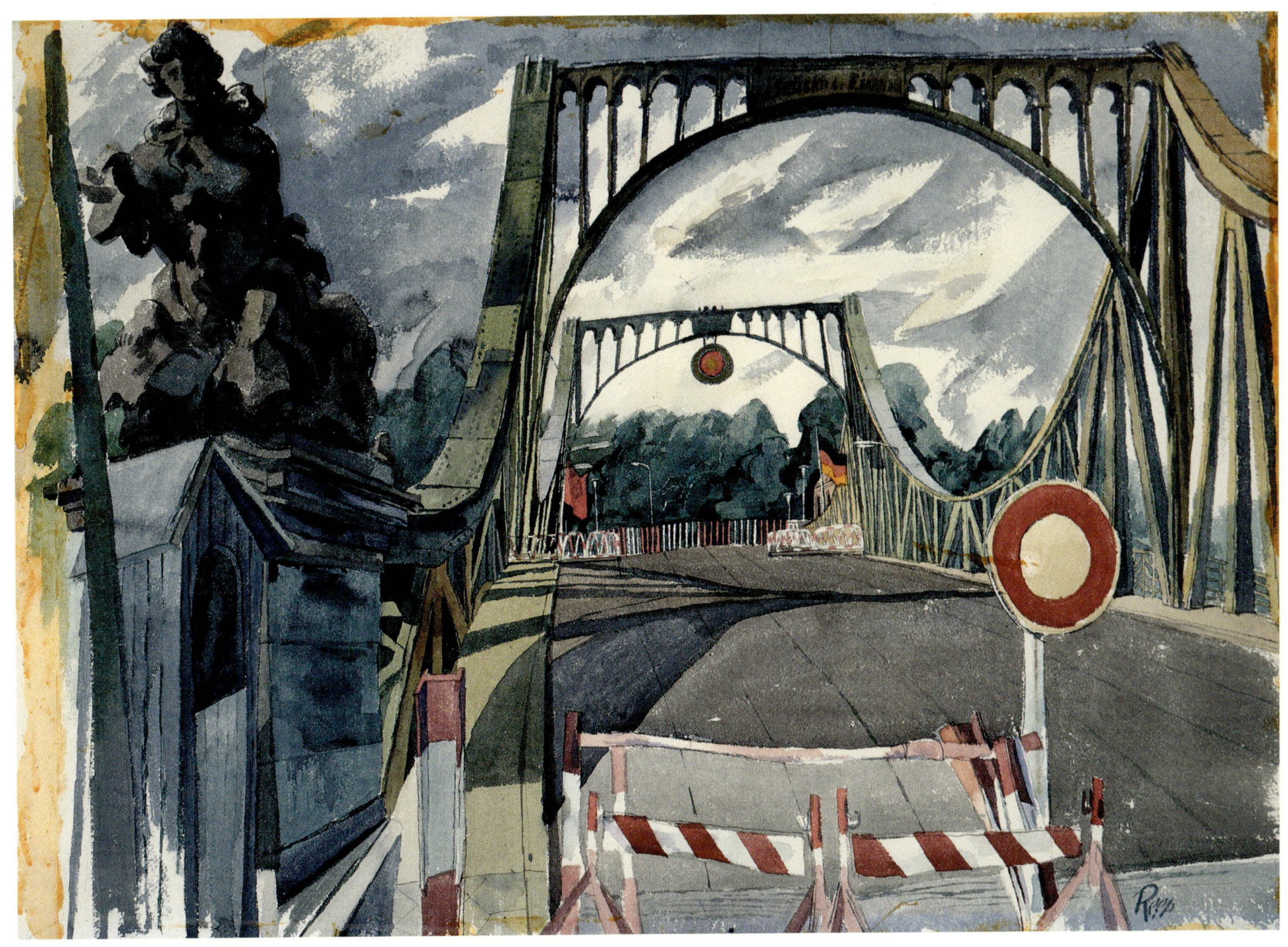

FREEDOM BRIDGE
Berlin, Germany
Edward A. Reep, 1972
Watercolor, 21″ x 29″

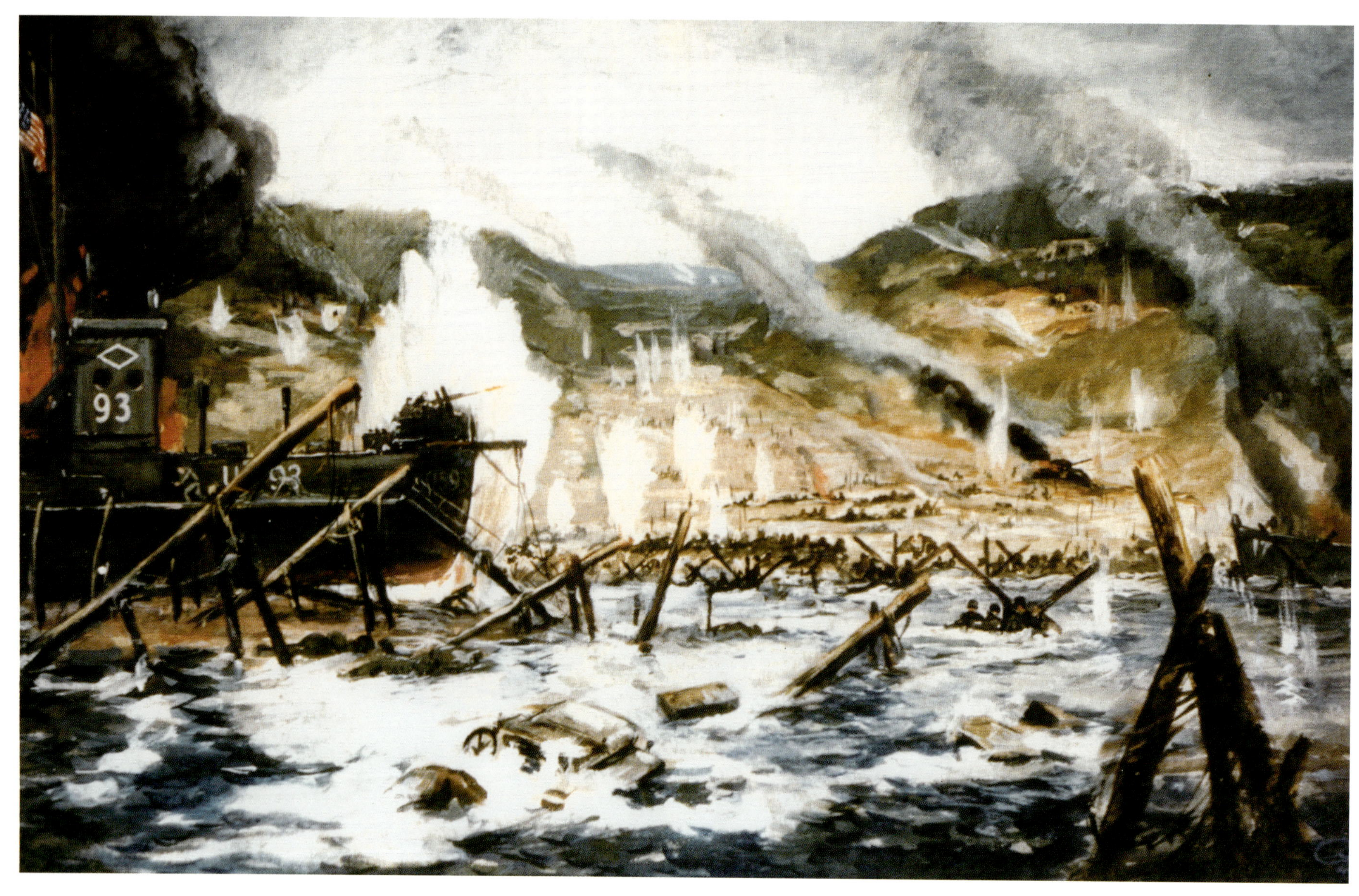

OMAHA BEACH
France
Joseph Gary Sheahan, 1944
Watercolor, 30" x 19 ½"

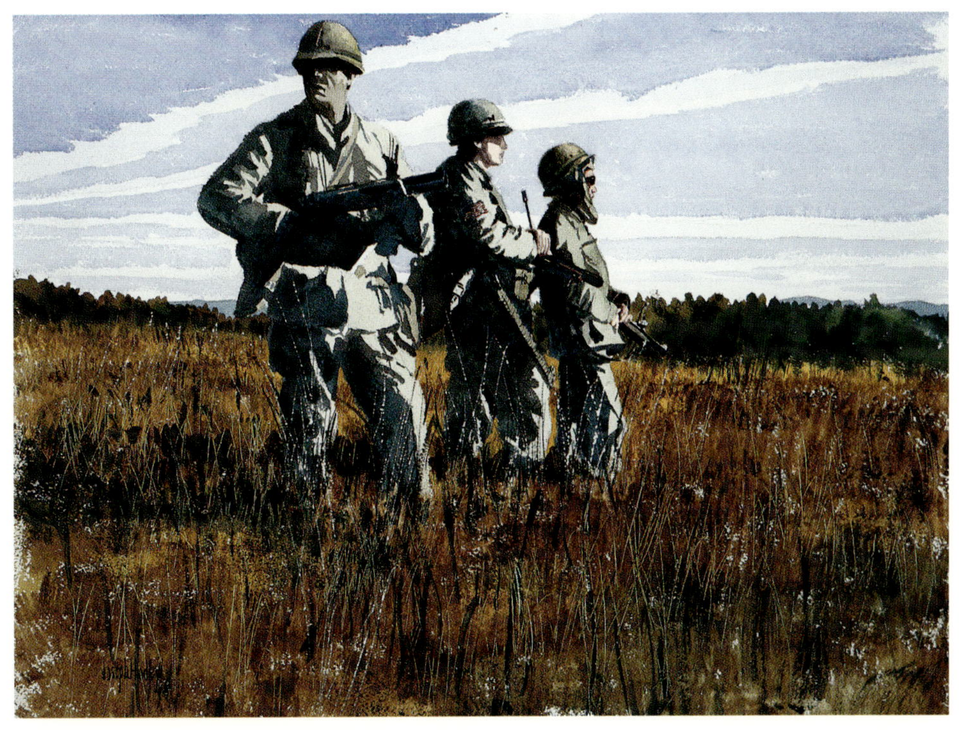

LOOK AND LISTEN
Baumholder, Germany
Joseph S. Hindley, 1972
Watercolor, 18" x 24"

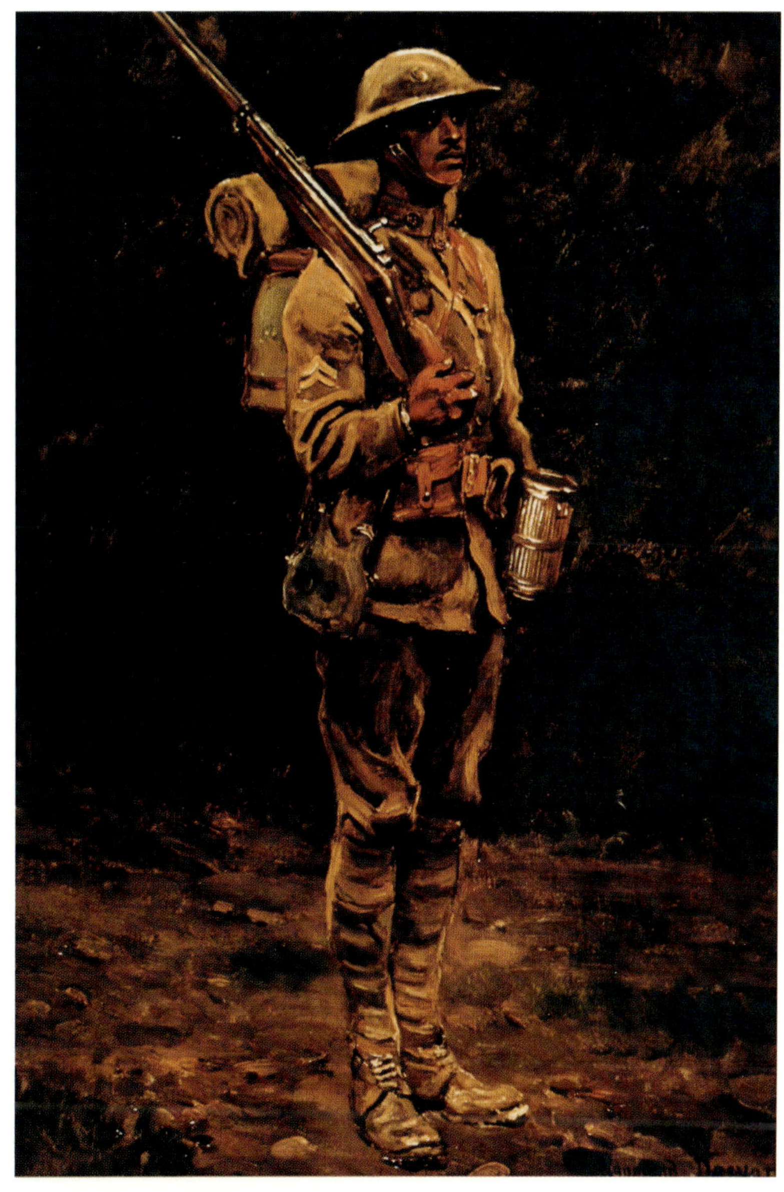

FULL STUDY OF CORPORAL, 15TH NEW YORK INFANTRY
Raymond Desvarraus, 1918
Oil, 24" x 35"

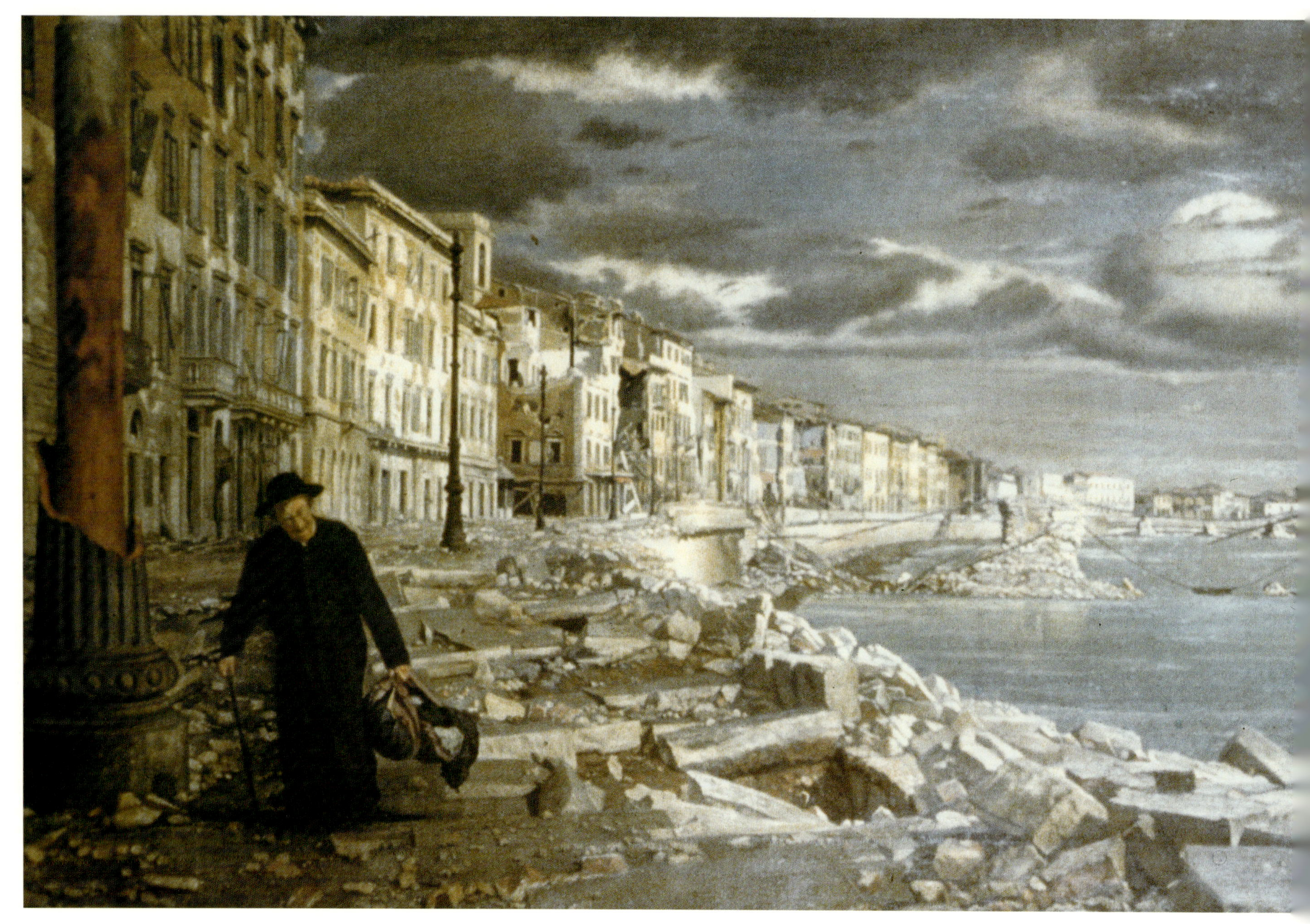

FAREWELL TO PISA
Italy
Edward R. Laning, 1944
Oil, 24" x 60"

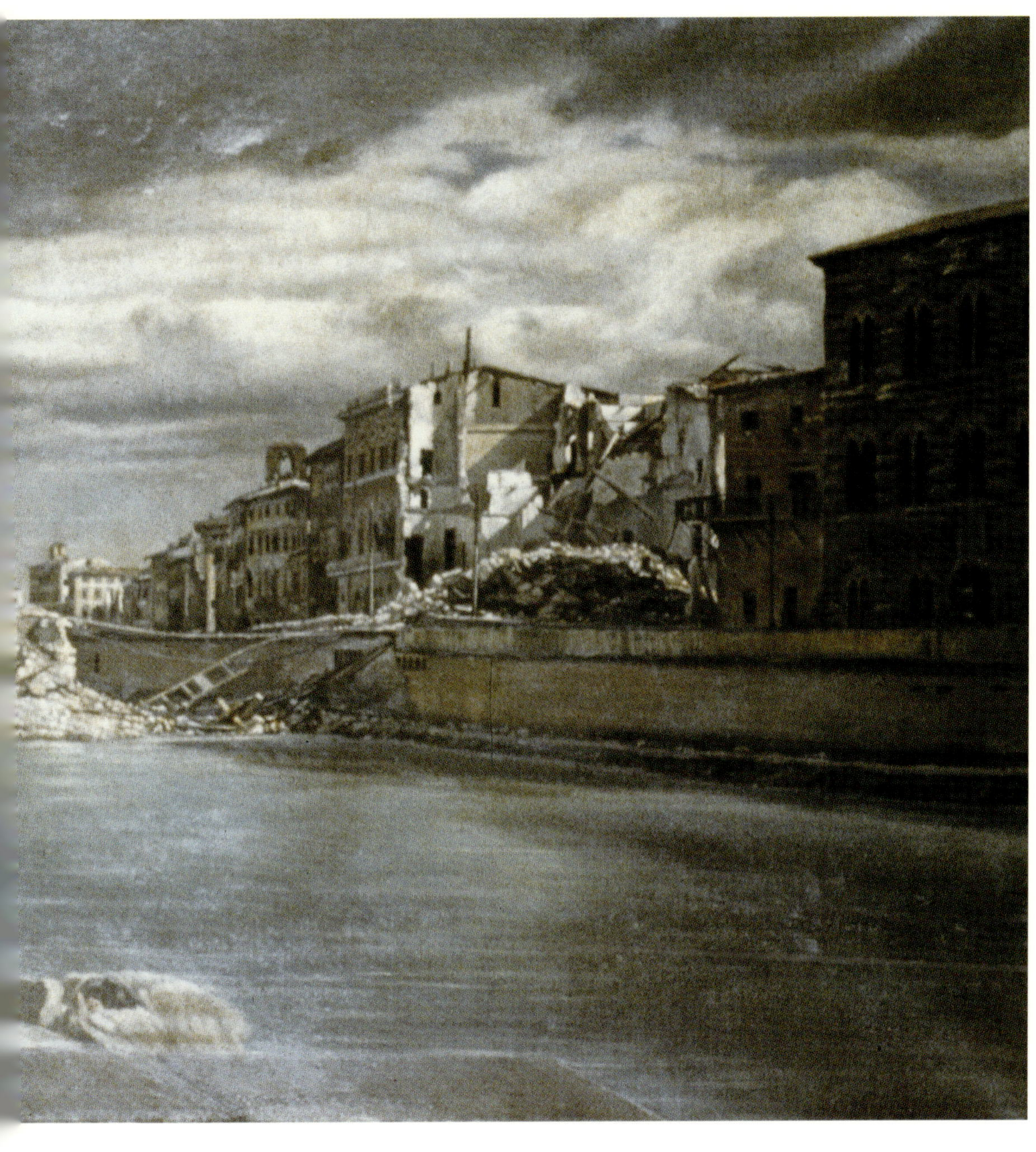

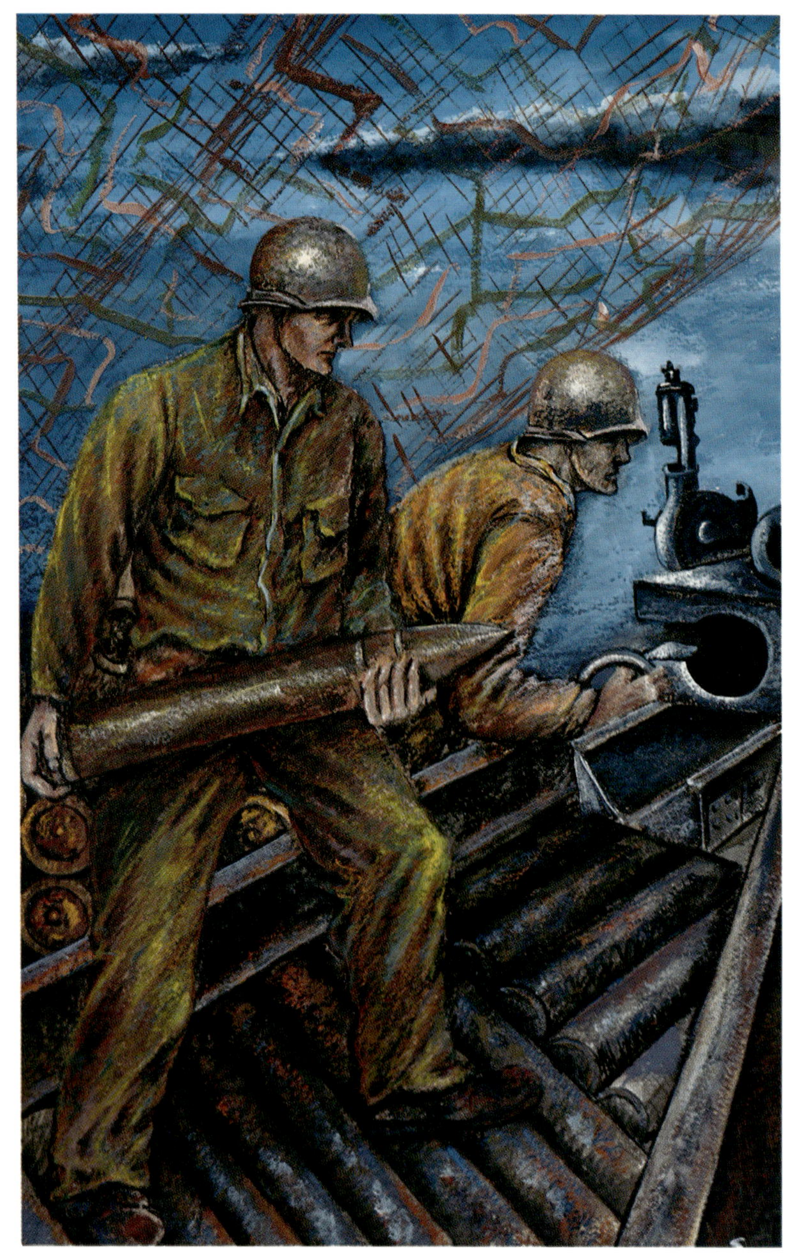

LOADING ARTILLERY PIECE AT ANZIO
Italy
Savo Radulovic, 1944
Watercolor, 22 ½" x 14 ½"

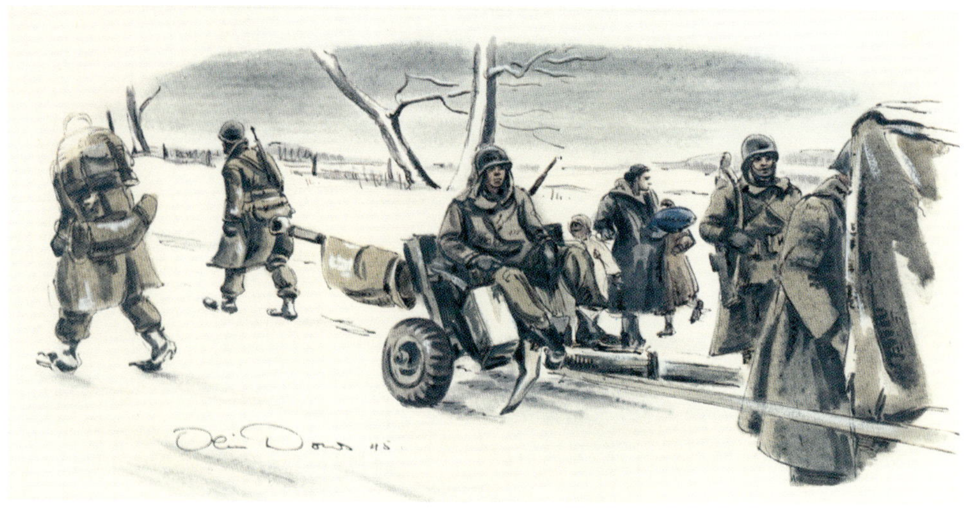

TWO WAY TRAFFIC, BASTOGNE
Belgium
Olin Dows, 1945
Watercolor, 9 ¾" x 17 ¾"

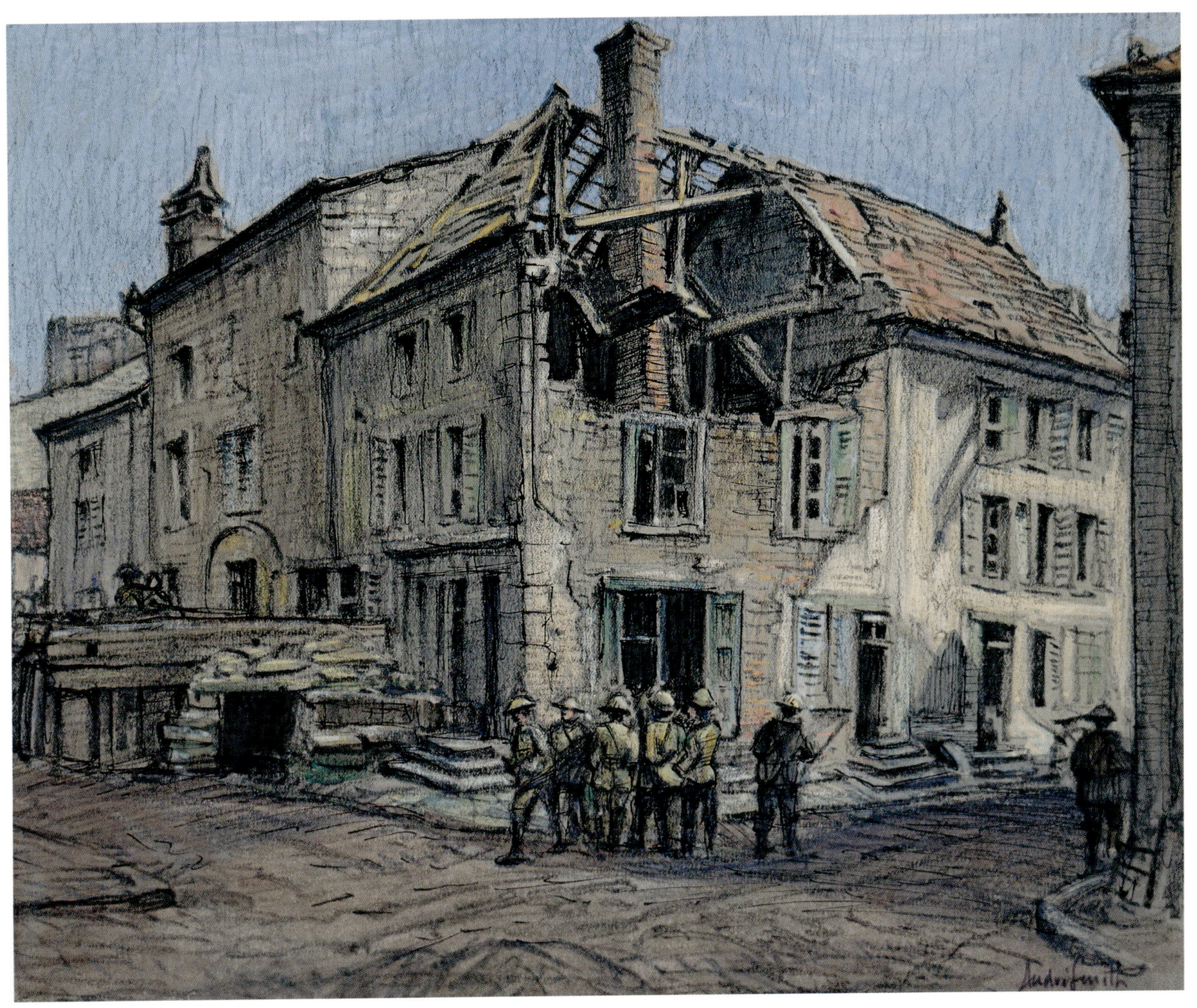

BADONVILLER
France
Jules Andre Smith, 1918
Pastel, 9" x 11 ⅛"

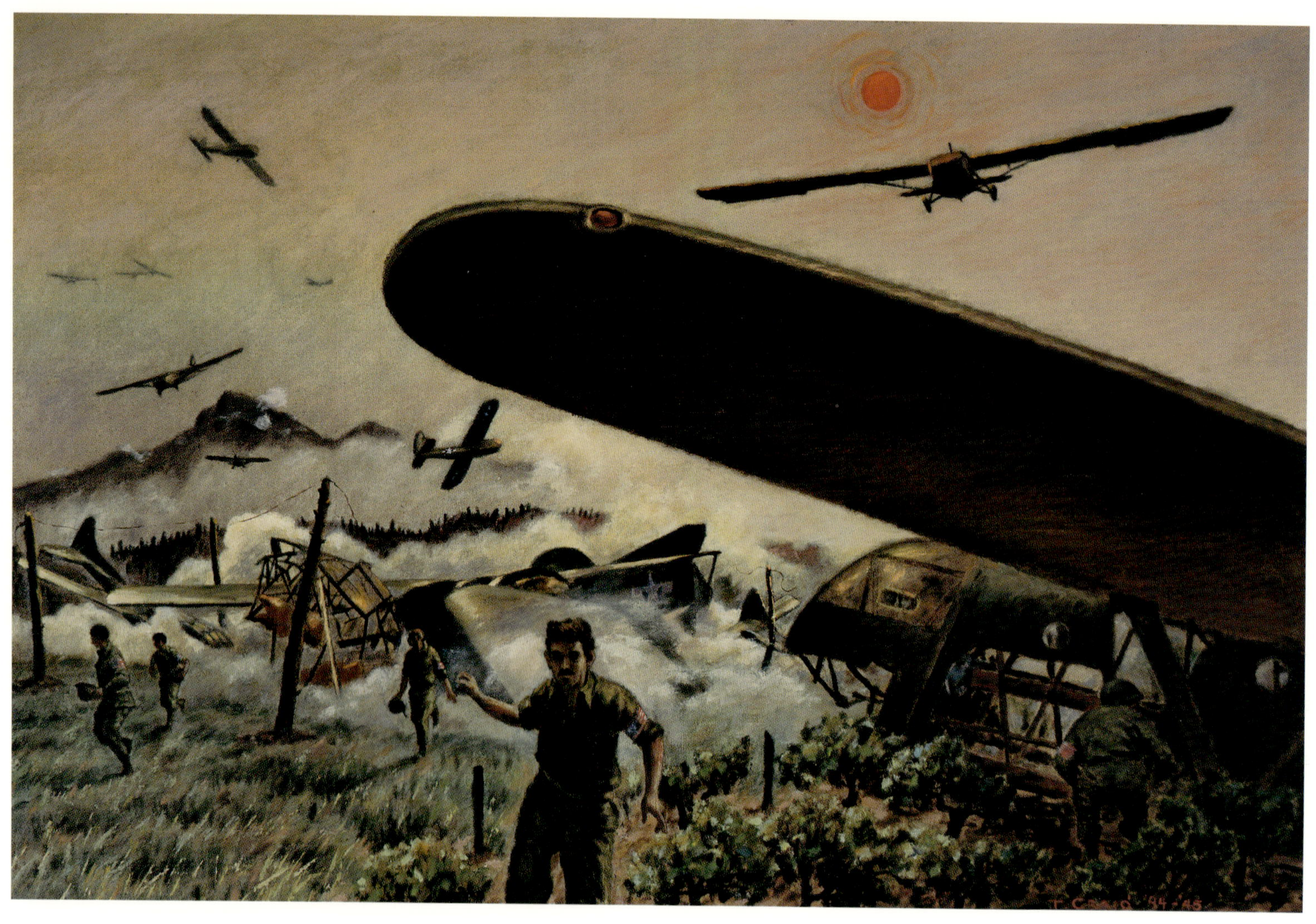

GLIDER LANDING IN SOUTHERN FRANCE
France
Tom Craig, 1944
Oil, 20" x 30"

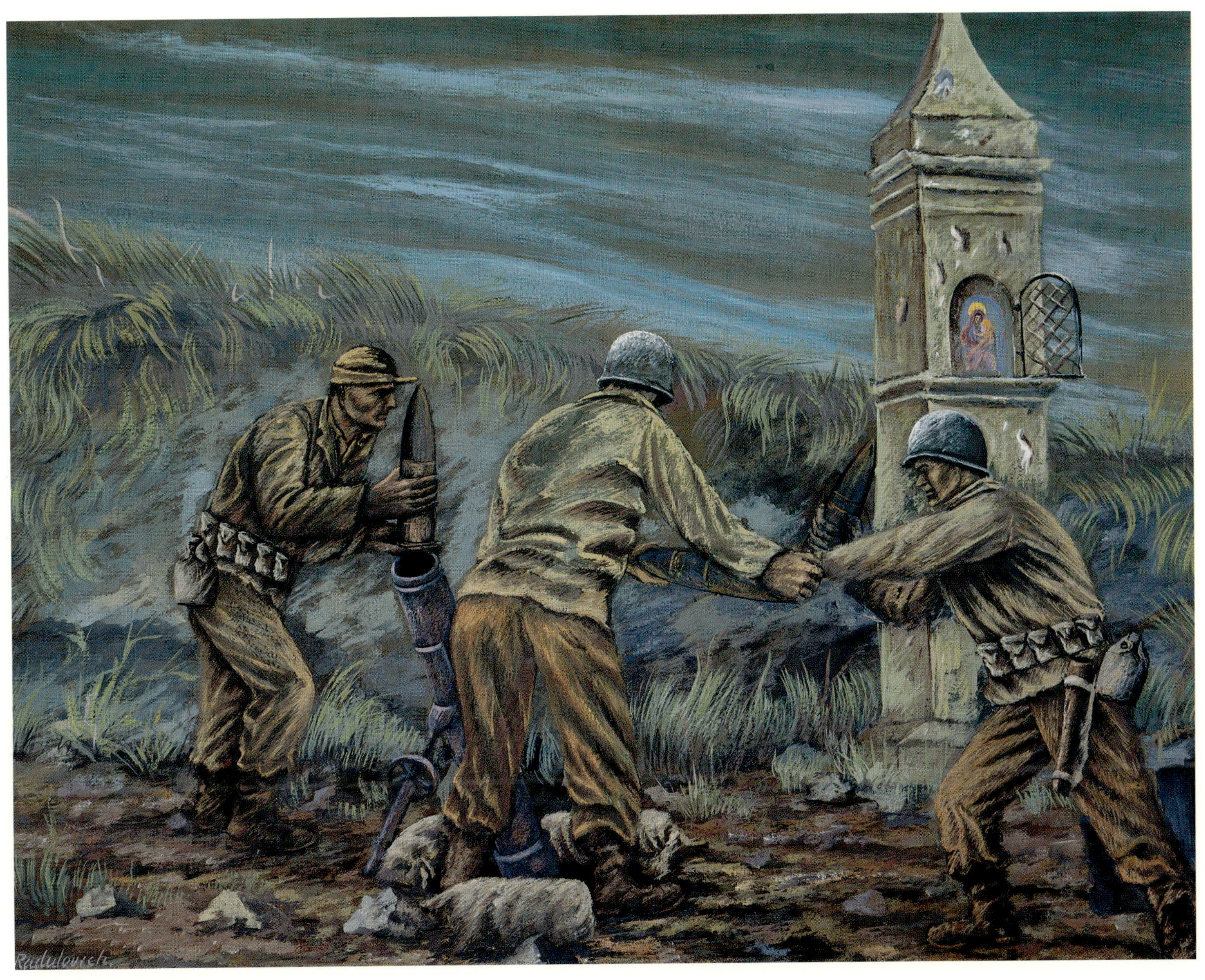

CHEMICAL MORTARMEN
Lizano, Italy
Savo Radulovic, 1945
Watercolor, 18 ⅞" x 23 ¾"

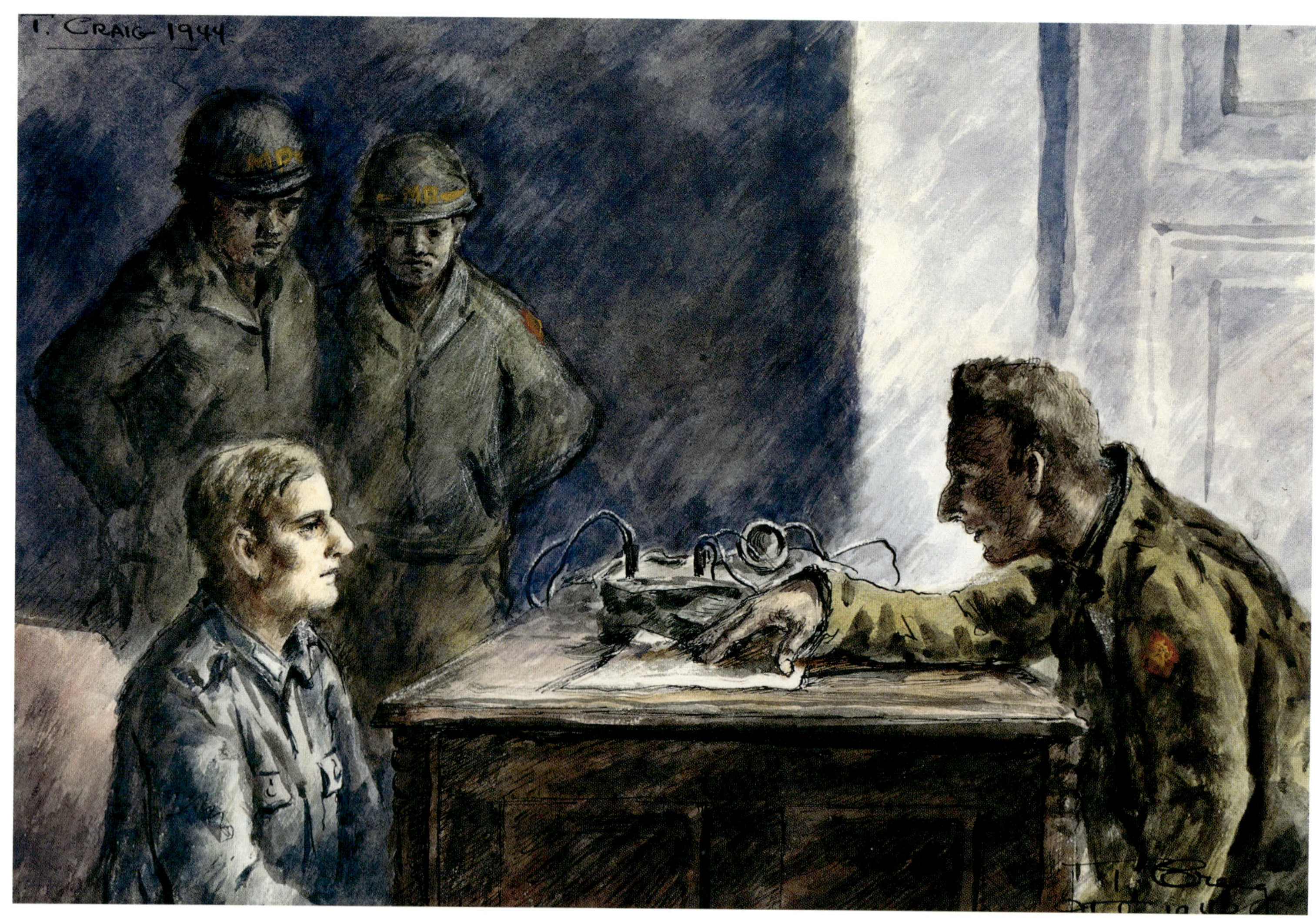

LT. ZACHARIAI
Italy
Tom Craig, 1943
Watercolor, 15" x 22"

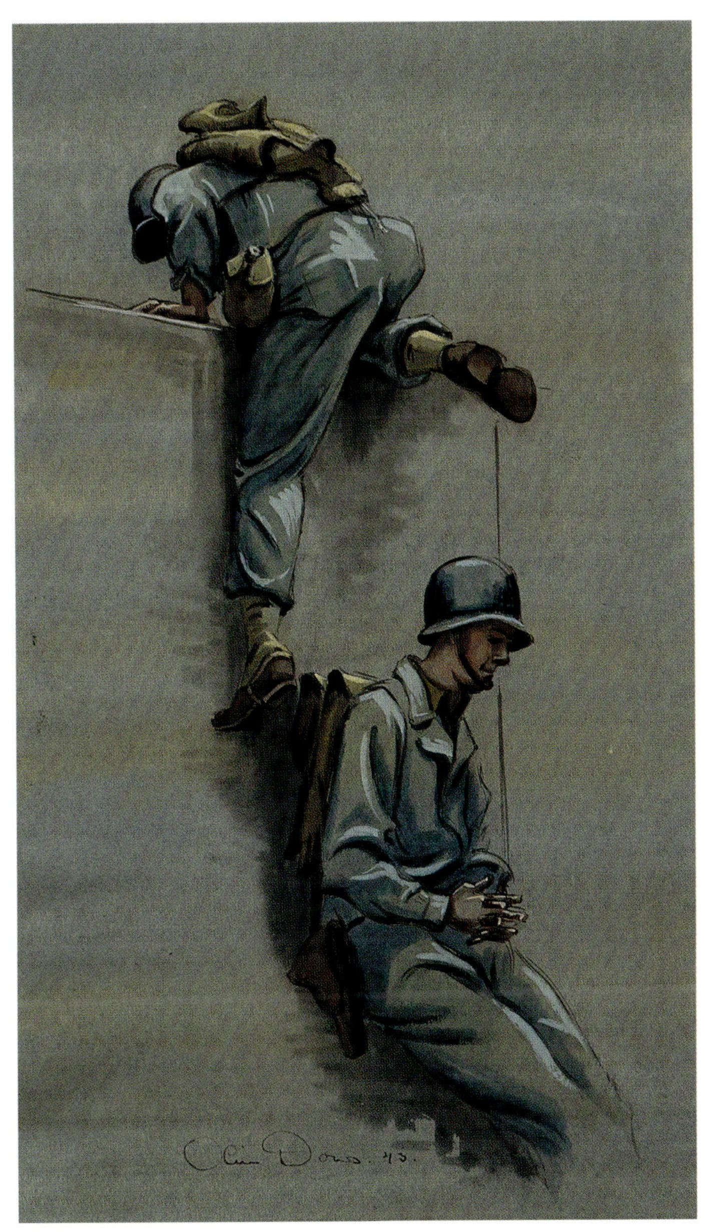

CLIMBING THE WALL
England
Olin Dows, 1943
Watercolor, 19" x 12 ¼"

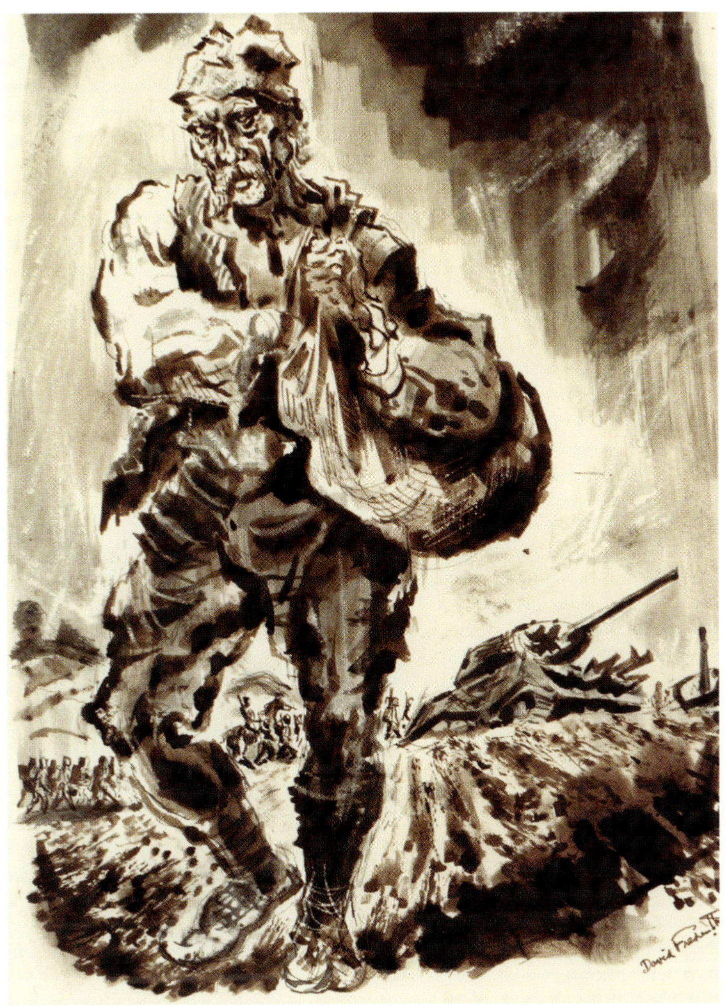

PEASANT SOWING DURING BATTLE
Yugoslavia
David Fredenthal, 1944
Watercolor, 9 ½" x 12 ½"

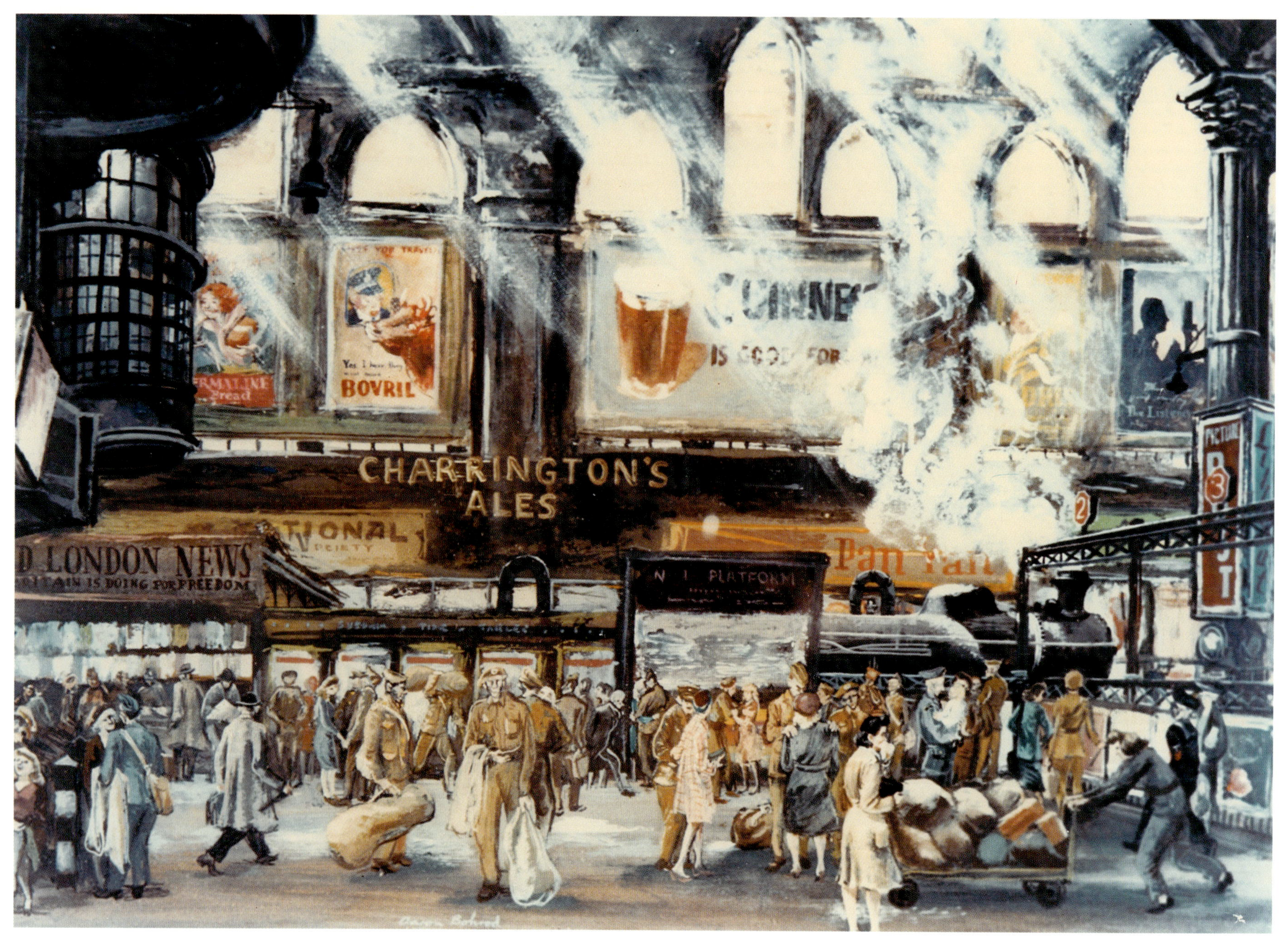

PADDINGTON RR STATION
London, England
Aaron Bohrod, 1944
Gouache, 13" x 19"

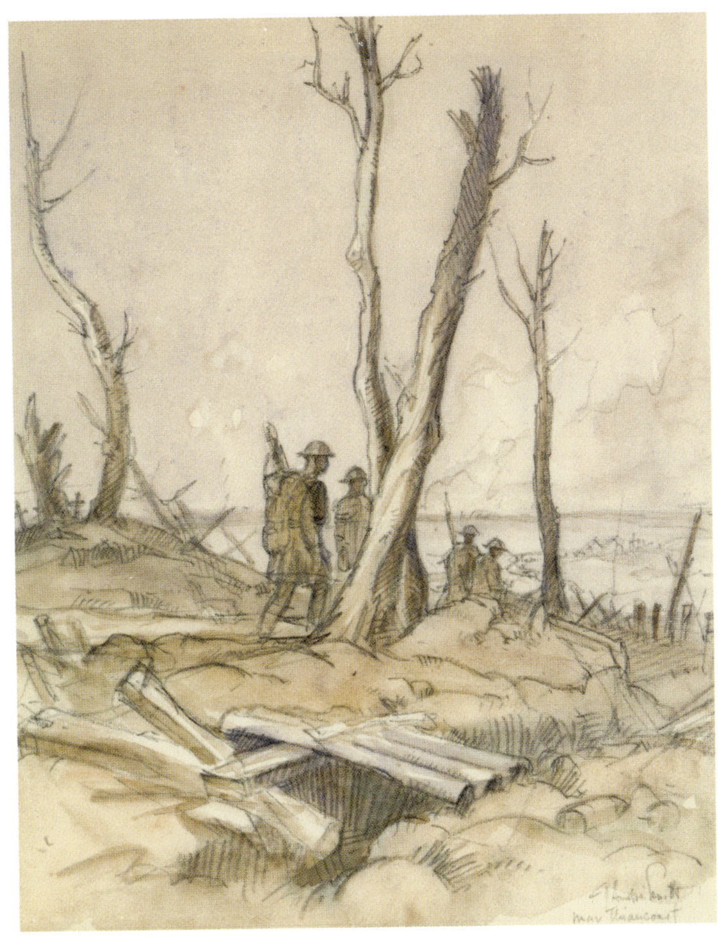

NEAR THIAUCOURT
France, World War I
Jules Andre Smith
Watercolor, 9" x 7"

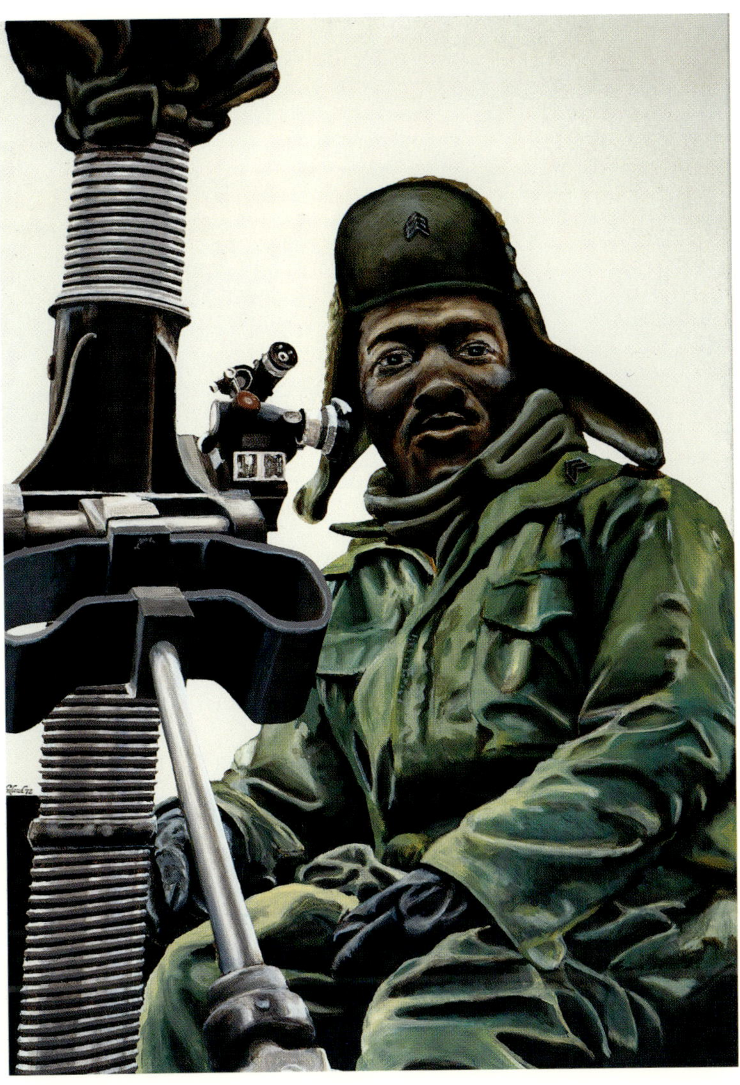

FOUR DEUCE
Germany
William F. Voiland, 1972
Acrylic, 42" x 30"

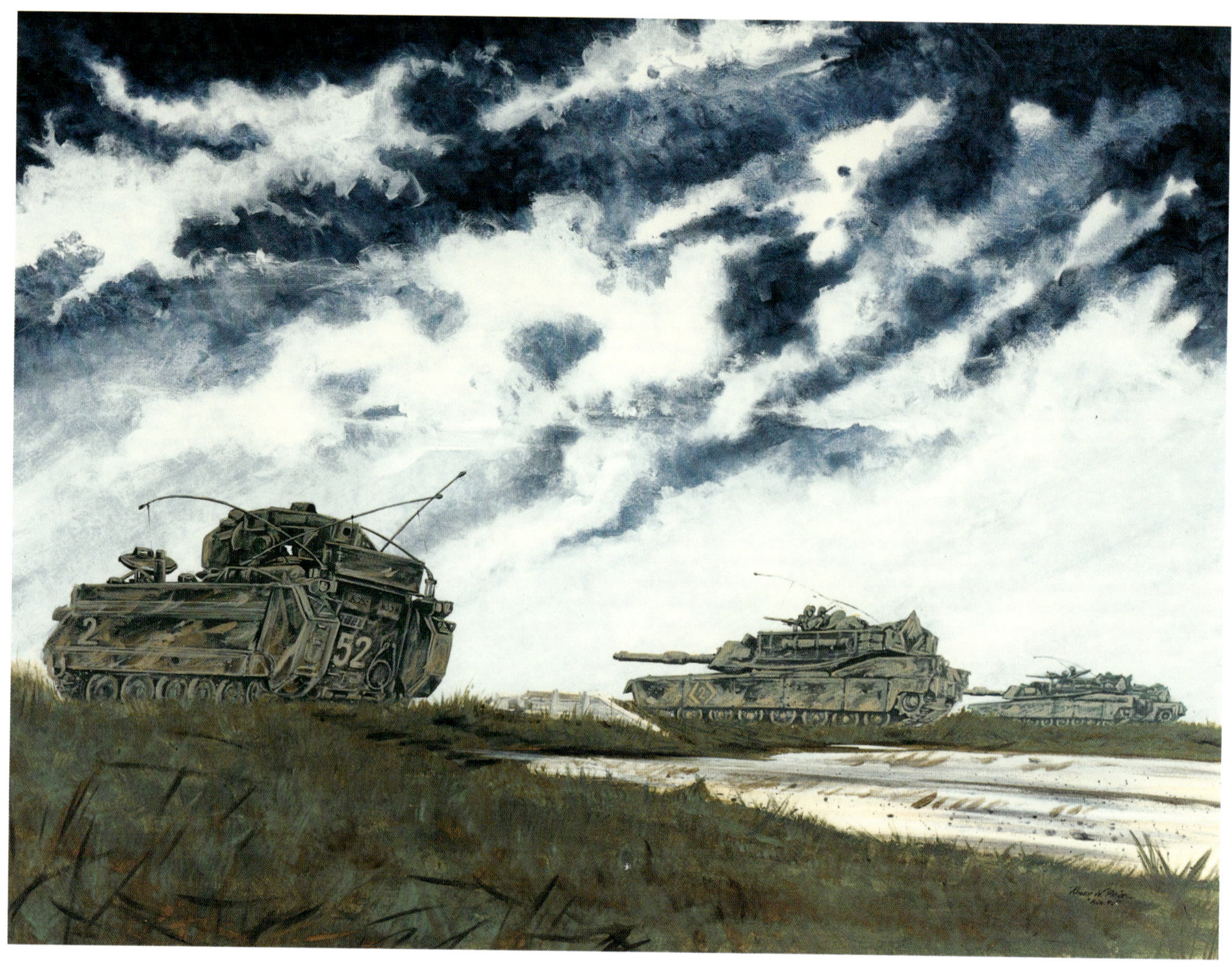

ON LINE
Germany
Roger W. Price, 1990
Oil, 30" x 40"

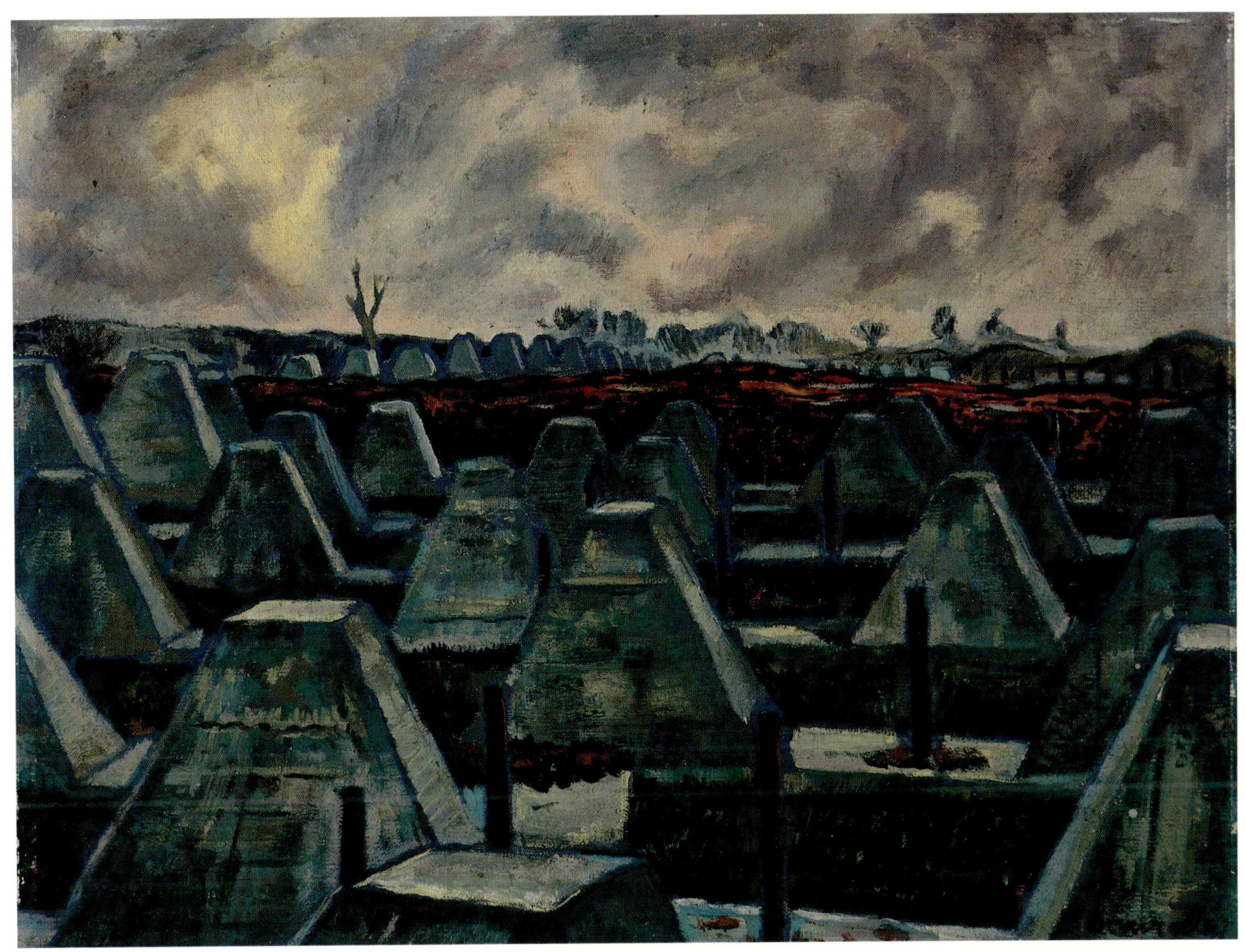

THE SIEGFRIED LINE
Belgium
Harrison Standley, 1944
Oil, 12" x 15 ¾"

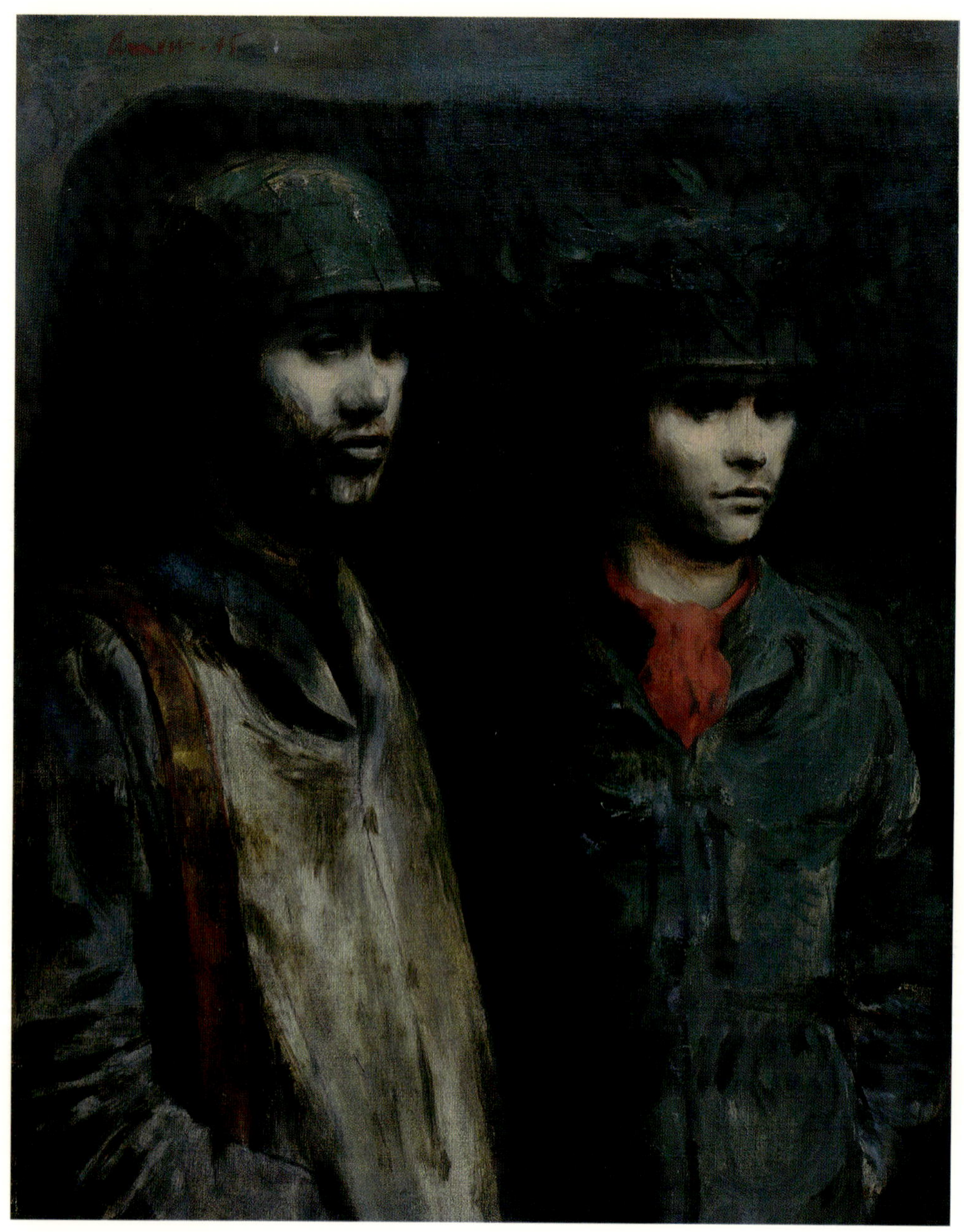

TWO SOLDIERS
Vossenack, Germany
Bernard Arnest, 1944
Oil, 21 ½" x 17 ½"

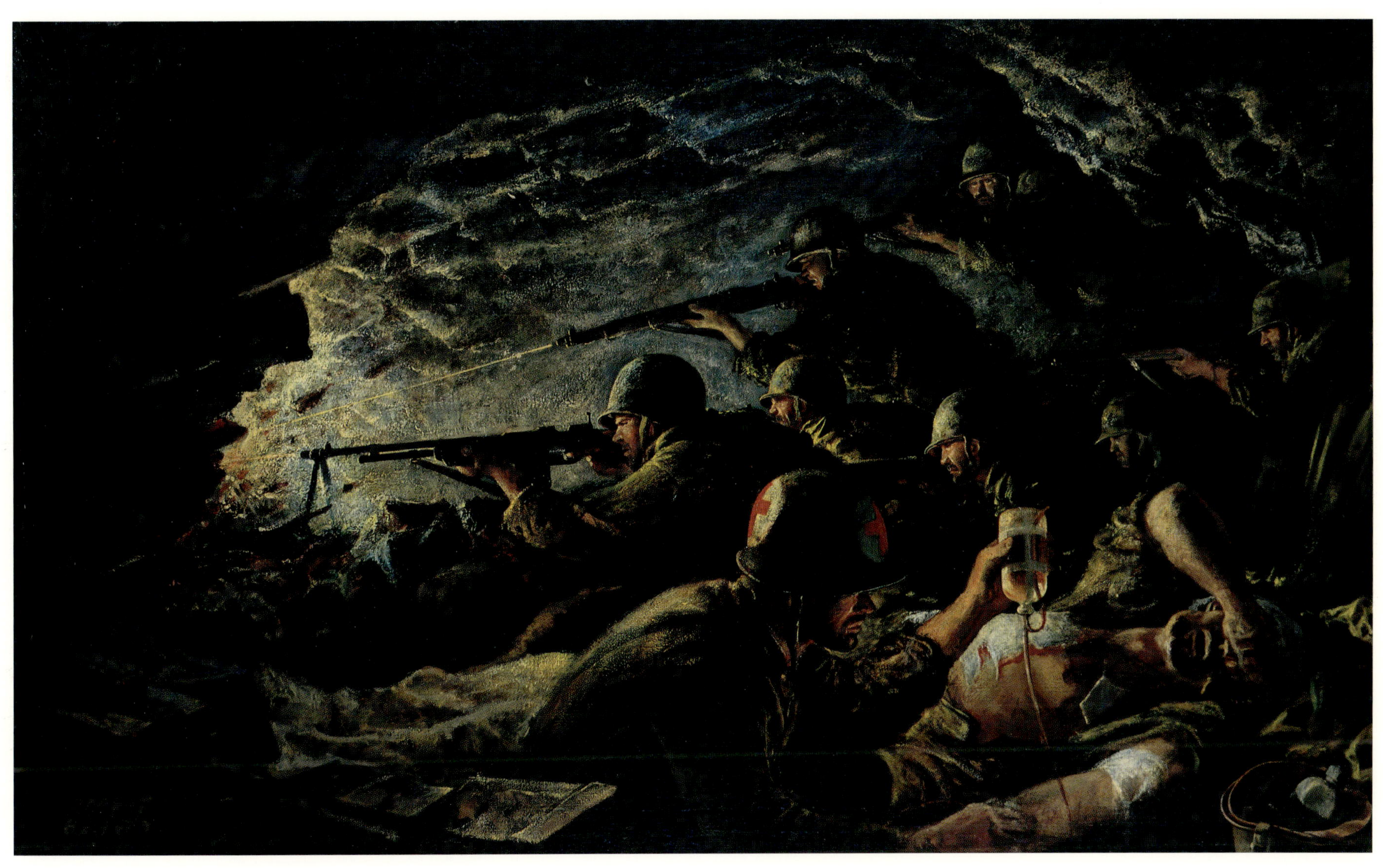

BATTLE OF THE CAVES
Anzio, Italy
Robert Benney, 1944
Oil, 22" x 36"

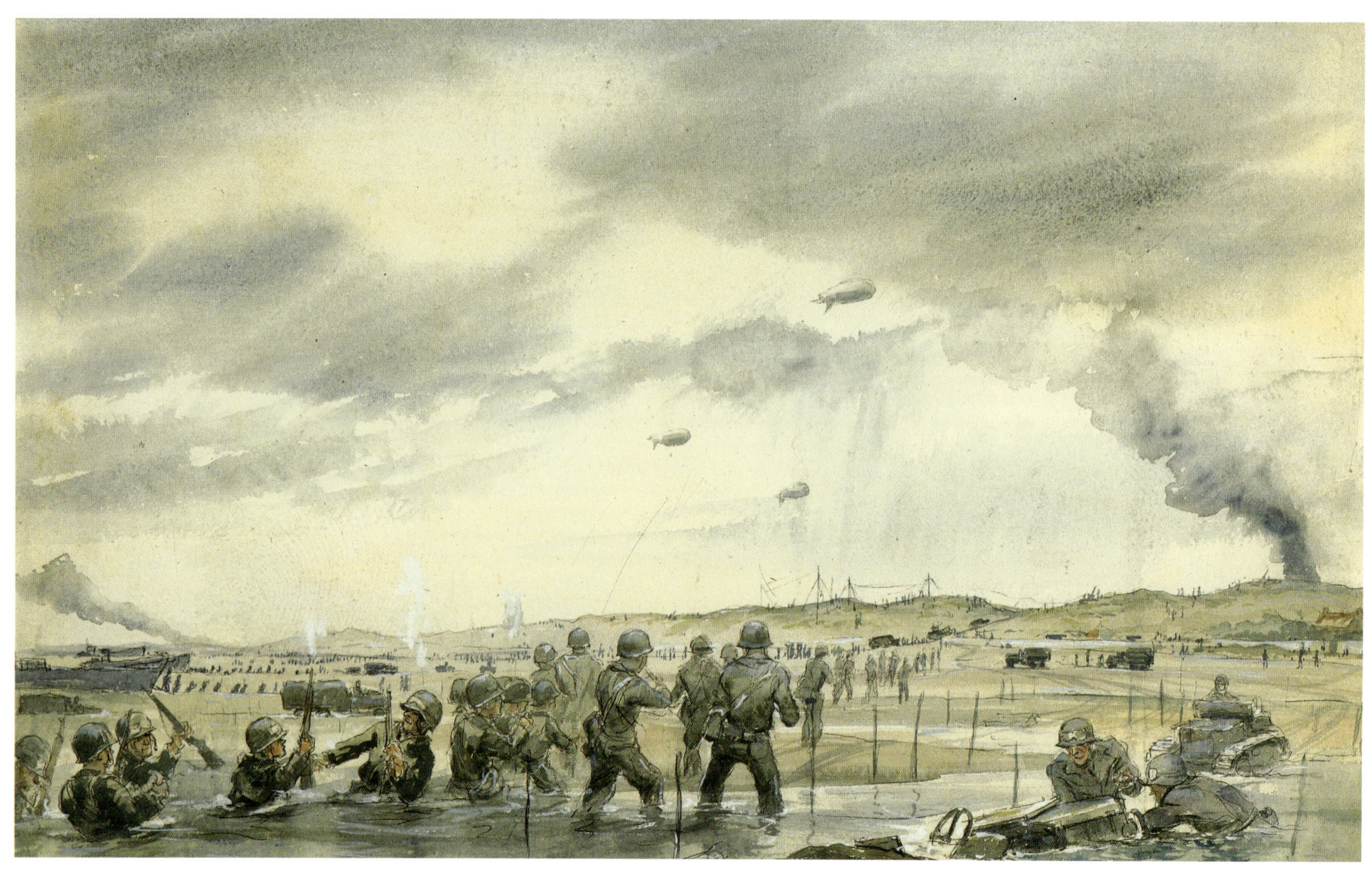

UTAH BEACH
France
Joseph Gary Sheahan, 1944
Watercolor, 22 ½" x 18"

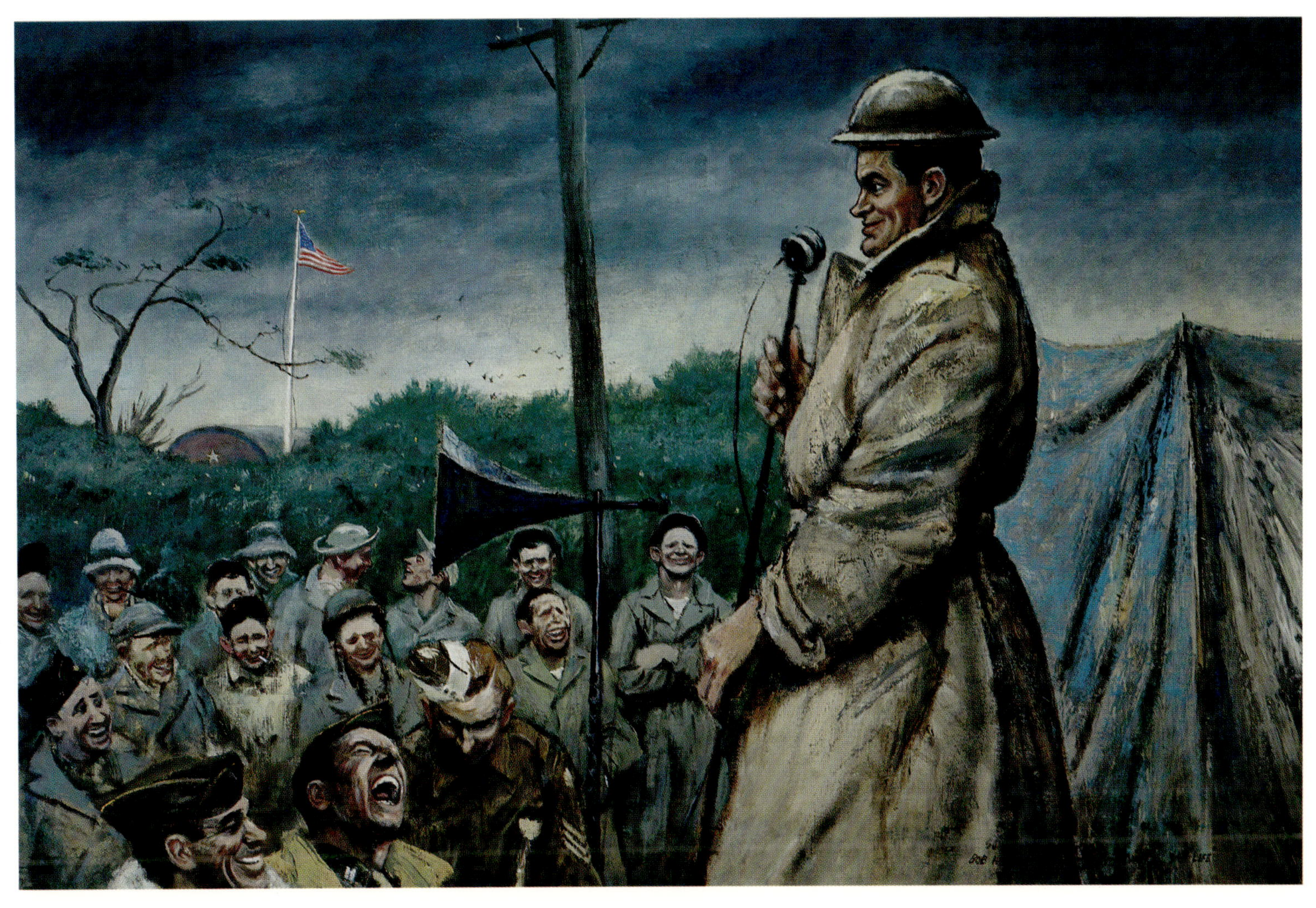

BOB HOPE ENTERTAINING TROOPS SOMEWHERE IN ENGLAND
England
Floyd Davis, 1943
Oil, 21″ x 30″

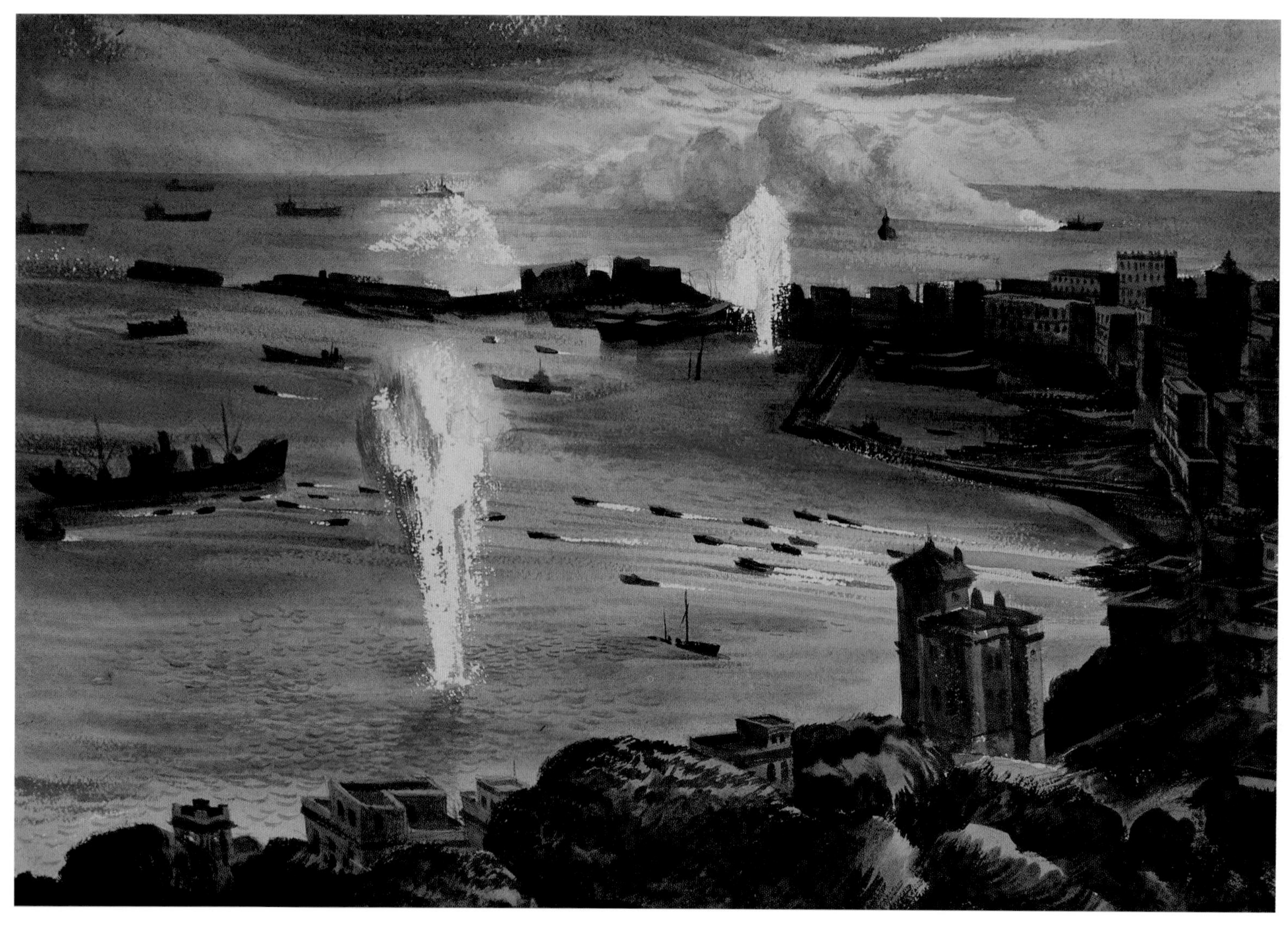

ANZIO HARBOR UNDER GERMAN BOMBARDMENT
Italy
Edward A. Reep, 1944
Watercolor, 15 ⅝" x 22 ¾"

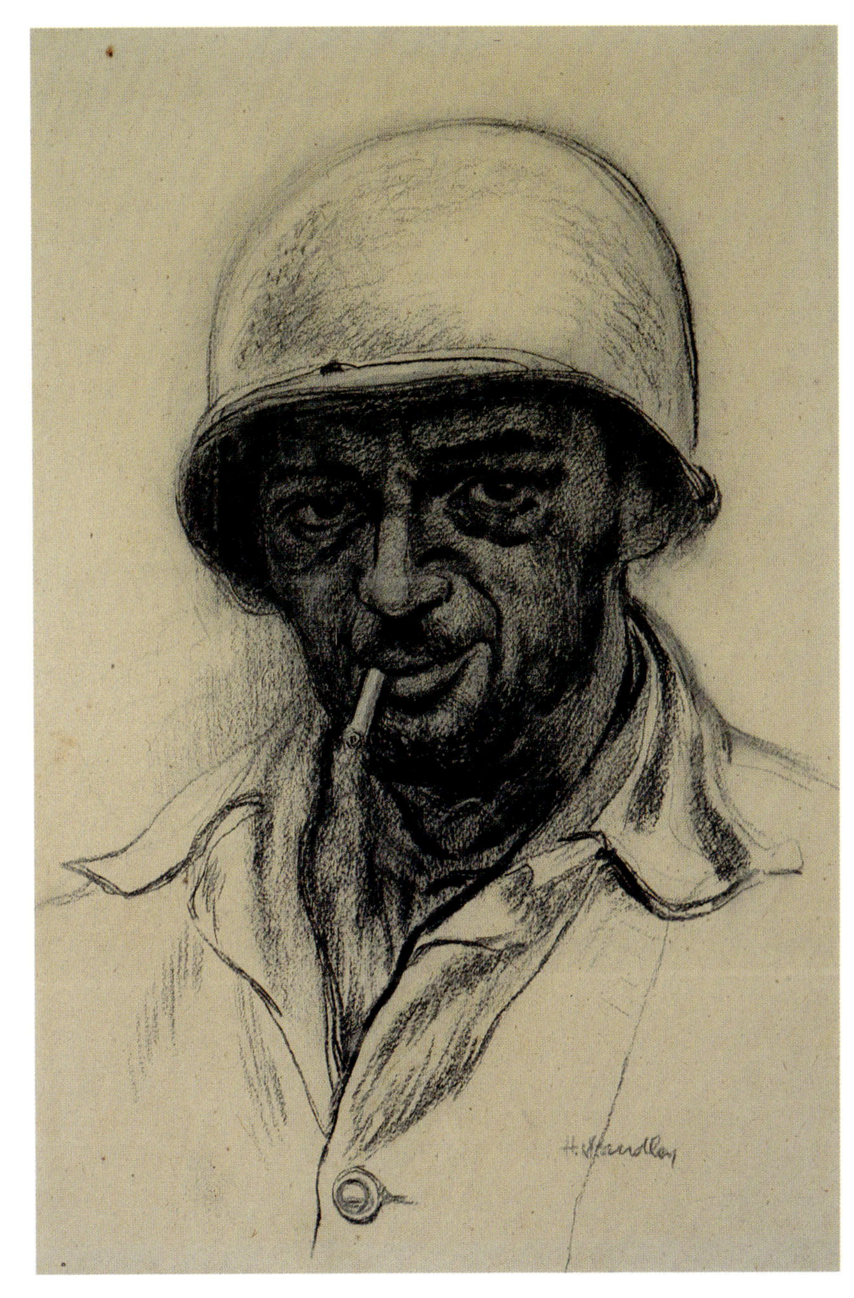

AFTER SIXTY-ONE DAYS AT THE FRONT
Belgium
Harrison Standley, 1944
Charcoal, 15 ¼" x 22 ⅝"

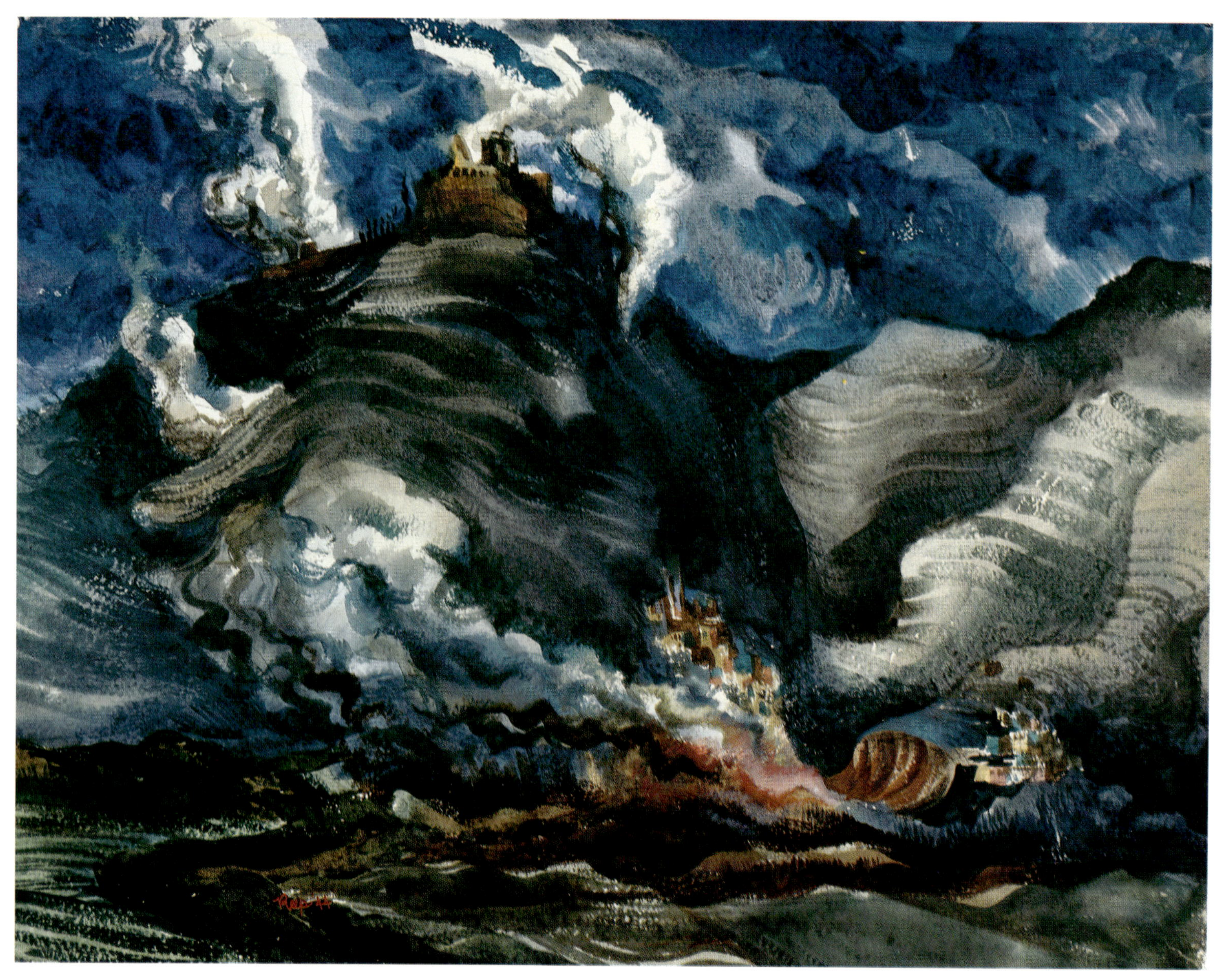

BOMBING OF THE ABBEY
Cassino, Italy
Edward A. Reep, 1944
Watercolor, 17 ½" x 22 ¼"

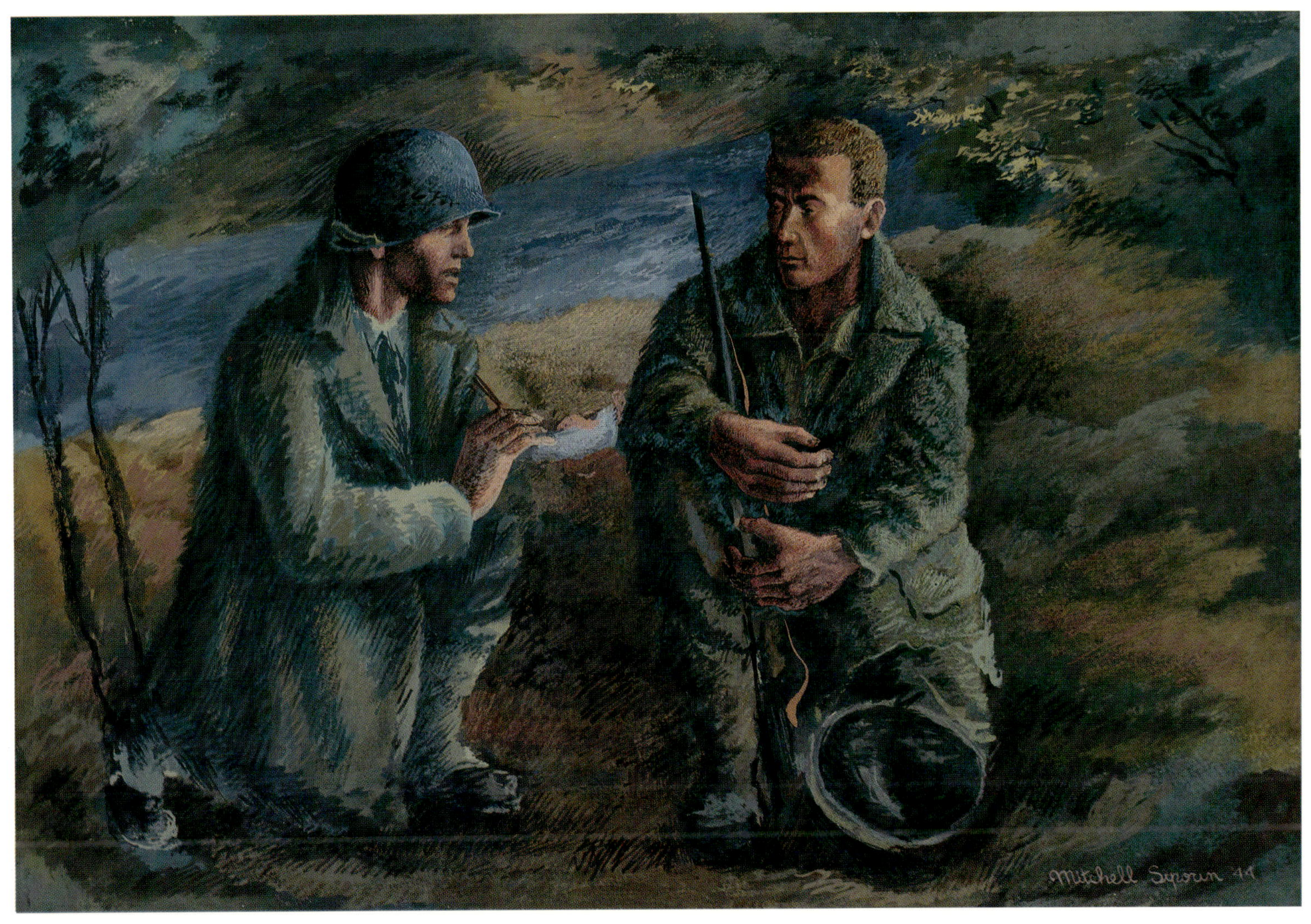

RECONNAISSANCE REPORT
Castelnuevo, Italy
Mitchell Siporin, 1944
Gouache, 14" x 19 ⅞"

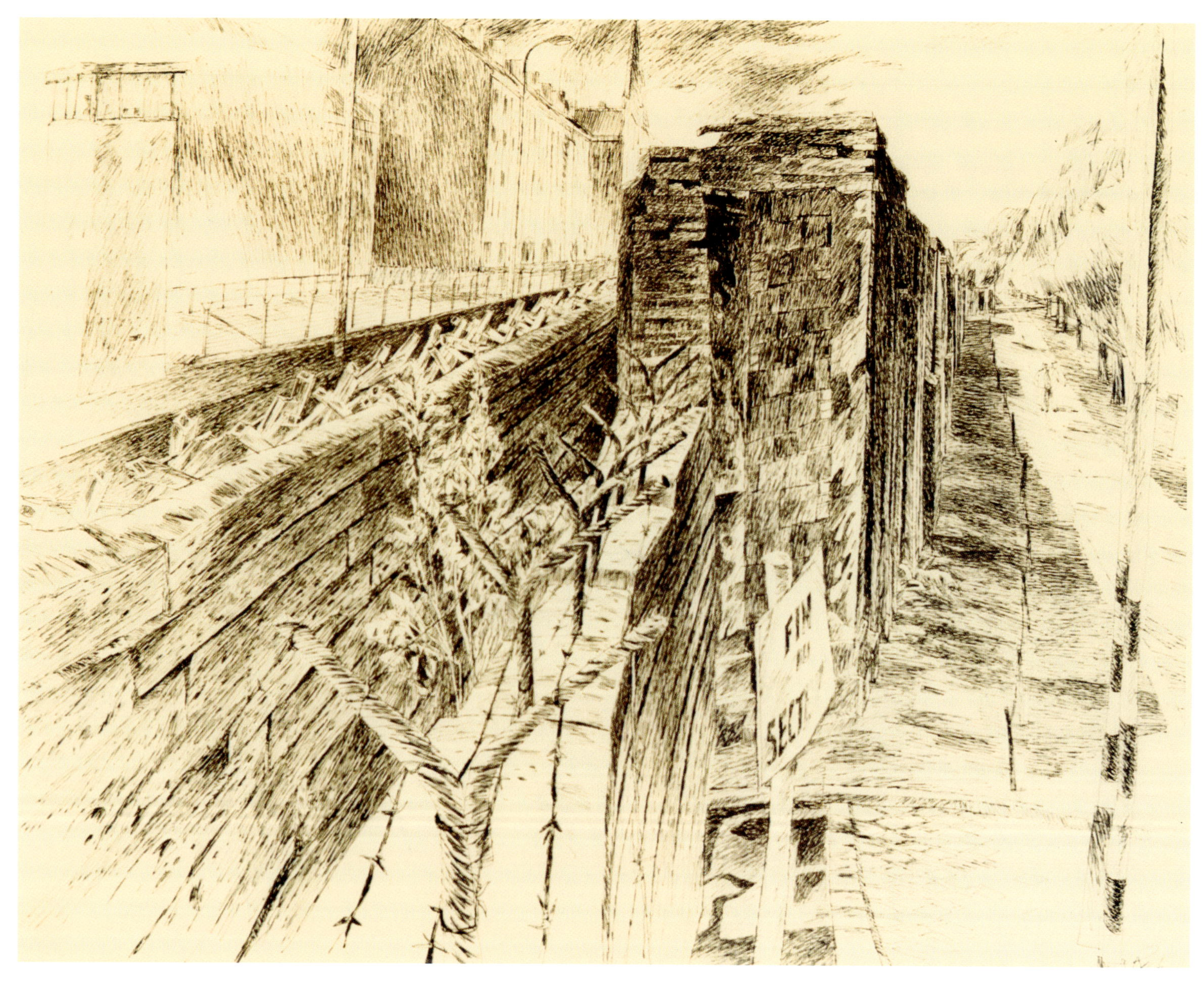

BERNHAUER STRASSE, AT THE END OF THE FRENCH SECTOR
Berlin, Germany
Edward A. Reep, 1972
Ink, 21 ½" x 26 ½"

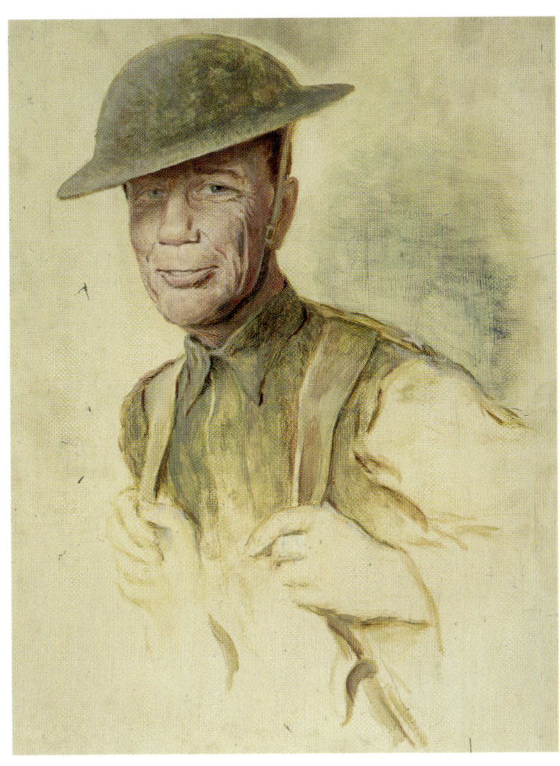

THEODORE ROOSEVELT, JR.
Joseph Cummings Chase
Oil, 24" x 18"

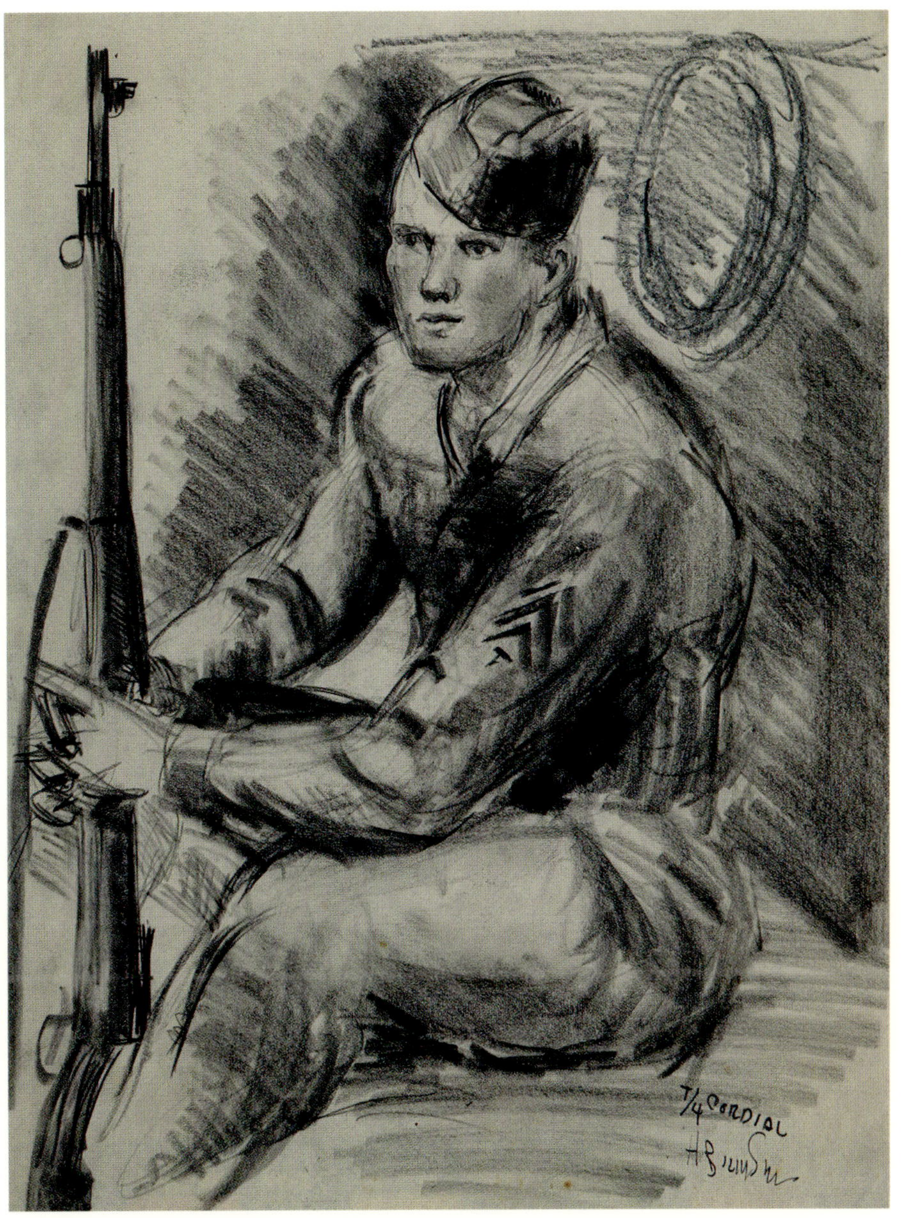

QUEEN MARY CROSSING #37
Atlantic Ocean
H. Robert Bizinsky, 1942
Charcoal on paper, 11" x 8 ½"

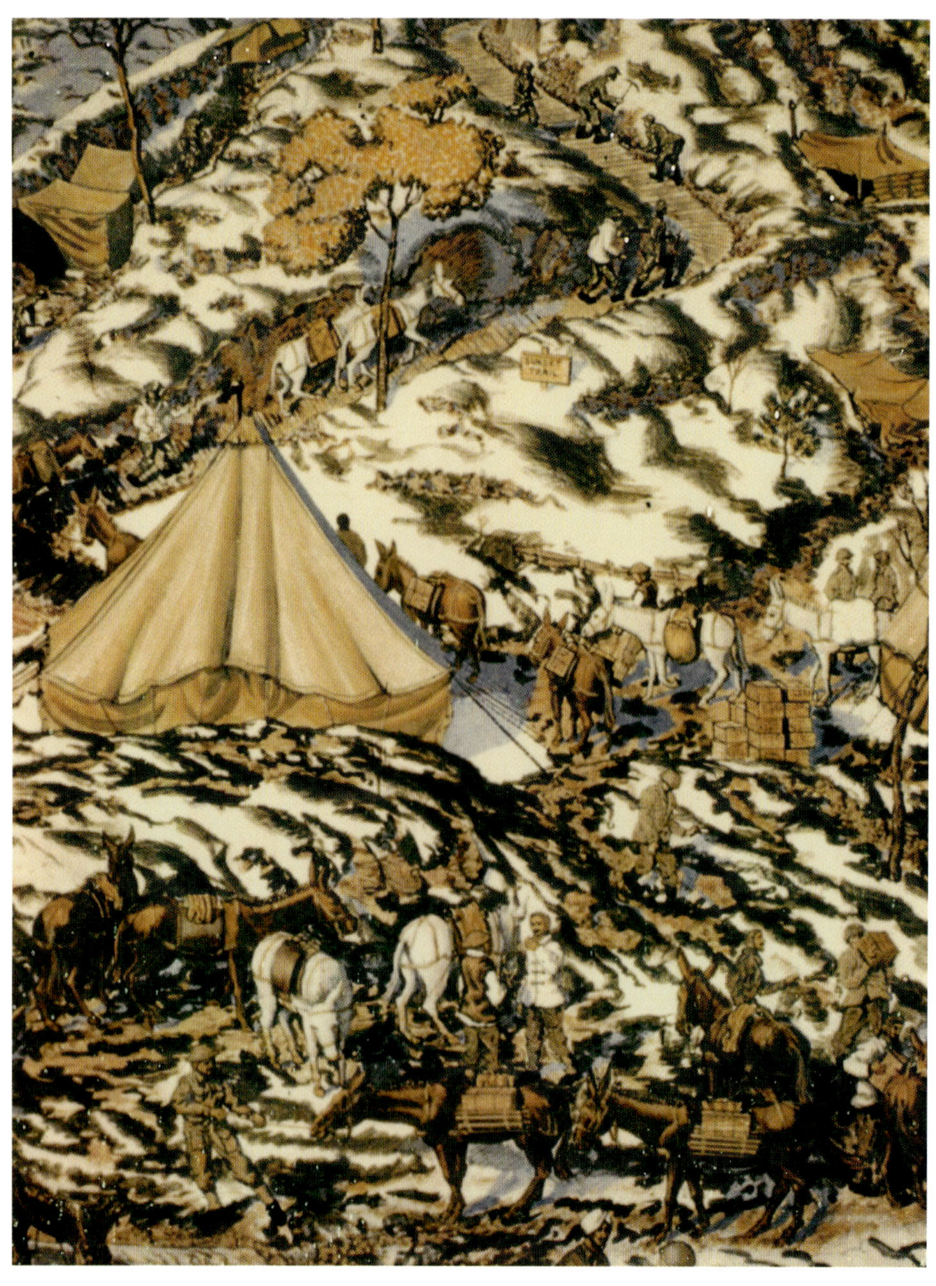

SUNSET TRAIL
Italy
William V. Caldwell, 1945
Gouache, 23 ¼" x 17 ½"

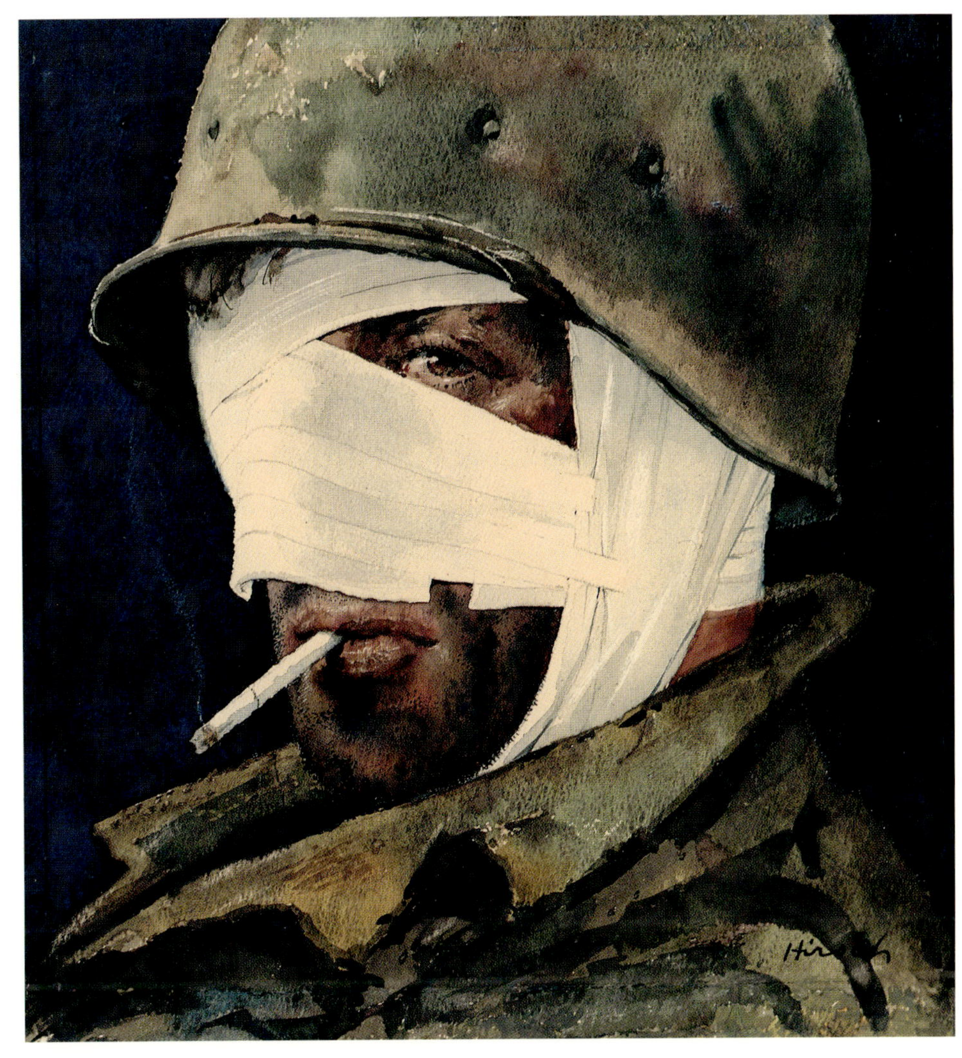

HIGH VISIBILITY WRAP
Italy
Joseph Hirsch, 1944
Watercolor, 9 ⅞" x 9"

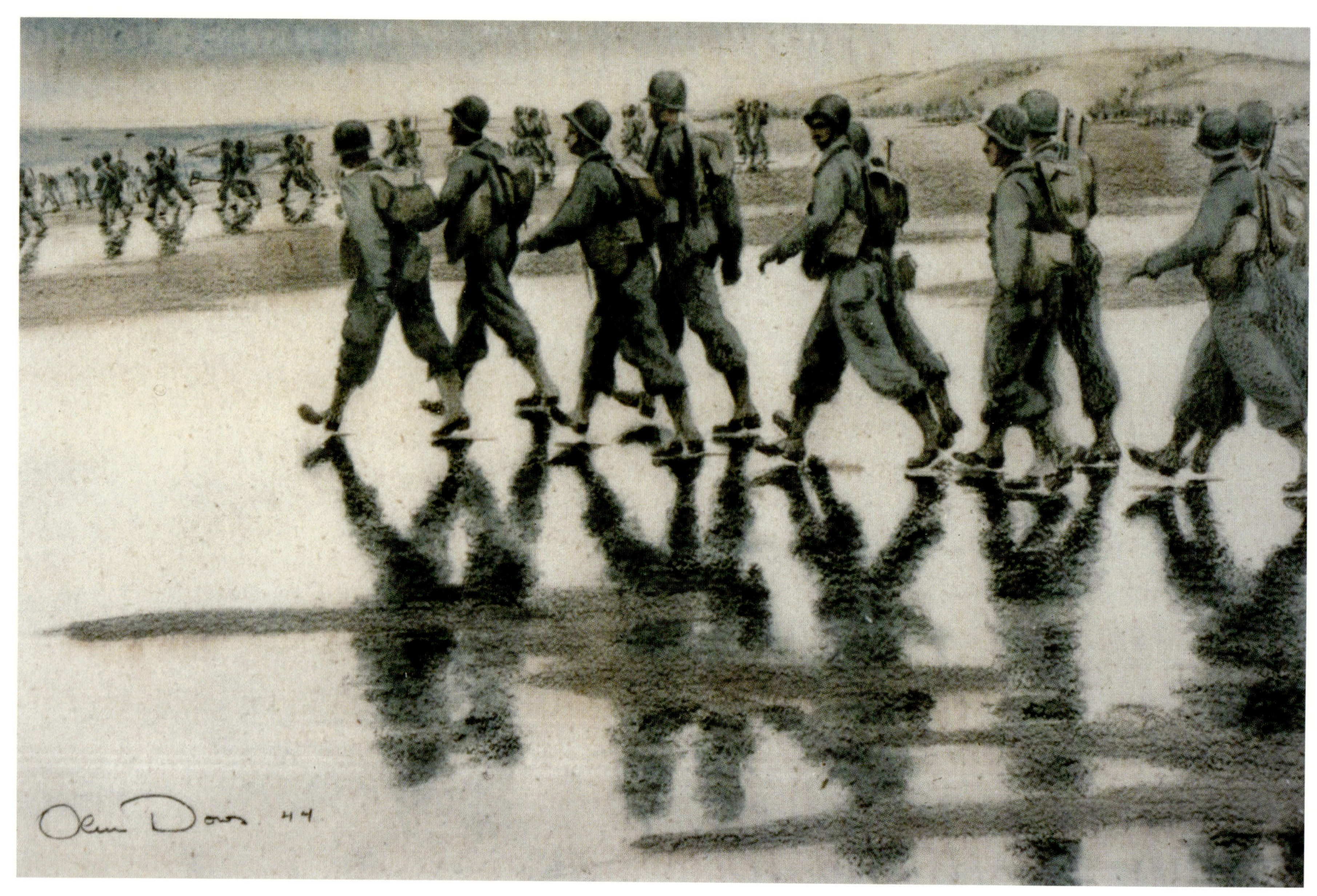

ON THE WAY TO THE ASSAULT BOATS
England
Olin Dows, 1944
Watercolor, 14" x 21 ¾"

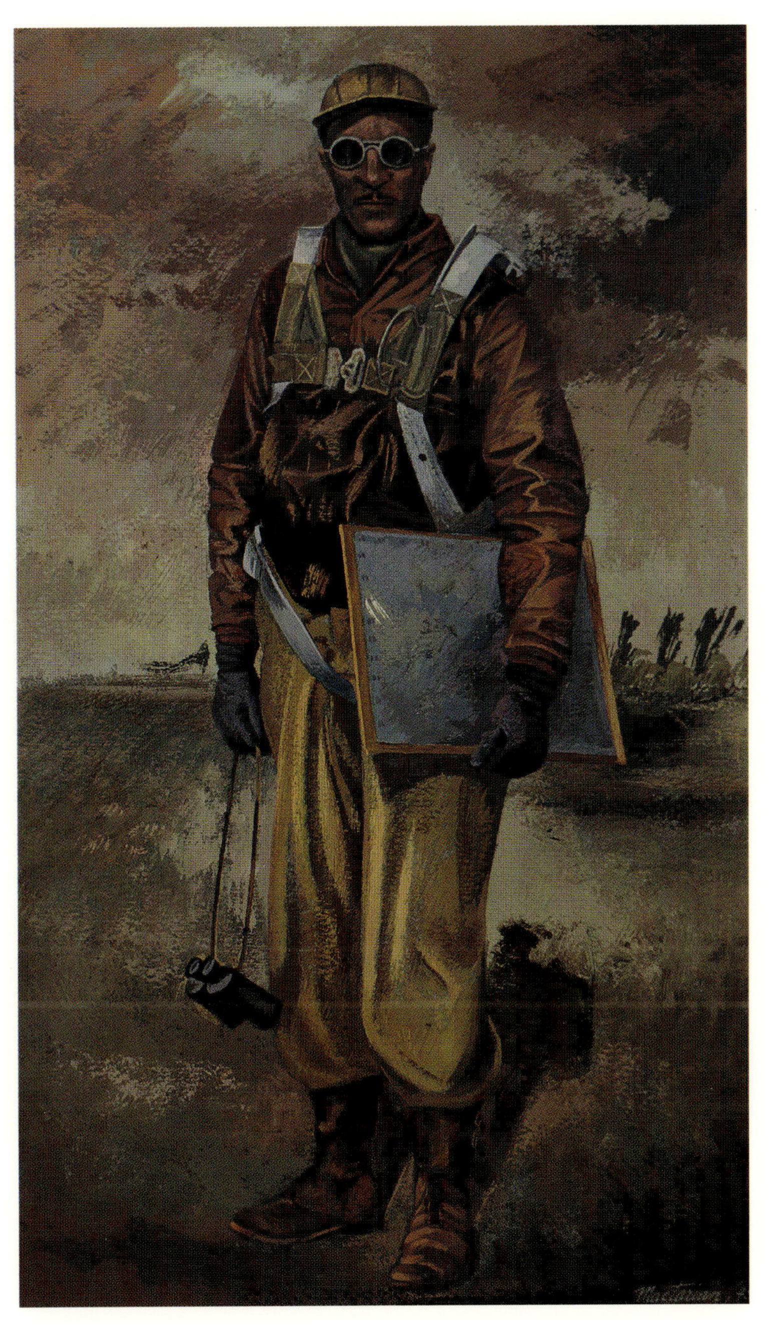

OBSERVATION PILOT
Viareggio, Italy
Ludwig Mactarian, 1945
Gouache, 15 ¾" x 9 ¾"

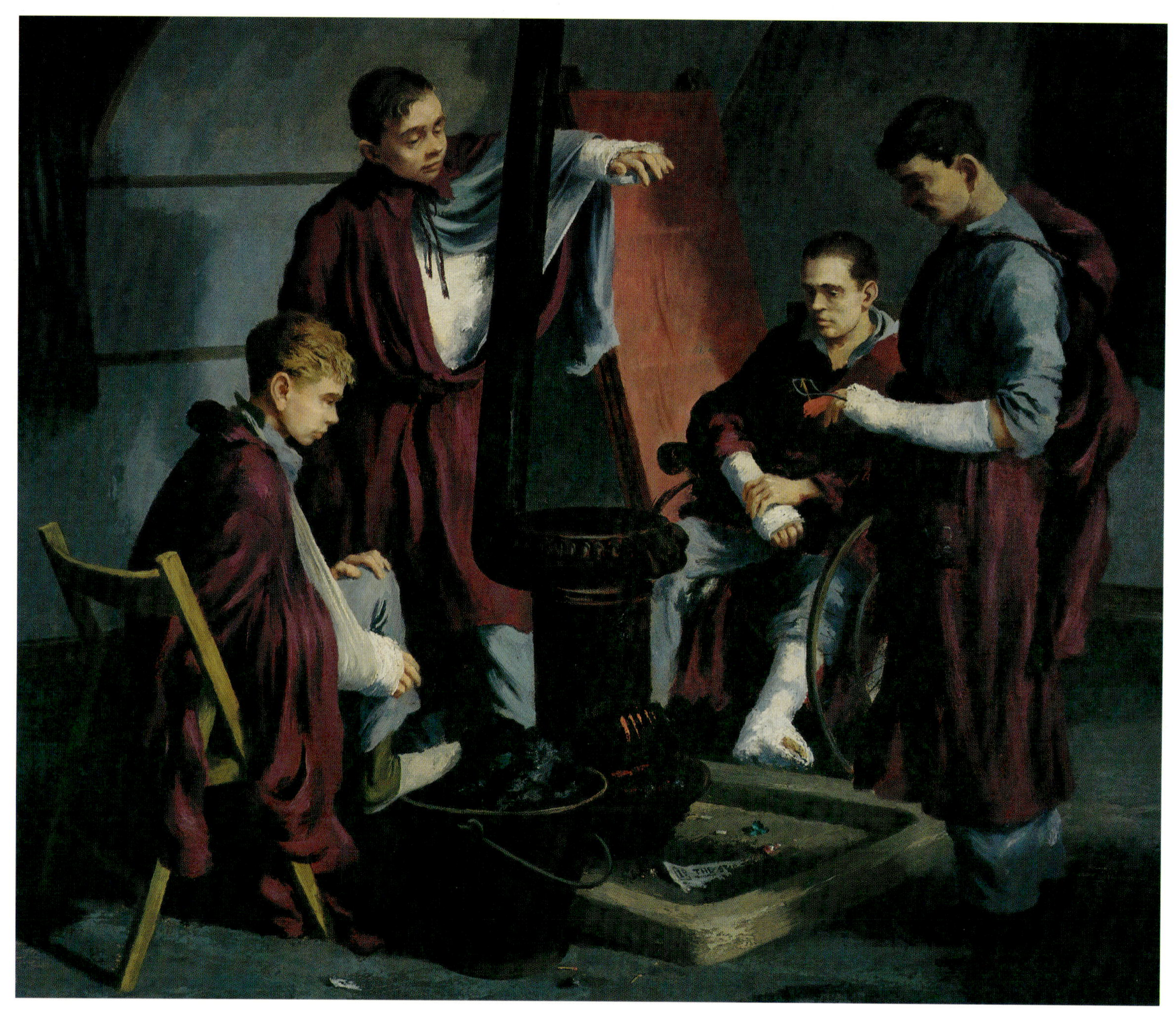

FIRESIDE COMFORT
England
Lawrence Beall Smith, 1944
Oil on masonite, 25″ x 29 ½″

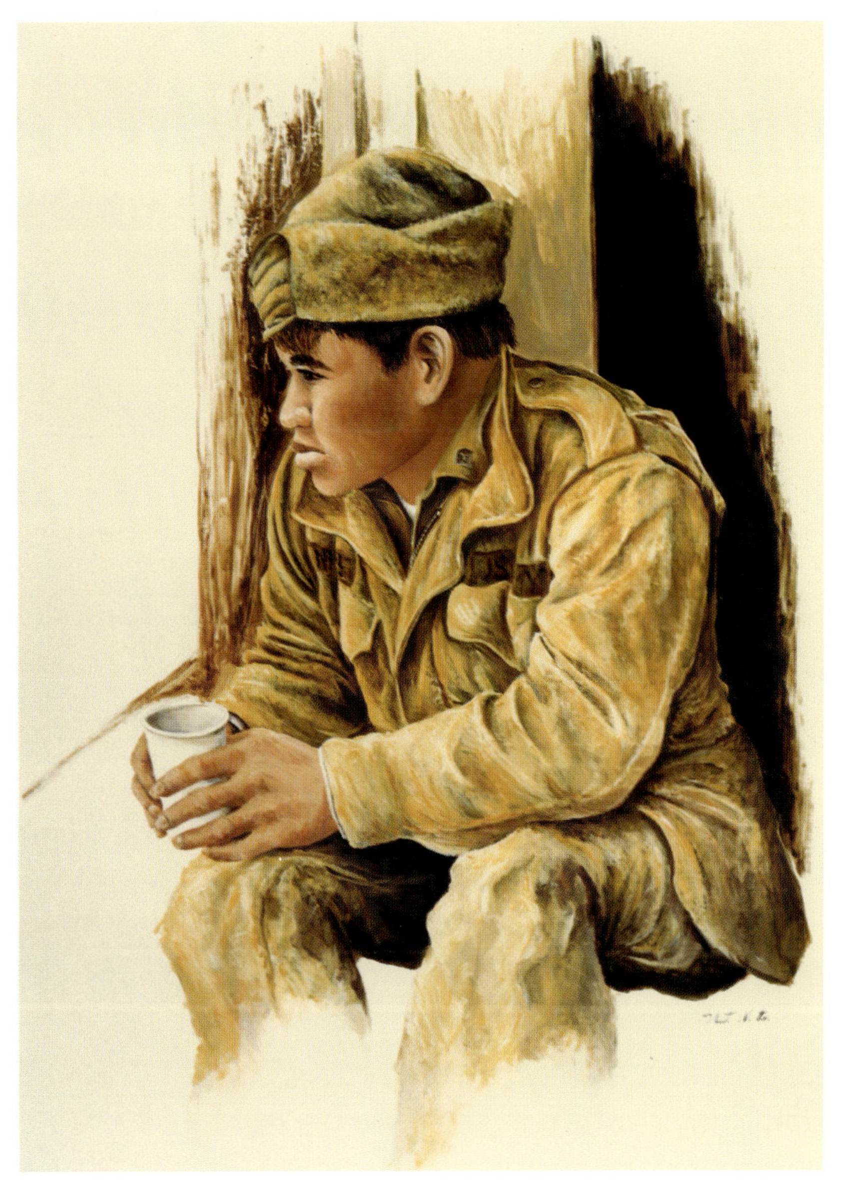

A GI SITTING IN AN APC
Germany
Robert A. Winter, 1972
Acrylic, 26" x 18"

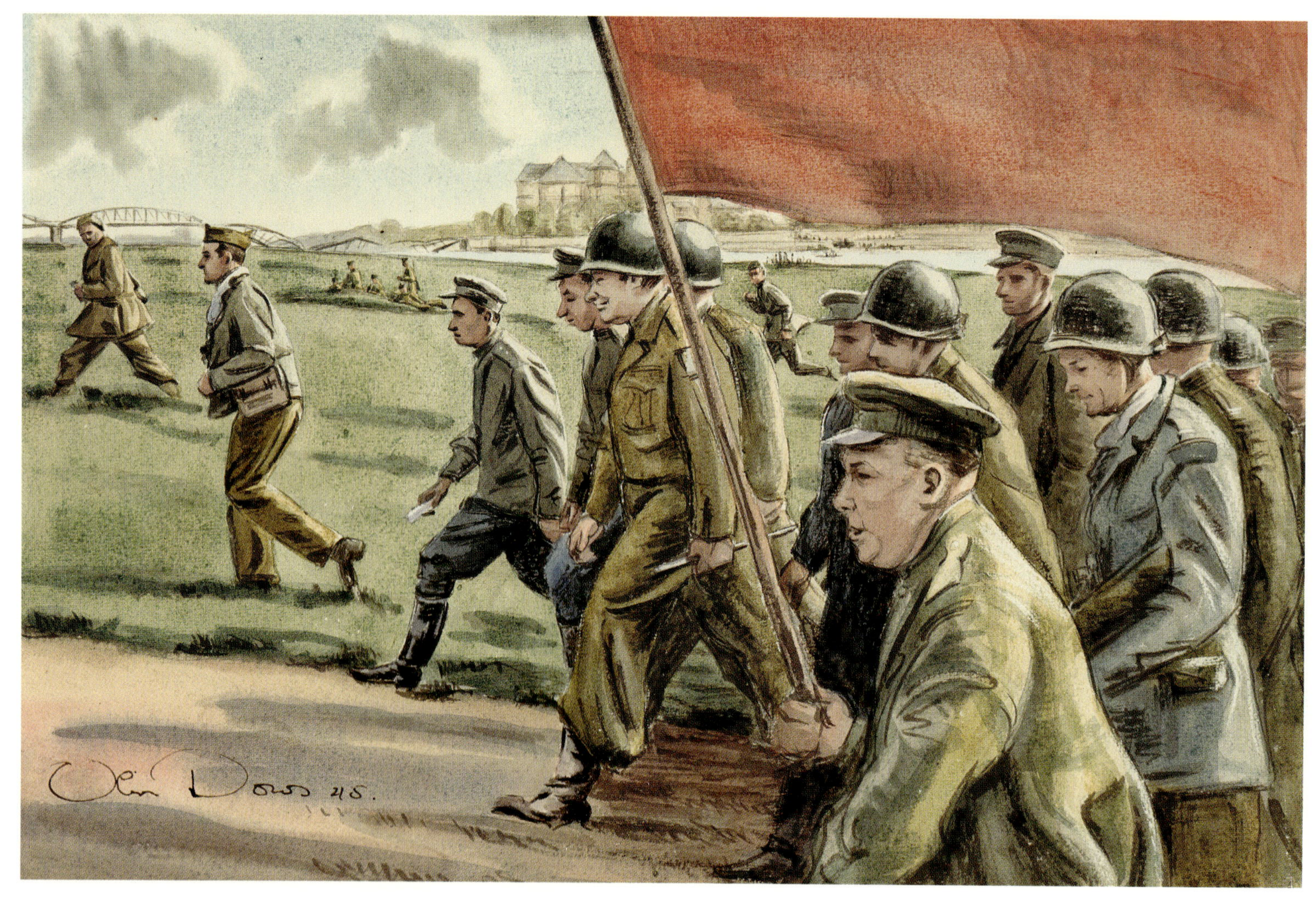

MEETING WITH THE RUSSIANS AT TORGAU
Germany
Olin Dows, 1945
Watercolor, 16 ½" x 21 ⅞"

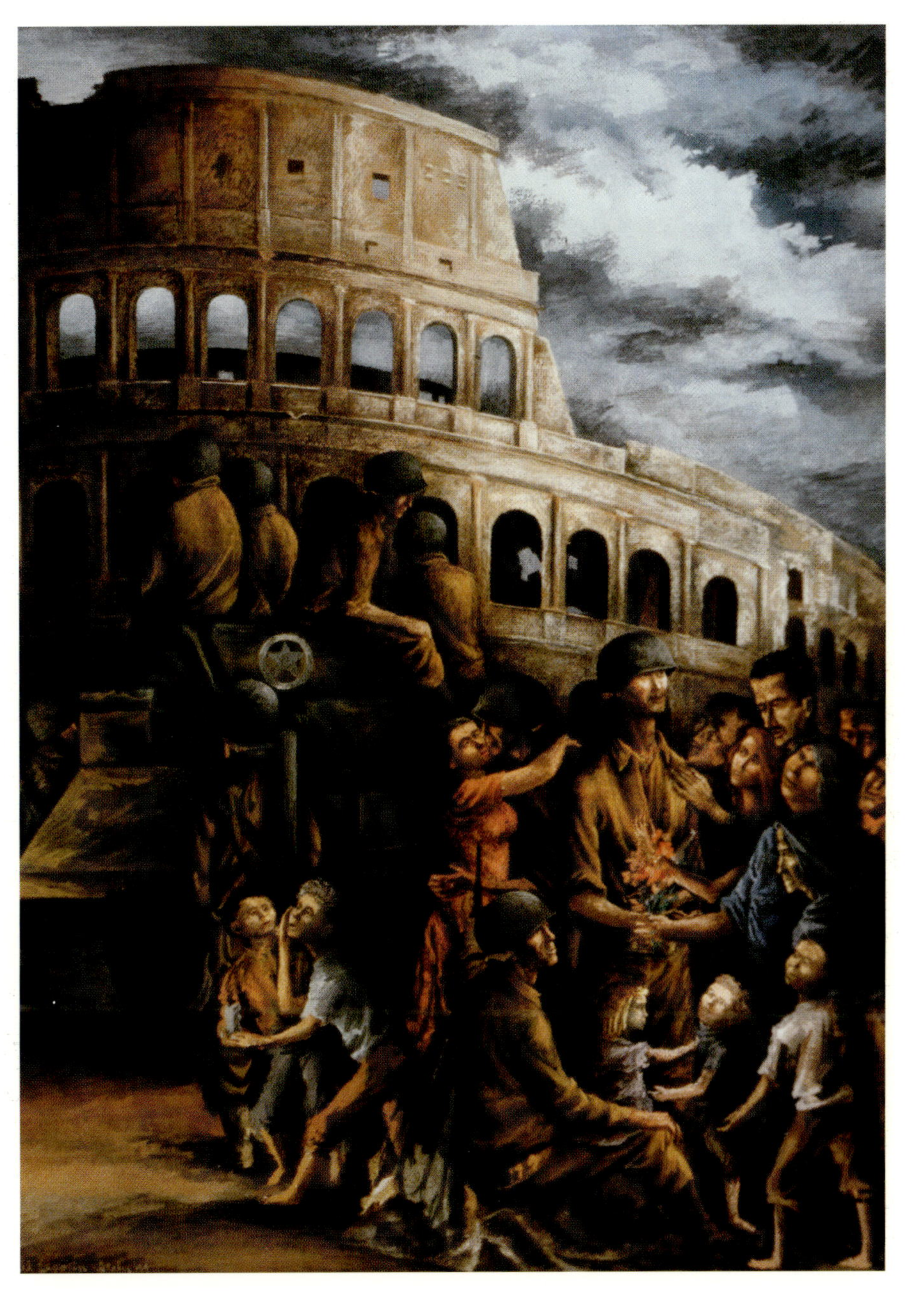

ROMAN HOLIDAY
Italy
Mitchell Siporin, 1944
Gouache, 25 ⅞" x 20 ⅜"

The Pacific and Asia

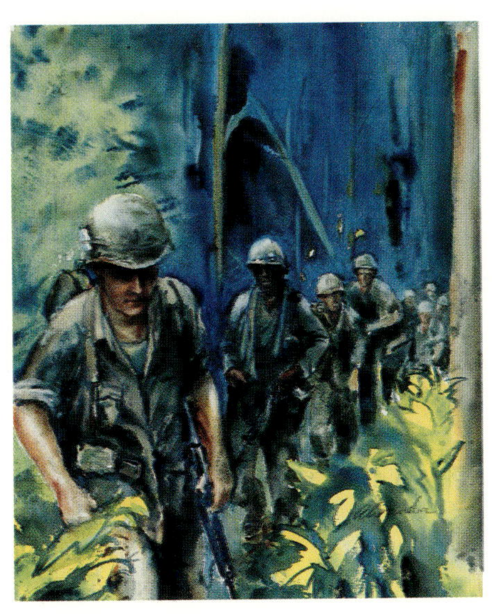

JUNGLE COLUMN
Vietnam
Samuel E. Alexander, 1967
Watercolor, 15 ½" x 22 ⅛"

THE SPANISH-AMERICAN WAR AT THE END OF THE NINETEENTH century brought the United States as a military power into the Pacific. With the arrival of U.S. Army regulars and volunteers in the Philippines in July 1898, the Army began a presence in the Pacific, and shortly thereafter on the mainland of Asia, that continues unbroken almost a hundred years later. Nowhere else outside the Western Hemisphere is there such a long history of continuous U.S. Army service to the nation in peace and war.

American soldiers have served in every region of the Pacific and Asia. They left their boot prints on the frozen tundra of Russian Siberia and in the tropics of the Pacific islands, on the jungle trails of Burma and the training areas of Australia, on the banks of the Yalu River in North Korea, and in the cane fields of Hawaii and the highlands of Vietnam. They fought Spanish soldiers, native insurrectionists, Boxer revolutionaries, North Vietnamese regulars, and South Vietnamese guerrillas. They marched to the relief of Tientsin and Peking and secured the Russian Trans-Siberian Railroad. They fought until they could fight no more down the length of Bataan, then marched back through hell to prison camps, and yet ultimately brought democracy and freedom to the oppressed throughout the Pacific. They garrisoned Shanghai, built the Ledo Road, fought aggressors shoulder-to-shoulder with their allies on the Korean front, and assaulted enemy bases in Laos and Cambodia. They defended their homes at Pearl Harbor and parachuted onto the Rock in Manila Harbor. They went ashore on the hostile beaches of innumerable Pacific islands, and they air-assaulted into the rice fields and hills of Vietnam.

Over the years American soldiers also performed many roles other than combat in this vast area. Whether imposing the authority of military occupation or providing military advice to friendly governments, they brought stability and reassurance. They helped rebuild homes, schools, and cities, assisted in caring for the sick and wounded and in feeding the hungry, and discovered shared interests, such as baseball in Japan. Their presence along the often cold and harsh demilitarized zone in Korea continues as a model for successful international peacekeeping.

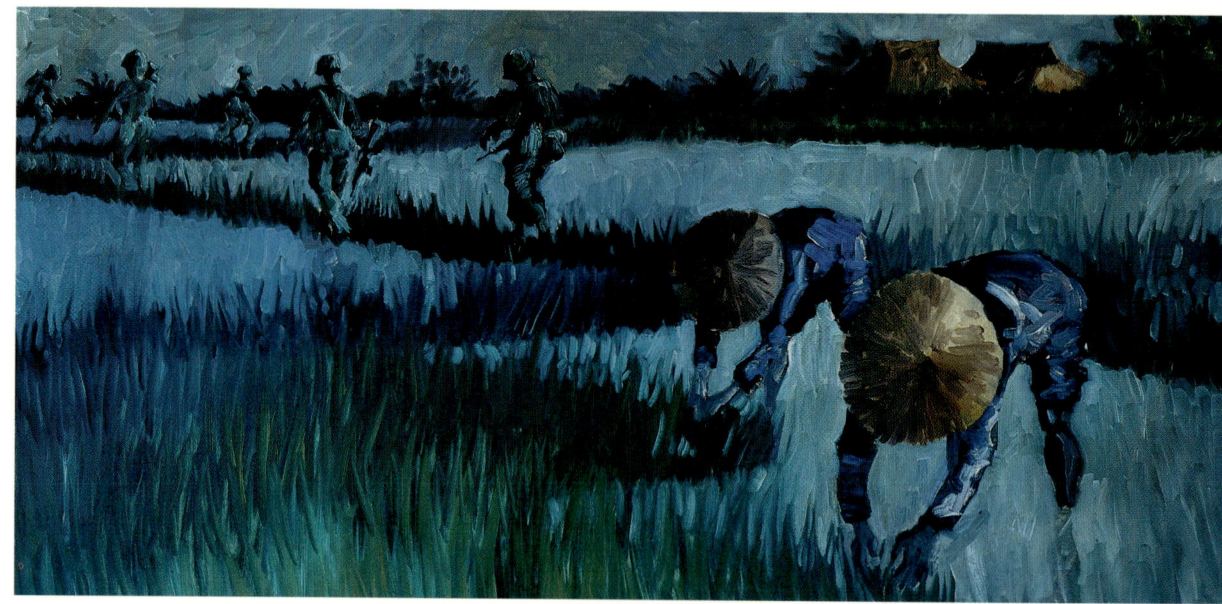

FRIEND TODAY—FOE TONIGHT
Vietnam
Augustine Acuna, 1966
Oil, 24" x 46"

American soldiers in the Pacific and Asia often had to struggle to pronounce place names they had never heard before. With the self-deprecating humor of soldiers, they called themselves "jungle rats," "old China hands," "the frozen chosen," and "grunts." But by any name, and in whatever place, they made the fullest commitment to accomplishing what their nation called upon them to do.

The holdings of the Army Art Collection are particularly rich concerning the Army's activities in the Pacific and Asia during World War II and the Vietnam War. During those years a large number of talented artists were given the opportunity to serve with Army units. They caught the many different sides of the soldier's experience wherever it was, from the dank gloom of the jungle to the bright sunlight of an Oriental marketplace, and they often captured those individual expressions that speak volumes about war from the soldier's perspective. One such depiction in this section, John Pike's *A Morning with the Russians*, stands apart because of what would be its later poignancy. At the end of World War II, the U.S. Army had the responsibility, in coordination with the Soviet Army, of disarming Imperial Japanese forces in Korea. The painting shows the victorious American and Russian soldiers celebrating together, unaware that events would soon put them on opposite sides in a radically changed, and dangerous, new global political order.

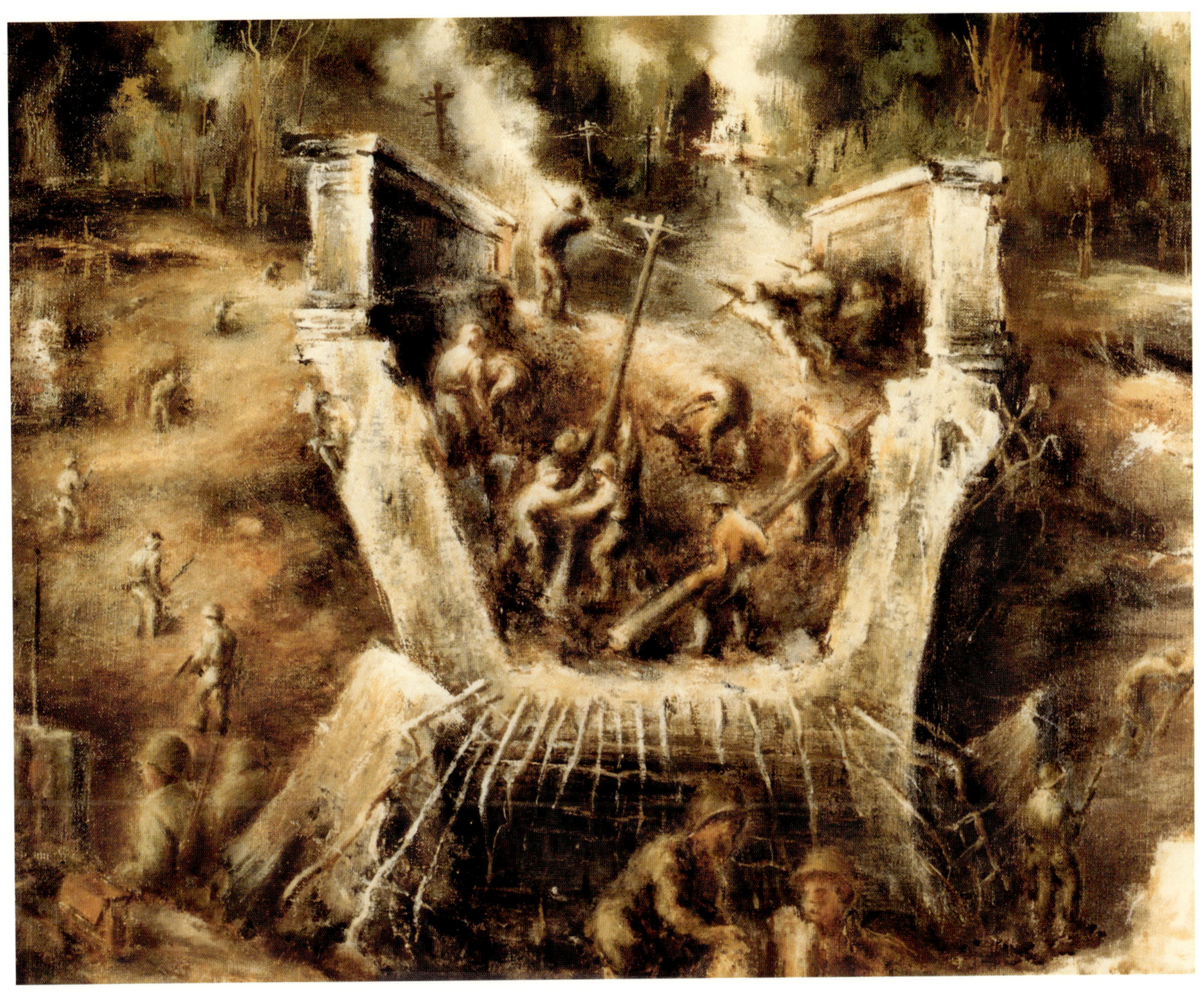

BATTLE FOR MANILA
Philippines
Frede Vidar, 1945
Oil, 24" x 32"

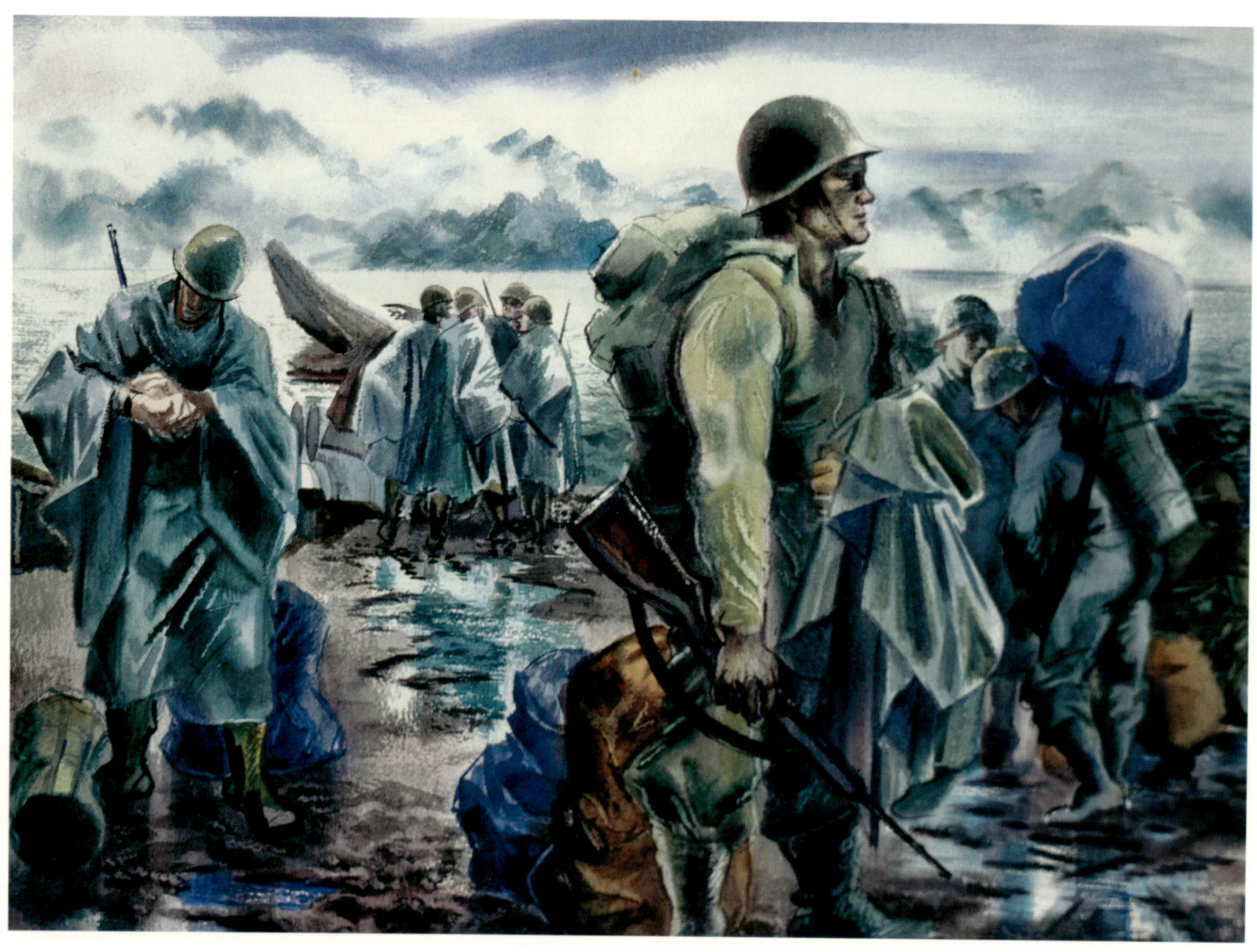

WAITING FOR EMBARKATION
Milne Bay, New Guinea
David Fredenthal, 1943
Watercolor, 21" x 29 ½"

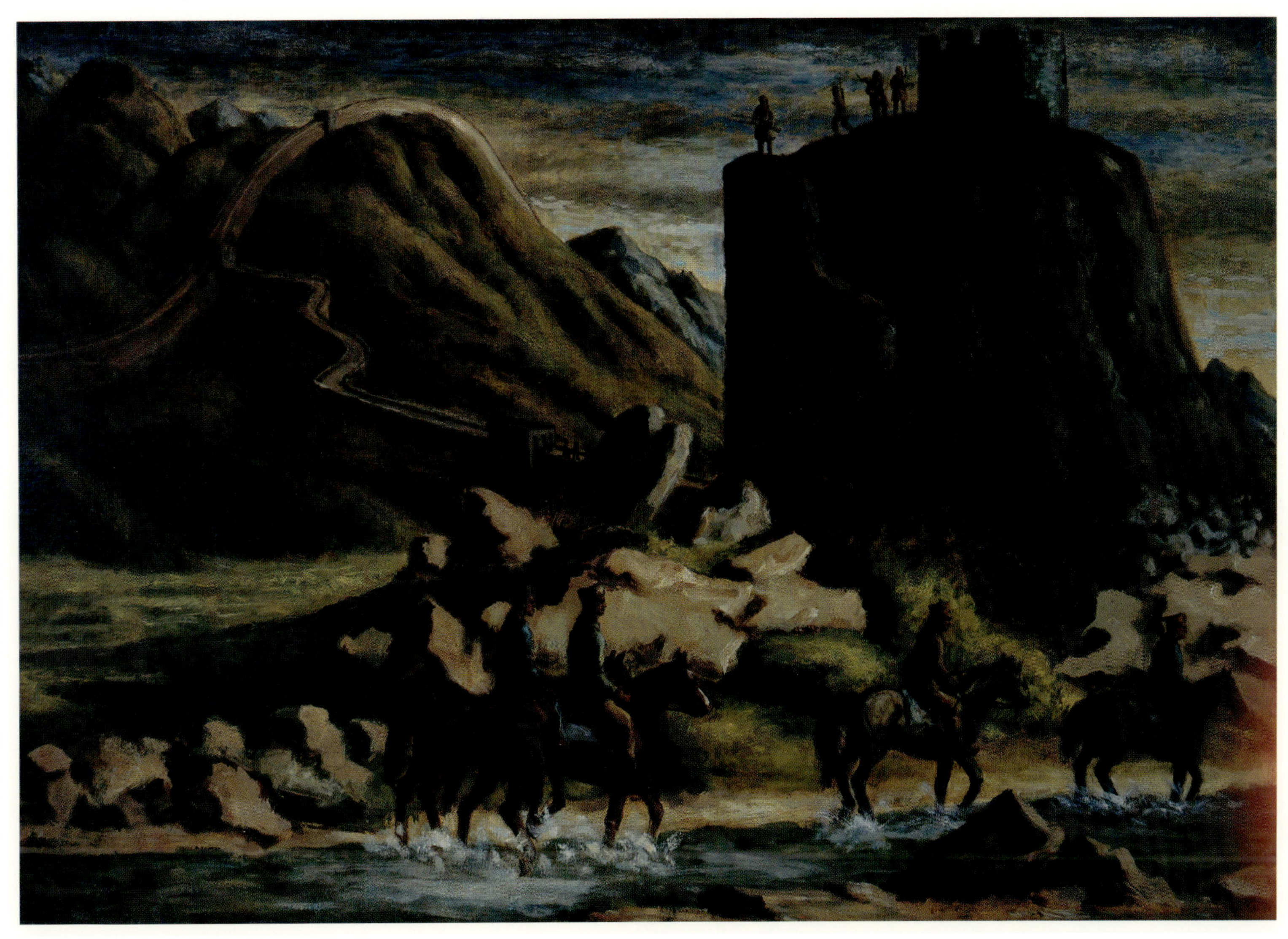

GREAT WALL OF CHINA
China
Wayne D. Larabee, 1946
Oil, 24" x 34"

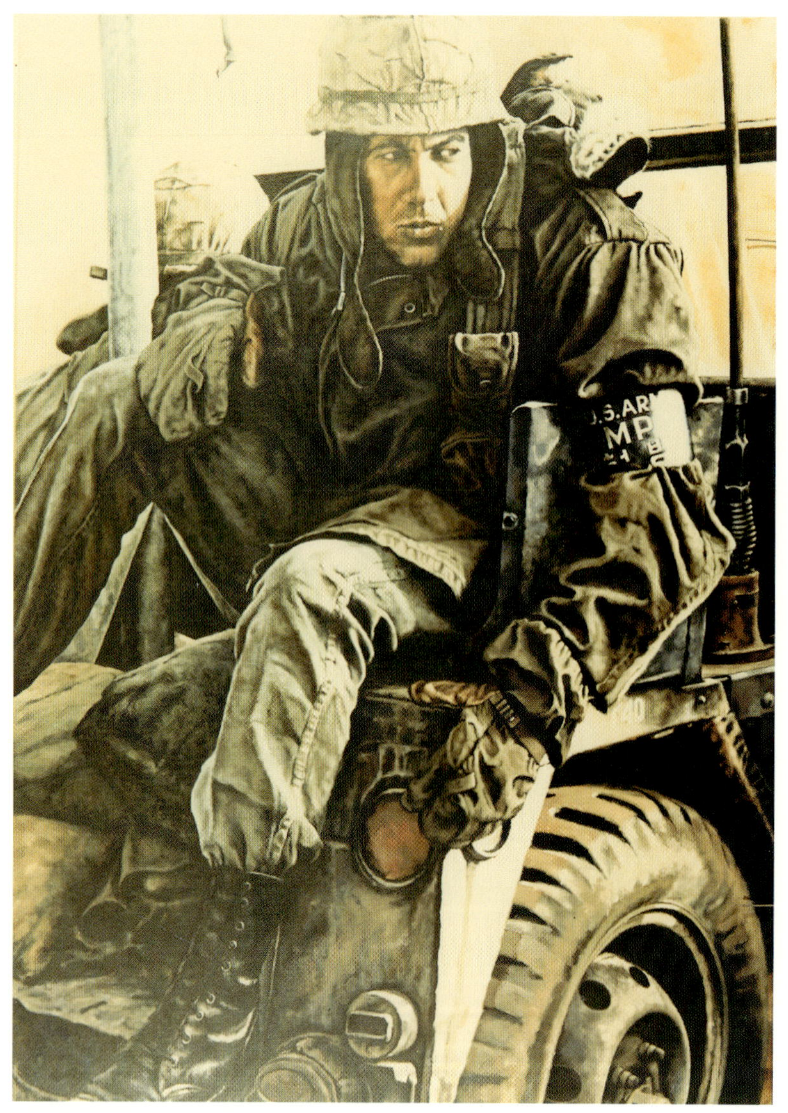

THE CHARIOTEERS
Korea
Chester Jezerski, 1970
Acrylic, 42" x 60"

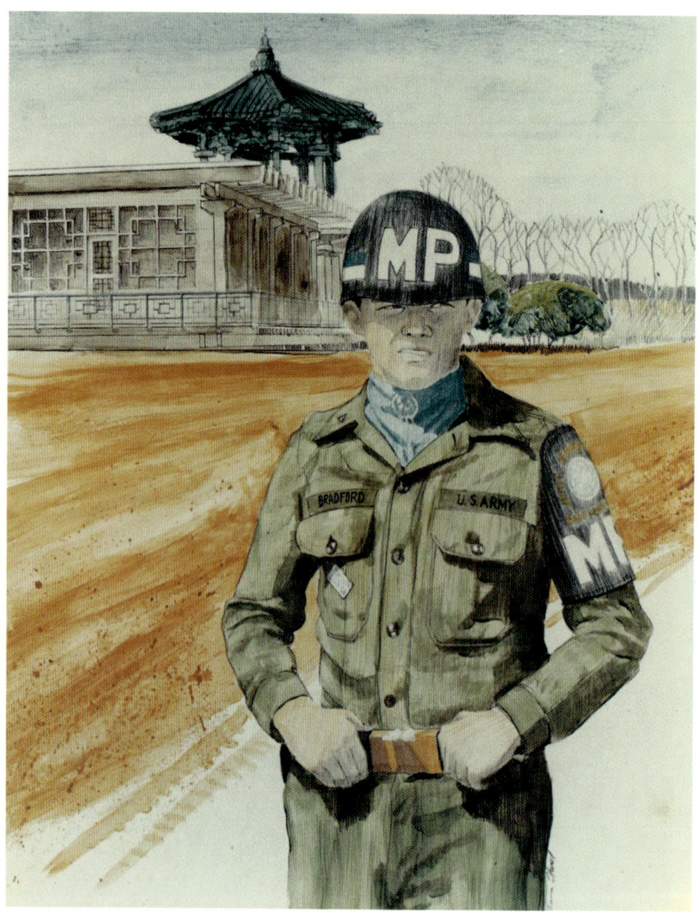

SIX FOOT MINIMUM
Korea
William H. Steel, 1970
Pencil, 22" x 30"

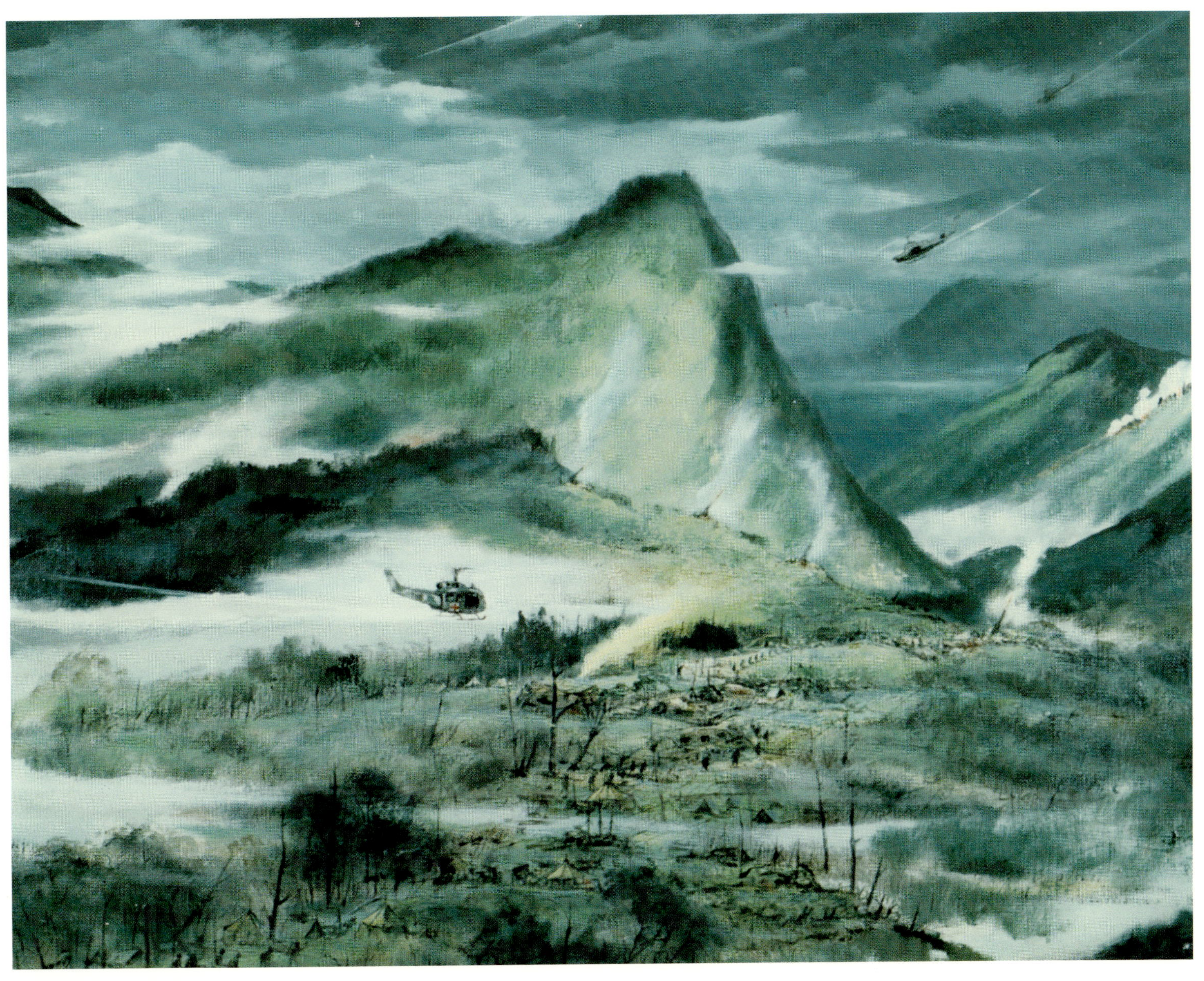

BRINGING THEM IN
Vietnam
John Wheat, 1968
Acrylic, 27 ¾" x 47 ½"

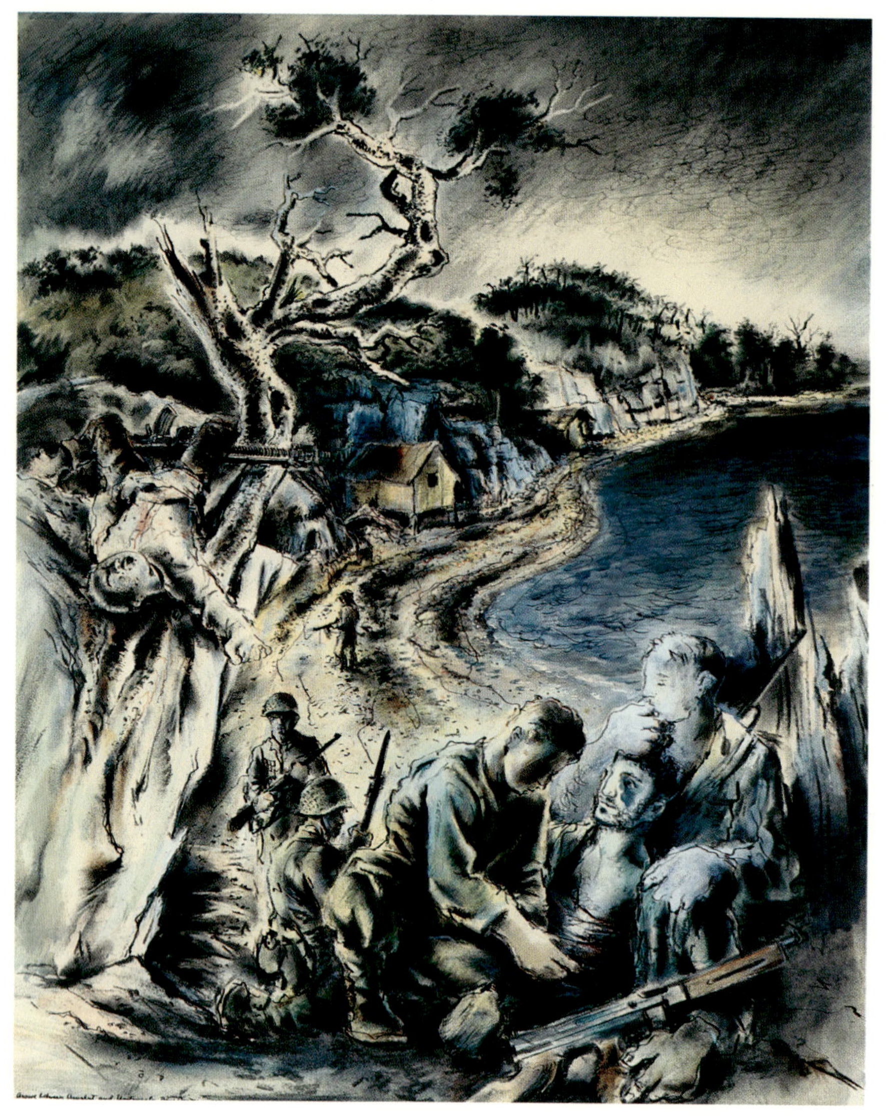

BEACH OF ARAWE
New Britain, World War II
Frede Vidar
Ink and watercolor, 17 ½" x 21"

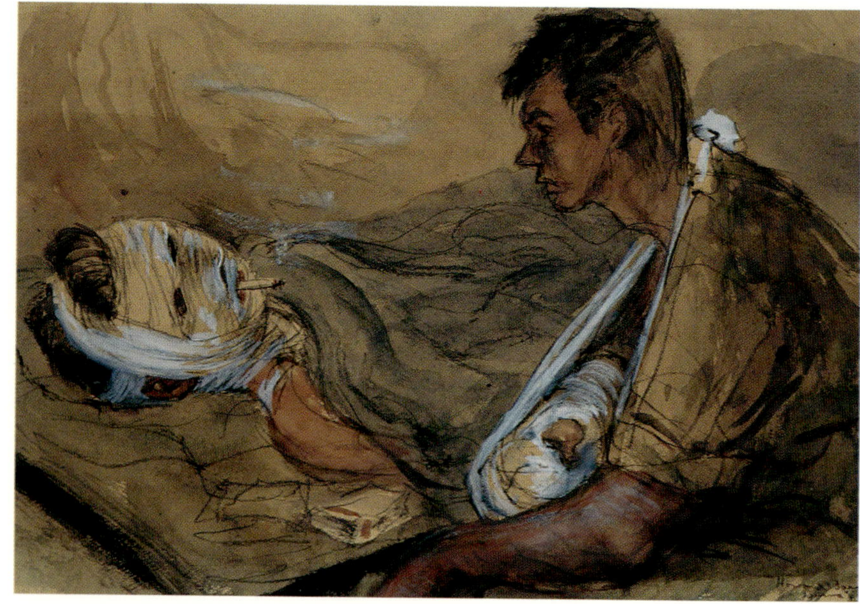

AMERICAN TANK MAN WOUNDED
Burma
Howard Baer, 1944
Watercolor, 11 ½" x 17 ½"

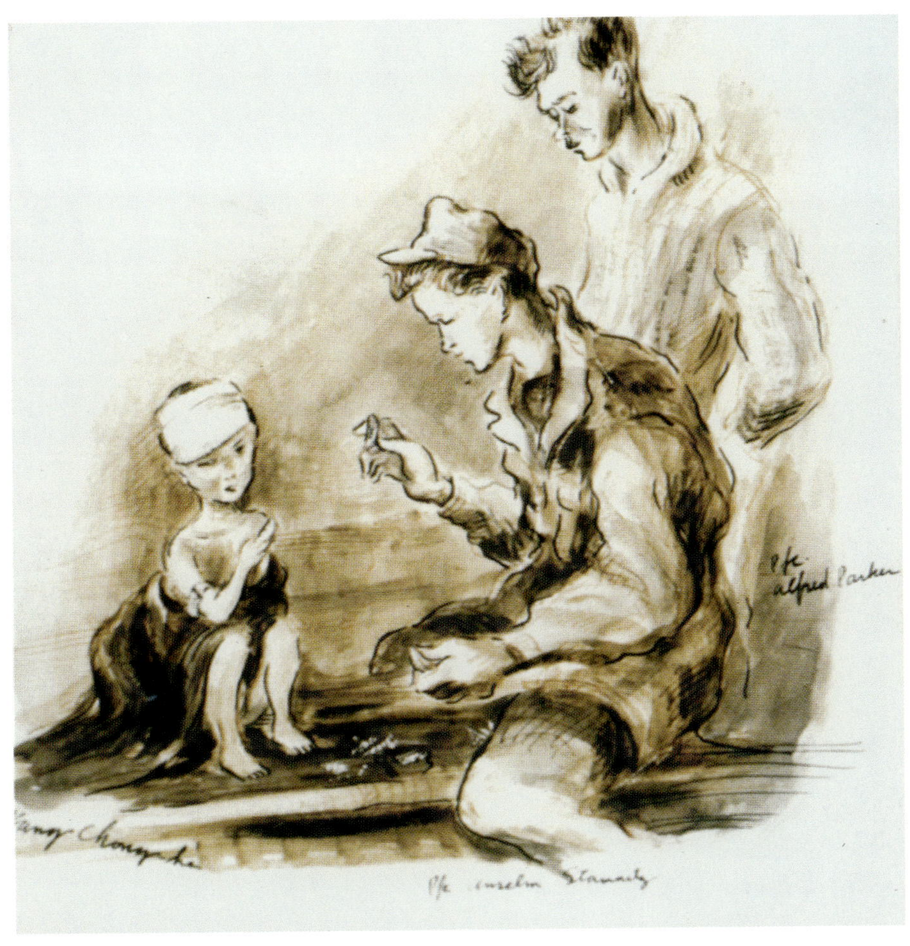

PFC. PARKER AND PFC. STAMNITZ
Korea
John Groth, 1950
Watercolor, 20" x 20"

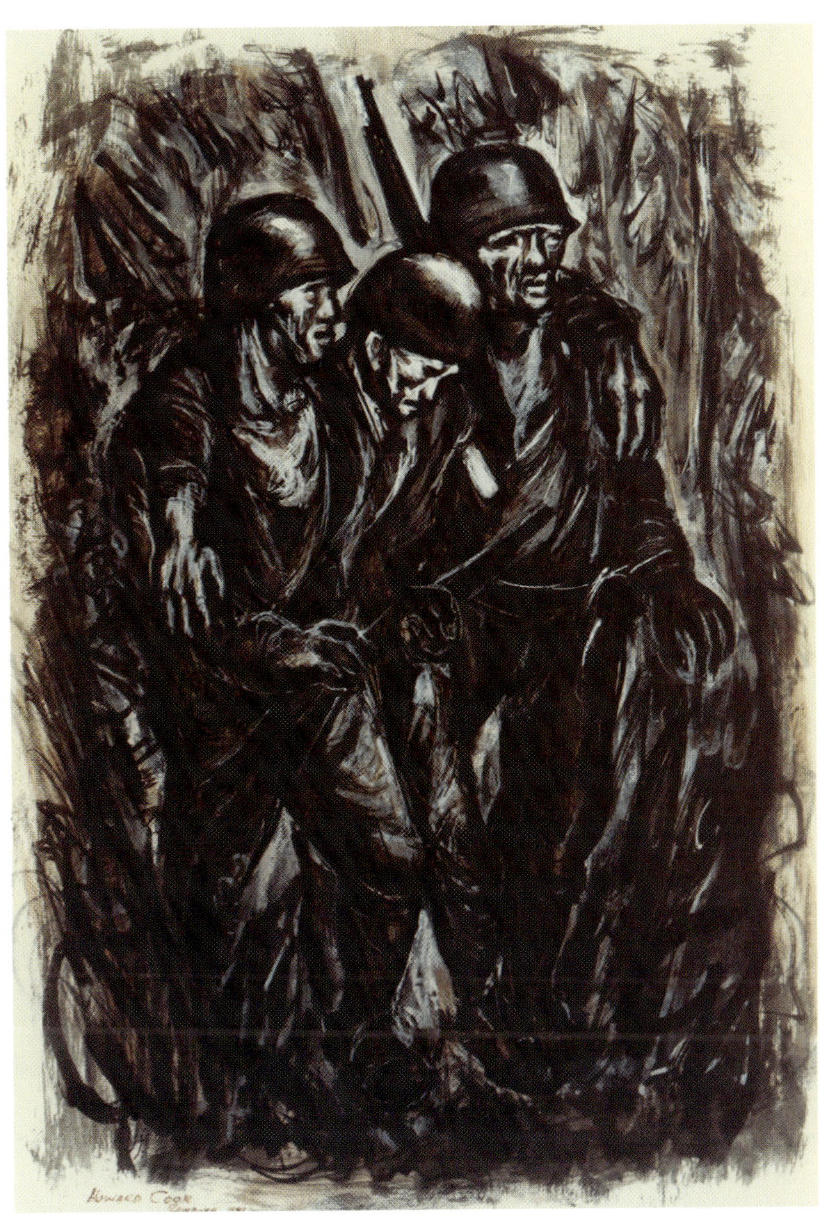

WALKING CASUALTY
Rendova
Howard Norton Cook, 1943
Watercolor, 14" x 9 ½"

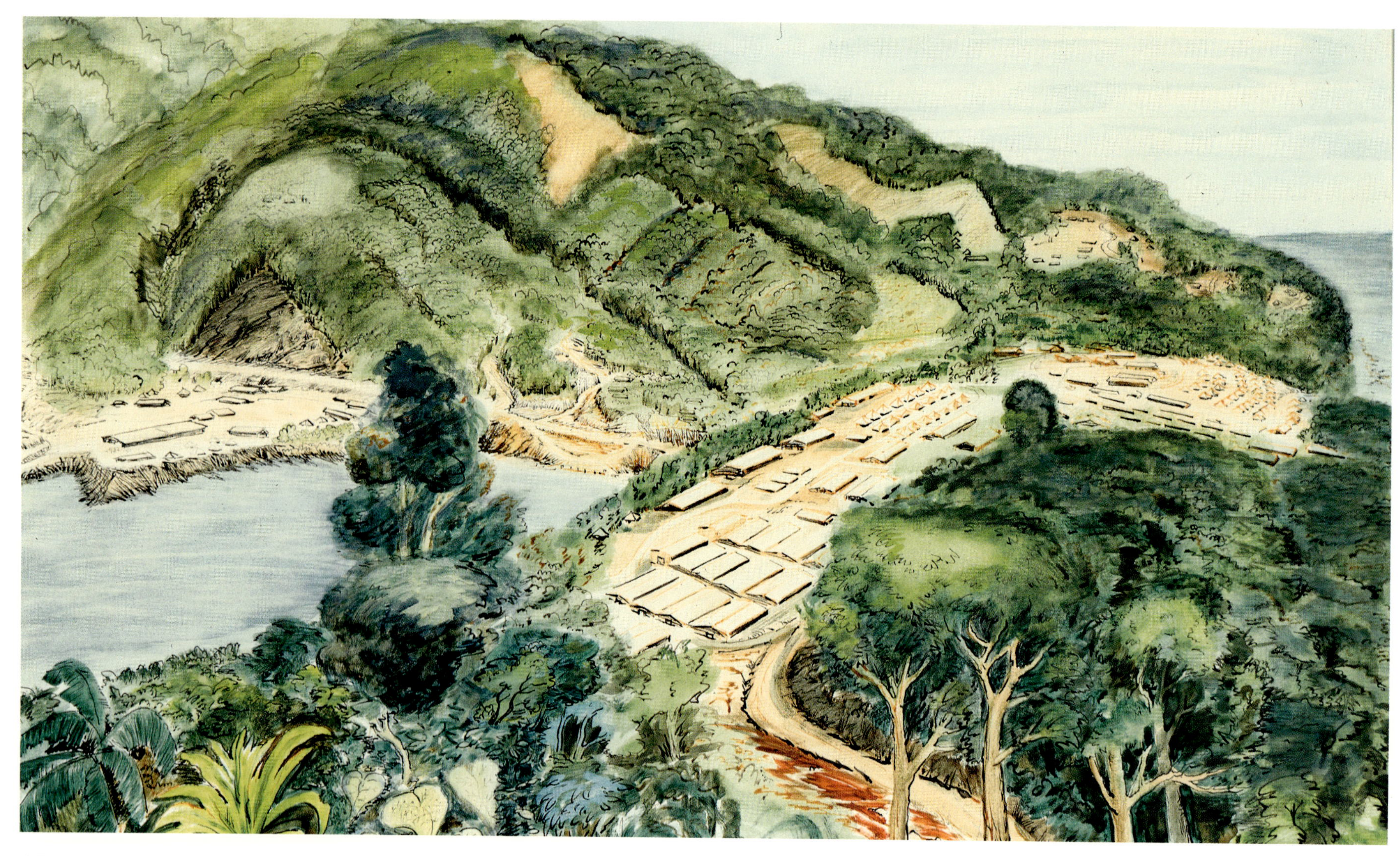

ARMY BASE IN THE JUNGLES
Pacific, World War II
Leslie E. Anderson
Watercolor, 14 ¼" x 22 ½"

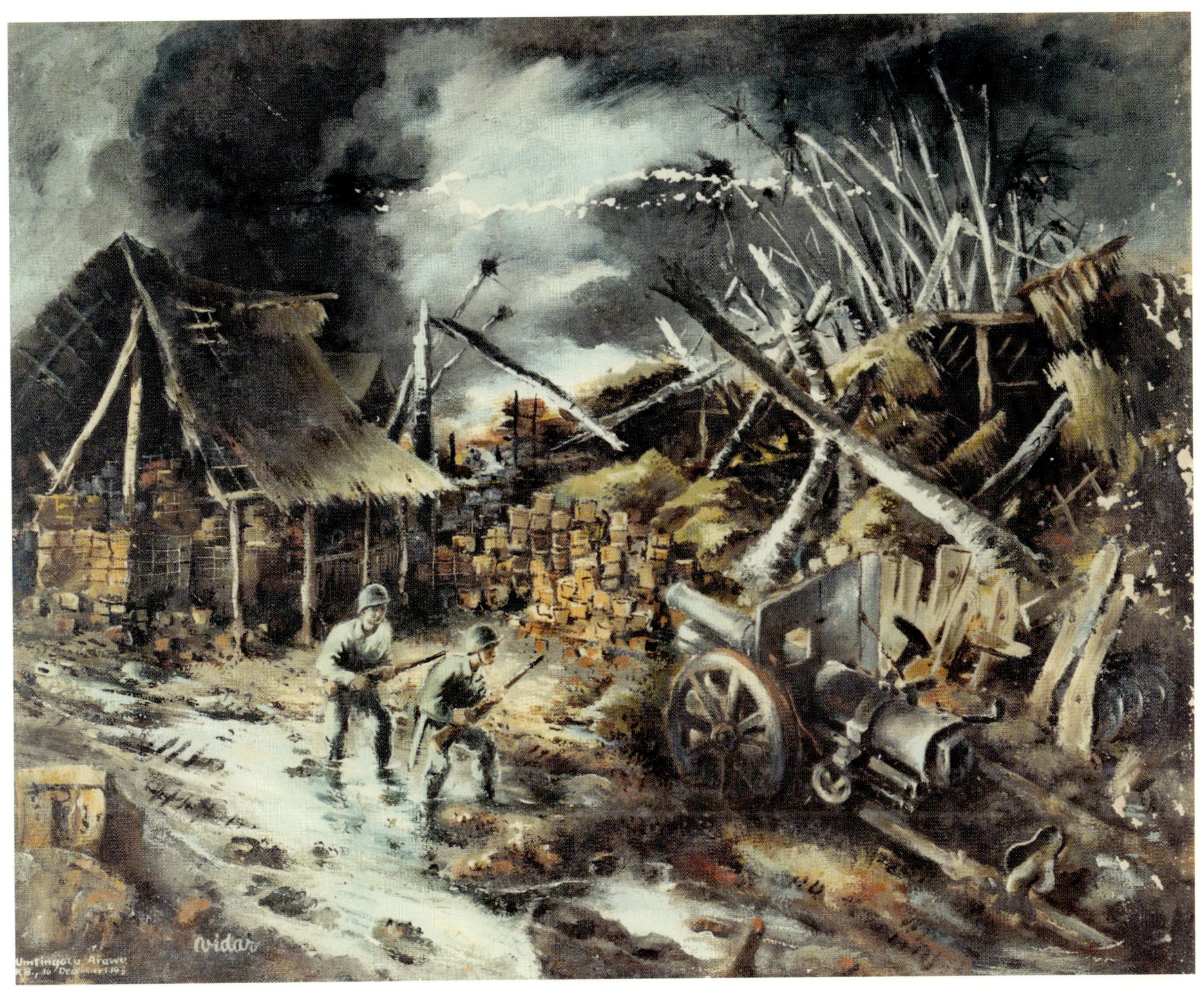

112TH CAVALRY PATROL AT UMTINGALU
New Britain
Frede Vidar, 1943
Oil, 20″ x 25″

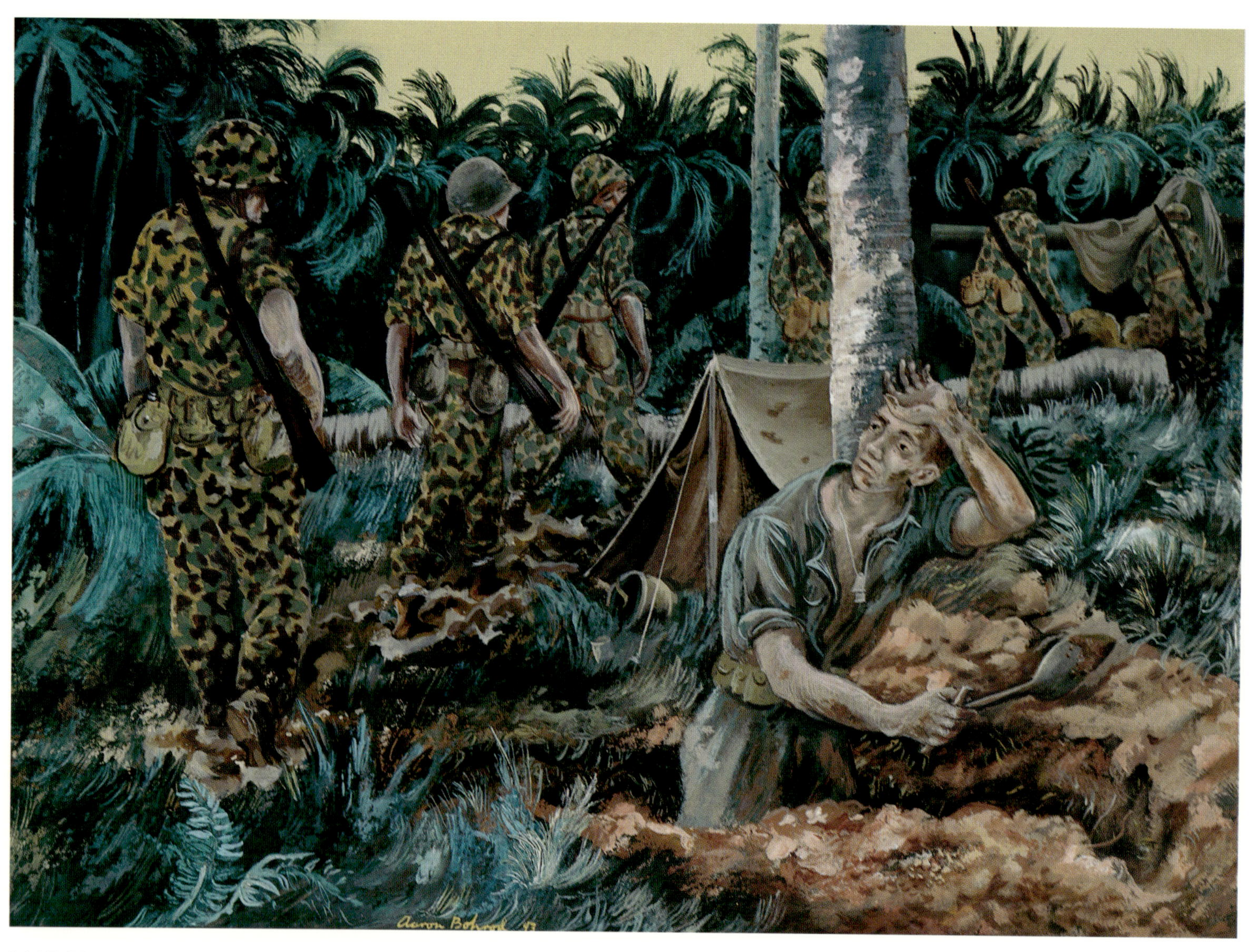

MARCHING THRU NEW GEORGIA
South Pacific
Aaron Bohrod, 1943
Gouache, 13 ½" x 17 ½"

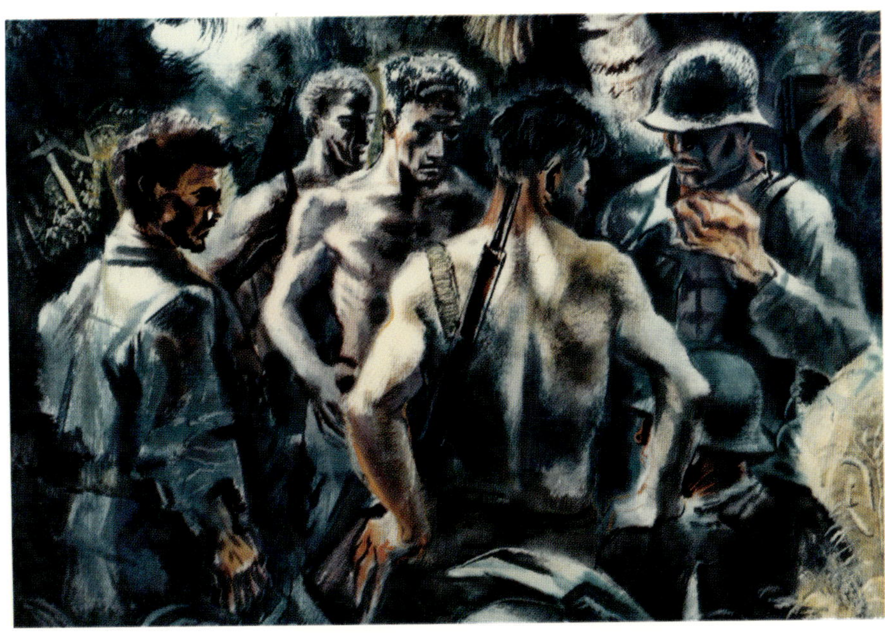

IN THE JUNGLES OF ARAWE
New Britain
David Fredenthal, 1943
Watercolor, 21" x 29 ½"

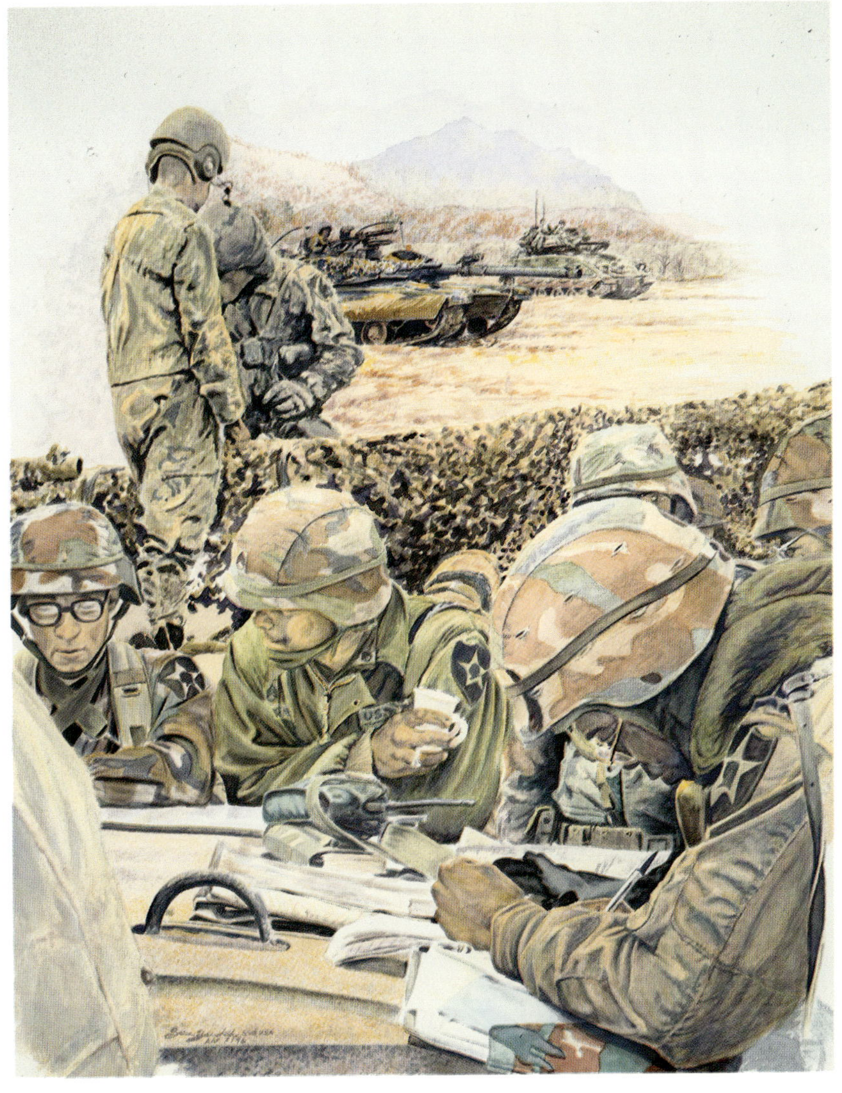

READY, SET, GO!
Korea
Brian Fairchild, 1991
Watercolor, 22" x 17"

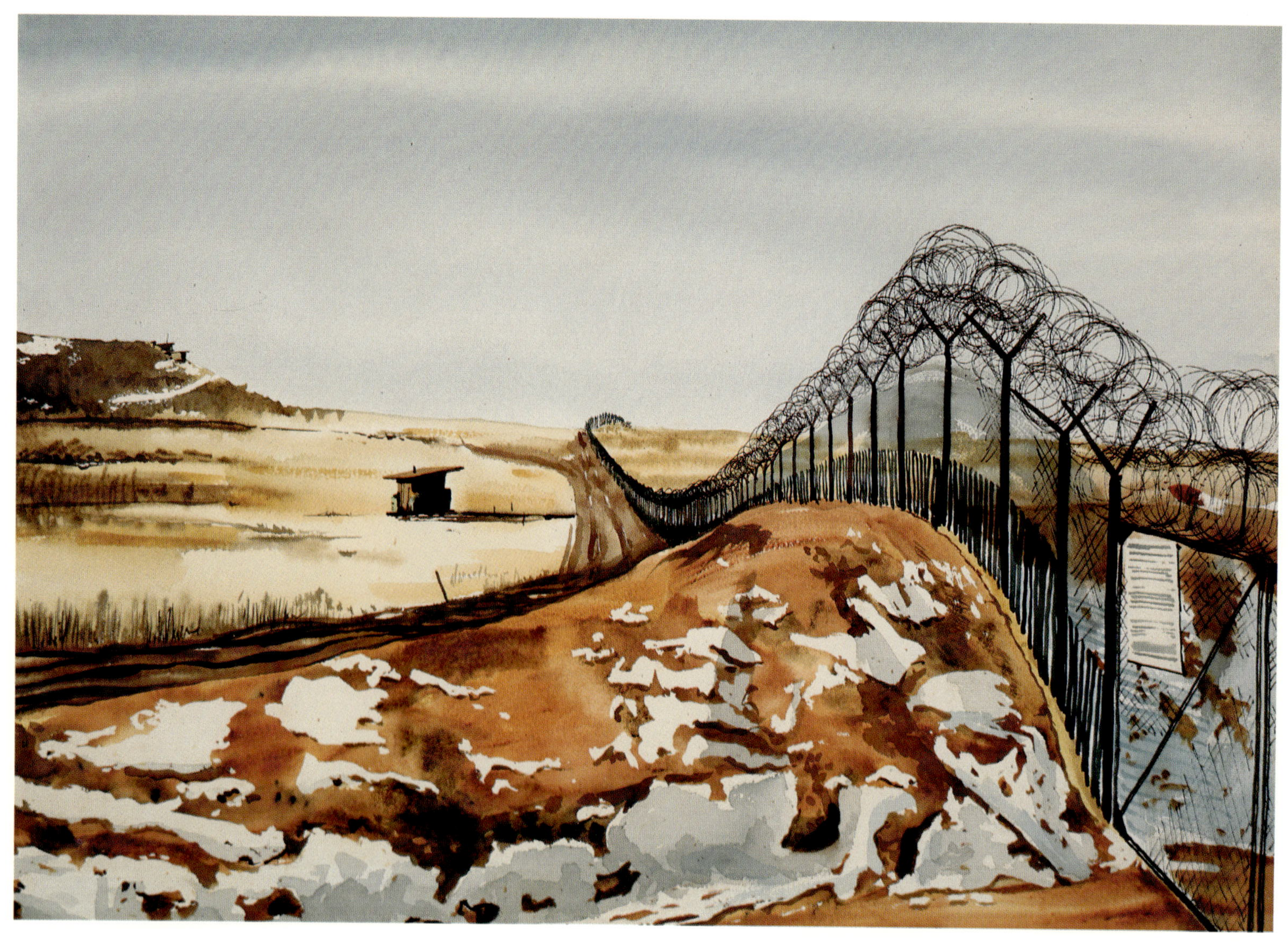

"MINI" TOWER, DMZ
Korea
William H. Steel, 1970
Watercolor, 22" x 30"

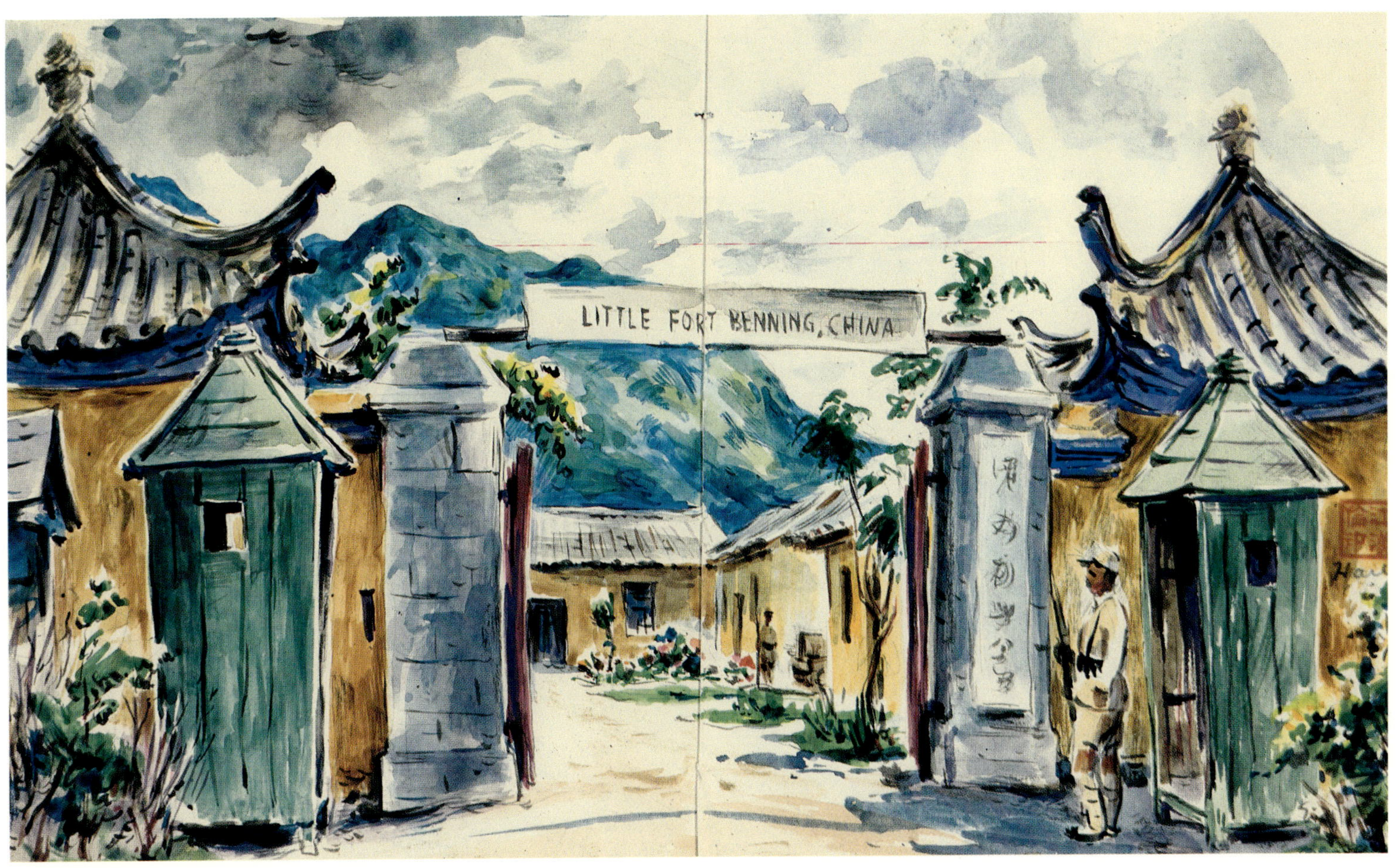

LITTLE FORT BENNING—CAMP GATE
Datun, China
John G. Hanlen, 1945
Watercolor, 7 ⅞" x 13"

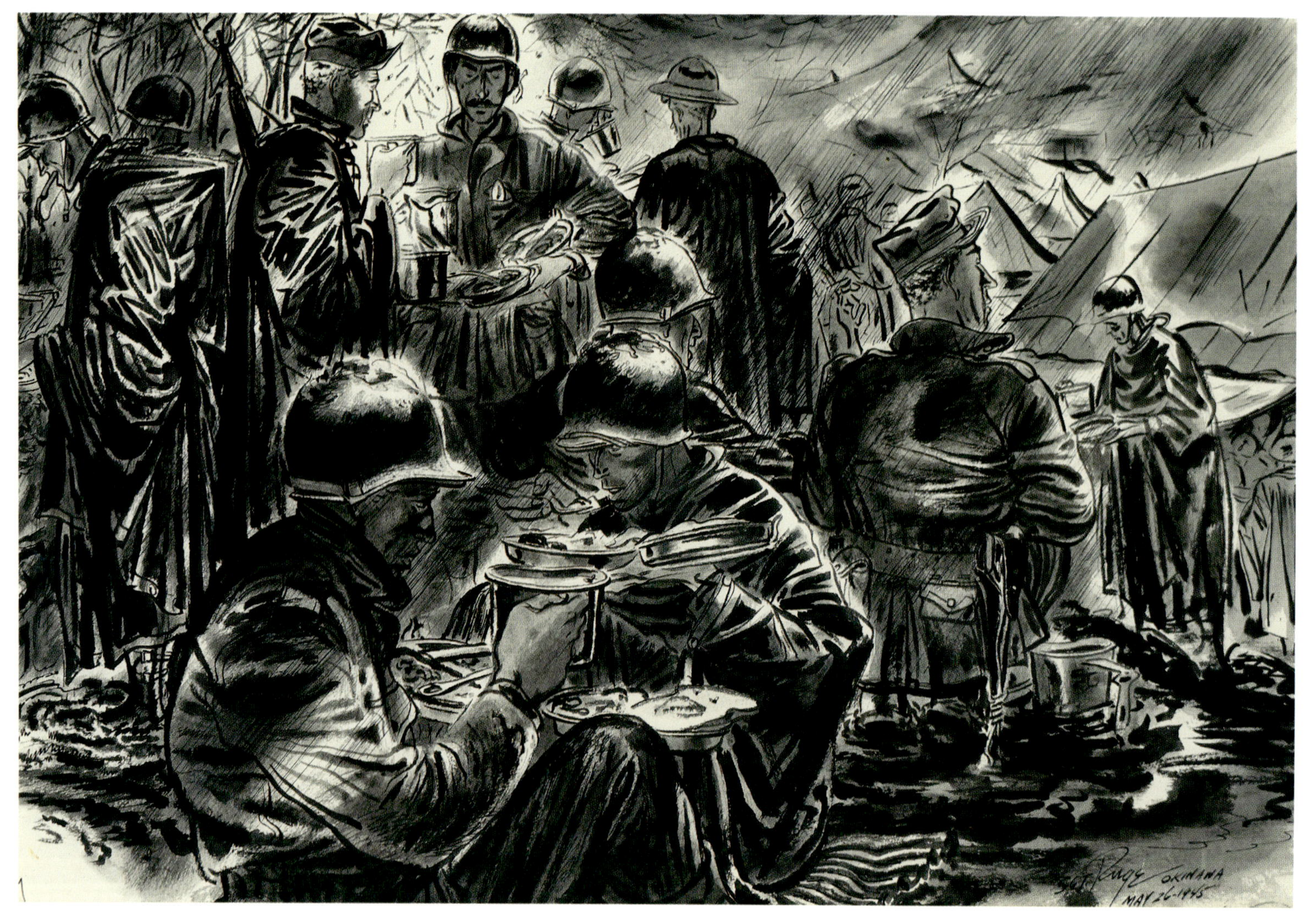

MESSING IN THE OPEN IN OKINAWA
Okinawa
John A. Ruge, 1945
Ink, 15" x 21 ¾"

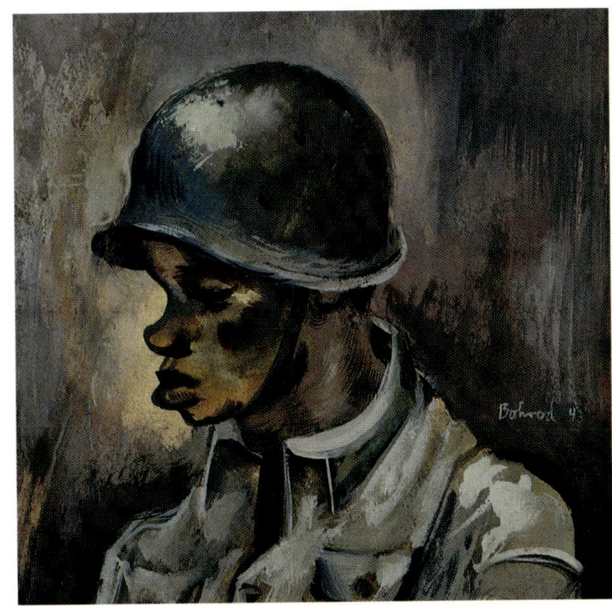

NEGRO SOLDIER
The Pacific
Aaron Bohrod, 1943
Gouache, 14" x 12 ⅞"

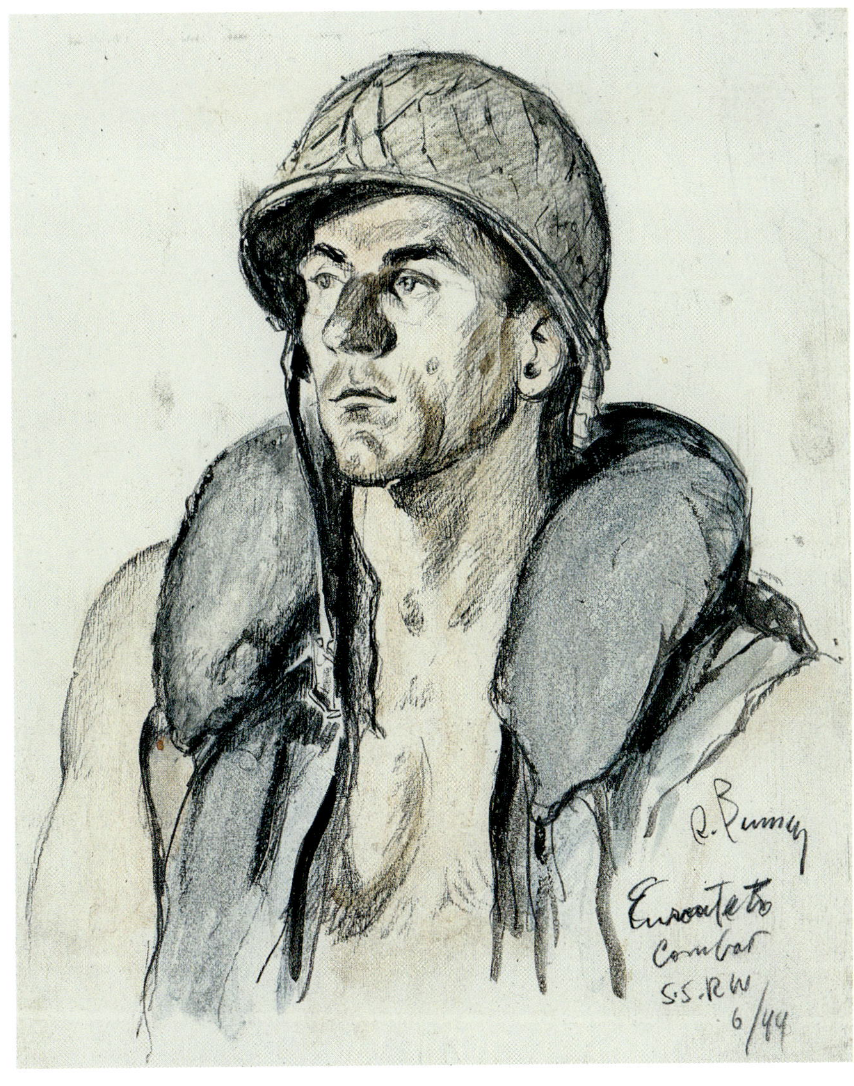

ENROUTE TO COMBAT
The Pacific
Robert Benney, 1944
Pencil and watercolor, 10" x 7 ⅞"

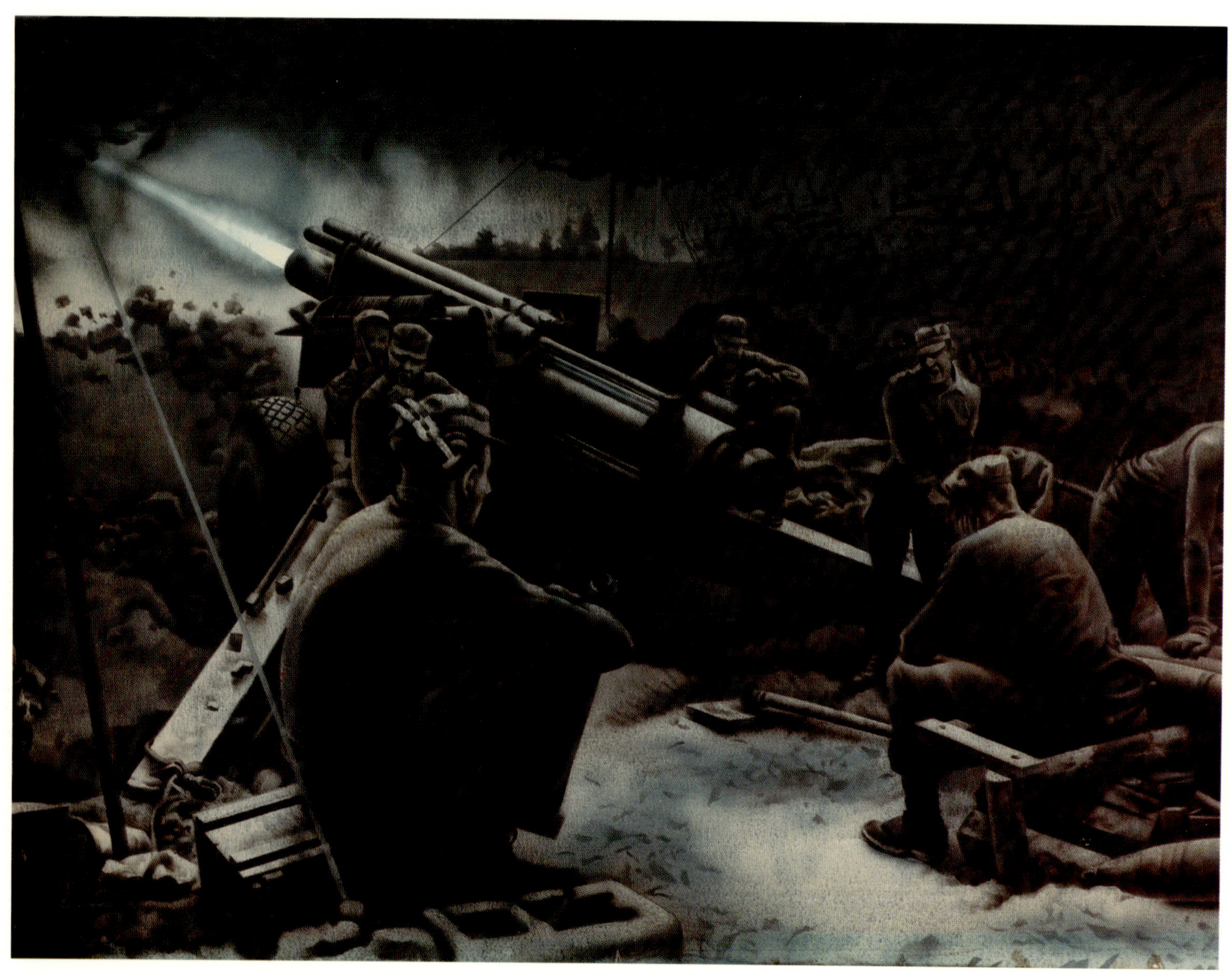

FIRE MISSION
Okinawa, World War II
Gerald W. Ferguson
Watercolor, 19" x 13"

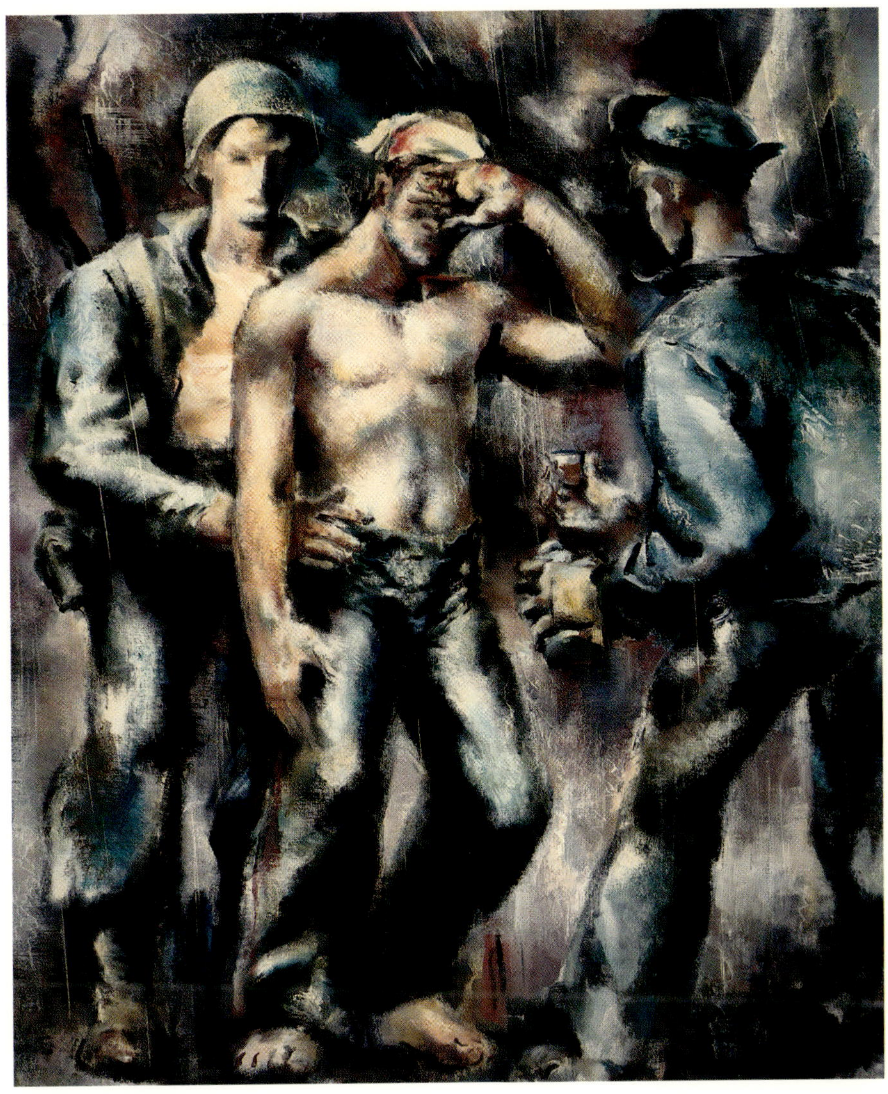

WOUNDED MAN, TARGET HILL
Cape Gloucester
Barse Miller, 1944
Oil, 36" x 30"

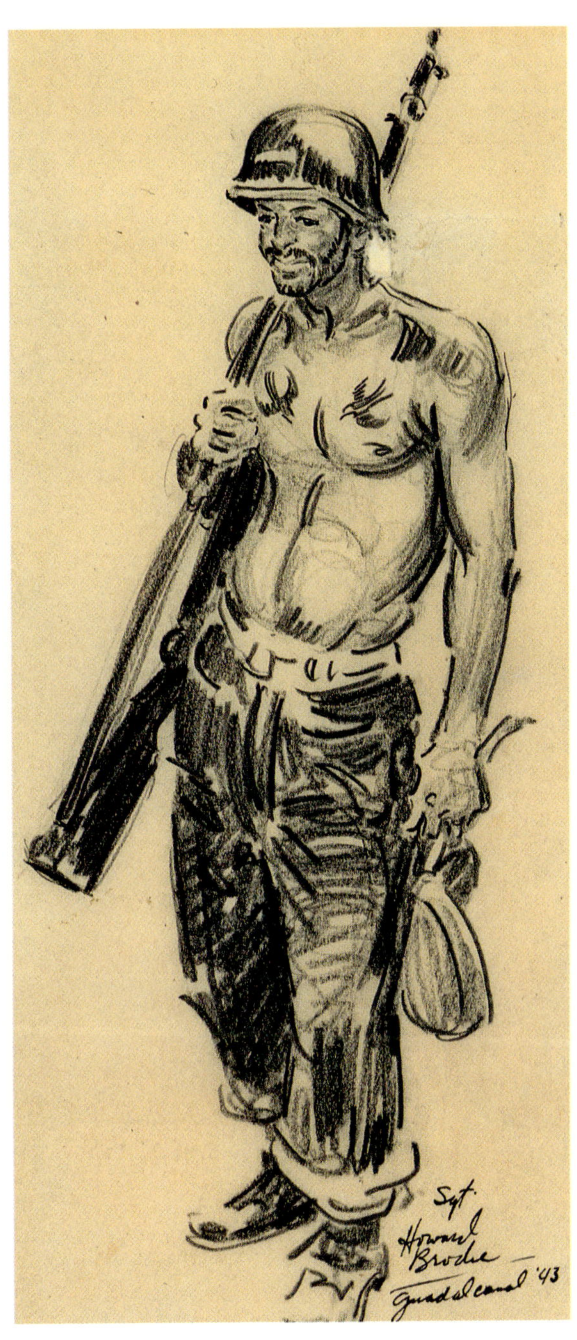

CANNONEER STEVEN "BLUE-BIRDS" KITT
Guadalcanal
Howard Brodie, 1943
Pencil, 15" x 8"

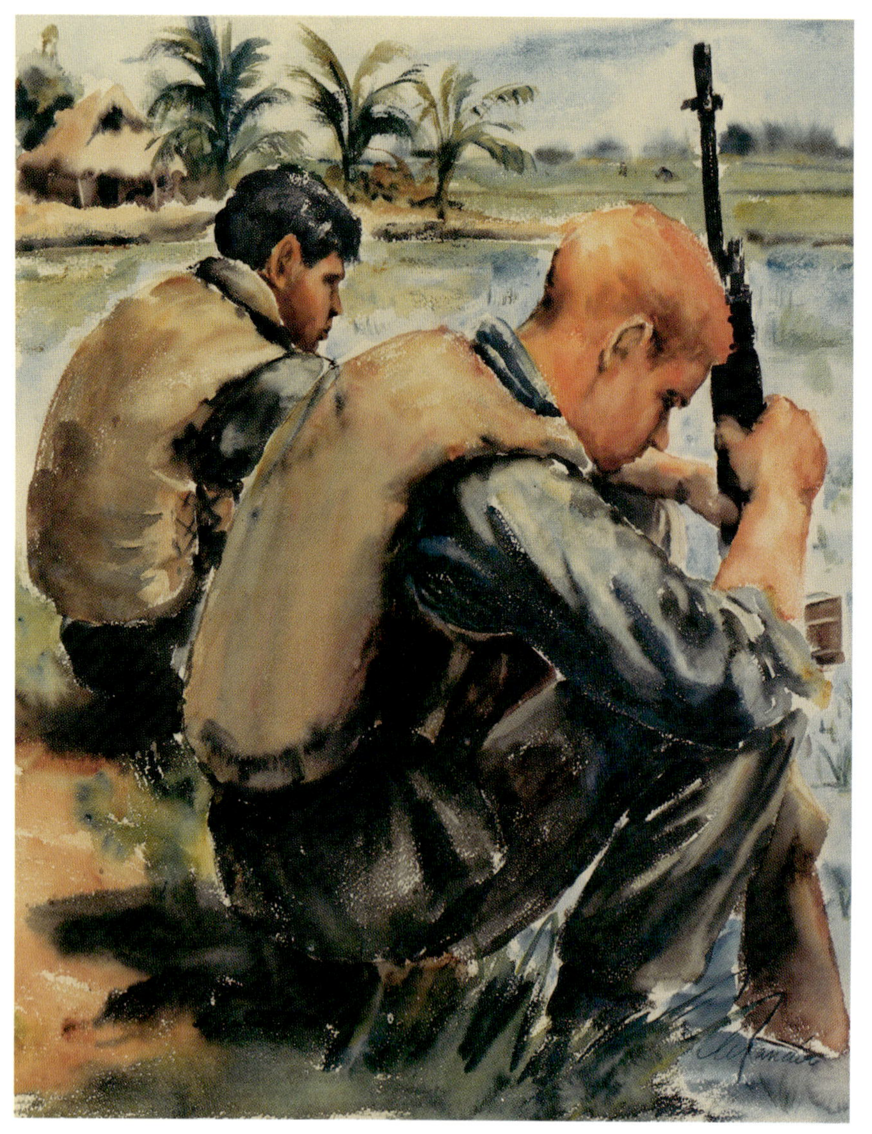

TEN MINUTE BREAK
Thach Tru, Vietnam
Samuel E. Alexander, 1968
Watercolor, 29 ½" x 22"

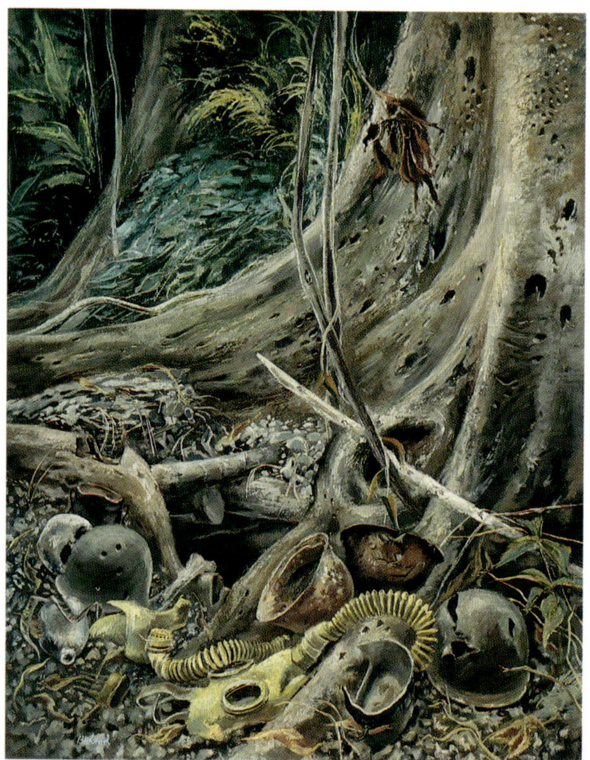

STILL LIFE
Guadalcanal
Aaron Bohrod, 1943
Oil, 19 ½" x 15 ½"

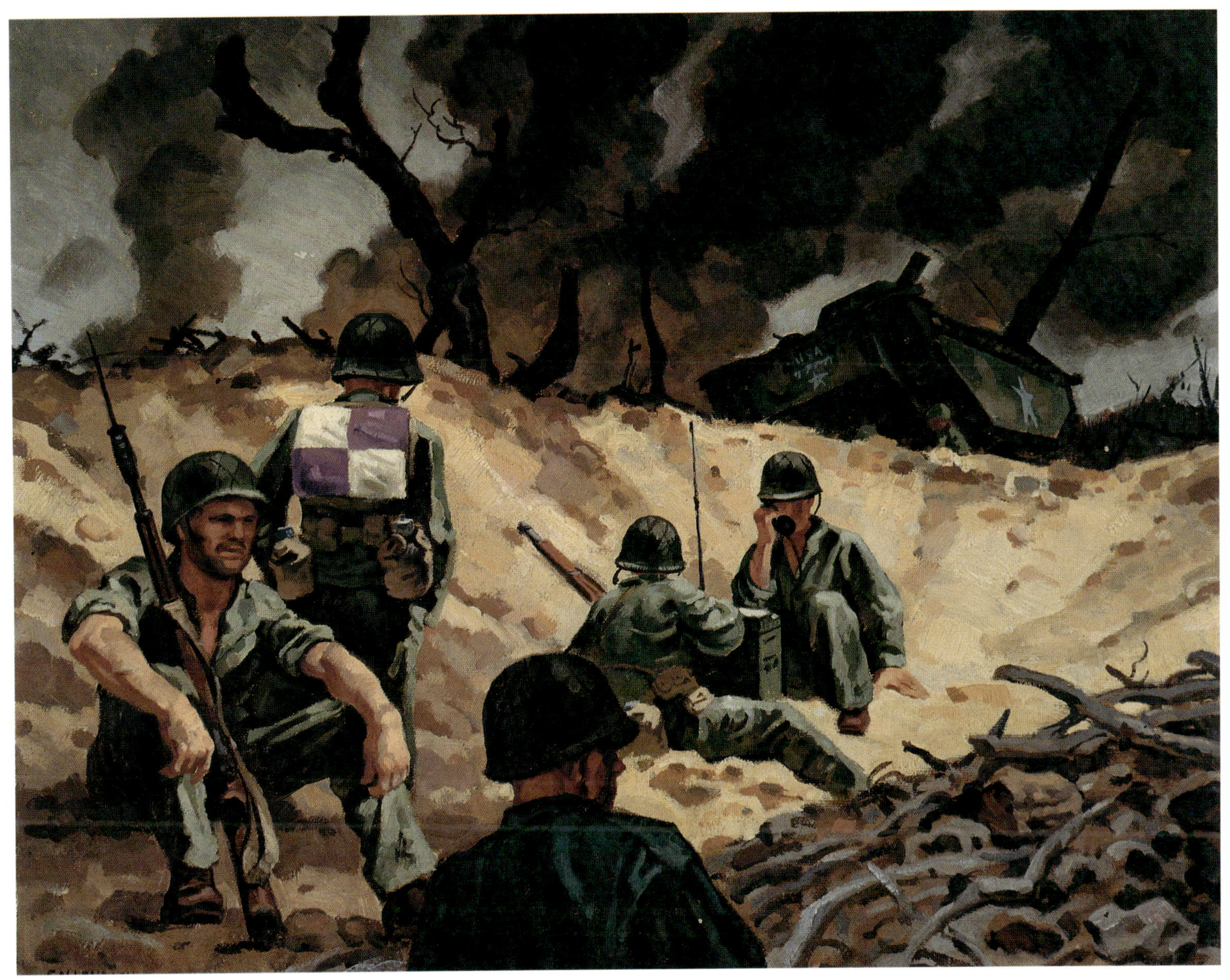

RADIO COMMUNICATIONS
Kwajalein, World War II
Edward A. Sallenback
Oil, 14 ¾" x 19 ½"

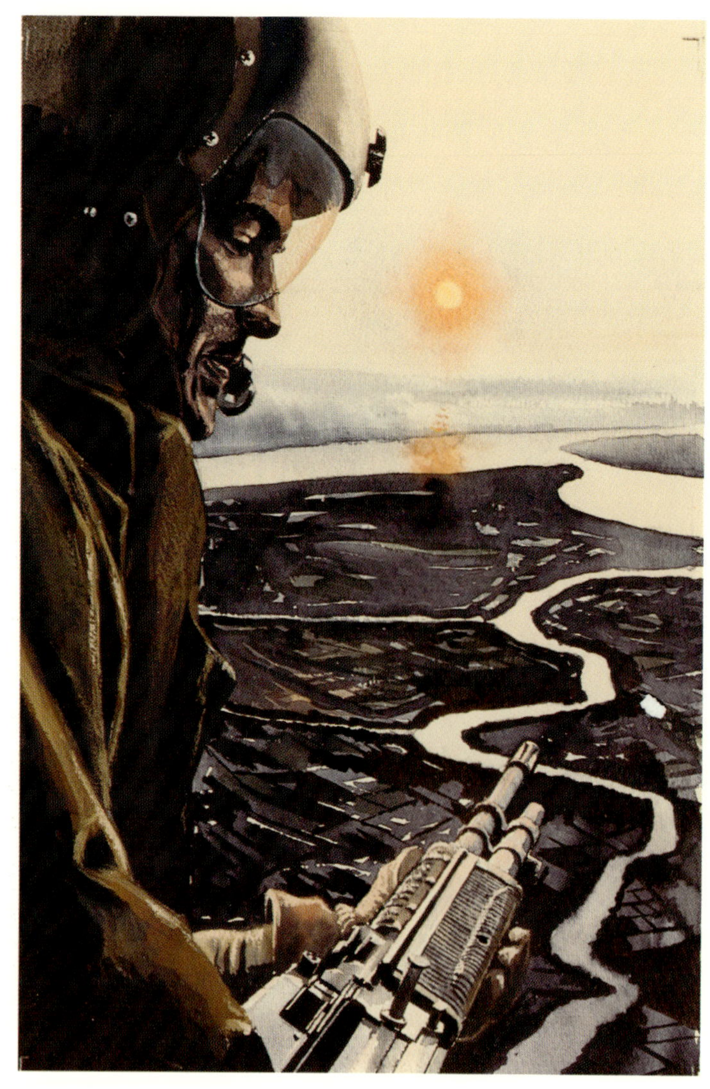

DELTA SUNRISE
Vietnam
Stephen H. Sheldon, 1967
Watercolor, 15 ½" x 13"

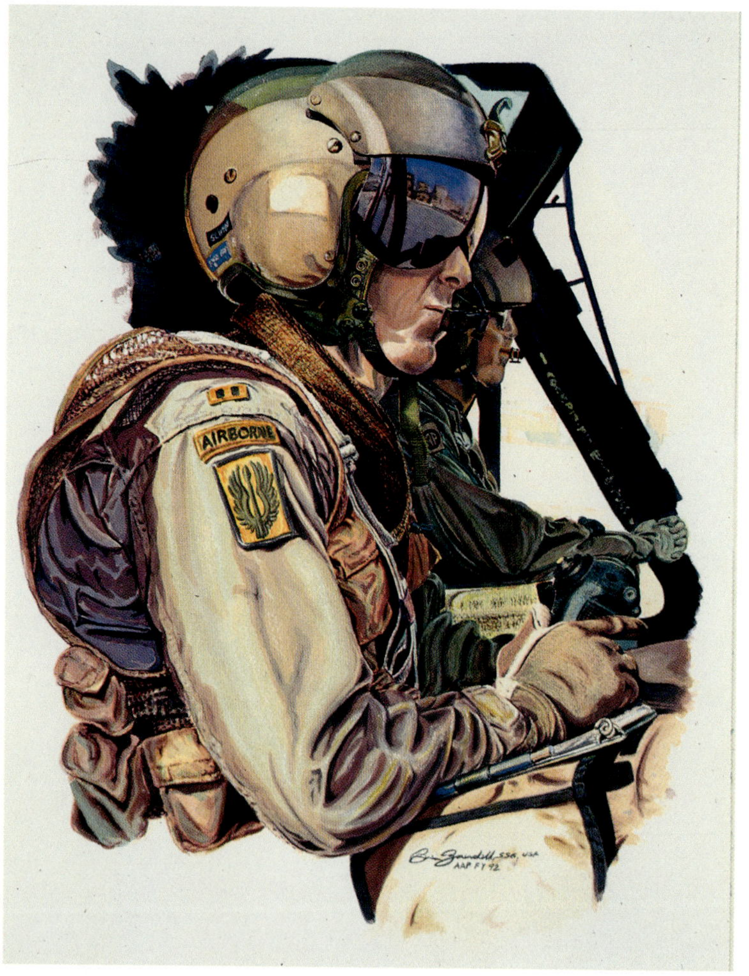

AWAITING CLEARANCE
Korea
Brian Fairchild, 1992
Watercolor, 20" x 14 ⅞"

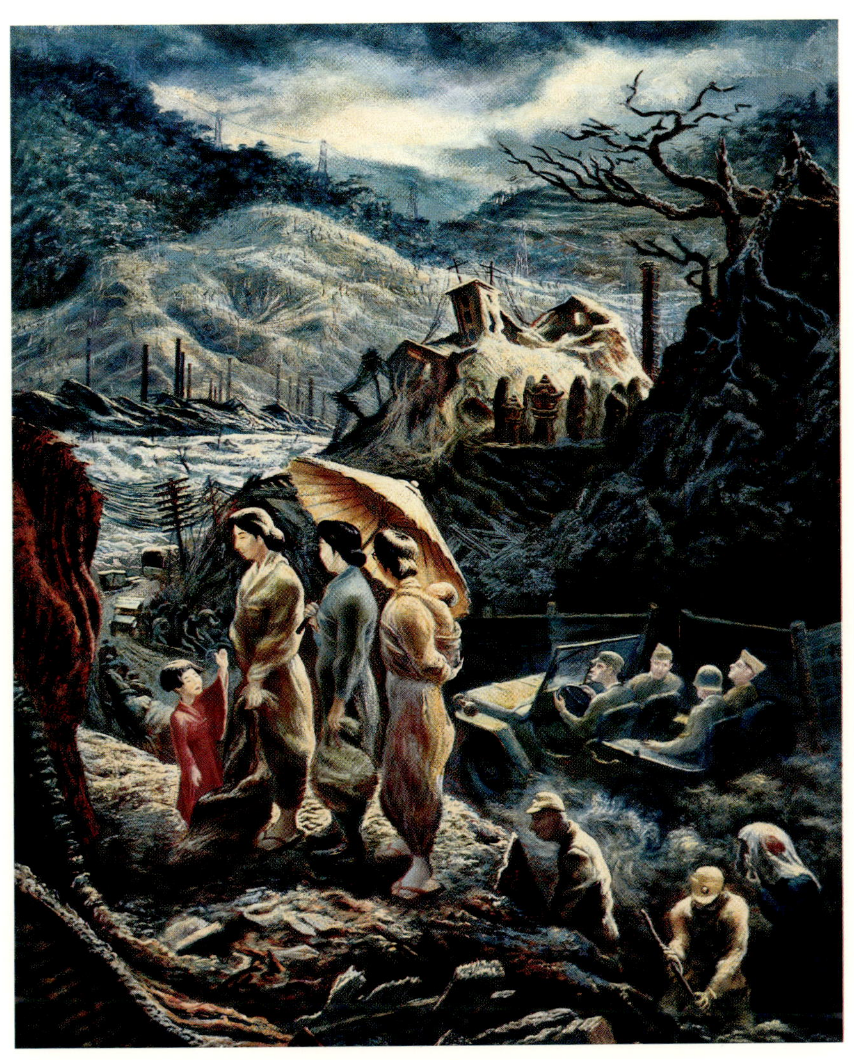

RESPECT FOR NEW EMPERORS
Japan
Robert MacDonald Graham, Jr., 1946
Oil, 24" x 30"

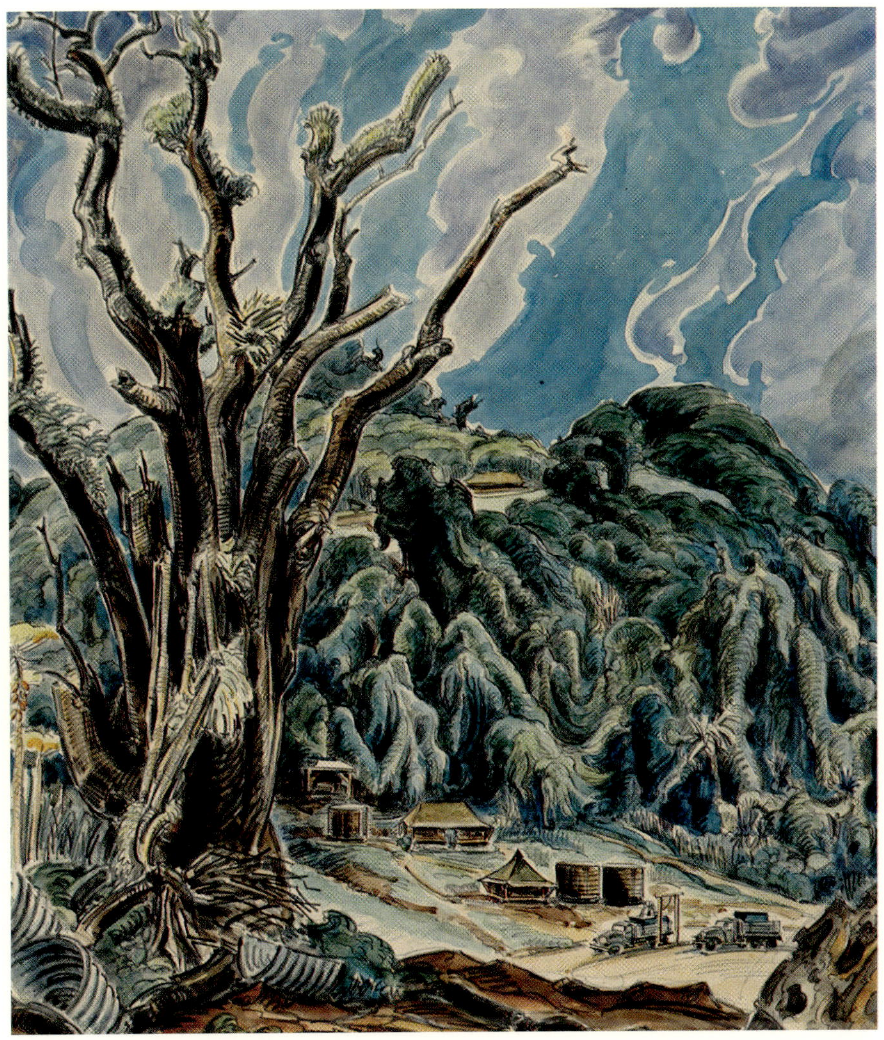

NICHLESON SPRINGS ON SAIPAN
Saipan
Hans Mangelsdorf, 1945
Watercolor, 12 ½" x 10 ½"

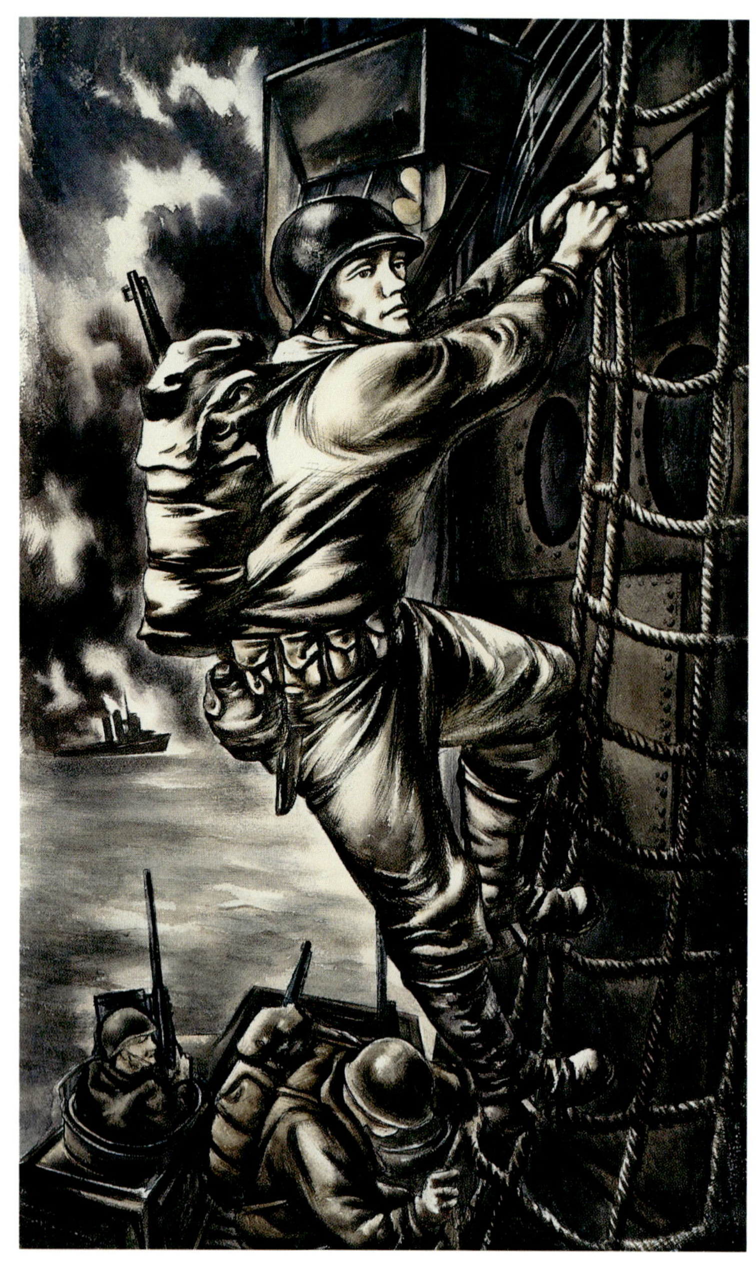

GOING OVERSIDE IN THE NEW GEORGIAS
South Pacific
Howard Norton Cook, 1943
Ink and watercolor, 25 ¾" x 16 ½"

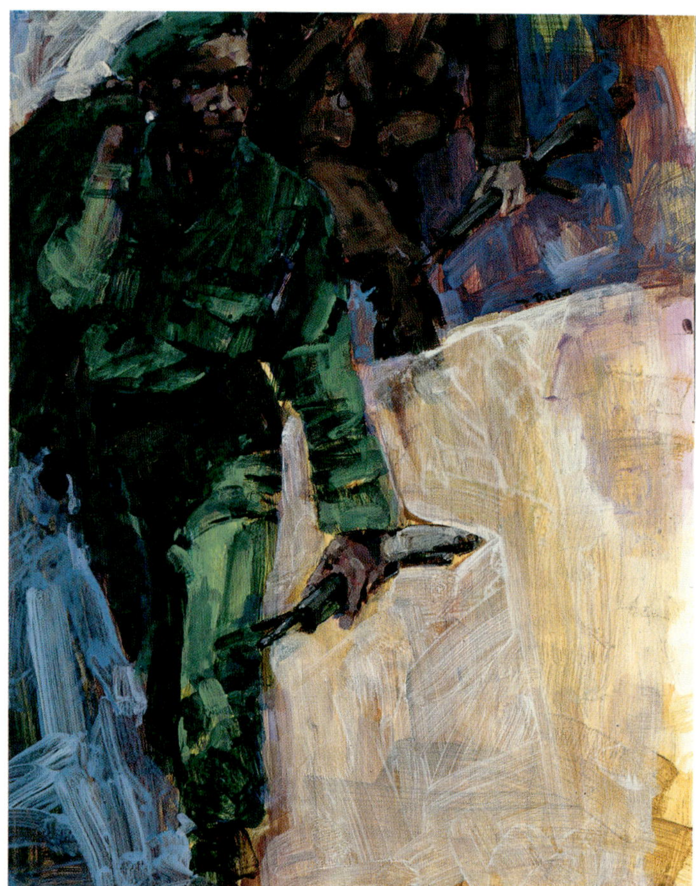

GREEN BERET
Vietnam
Paul Rickert, 1966
Acrylic, 29" x 22 ⅞"

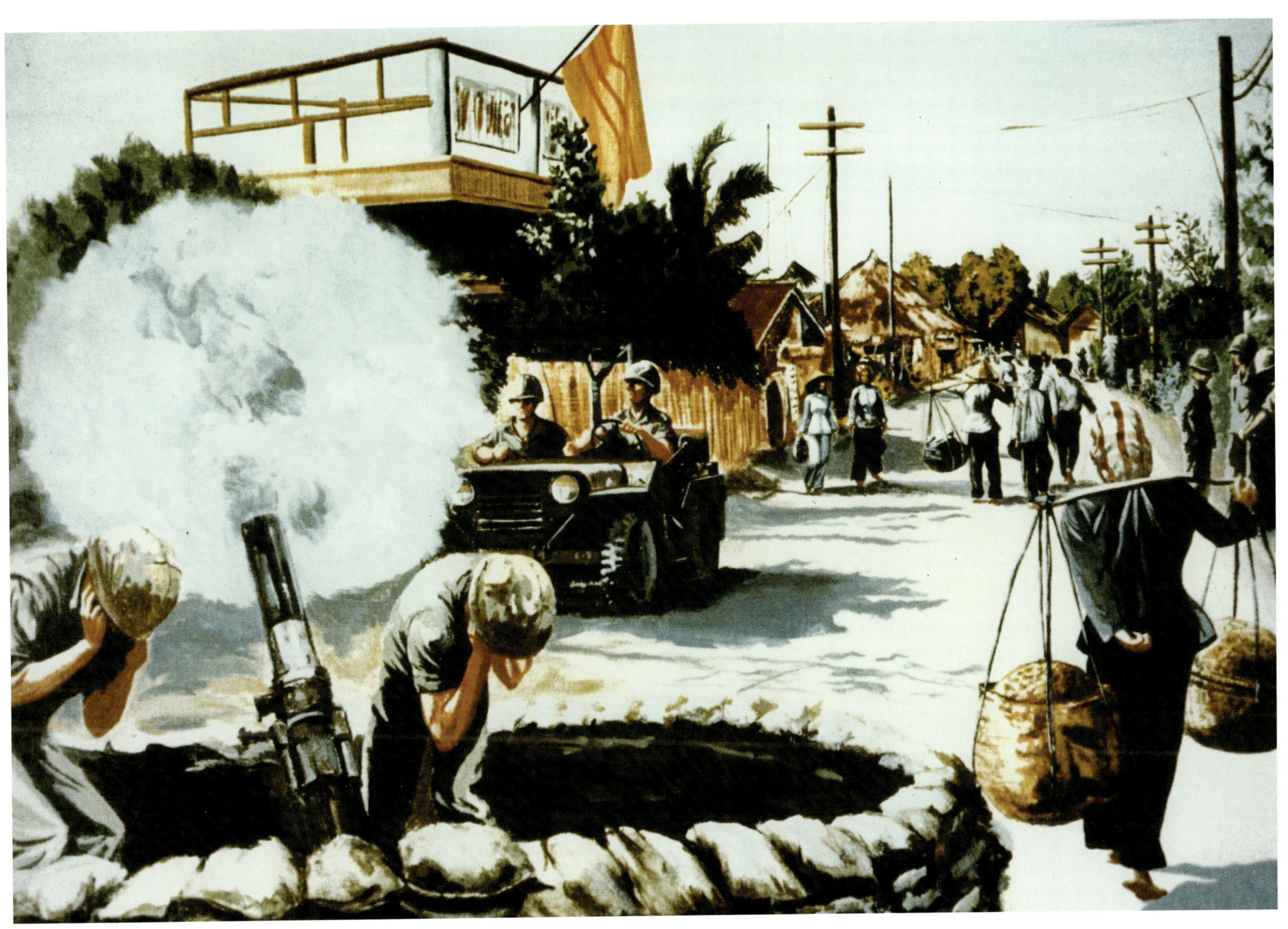

STREET SCENE
Vietnam
Kenneth J. Scowcroft, 1967
Acrylic, 28" x 24"

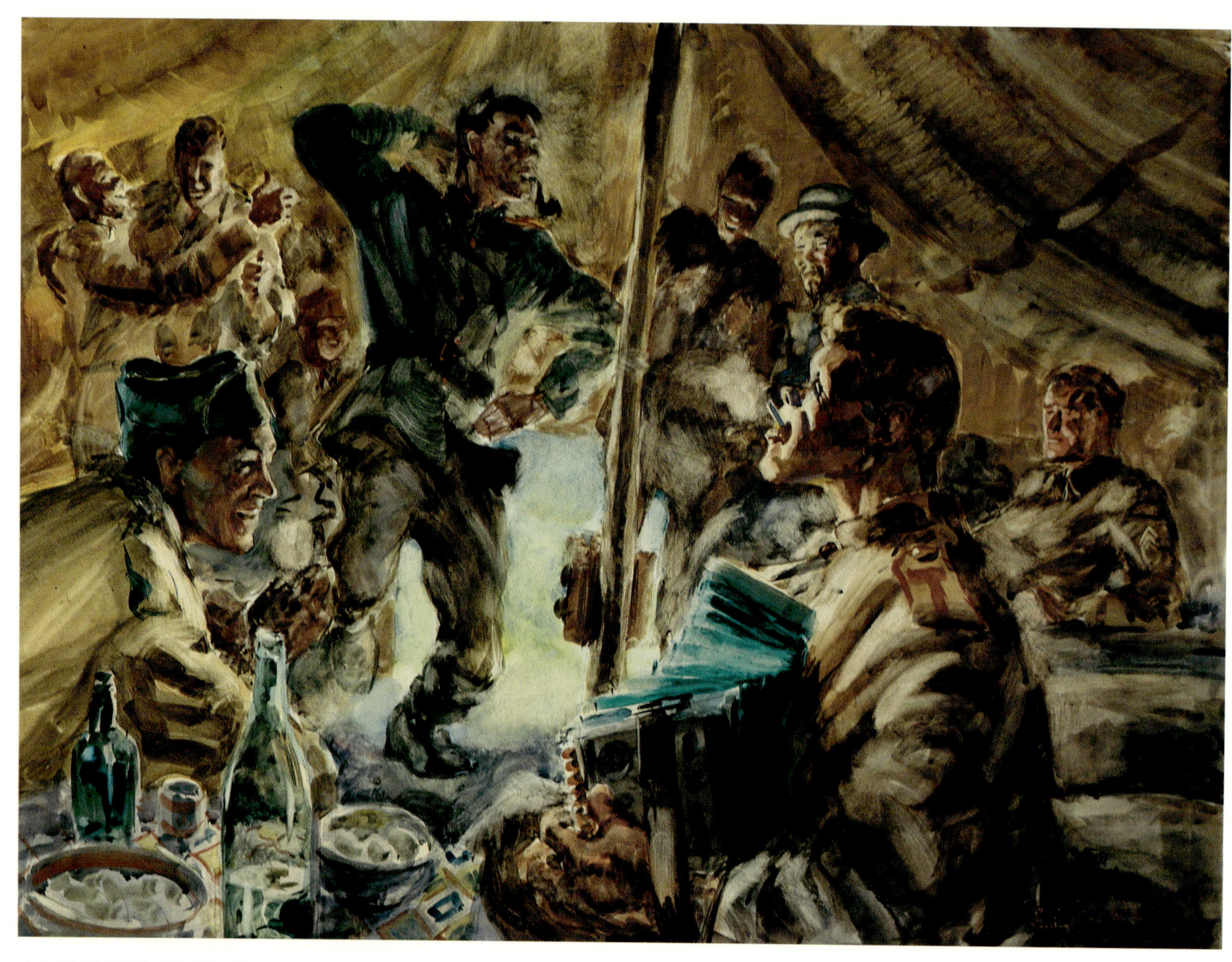

A MORNING WITH THE RUSSIANS
Korea
John Pike, 1945
Watercolor, 20 ½" x 26 ¼"

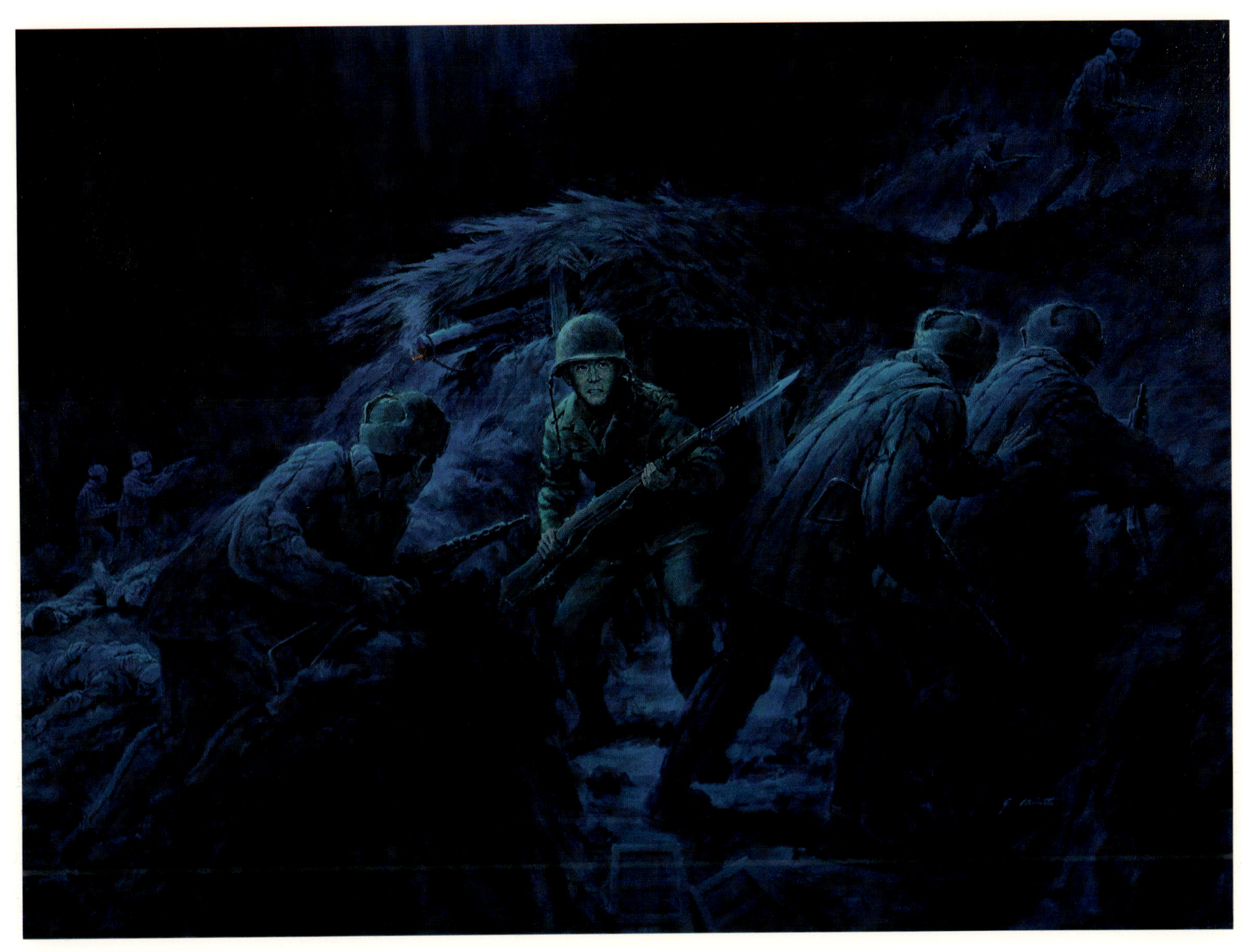

CORPORAL HIROSHI N. MIYAMURA
Korean War
George Akimoto, 1977
Oil, 36″ x 48″

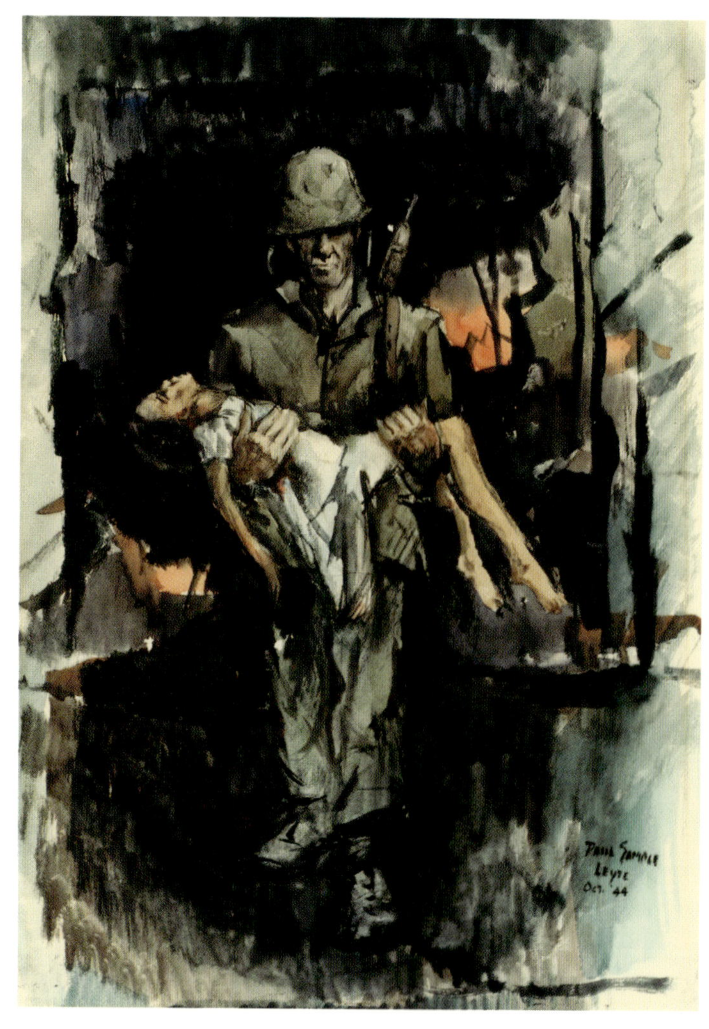

SOLDIER CARRYING WOUNDED CHILD
Leyte, Philippines
Paul Sample, 1944
Watercolor, 11" x 17"

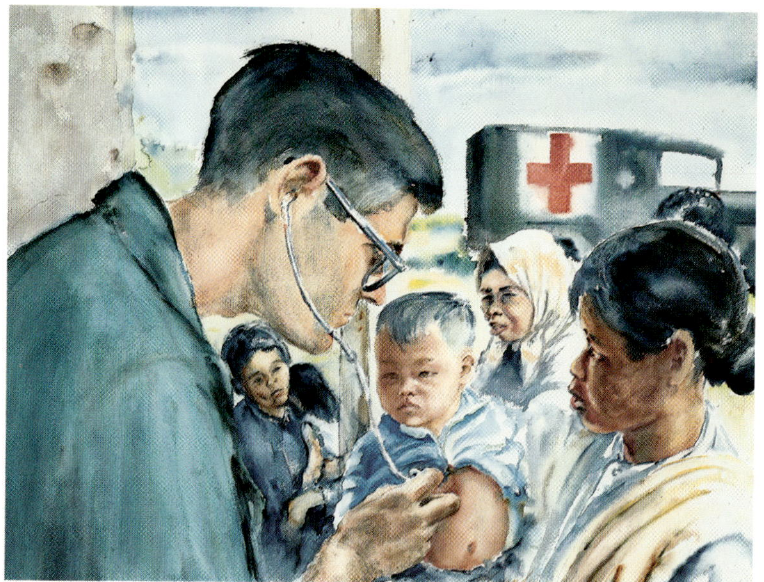

AMERICAN DOCTOR EXAMINES VIETNAMESE CHILD
Vietnam
Samuel E. Alexander, 1967
Watercolor, 22" x 30"

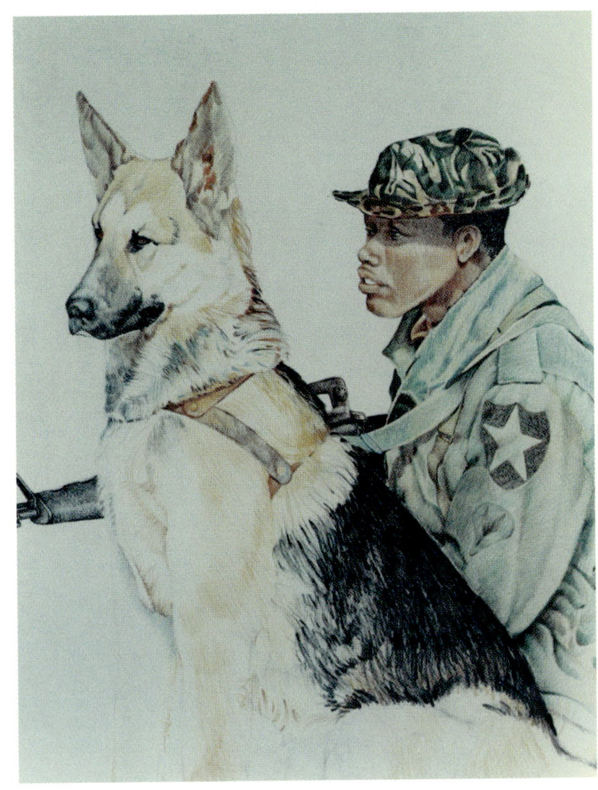

ALERT
Korea
David Grinstein, 1970
Watercolor, 22"x 30"

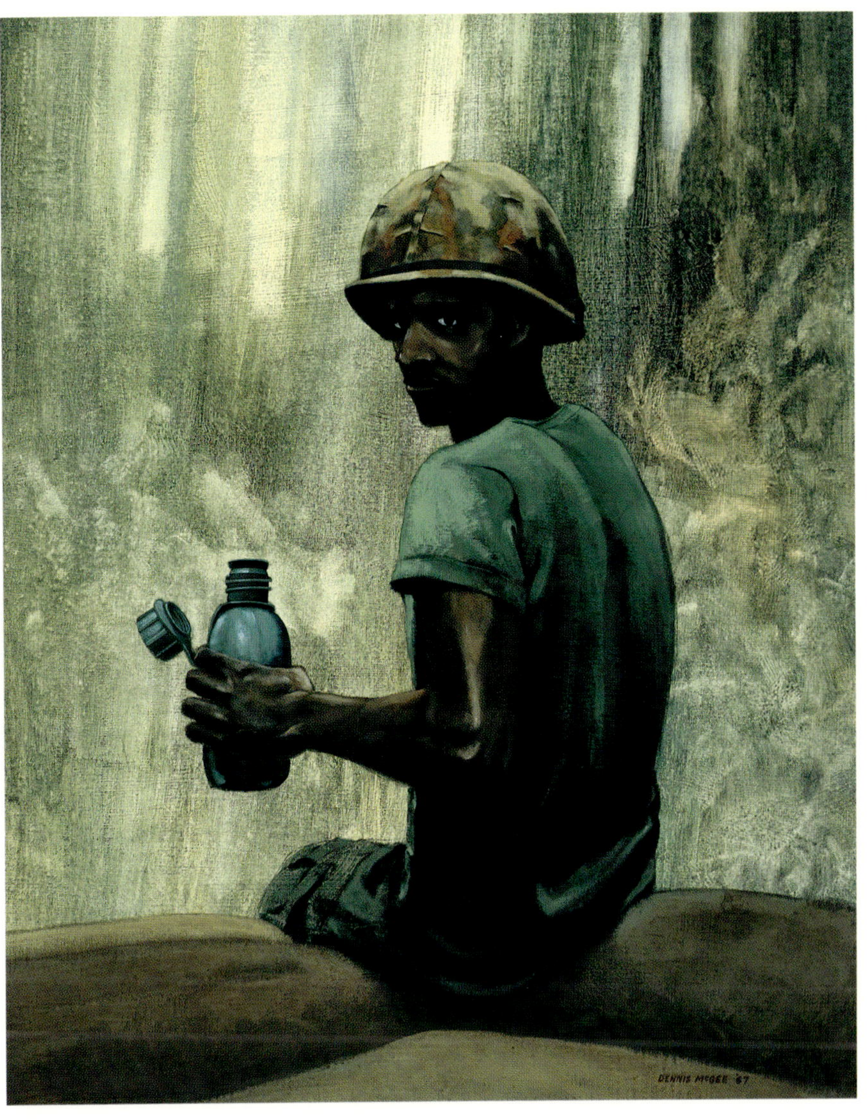

THE PAUSE THAT REFRESHES
Vietnam
Dennis O. McGee, 1967
Acrylic, 30"x 34"

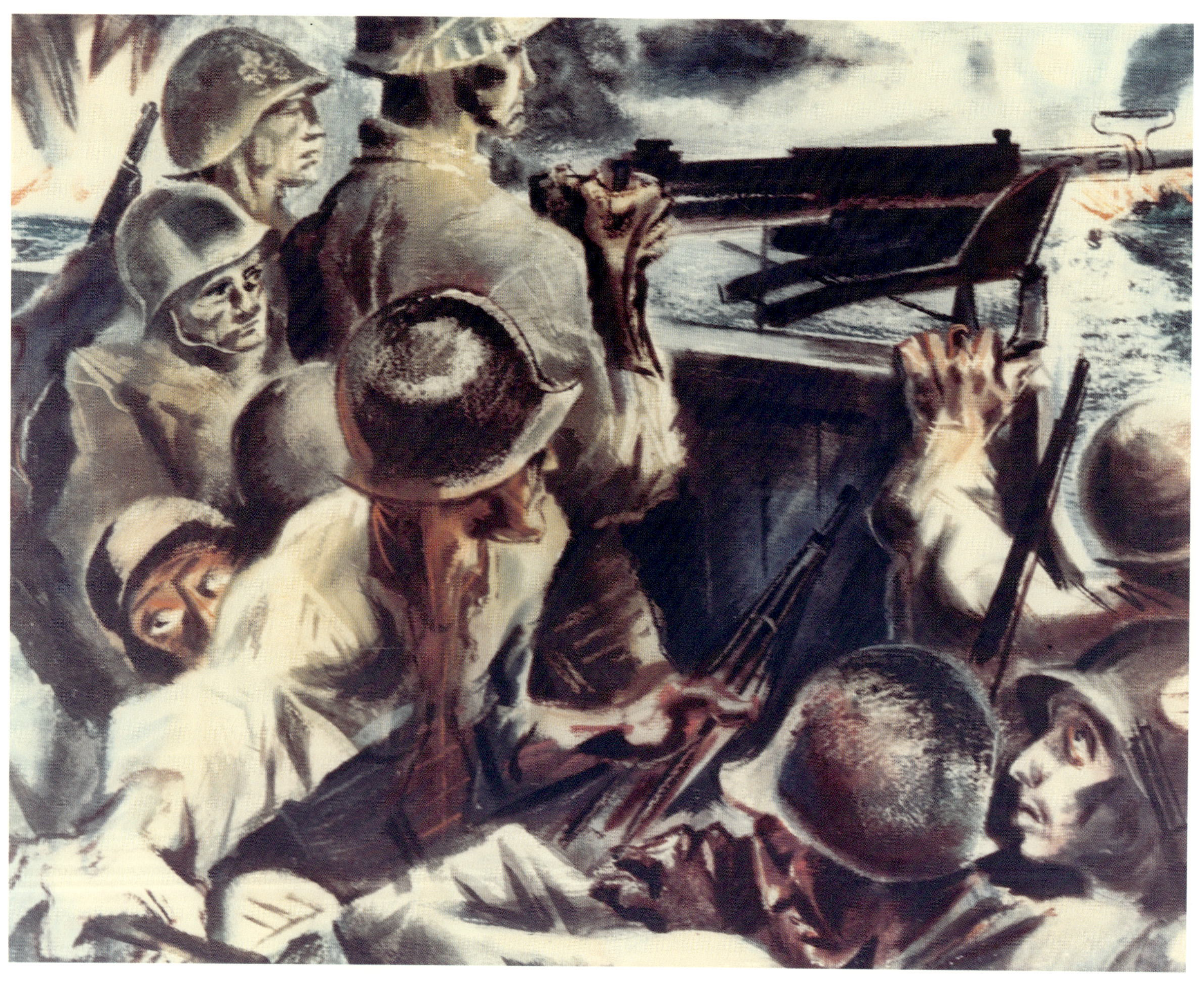

GUN CREWS COVER THE LANDING CRAFT
Arawe, New Britain
David Fredenthal, 1943
Watercolor, 21" x 29 ½"

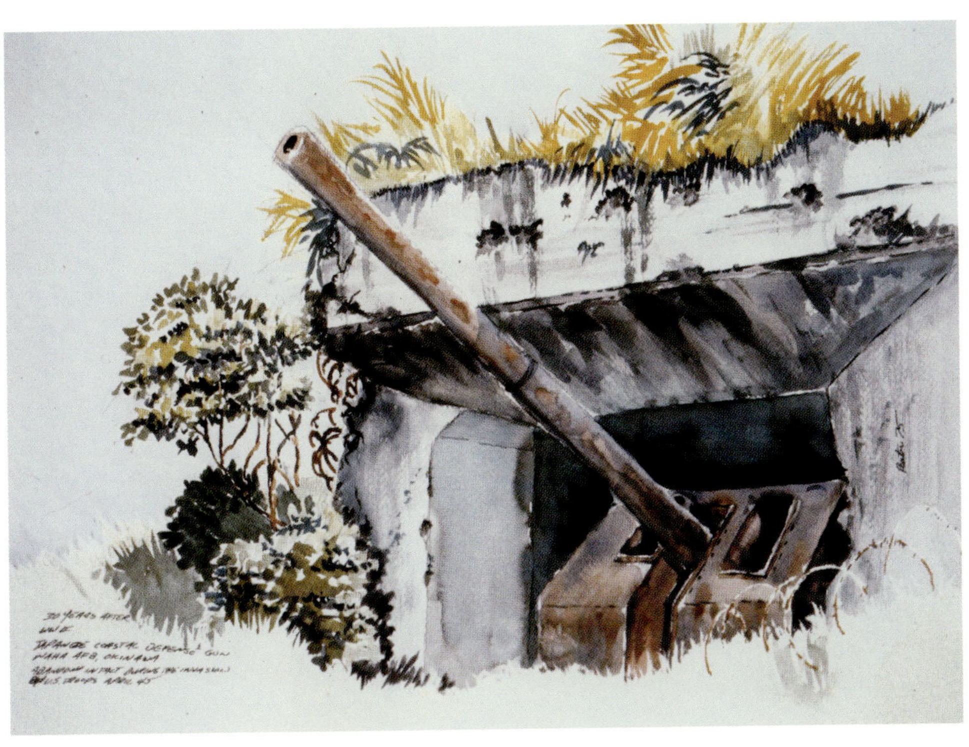

30 YEARS AFTER—OKINAWA
Okinawa
Raymond R. Reuter, 1975
Watercolor, 18" x 24"

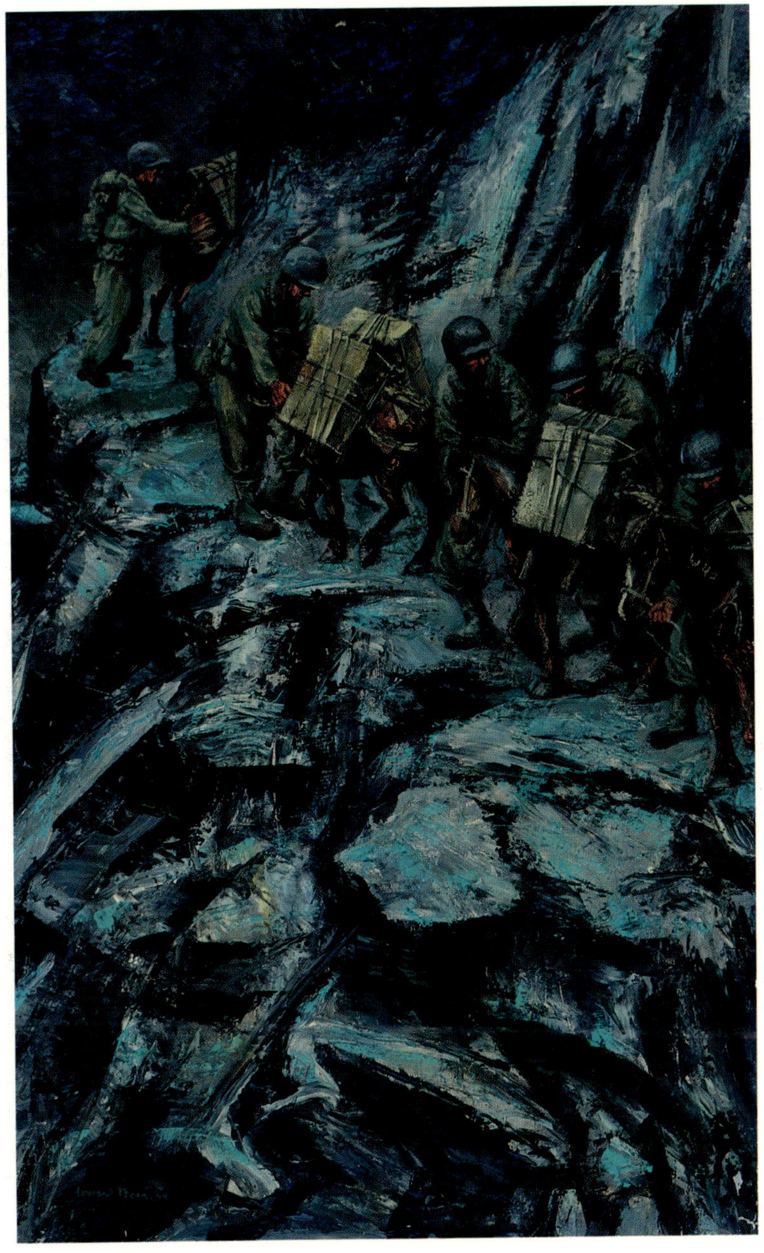

PACK TRAIN IN CHINA
China
Howard Baer, 1944
Oil, 31 ¾" x 19 ⅜"

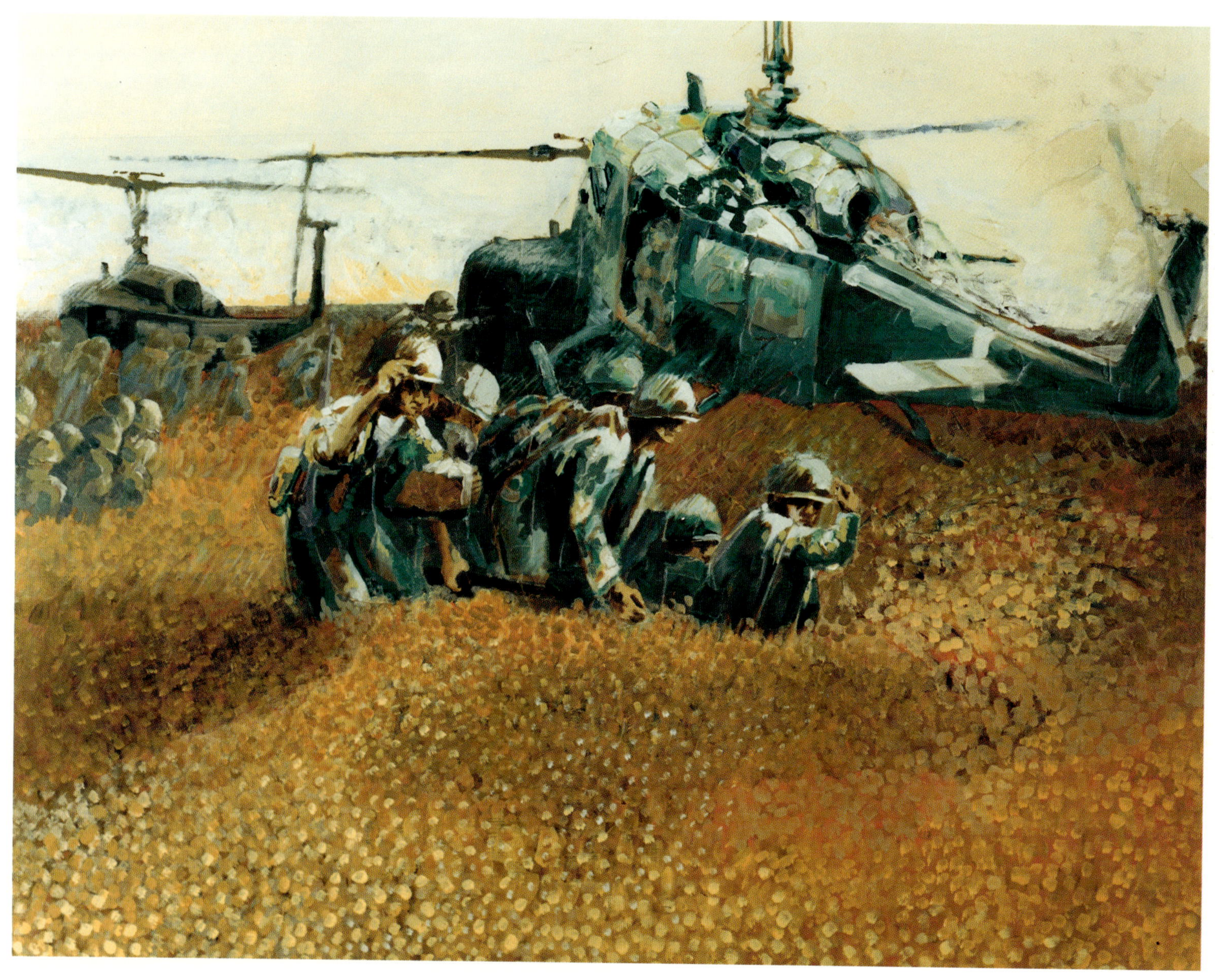

CHOPPER PICK-UP
Vietnam
Brian H. Clark, 1968
Acrylic, 36″ x 48″

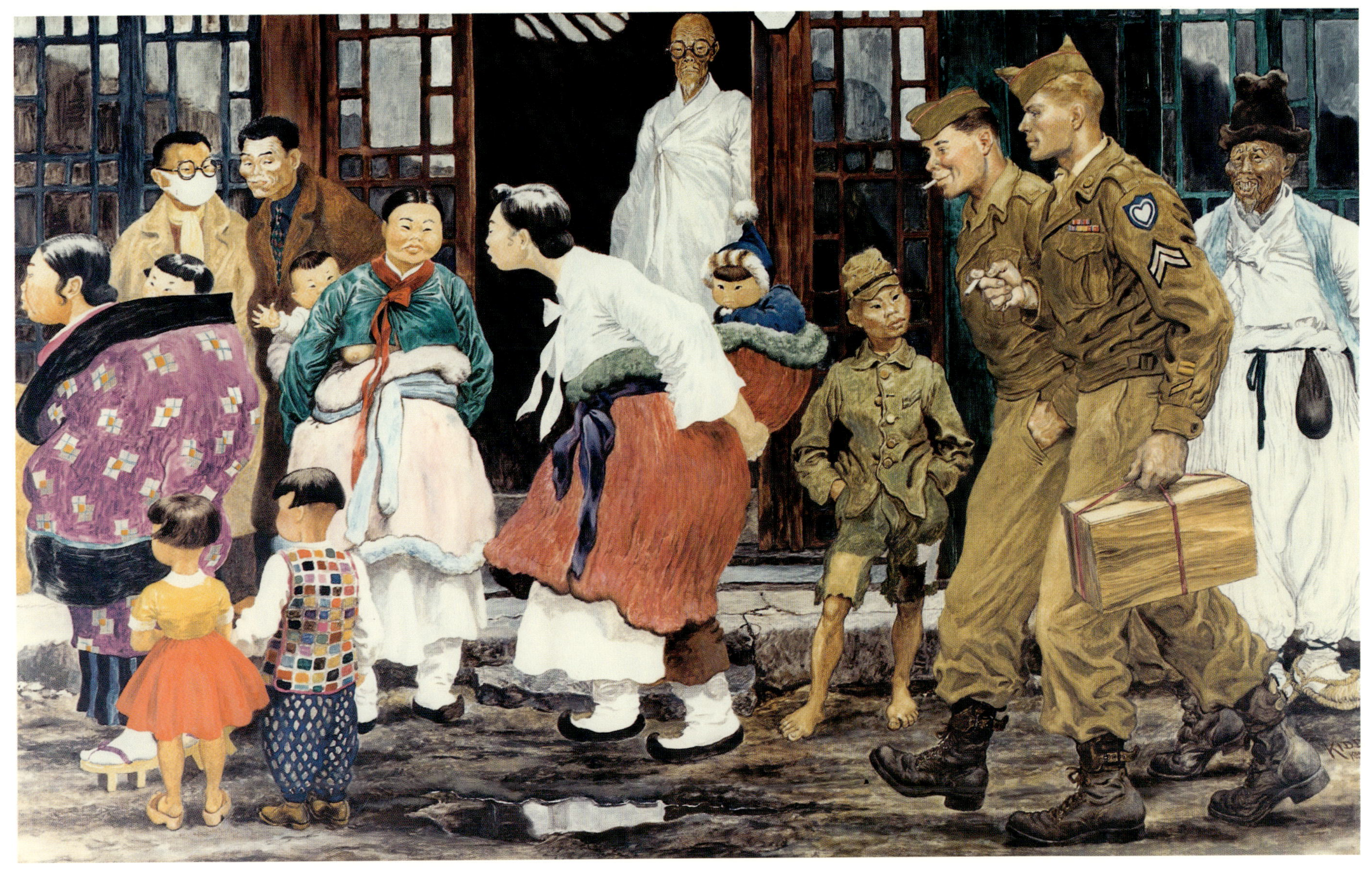

SEOUL STREET SCENE
Korea
Steven R. Kidd, 1945
Oil, 25" x 41"

Africa and the Middle East

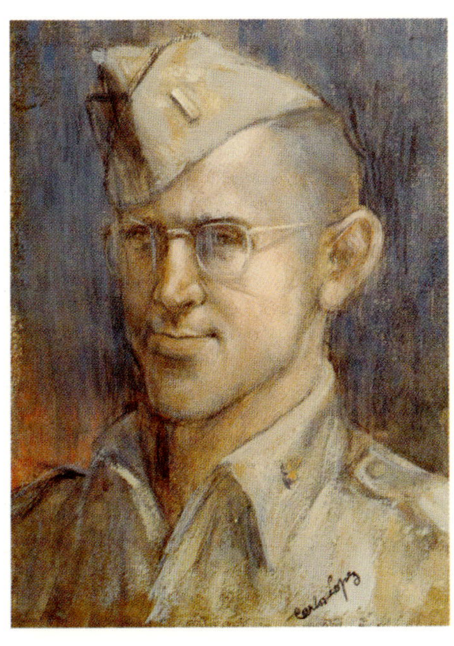

LT. A. C. MEYERS
Africa
Carlos Lopez, 1943
Watercolor, 7" x 4 ½"

THE HISTORY OF THE U.S. ARMY'S PRESENCE IN AFRICA AND the Middle East is relatively short, but it has involved important and demanding missions in many places. American soldiers have served from North Africa to Somalia, from Liberia to Eritrea, from Kuwait to Iran. The Army's experience in the area, however, has been concentrated in two time periods, World War II and the 1990s. During both periods American soldiers stopped aggression by the forces of ambitious tyrants who invaded and sought to dominate their neighbors. Twice within fifty years American tanks and armored vehicles raced over African and Middle Eastern desert sands to confront a marauding enemy, and twice they defeated the foe.

In early 1941 the successes of German forces in France, the Balkans, and North Africa, combined with submarine warfare in the Atlantic, threatened to give the Axis Powers total control of the Mediterranean. Although the United States was not yet a combatant in World War II, by midyear American soldiers were being sent to establish a series of bases on small, isolated South Atlantic islands. The objective was to create an air and sea bridge to maintain American links with the struggling British forces. The route went south to Brazil and then across the South Atlantic to the Azores and Europe. American soldiers soon found themselves serving on tiny way stations in the Atlantic with names like Ascension Island—places small in size but large in their strategic importance to the Allied war effort.

The United States entered the war after the Japanese attack on Pearl Harbor in December 1941, but events and resource limitations prevented any immediate Allied assault on the European continent. A decision was then made to attack the German and Italian forces in French North Africa. The subsequent landings in November 1942 brought American soldiers into places that had not seen an American force since naval activity against pirates in the early days of the republic. The initial resistance by the Vichy French was brief, and Casablanca, Oran, and Algiers became liberated cities and gateways into the interior. The Allied forces then began moving east toward British forces advancing out of Egypt.

For the American soldier the first real test came at two mountain passes southwest of Tunis, Kasserine and Sbiba. Here, despite the courage of many individual soldiers, untried American units were shattered by the Germans, and the Army learned some hard lessons. Within weeks, however, American soldiers were striking back. Battles at places with names like El Guettar, Maknassy, the Gabes-Gafsa Road, and Fondouk Gap were interspersed with equally fierce fights for ridges and hills remembered by the surviving soldiers only as numbers—Hill 290, Hill 306, Hill 396, and dozens of others. In all of these engagements, American soldiers showed that spirit of courage and determination that has always been their trademark, as well as a real concern for the well-being of North African civilians caught in the battle areas. By the end of May 1943, less than three months after the debacle at Kasserine, the Allied forces had linked, and the remaining elements of the Axis forces in North Africa surrendered. The Axis threat to dominate the Mediterranean was over. American ships landed cargo after cargo of supplies and equipment as the local ports were transformed into giant staging areas for the planned future invasions across the Mediterranean into Sicily and the rest of Europe.

In the meantime, the unbroken flow of lend-lease supplies had been critical to the success of the British fighting in the Middle East and would continue to be so for the Soviet armies on the Eastern Front. The ports of the Persian Gulf offered a back door into the area, and American soldiers were sent to prepare routes for the reception and movement of lend-lease assistance throughout the region. New places were added to the Army's lexicon—Basra, Baghdad, Umm Qasr, and Tehran. A Persian Gulf Command was established, and Army transportation and logistics specialists kept the stream of war materials moving from the Gulf ports onto trains and then north to the Russians to the end of the war.

In the late summer of 1990, almost fifty years after the defeat of the German Afrika Korps, American soldiers were again called to the Middle East to serve their nation. Brought from garrisons in the United States as well as Europe, the men and women of the Army once more stood on a desert battle line facing the invading

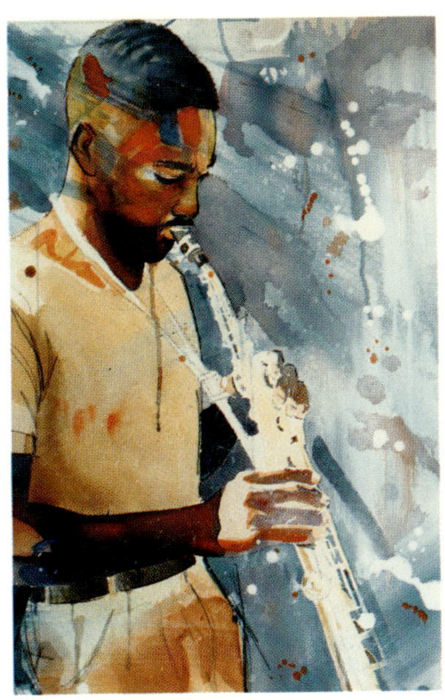

SAUDI JAZZ ON SUNDAY
Saudi Arabia
Peter G. Varisano, 1990
Watercolor, 30" x 22"

forces of a tyrant. The Iraqi Army had advanced into Kuwait, and it appeared to be preparing to continue into Saudi Arabia. This time American soldiers faced T–72 tanks and Scud missiles instead of panzers, but instead of Sherman tanks, jeeps, and half-tracks, the Army was now armed with Abrams tanks, high mobility multipurpose wheeled vehicles ("humvees"), Bradley fighting vehicles, and multiple launch rocket systems (MLRS). And another dimension was also present on this modern battlefield, as the Army filled the sky with heavily armed Black Hawk and Apache helicopters.

The Army had honed its units to a sharp edge of readiness on training grounds in Germany and the California desert. When the signal to attack was given, new names were quickly added to the list of the Army's battle honors. American soldiers found themselves fighting for their lives in fast-moving tank battles at places like 73 Easting, Norfolk, and Medina Ridge. Sustained by a combination of Army field rations and fast food from Saudi-supplied mobile trucks, the American-led coalition rolled to an overwhelming victory in 100 hours.

Just as critical to the combat effort as the combat forces were the thousands of soldiers in support units who served in places like King Khalid Military City, Pipe Line Road, Dhahran, and in a whole network of temporary camps and nameless supply depots. Even after the end of hostilities, a number of these soldiers have remained to maintain a stock of supplies and equipment to ensure a rapid redeployment in any future emergency in the area. Most recently American soldiers also have served in humanitarian relief operations in Somalia and Rwanda. The Somalia mission in particular was extremely dangerous because of the lack of local political stability, but it saved the lives of literally thousands of people.

The art in this section shows the American soldier in many moods and circumstances, in danger and relaxing. Here one can also glimpse the types of far-flung settings experienced by the soldiers, from desert to offshore island to bustling ports and railheads, all of them far from home and loved ones. For today's soldier, Operation DESERT STORM in particular, despite its huge scale, was but one more call to duty, one more chance to demonstrate an unbroken commitment on the individual level to the nation and to the Army's assigned role.

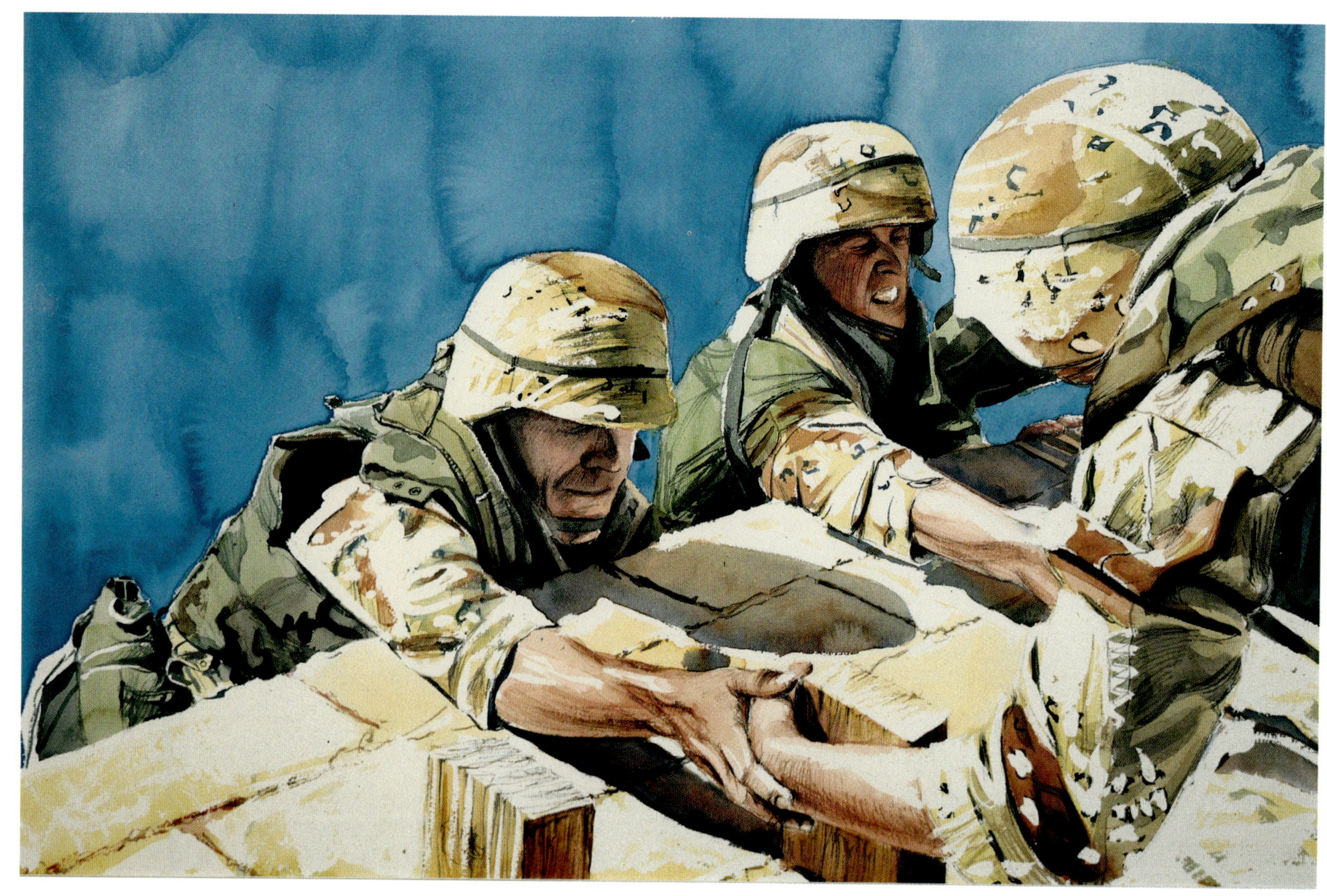

SCALING THE WALL WITH A LITTLE HELP
Saudi Arabia
Sieger Hartgers, 1990
Watercolor, 24" x 36"

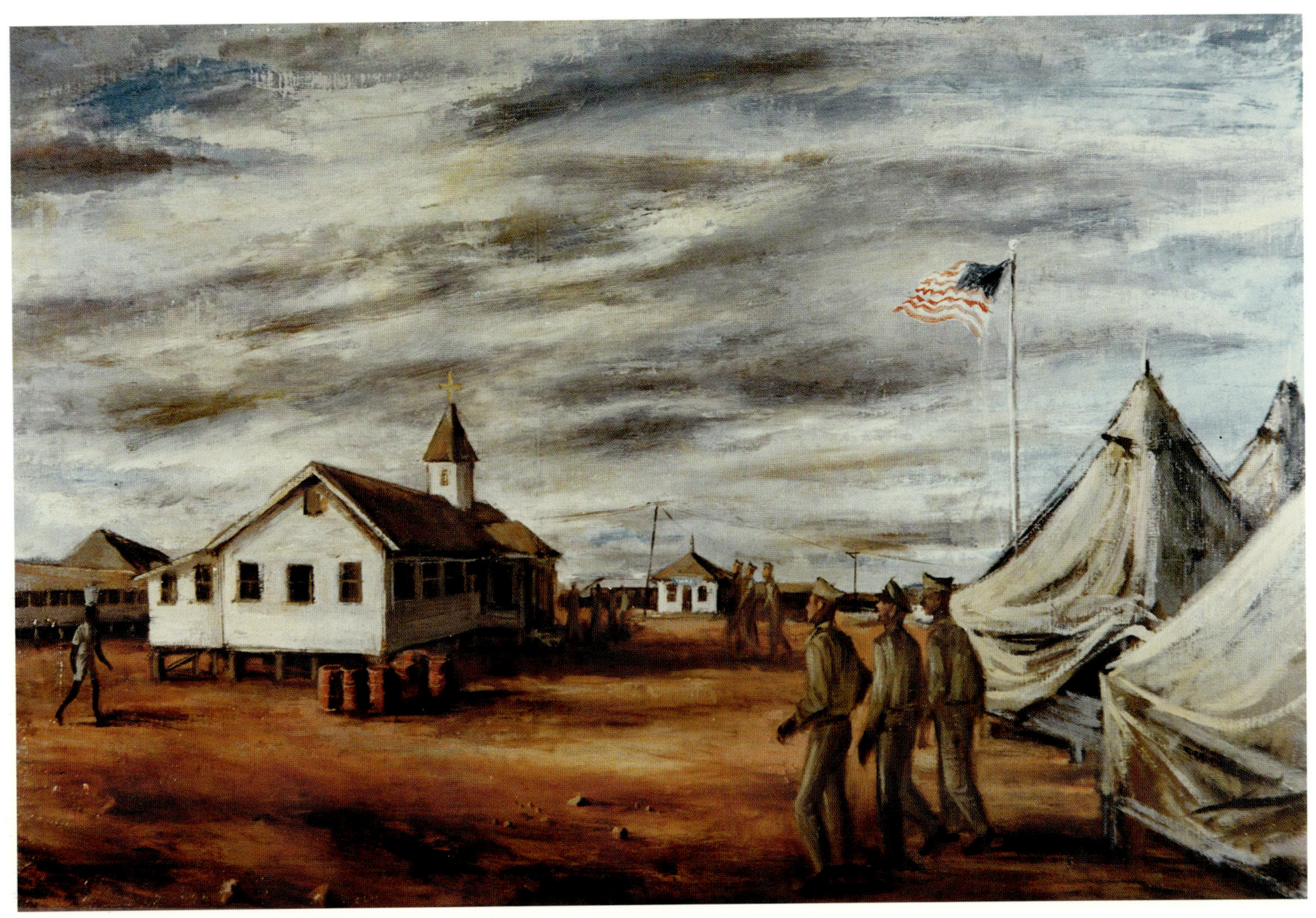

CHURCH AT BUSHTOWN
Accra, Gold Coast
Carlos Lopez, 1943
Oil, 20" x 30"

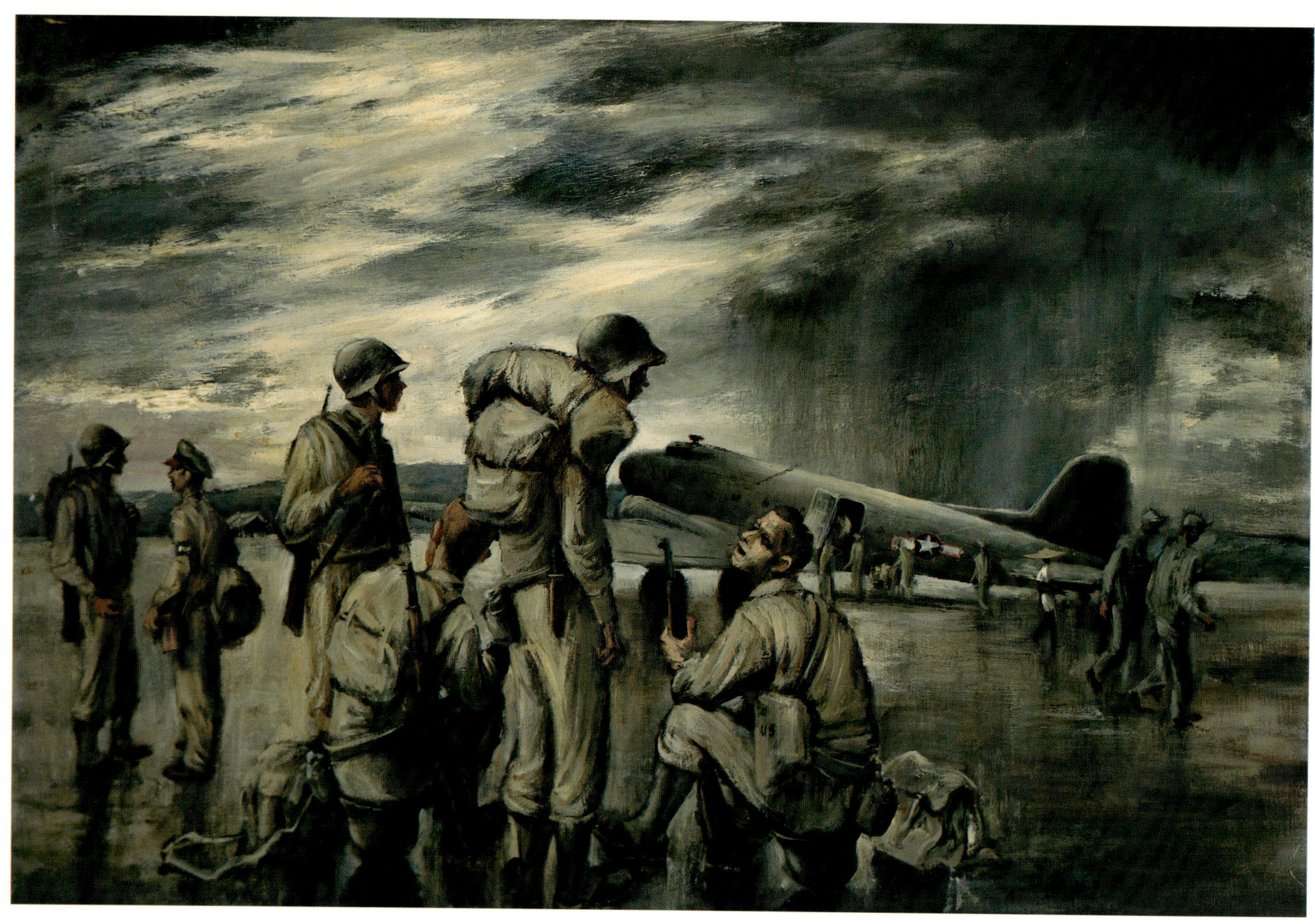

ROBERTS FIELD
Liberia
Carlos Lopez, 1943
Oil, 22" x 32"

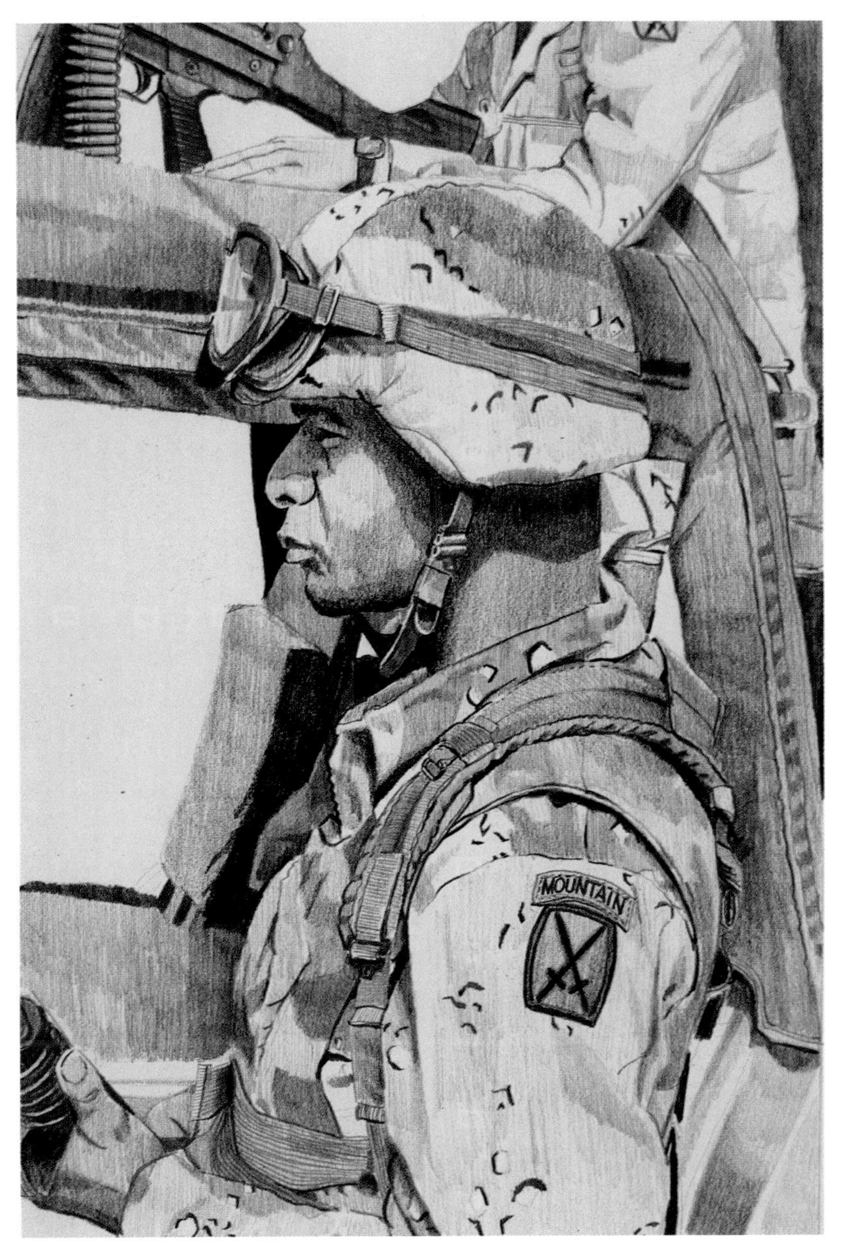

10TH MOUNTAIN TROOPS
Somalia
Peter G. Varisano, 1993
Pencil, 17" x 13 ½"

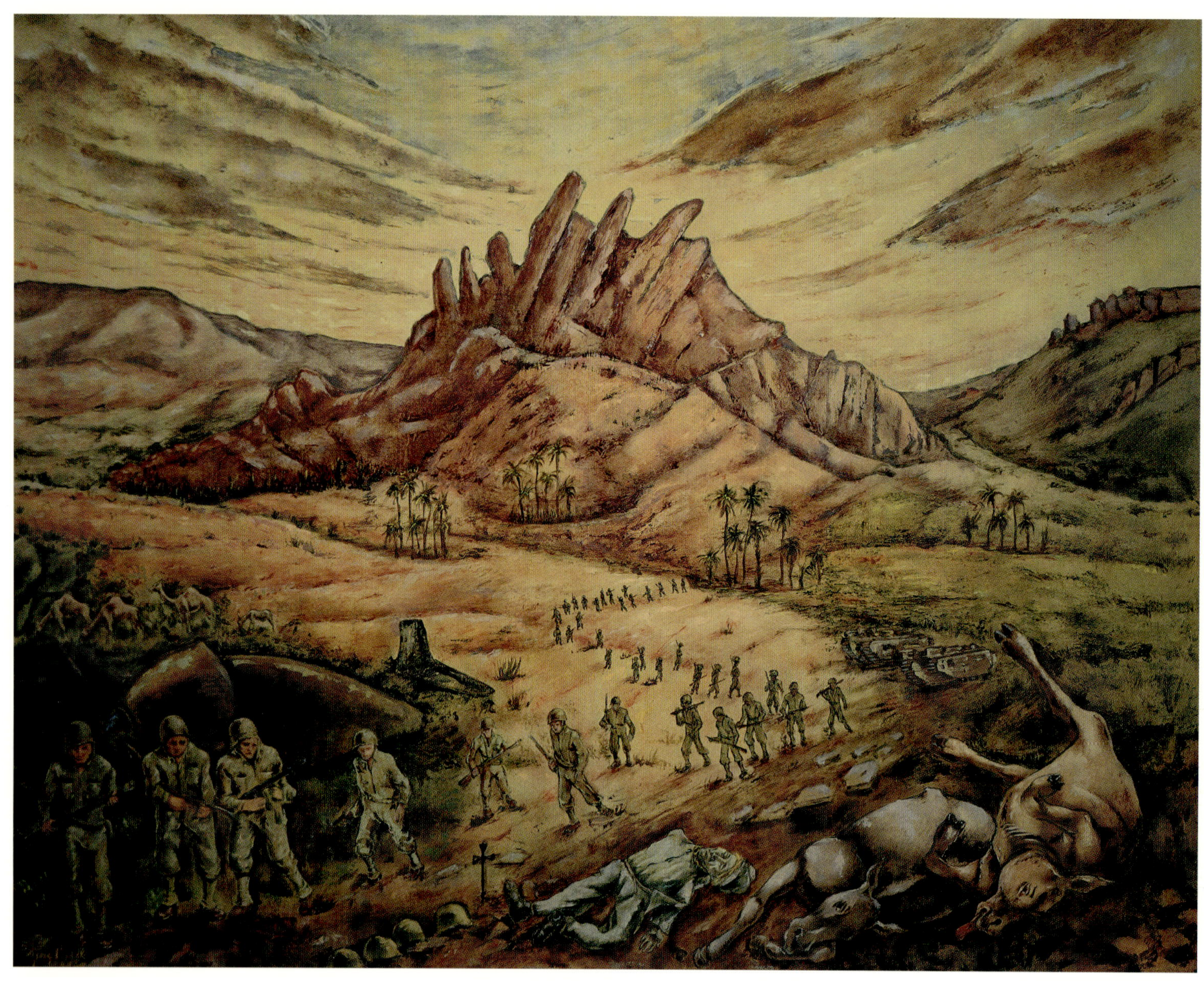

FAID PASS
Tunisia
George Biddle, 1943
Oil, 40" x 50"

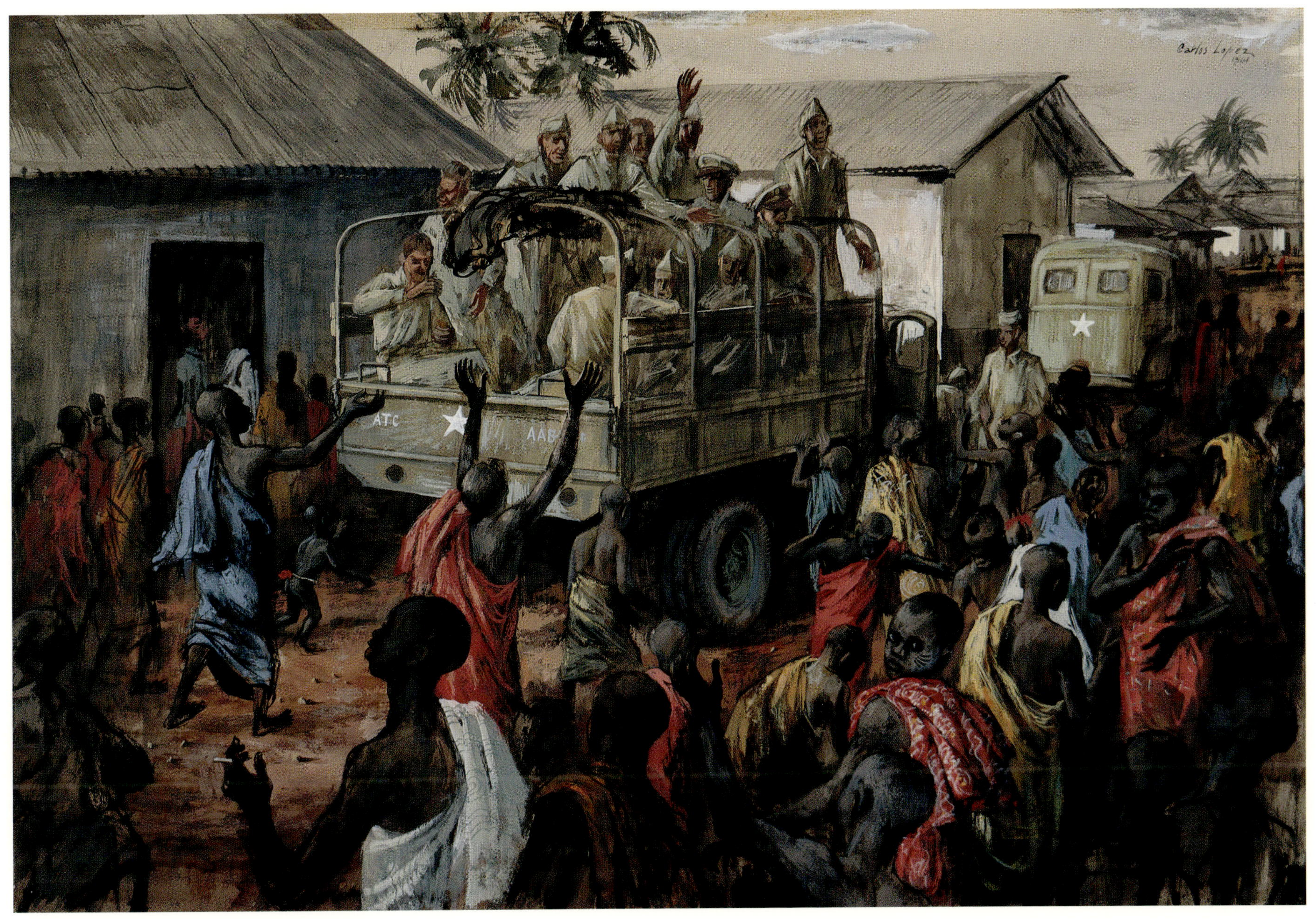

ON A BUSH TRIP
Dakar, French West Africa
Carlos Lopez, 1943
Watercolor, 16" x 24"

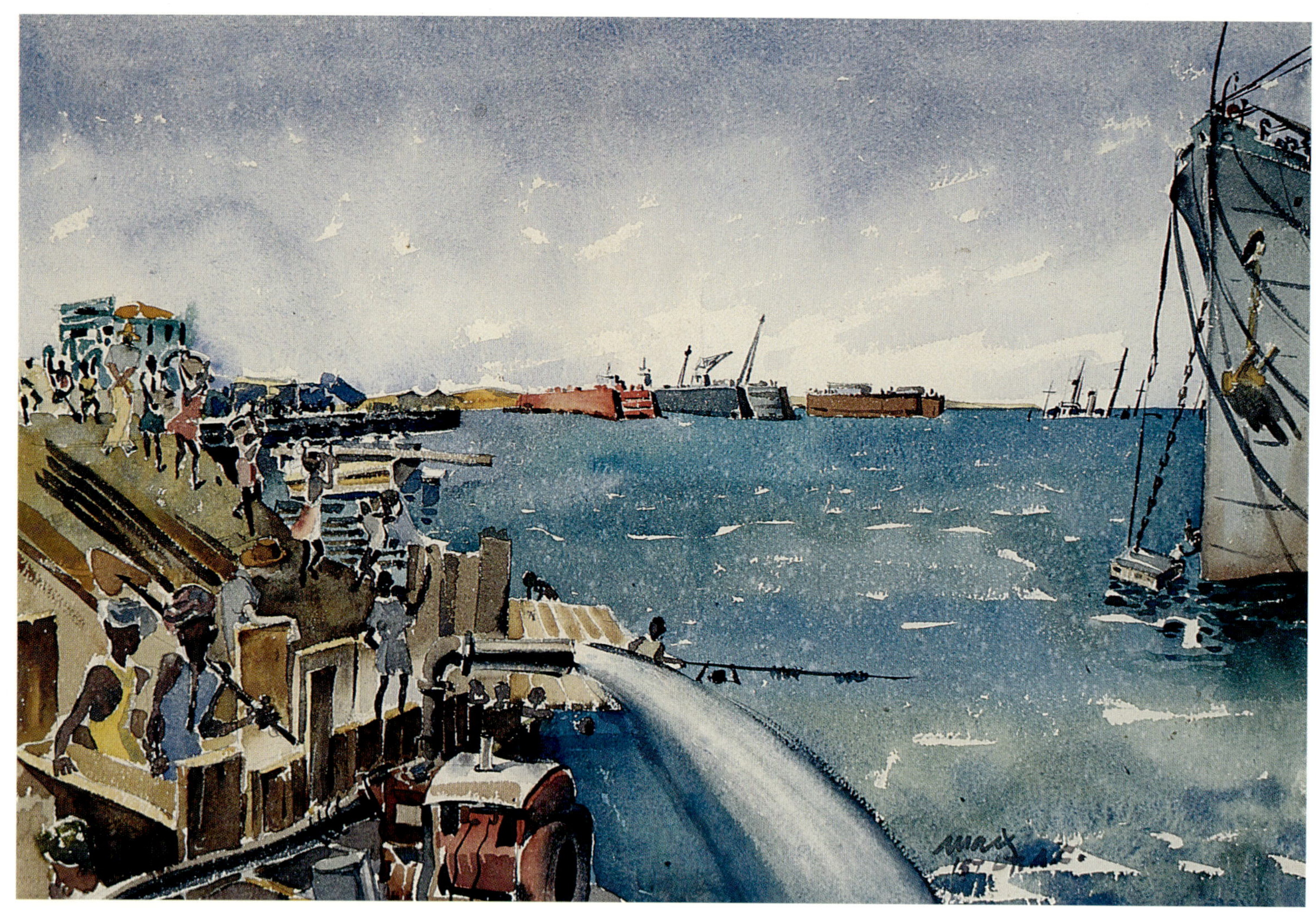

AMERICAN BUILT PIER AT MASSAWA
Eritrea
Milton Marx, 1943
Watercolor, 13 ⅛" x 19 ⅜"

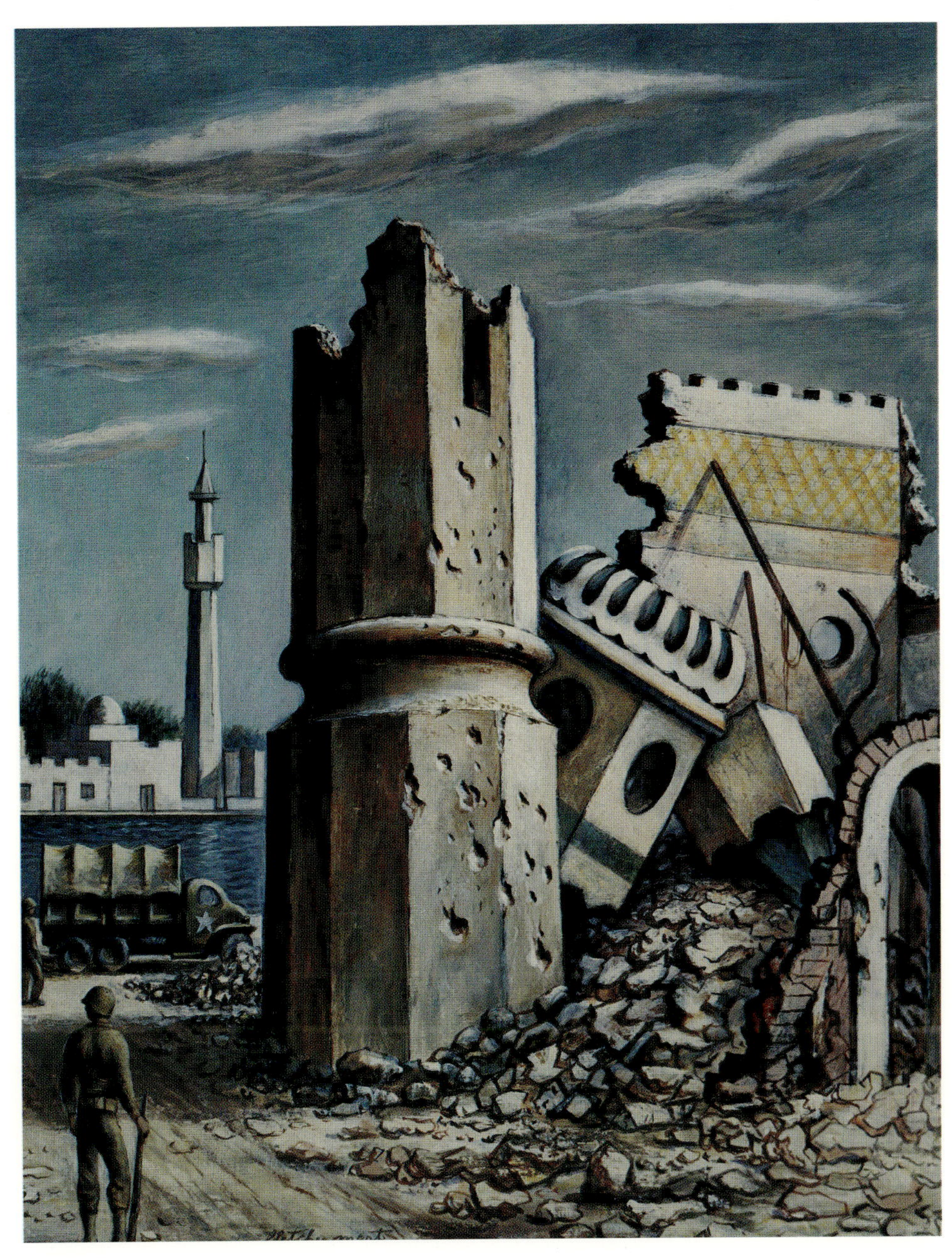

BIZERTE
Tunisia
Fletcher Martin, 1943
Oil, 21 ½" x 28"

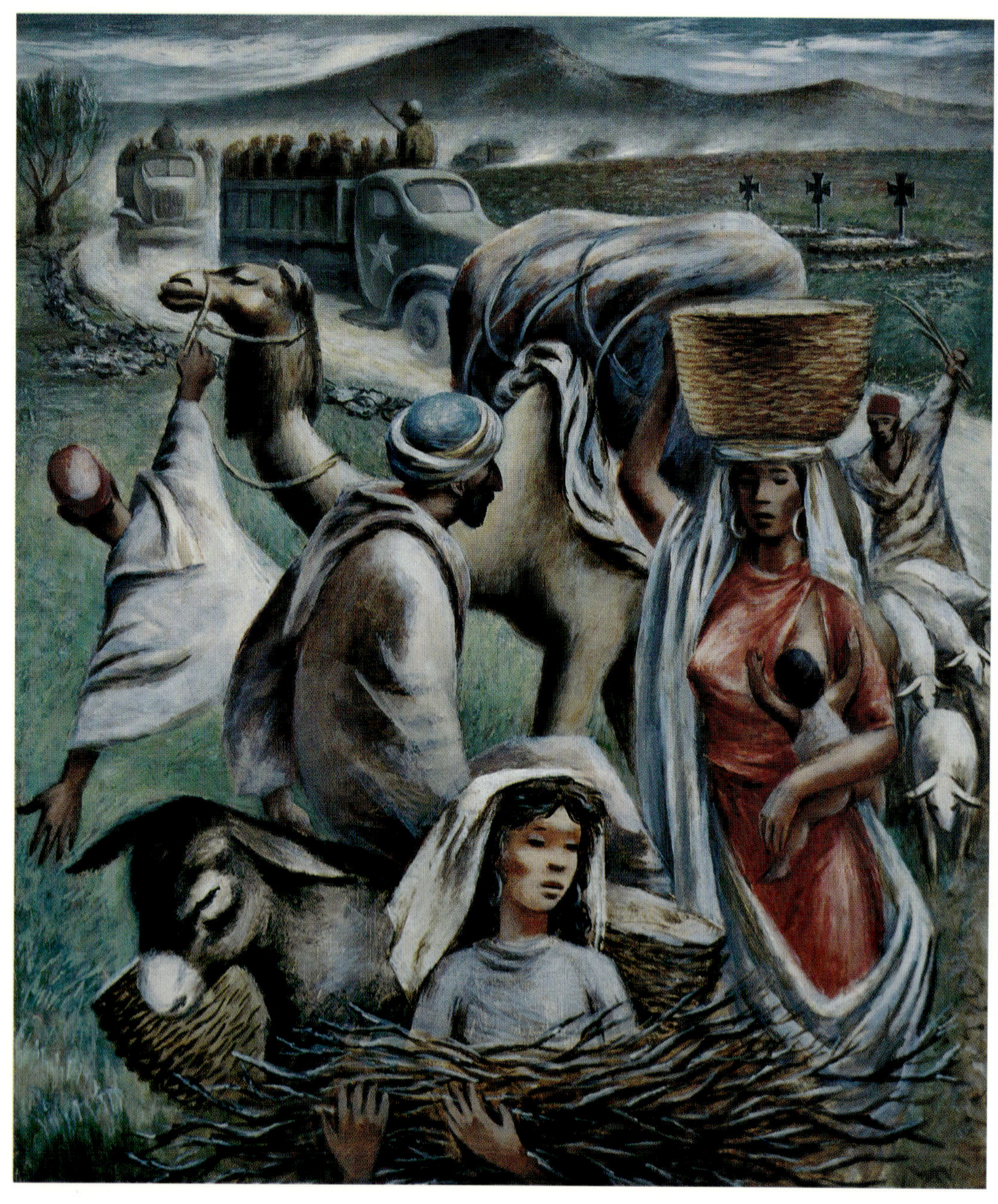

PRISONERS FROM CAPE BON
Tunisia
Fletcher Martin, 1943
Oil, 17" x 20 ½"

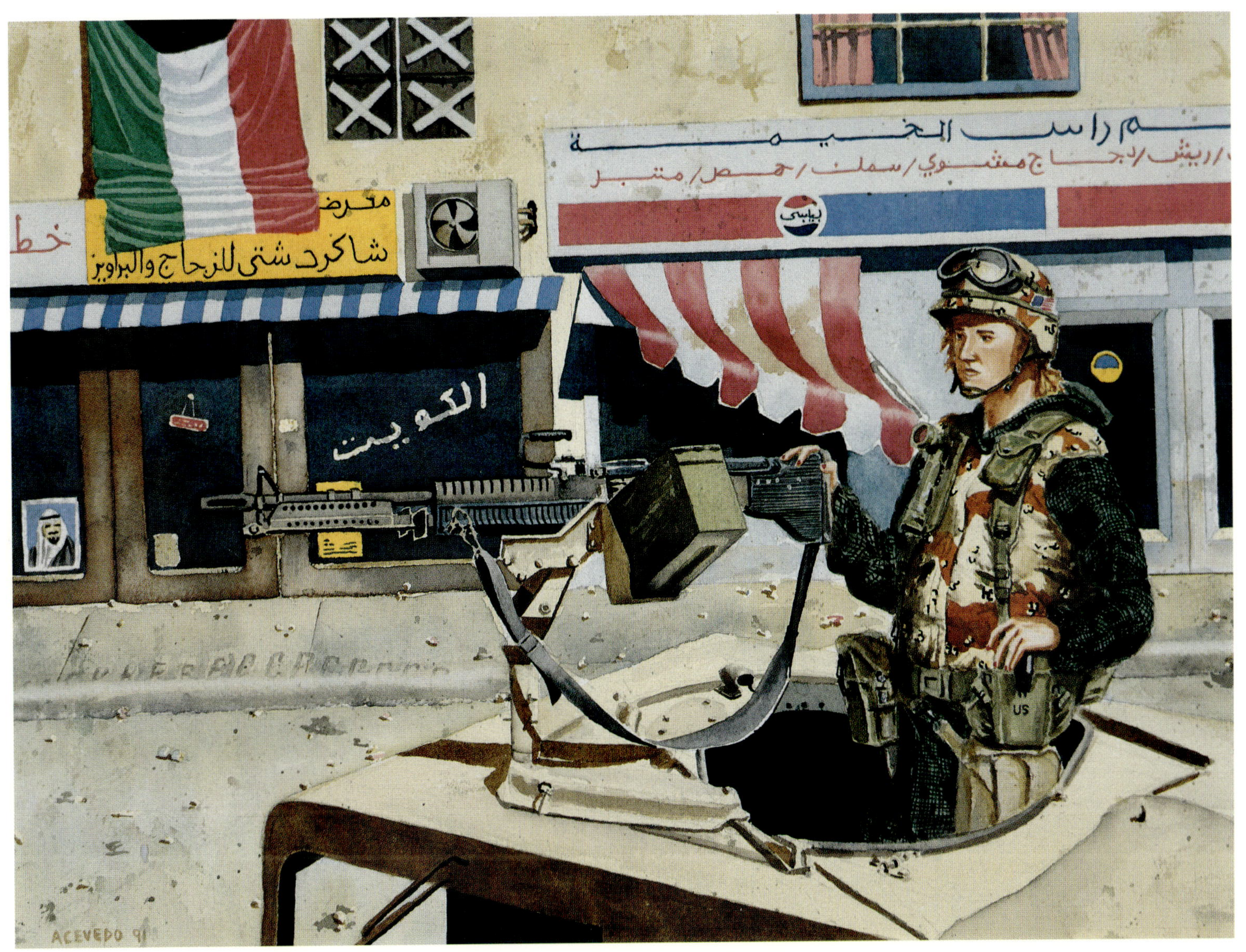

PATROL DUTY IN KUWAIT CITY
Kuwait
Mario H. Acevedo, 1990
Watercolor, 12 ¼" x 16 1/16"

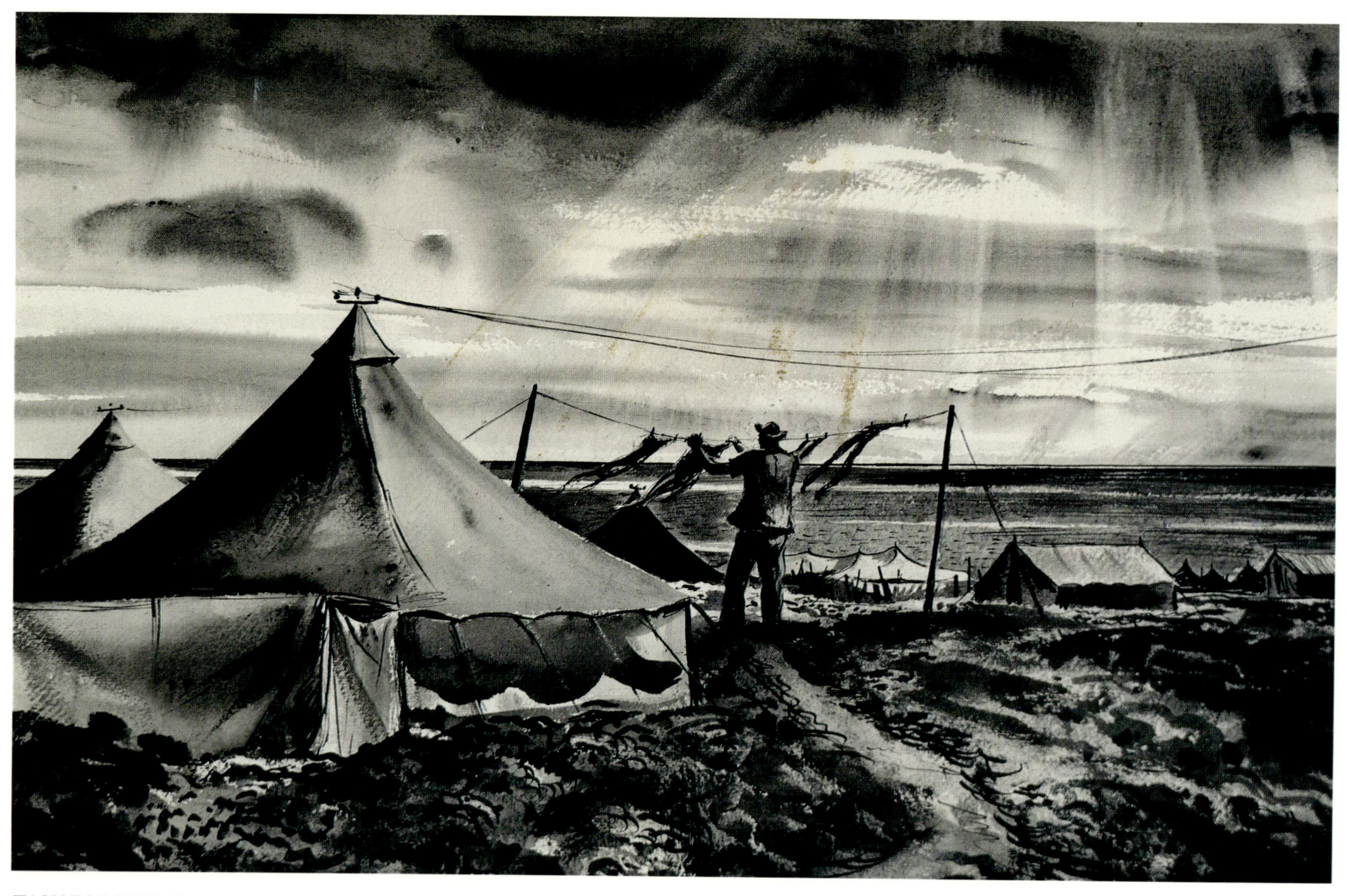

TASK FORCE ENCAMPMENT ON THE LAVA ROCK
Ascension Island
Peter Hurd, 1944
Watercolor, 14" x 21 ½"

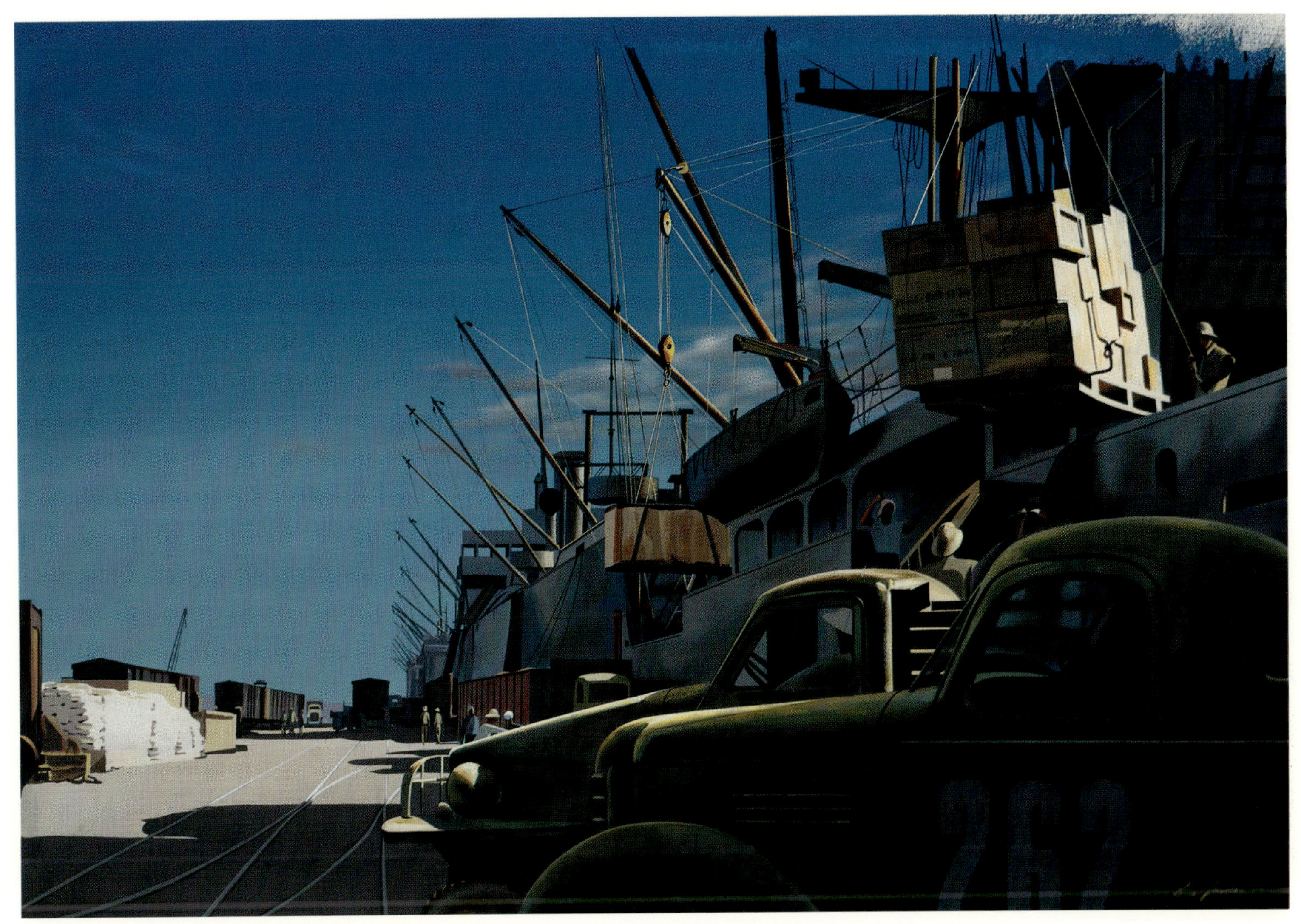

UNLOADING LIBERTY SHIPS
Khorramshahr, Iran
Richard H. Jansen, 1944
Gouache, 26" x 36"

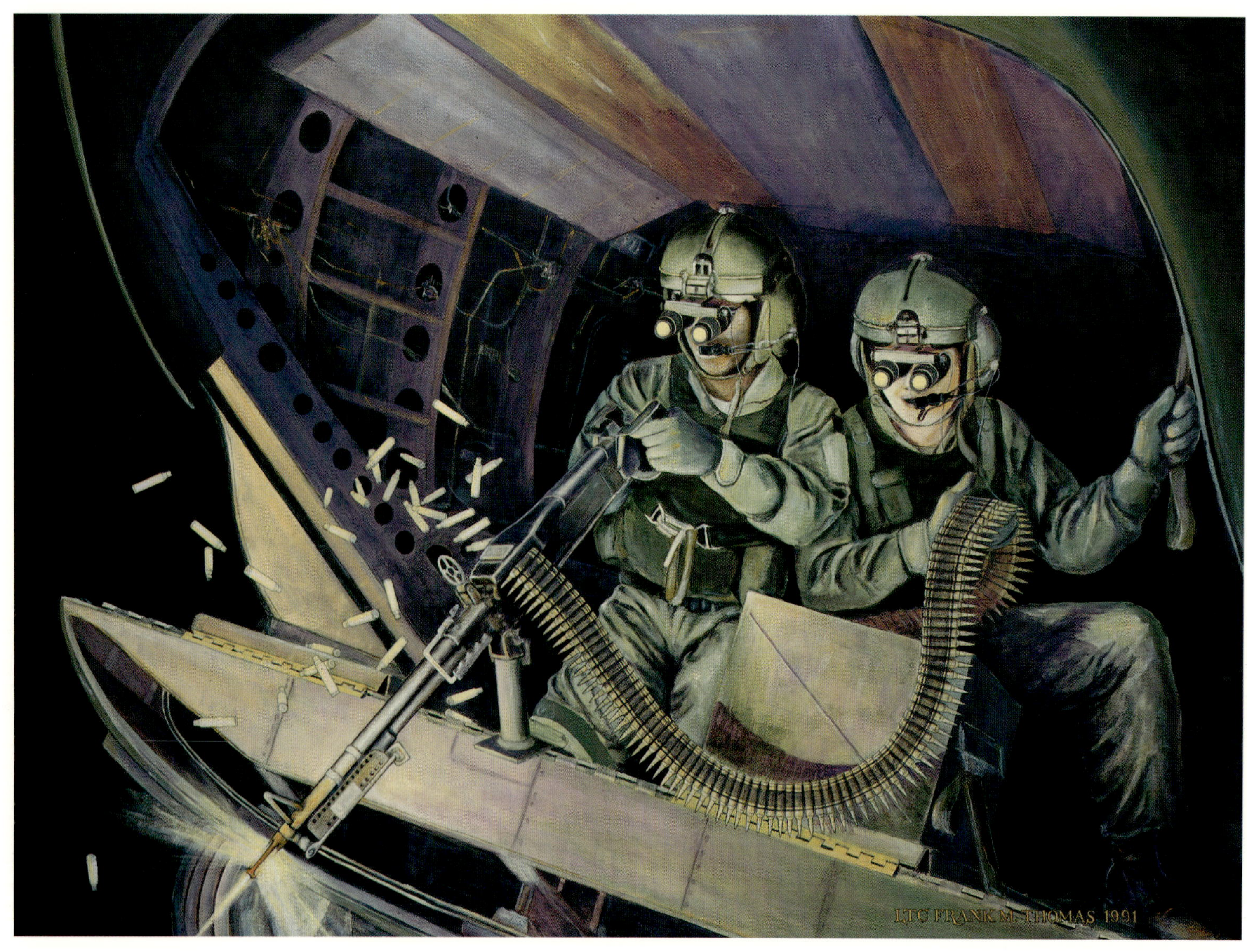

NIGHT RUN
Iraq
Frank M. Thomas, 1991
Acrylic, 36" x 48"

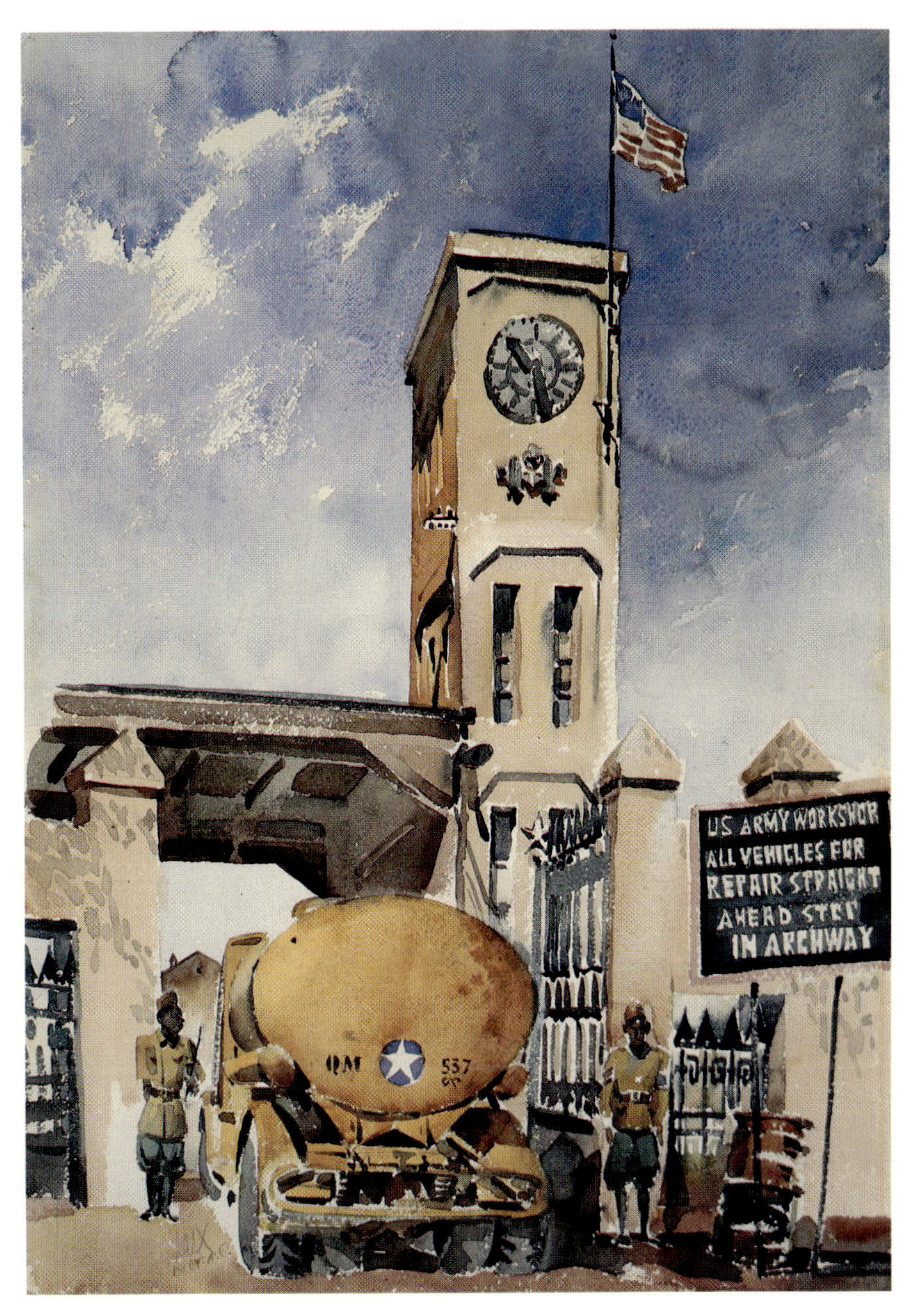

ENTRANCE TO THE ASMARA ARSENAL
Eritrea
Milton Marx, 1943
Watercolor, 20 ⅞" x 14 ⅝"

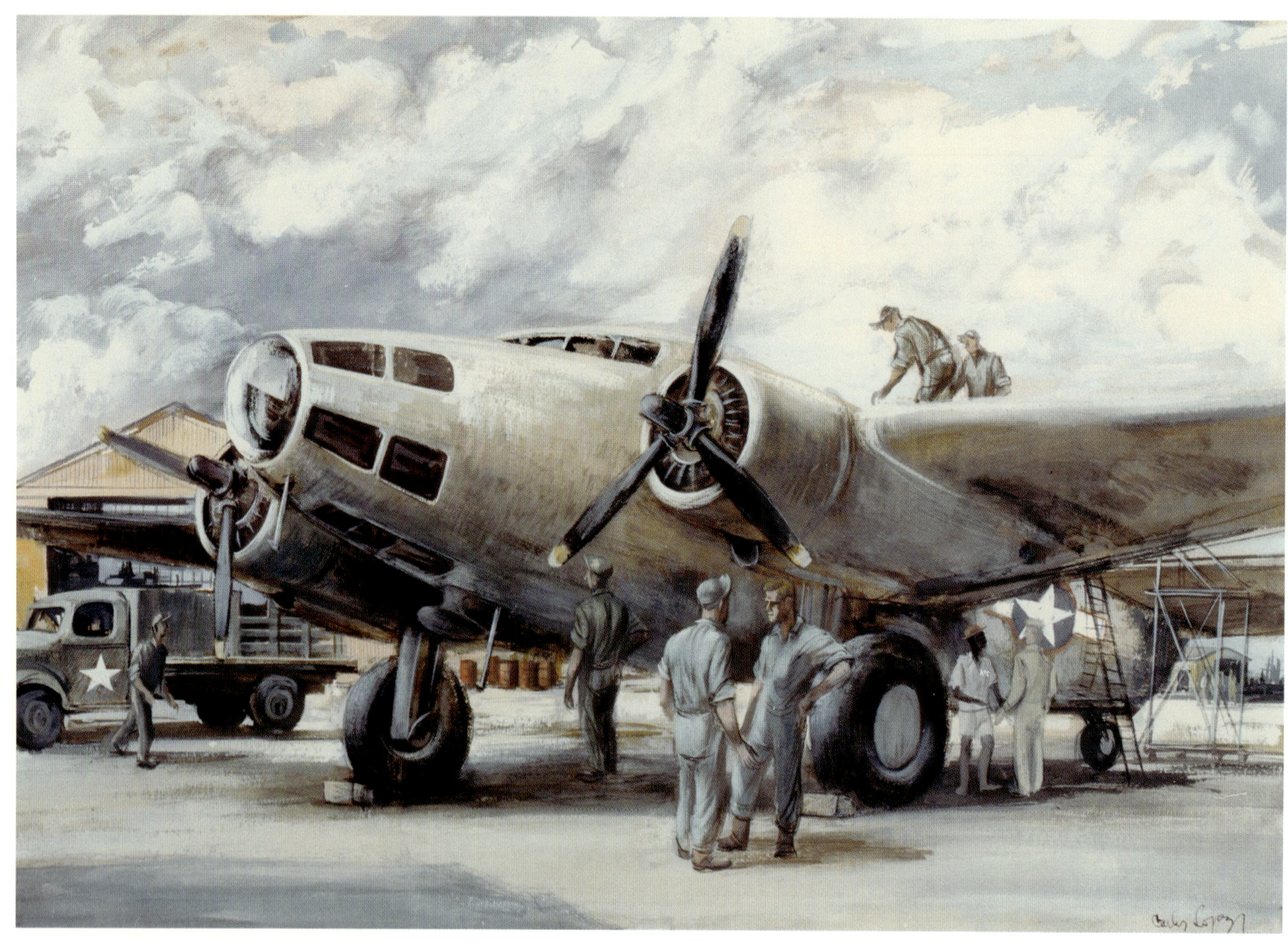

IN GOOD WEATHER
Africa
Carlos Lopez, 1943
Watercolor, 20″ x 30″

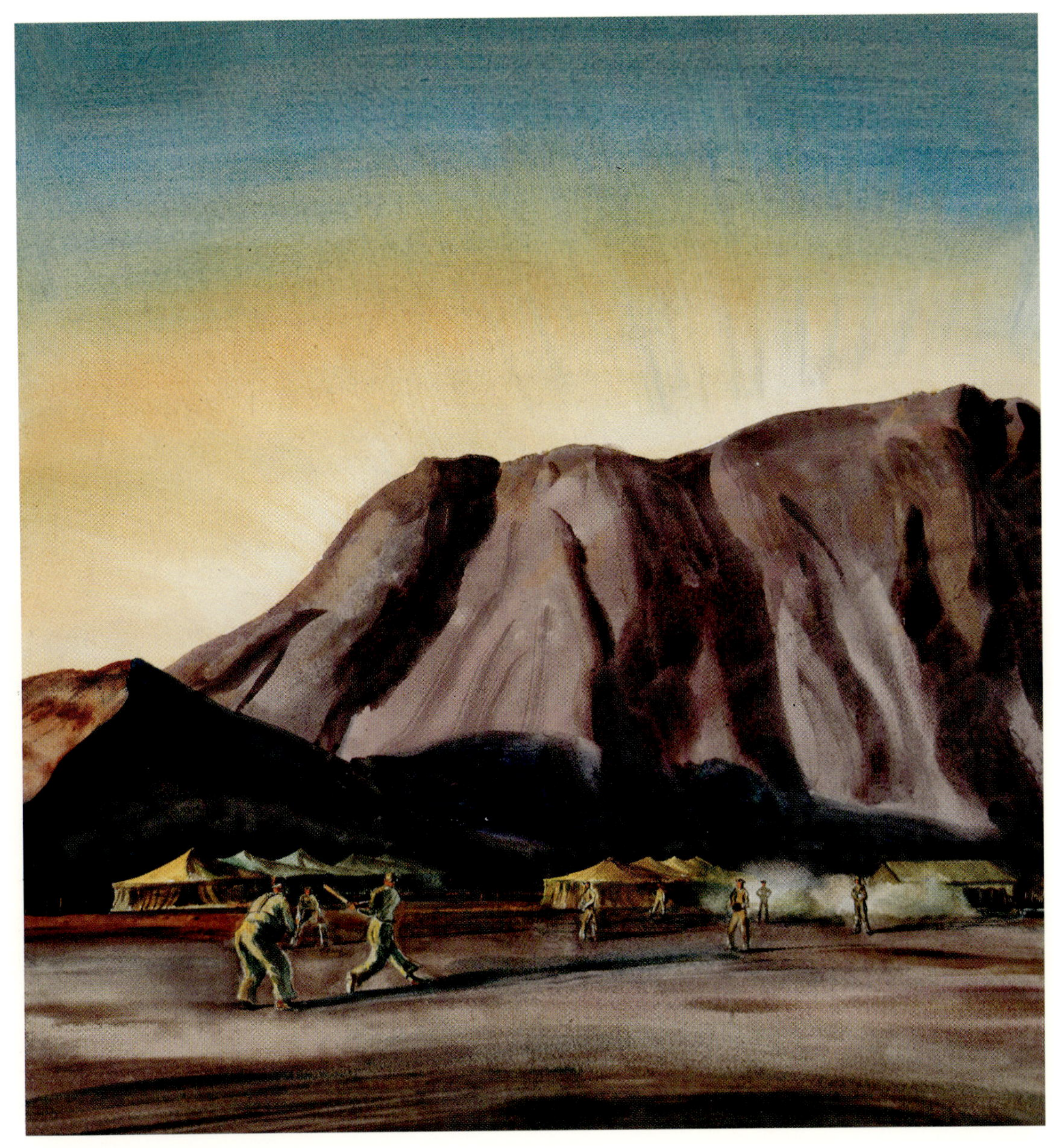

BASEBALL PRACTICE
Ascension Island
Peter Hurd, 1944
Watercolor, 19 ½″ x 21″

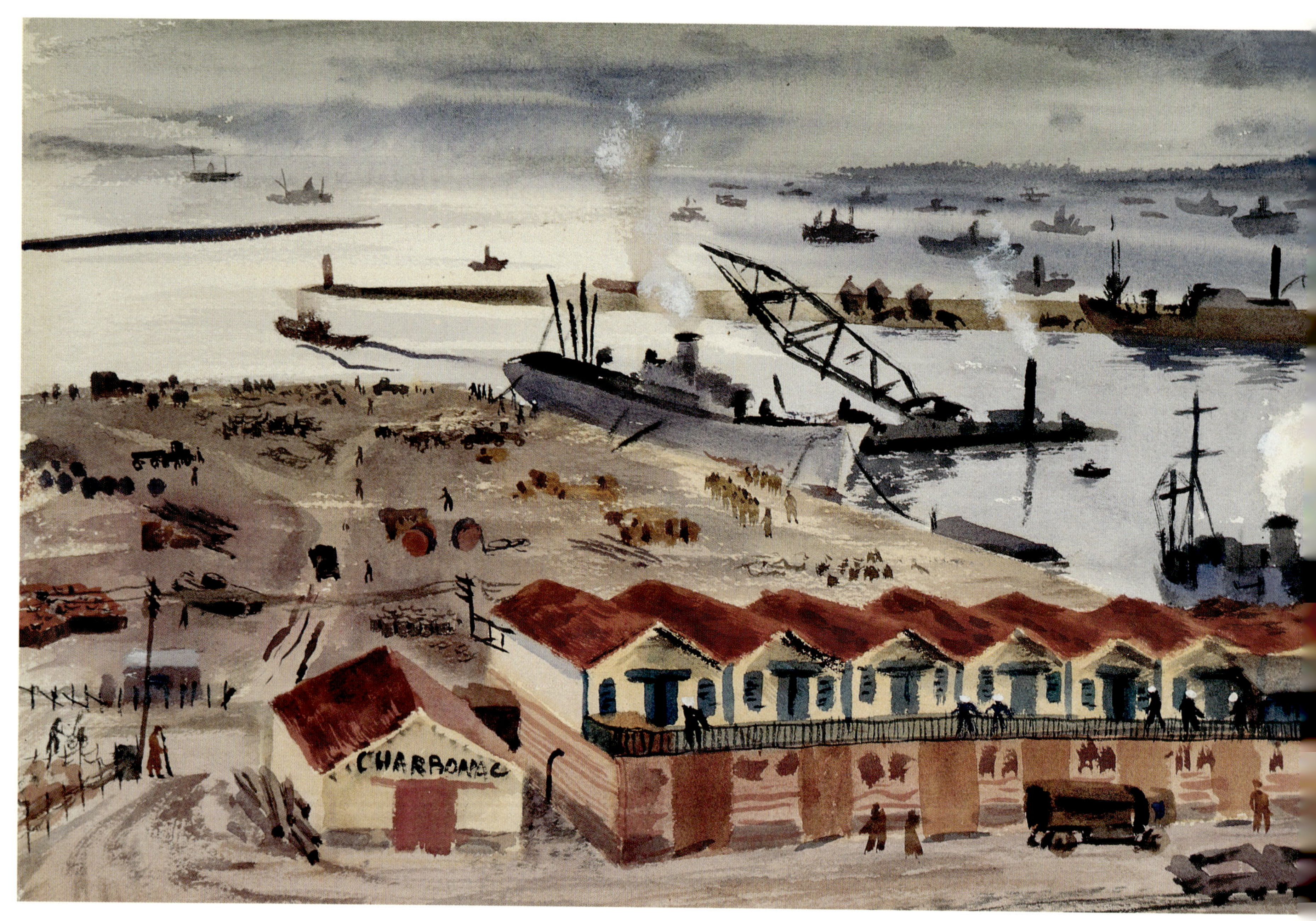

ALGIERS HARBOR
Algeria
Tom Craig, 1943
Watercolor, 9 ½" x 22"

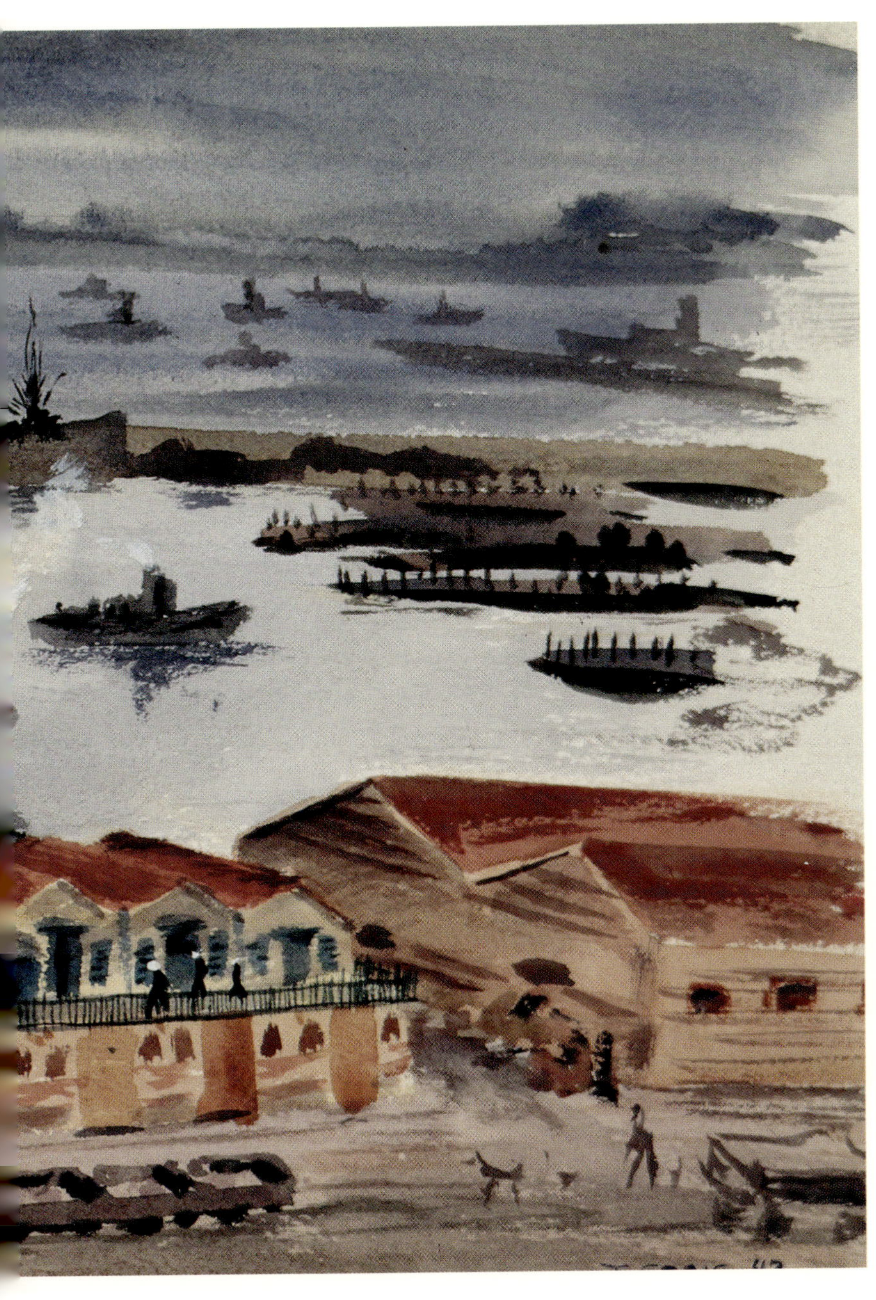

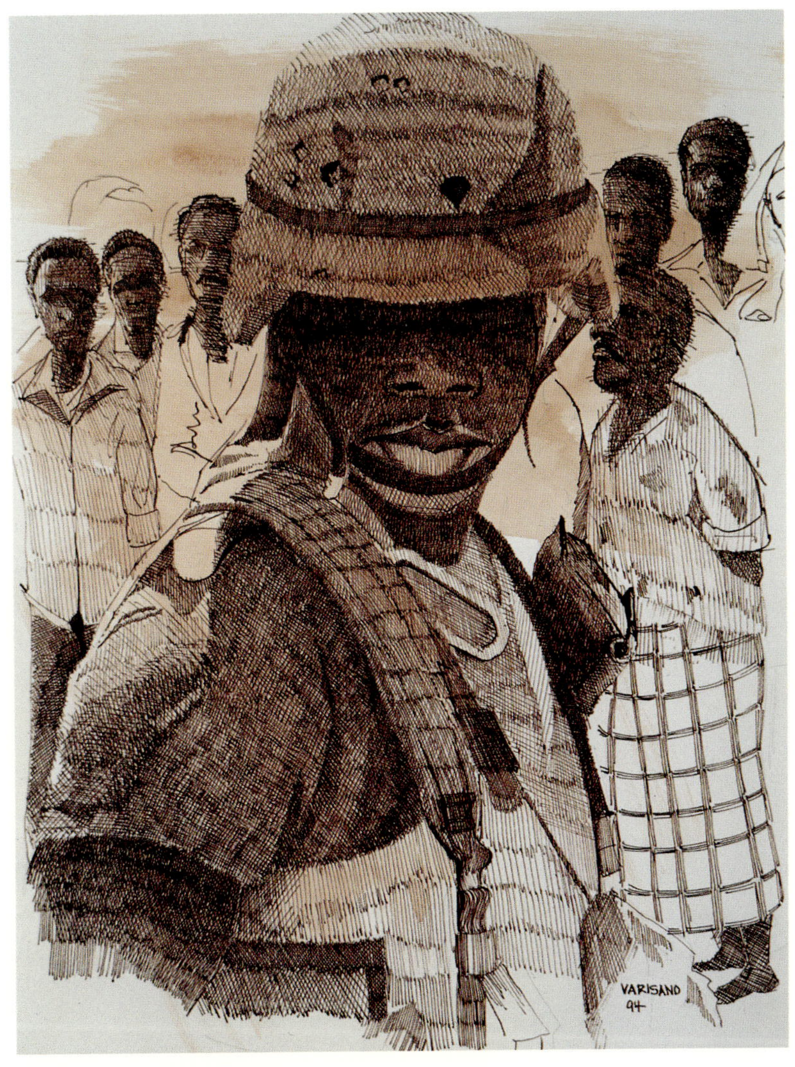

MP AT UNIVERSITY GATE
Somalia
Peter G. Varisano, 1994
Ink, 16 ¼" x 12 ½"

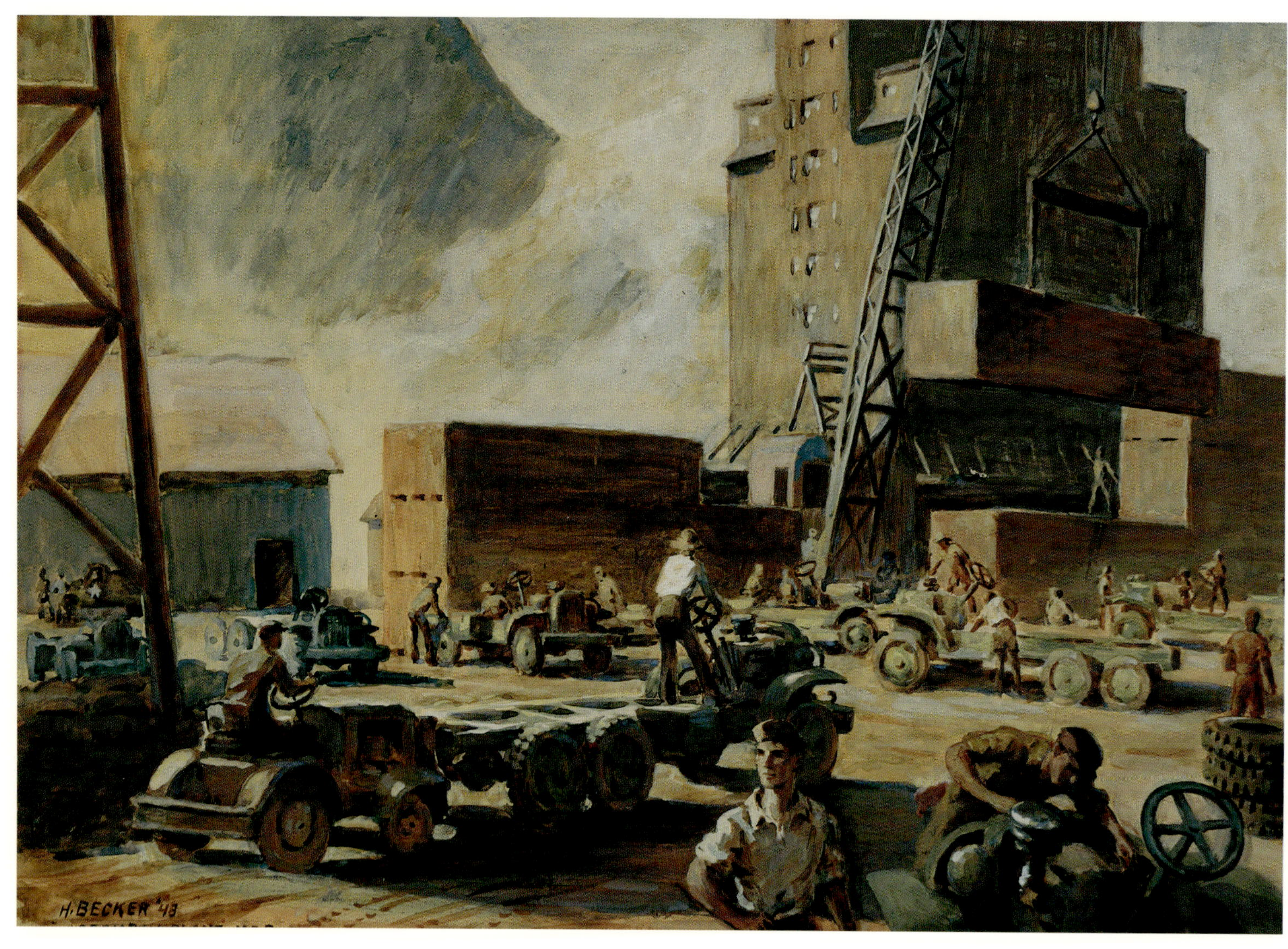

ASSEMBLY PLANT
Cazes, Morocco
Howard D. Becker, 1946
Watercolor, 12 ½" x 17 ¼"

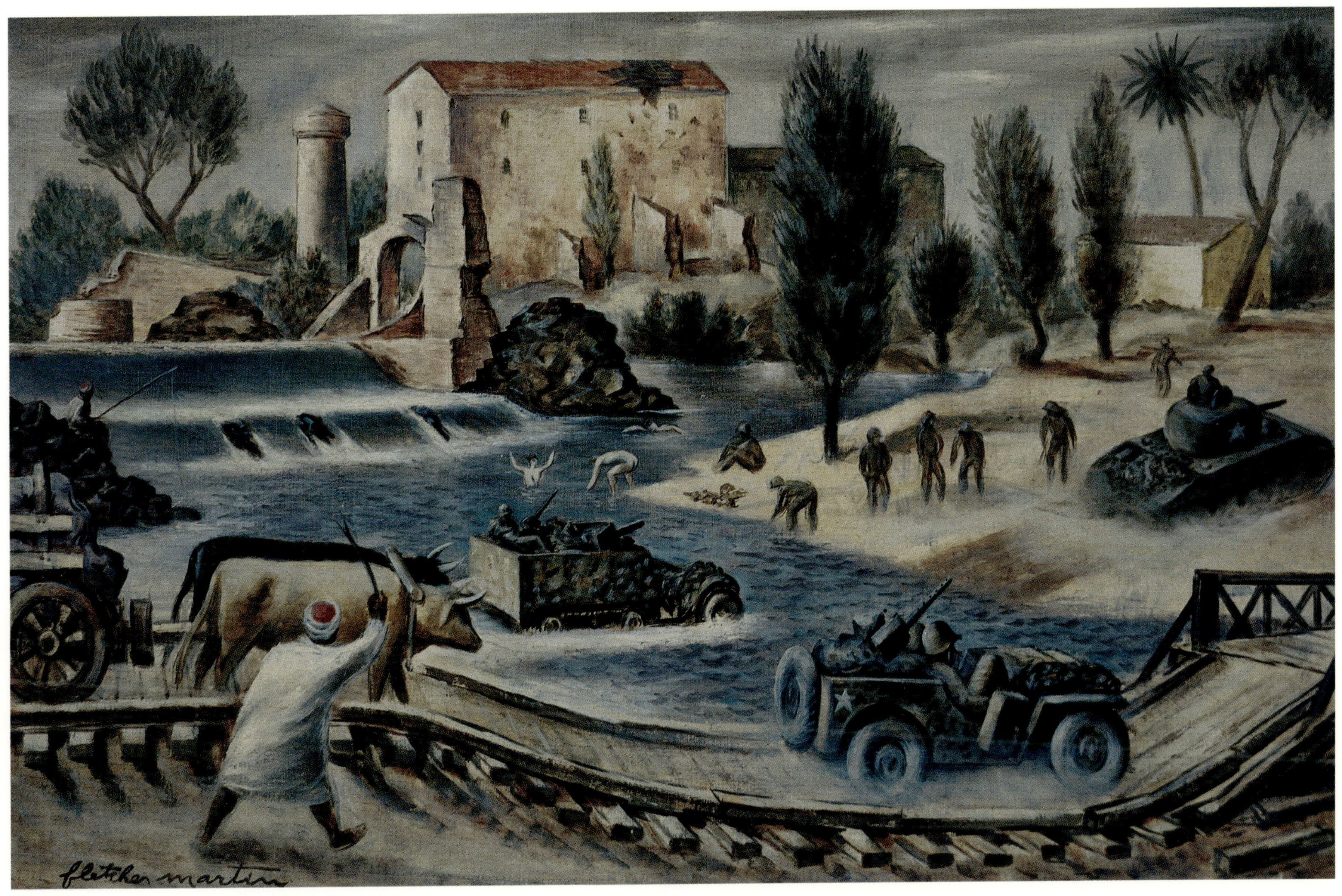

RIVER CROSSING
North Africa
Fletcher Martin, 1943
Oil, 21" x 32"

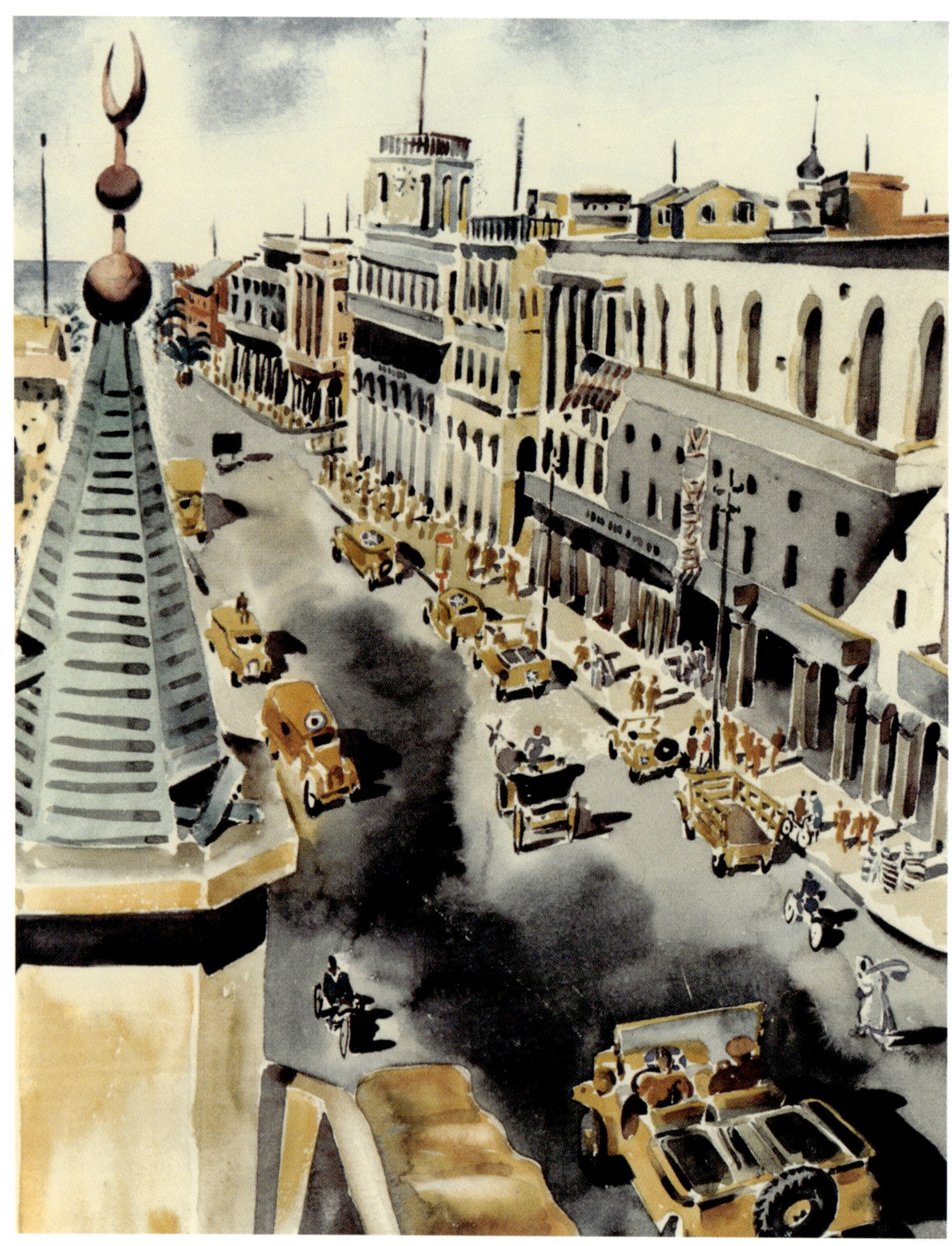

AMERICAN HEADQUARTERS IN TRIPOLI
Libya
Milton Marx, 1943
Watercolor, 20 ½" x 14 ½"

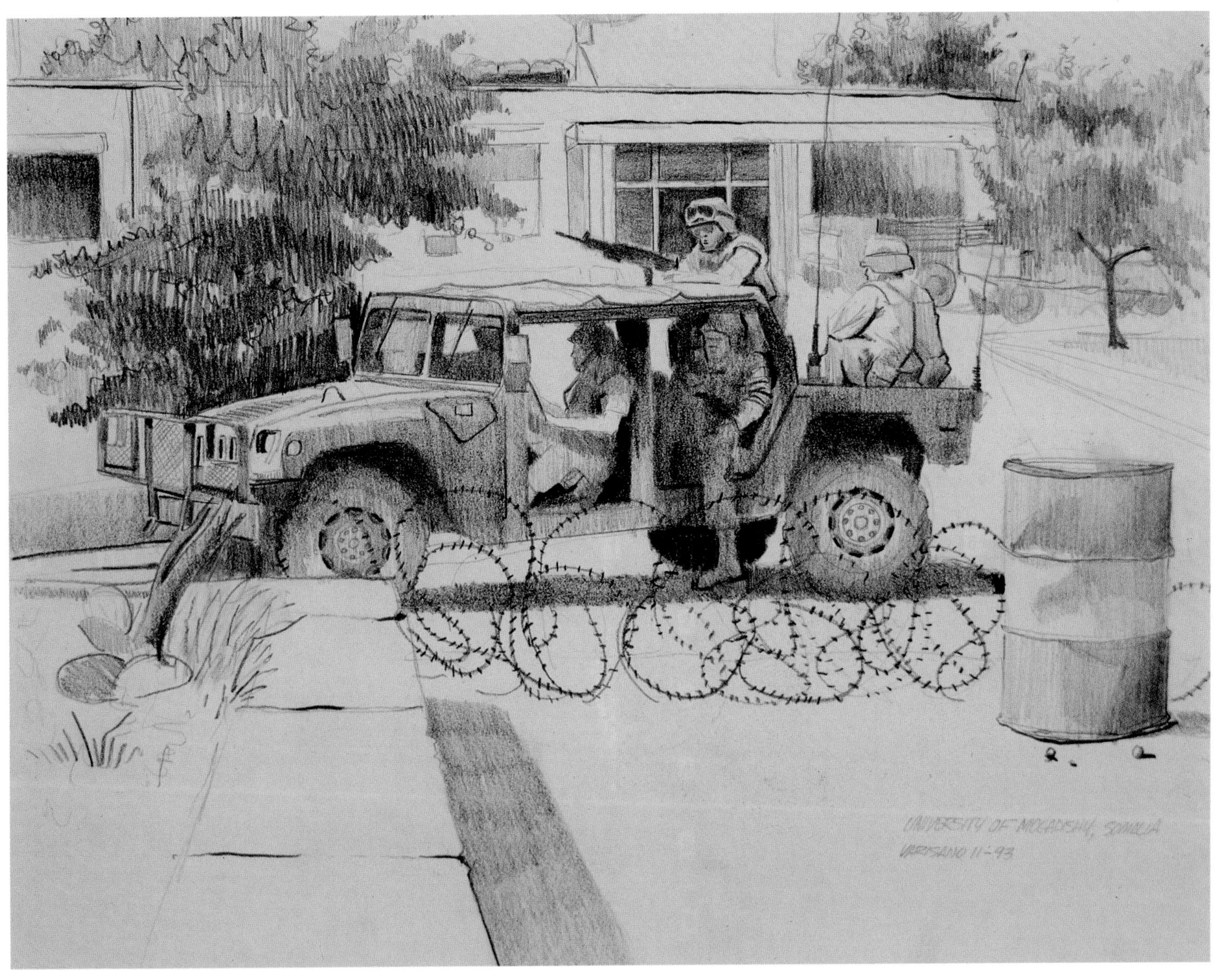

UNIVERSITY OF MOGADISHU
Somalia
Peter G. Varisano, 1993
Pencil, 13 ½" x 17"

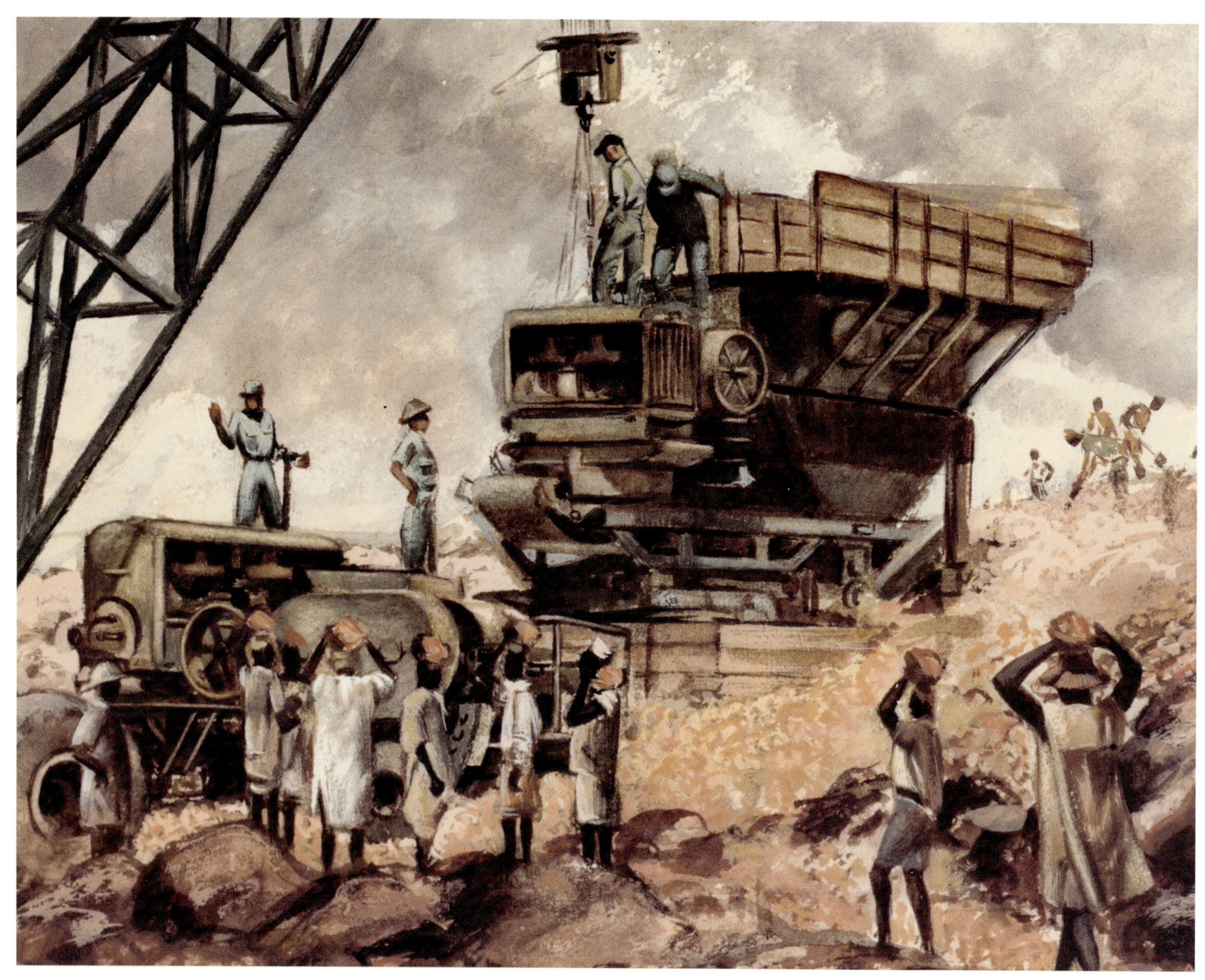

TWO CIVILIZATIONS
Africa
Samuel D. Smith, 1944
Watercolor, 9" x 11 ⅞"

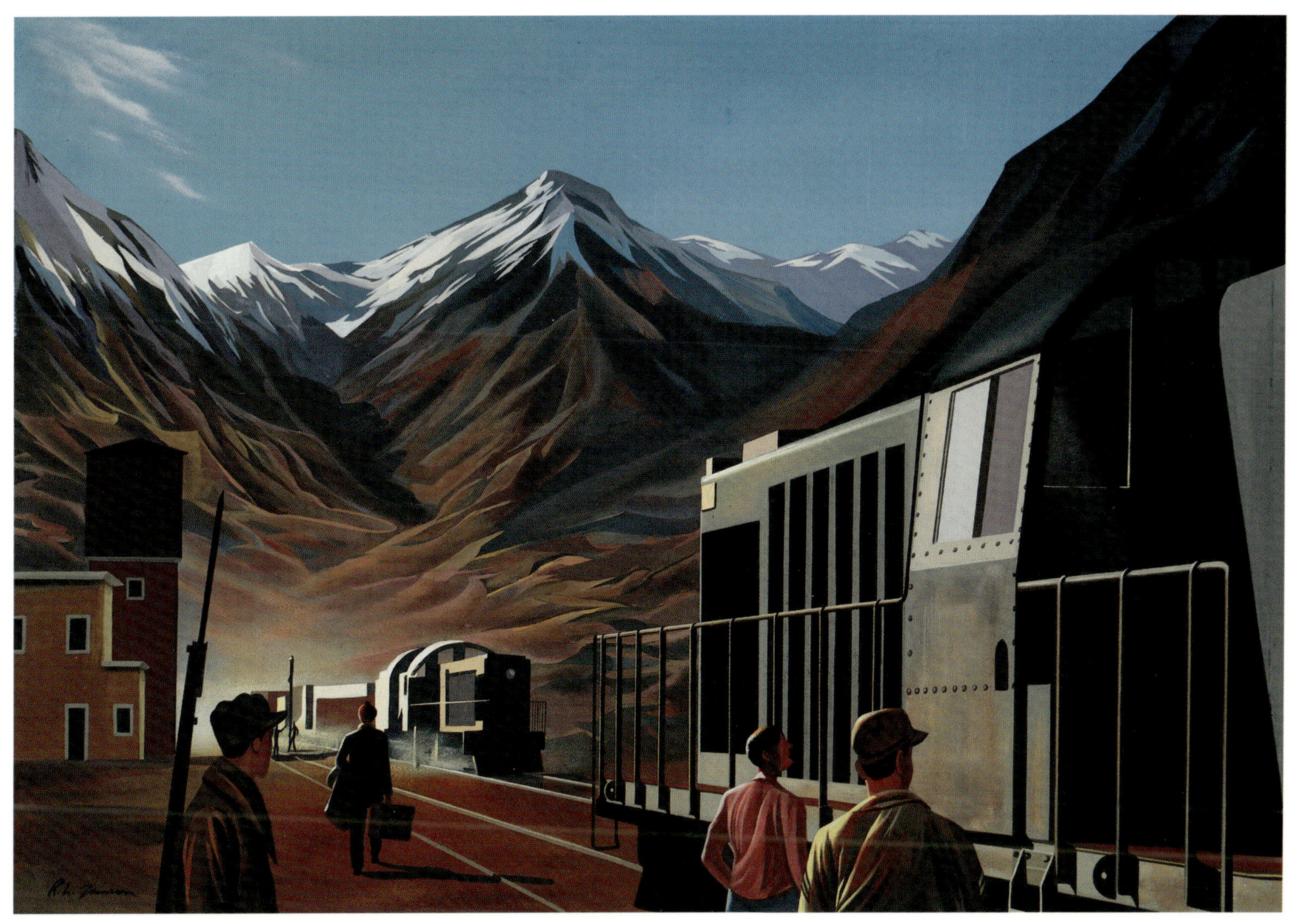

TRANS-IRANIAN RAILROAD
Daroud, Iran
Richard H. Jansen, 1944
Watercolor, 25 ½" x 34 ½"

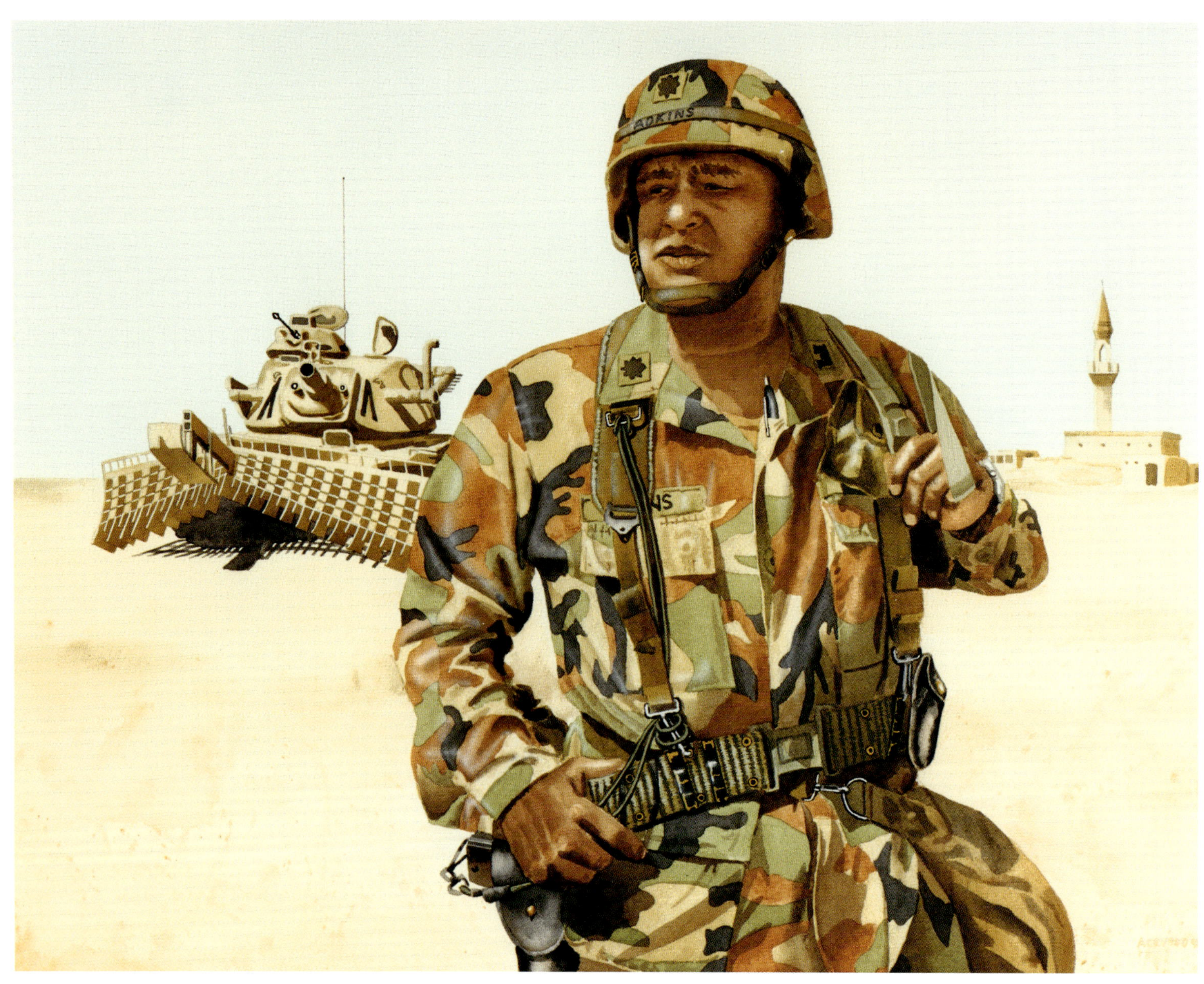

THE DIVISION ENGINEER
Saudi Arabia
Mario H. Acevedo, 1991
Watercolor, 18" x 24"

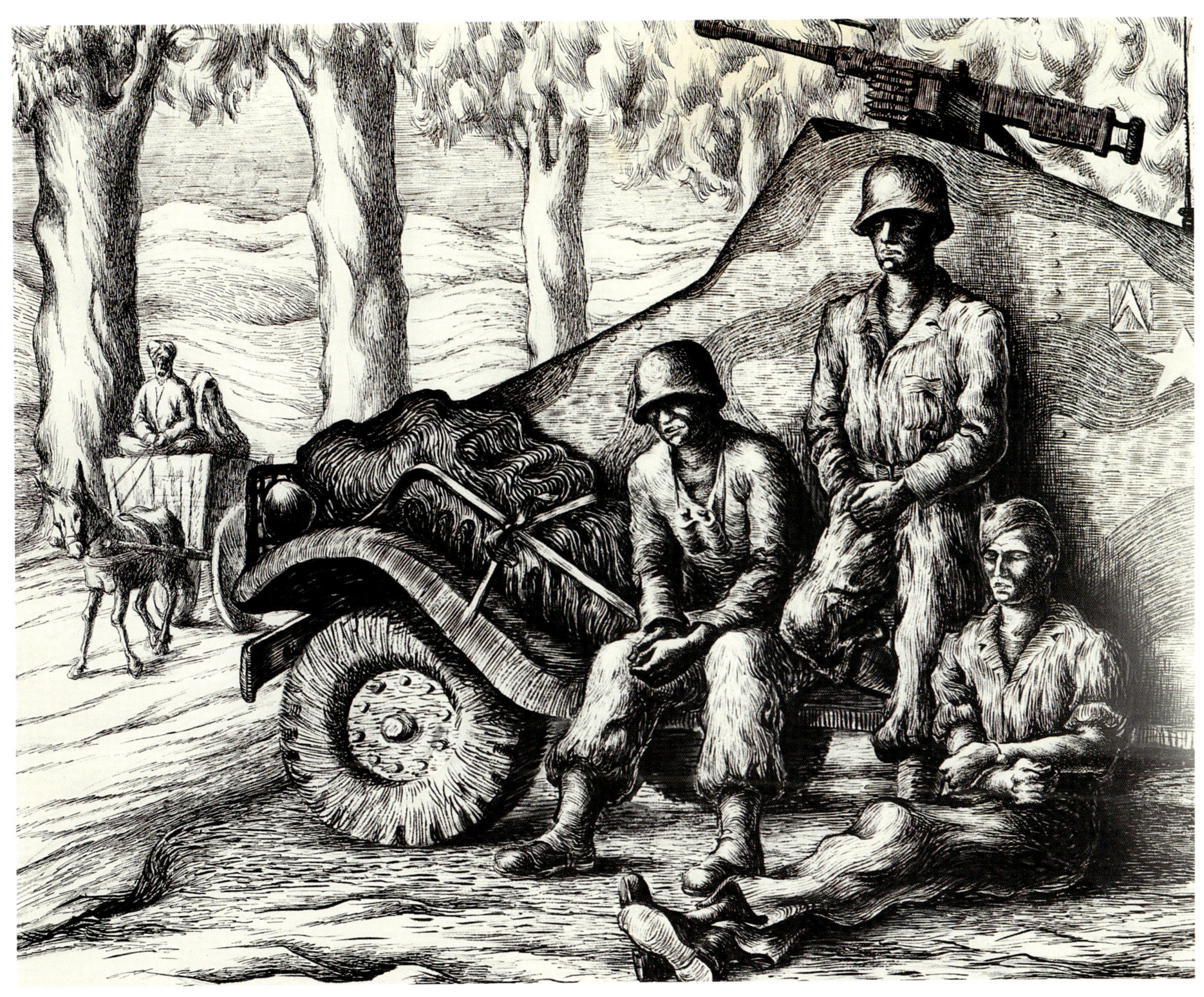

RECONNAISSANCE CAR CREW
Africa
Rudolph C. Von Ripper, 1943
Ink, 15" x 19"

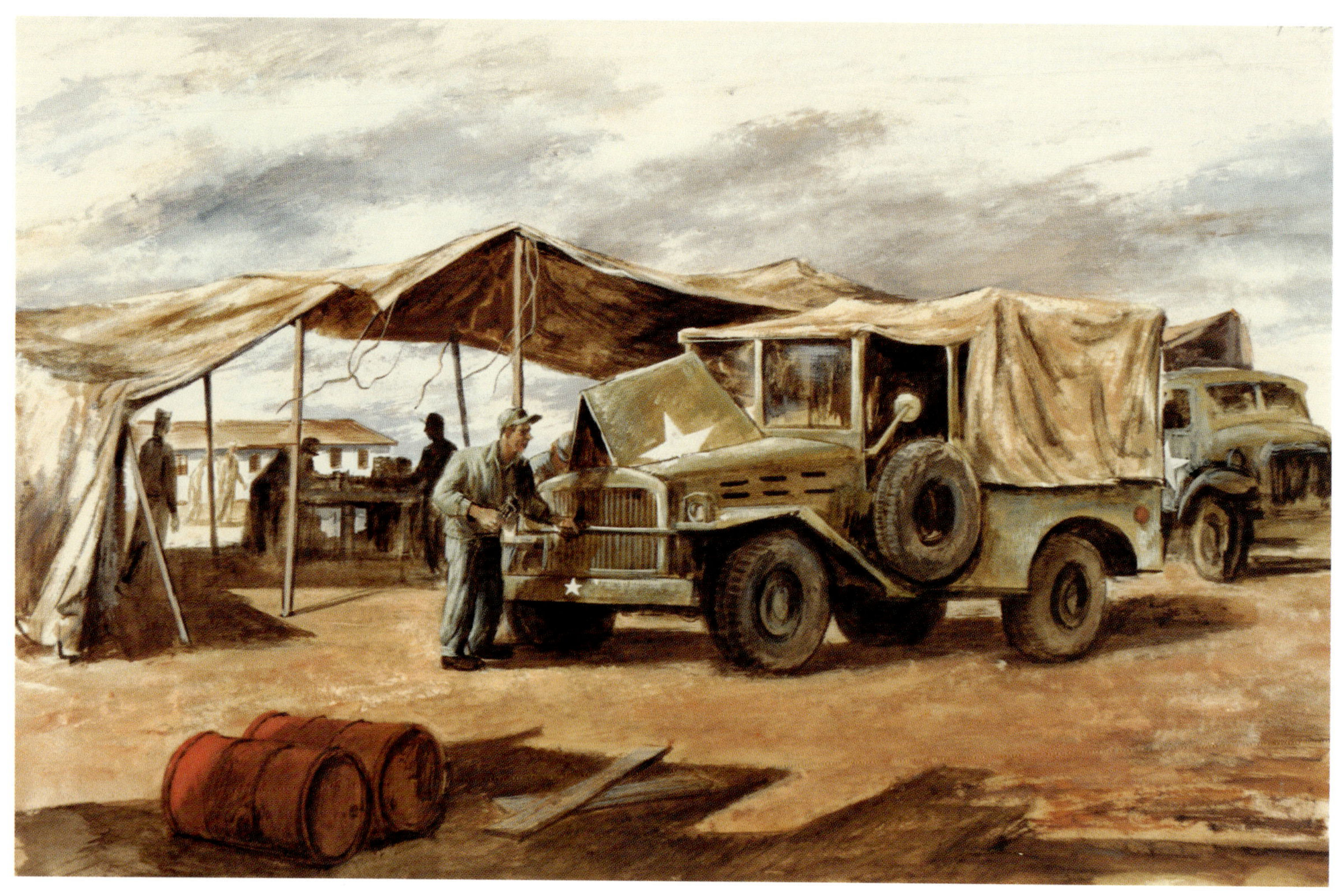

AT THE GARAGE
Central Africa
Carlos Lopez, 1943
Watercolor, 19" x 29"

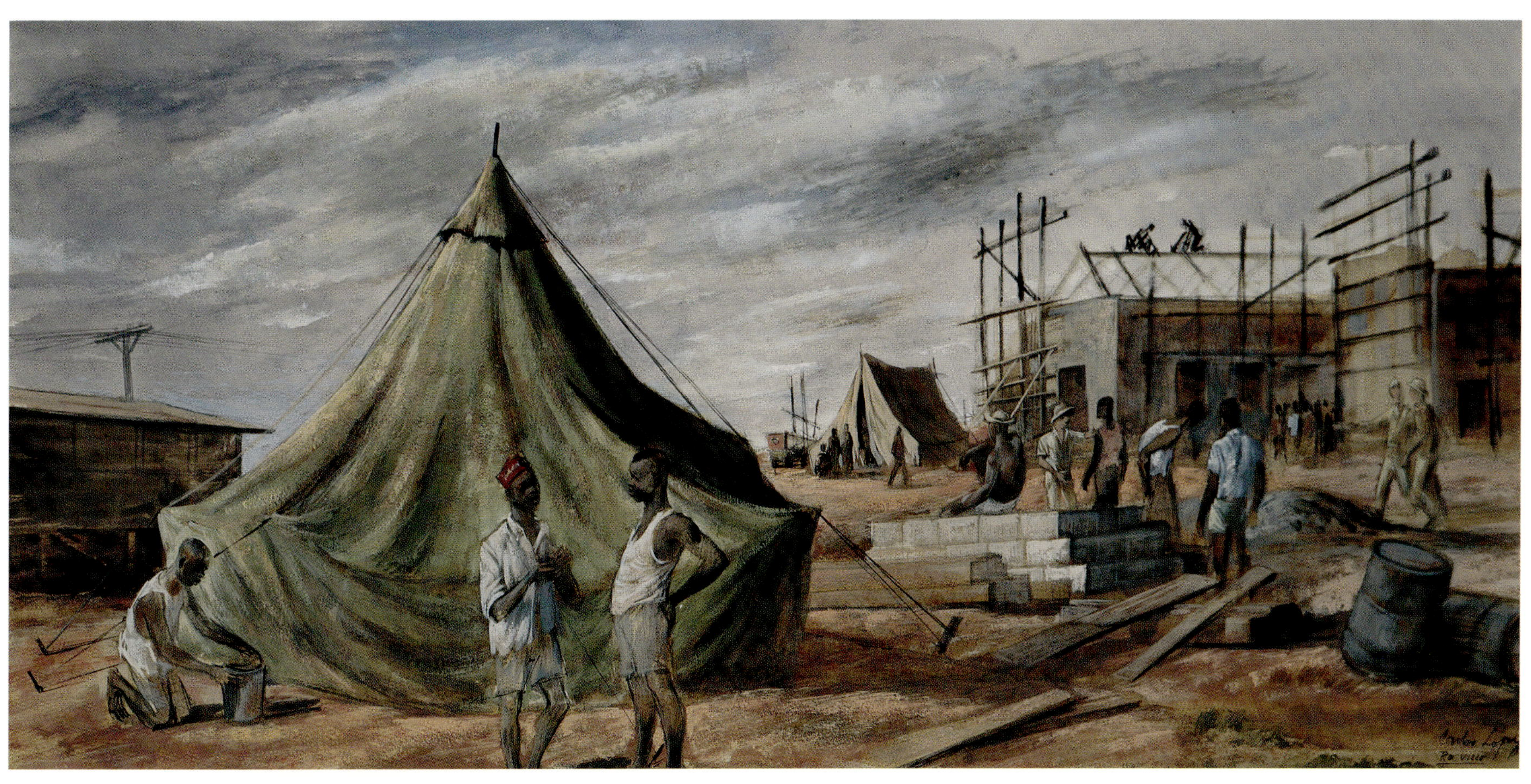

NATIVE LABOR
Africa
Carlos Lopez, 1943
Watercolor, 13 ½" x 27"

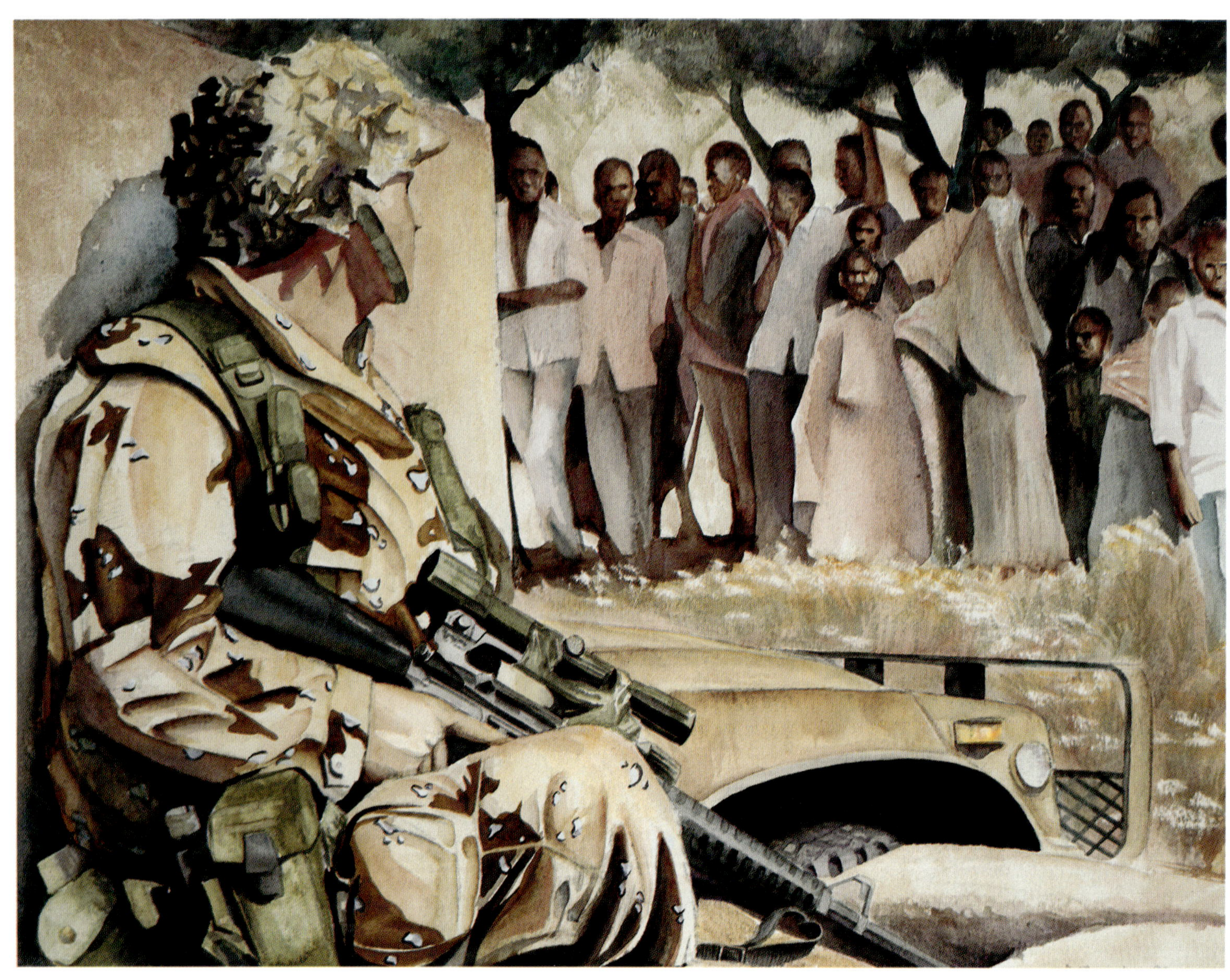

ON THE ALERT
Somalia
Jeffrey T. Manuszak, 1994
Watercolor, 18" x 24"

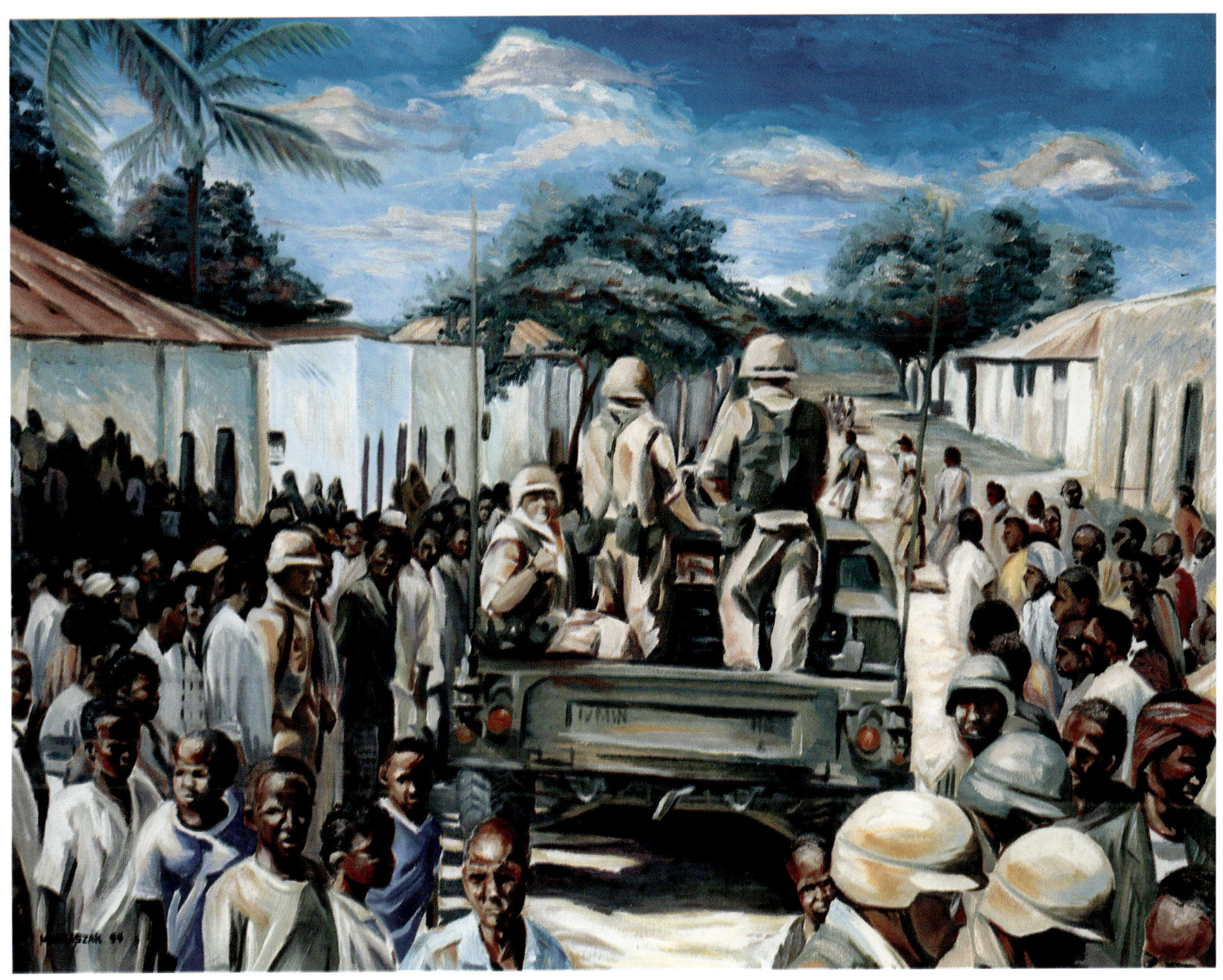

ON THE TOWN
Somalia
Jeffrey T. Manuszak, 1994
Oil, 22" x 28"

Appendixes

The Artists

Mario H. Acevedo was born in El Paso, Texas, in 1955 and studied at New Mexico State University. He describes himself as being self-taught in art. He was a captain in the Army Reserve when called to active duty to record DESERT STORM. He served six months as a soldier-artist. **(153, 168)**

Augustine Acuna studied at the University of Arizona. He was a second lieutenant when he served on Soldier-Artist Team 2 in Vietnam, October 1966–February 1967. **(108)**

George Akimoto was born in 1922 in Stockton, California. He was relocated to Rohwer Relocation Center, Arkansas, in 1942. From 1943–45, he studied at the Art Students League, and from 1945–48 he worked with an advertising company in Miami, Florida. After his return to California, he worked as an illustrator for Douglas Aircraft Company and as a free-lance advertising artist for motion picture companies. **(133)**

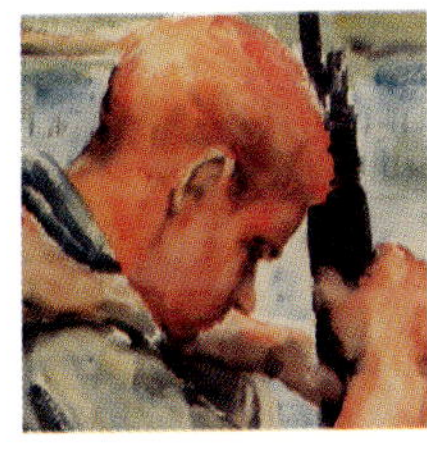

Samuel E. Alexander was born in 1943. He received his bachelor of fine arts degree from the Ringling School of Art in Sarasota, Florida, in 1966. At the time of his selection to Soldier-Artist Team 4, August–December 1967, he was assigned to the Information Office, Headquarters Company, U.S. Army, Vietnam. **(107, 126, 134)**

Leslie E. Anderson was born July 1, 1904, in Trent, South Dakota. He studied at the Minneapolis School of Art and the University of Minnesota with Cameron Booth. He entered the service in August 1942 with a direct commission as second lieutenant in the Air Corps. In January 1945 he was transferred to the Southwest Pacific, where he worked as a liaison officer and executed many drawings of Hollandia, New Guinea. In November 1945 he was detailed to the War Art Unit and transferred to Tokyo. **(116)**

Bernard Arnest was born February 19, 1917, in Denver, Colorado. He received degrees from the Colorado Springs Fine Arts Center, North Cascade, Colorado, and Colorado Springs College. Arnest entered the service November 1, 1941, and was discharged in February 1945 with the rank of first lieutenant. He was appointed official war artist in 1943 and was a member of the original War Art Unit sent to Iceland. He was Chief Artist, Historical Section, European Theater of Operations, from 1944–45. He covered the battle in the Ardennes and participated in one of the first patrols during the meeting of American forces with the Russians. Arnest died in 1985 in Colorado. **(66, 88)**

Numbers in parentheses indicate page where an artist's work appears.

Howard Baer was born in Pittsburgh, Pennsylvania, in 1907. He studied art at the Carnegie Institute, Pittsburgh. Baer was commissioned by Abbott Laboratories as an artist-correspondent to record the work of the WAVES in Aviation at the Anacostia Naval Base, Maryland, and at the WAVES Training Center, Norman, Oklahoma. His second assignment for Abbott Laboratories from April–September 1944 sent him to the China-Burma-India theater. There he traveled up and down the Burma Road, to the front with Stilwell's forces in Kunming and Chungking, with Merrill's Marauders, and to Calcutta depicting the work of the Army Medical Department. **(114, 137)**

George Banagis served in the U.S. Navy, 1968–72, where one of his duties was art director on the USS *Midway*. He joined the U.S. Army in 1981 as an illustrator. He was selected for Soldier-Artist Team 30 to document Army involvement in Panama and Honduras, September–December 1992. **(45, 48)**

Howard D. Becker was born January 21, 1914, in Albany, New York. He studied at the Pratt Institute, where he received the highest honors in pictorial illustration, Class of 1935. Becker was drafted May 9, 1941, at Camp Upton, Long Island, New York, and assigned to 6th Port Headquarters as documentary artist by Col. R. Hunter Clarkson. He left Naples, Italy, with 6th Port Headquarters in August 1944 and landed at Marseille, France, August 29, 1944. There he painted and sketched the history of the occupation and reconstruction of the port. He was discharged October 7, 1945, at Fort Dix, New Jersey. **(162)**

Robert Benney was born July 16, 1904, in New York City. He studied art at the Cooper Union, the Art Students League, the Grand Central School of Art, and the National Academy of Design, all in New York City. He served as art director to industry and publications. In that capacity he did free-lance work for Abbott Laboratories for which he contributed to the Abbott Collection of Paintings of Army Medicine. **(3, 6, 12, 89, 123)**

George Biddle was born January 24, 1885, in Philadelphia, Pennsylvania. He studied law at Harvard and art at the Pennsylvania Academy of Fine Arts and the Julien Academie in Paris as well as in Munich. Biddle was chairman of the War Art Advisory Committee, which helped the Army to select the artists to paint a record of the war. He reached North Africa just as the Tunisian campaign was coming to an end. About ten days after the first attack Mr. Biddle went to Sicily and covered the Sicilian campaign. He was then assigned to an American cruiser which landed English commando groups for the attack on Italy. Biddle died in 1973. **(148)**

H. Robert Bizinsky was born in Georgia in 1915. He studied at the High Museum of Art, Atlanta, Georgia, 1936–42 and the Art Students League, 1942–46. He served with the combat engineers assigned to lst Armored Division in North Africa, 1942–46. He also served as artist for Atlantic Base Section in North Africa, 1944. Bizinsky died in 1982. **(64, 97)**

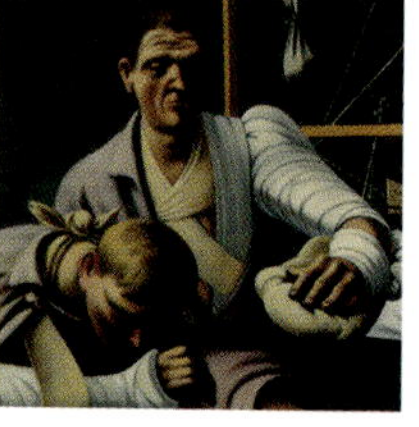

Peter Blume was born in Russia, October 27, 1906. He came to the United States with his family at the age of five. He received his art education from the New York City public schools, evening high school art classes, the Educational Alliance Art School, the Beaux Arts Institute of Design, and the Art Students League of New York. Abbott Laboratories commissioned him as an artist-correspondent to record the work of the Army Medical Corps. **(35)**

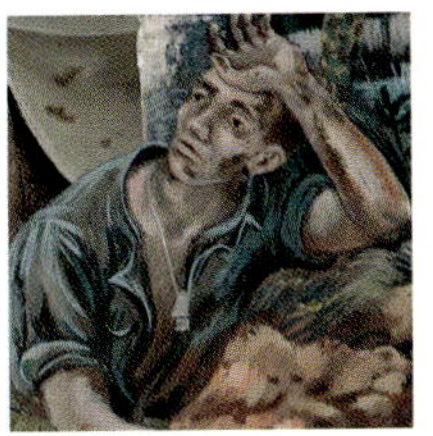

Aaron Bohrod was born November 21, 1907, in Chicago, Illinois. He studied at the Art Institute of Chicago and the Art Students League, New York City. In February 1943 he was engaged as an artist by the War Art Advisory Committee and assigned to the South Pacific Defense Command. When the program was suspended, he became an artist-correspondent with *Life* magazine, completing his assignment in the South Pacific before going to Europe, where he was assigned to the London office. He went to Normandy one week after the invasion and painted his way across northern Europe. Bohrod died in Madison, Wisconsin, in 1992. **(62, 65, 84, 118, 123, 126)**

Howard Brodie was born November 28, 1915, in Oakland, California. He studied at the California School of Fine Arts. Brodie enlisted August 1, 1942, and was discharged January 8, 1946, with the rank of technical sergeant. He was assigned to *Yank, The Army Weekly*, and sent to Guadalcanal as a combat artist in December 1942. In 1944 he was sent to Europe to cover the Ardennes and the Rhineland campaigns. He was awarded the Bronze Star for coverage of an assault. **(125)**

Alexander Brook was born in Brooklyn, New York, on July 14, 1898. He studied at the Art Students League with Kenneth Hayes Miller. He won many prizes for his work, including a Guggenheim Fellowship. He served on the staff of *Life* magazine as an artist-correspondent. Brook died in 1980 in Sag Harbor, New York. **(19)**

Robert C. Burns was born in 1916 in Lagrange, Illinois. He studied at the Yale Art School, graduating in 1939 with a bachelor of fine arts degree, and received a bachelor of arts degree in 1941 from Rollins College, Winter Park, Florida. He was inducted at Camp Blanding, Florida, in November 1941 and transferred to the 30th Topographic Engineers, Fort Belvoir, Virginia. In the capacity of artist, he worked on illustrations for training manuals, murals, charts, and film strips for the Division of Training Publications for Antiaircraft Artillery. Burns was discharged from Fort Bliss, Texas, with the rank of staff sergeant in November 1945. He retired from teaching at Trenton State College, Trenton, New Jersey, in 1977. **(41)**

William V. Caldwell was born December 9, 1914, in Pittsburgh, Pennsylvania. He studied at Carnegie Institute of Technology in Pittsburgh and at the Yale School of Fine Arts. He also studied under Samuel Rosenberg. He entered the service February 14, 1942. In September 1944 he was sent to Italy to illustrate activities of GIs at a replacement depot. Later he went with the 337th Infantry to the Apennines as the regimental artist. After V–E Day he was transferred to the Historical Section, G–3, AFHQ, to continue developing his sketches. Caldwell was discharged November 30, 1945, as a corporal. **(63, 98)**

Conrad Wise Chapman was born in Rome in 1842. His father, the artist John Gadsby Chapman, was his first teacher. When the Civil War started, Chapman joined the Confederate Army and made many pictures of army life. He died in Virginia in 1910. **(11)**

Joseph Cummings Chase was born May 5, 1878, in Kents Hill, Maine. He studied with Jean Paul Laurens and was the chairman of the Art Department at Hunter College in New York City. Chase is best known for his portraits of General John J. Pershing, Marshal Ferdinand Foch, and other officers of the American Expeditionary Forces in France. He also painted portraits of many of the presidents. Fifty of his portraits are in the Smithsonian Institution, Washington, D.C. Chase died in New York City in 1965. **(97)**

Brian H. Clark received his bachelor of fine arts degree from Wayne State University, Detroit, Michigan, in June 1965 and studied at the Academie de la Grande Chaumiere, Paris, from June –August 1965. He entered the Army in 1966 and was assigned to Psychological Operations, Fort Bragg, North Carolina, as an illustrator. Clark was selected for Soldier-Artist Team 7, which documented the war in Vietnam from August–December 1968. **(138)**

Howard Norton Cook was born in Springfield, Massachusetts, in 1901. He studied at the Art Students League in New York City from 1918–21. He painted murals in fresco for the Section of Fine Arts of the Treasury Department. He executed work for *Life* and *Colliers* magazines. Cook was an artist-correspondent under a War Department contract, assigned to the engineers and based at Noumea, New Caledonia, April–August 1943. He made a pictorial record of action at Guadalcanal, landing with the 43d Division on New Georgia Island, June 1943. He died in 1980. **(115, 130)**

Tom Craig was born in 1909 in Upland, California. He studied at Pomona College and the University of California. *Life* magazine assigned him to Italy during 1943–44 as an artist-correspondent. **(80, 82, 160)**

Floyd Davis was born in Chicago in 1896. He served with the Navy in World War I and was honorably discharged in 1918. Davis produced a series of nine paintings on Bermuda in 1942 for *Life* magazine. In 1943 and again in 1944 he went to England with his wife, artist Gladys Rockwell Davis, as a war correspondent to cover England and France after the Normandy invasion. Davis died in 1966. **(5, 67, 91)**

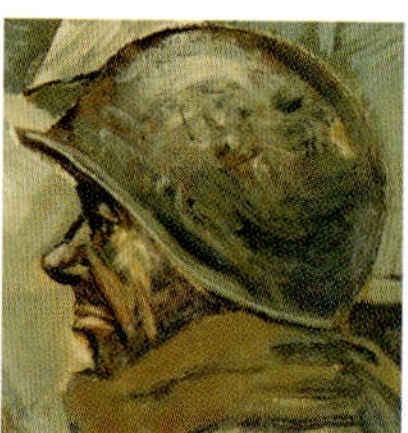

Raymond Desvarraus. Biographical information not available. **(75)**

Harry Dix was born in Seattle, Washington, in 1907. He studied at Eton College, England, and at the Art Students League, New York City. His first military assignment was at Keesler Field, Mississippi, where he executed murals and paintings for the day room. Later he was stationed in London, where he was attached to the Historical Section, G–3, AFHQ, as an artist and photographer. His assignments included England, France, and Germany. Dix died in 1968. **(61)**

Olin Dows was born August 14, 1904, in Irvington-on-Hudson, New York. He studied at the Harvard and Yale Departments of Fine Arts and at the Art Students League, New York City. Dows enlisted in June 1942. He gave up an opportunity for officer training to head a group of three war artists to cover the European Theater of Operations. One month after he arrived in England the program was suspended. He was then attached to the 166th Signal Photo Unit and went with it to Normandy in June 1944. Dows was also attached to the 35th Division from June–September 1944 and saw action at Bastogne and Metz and with the Third Army across Germany. He was present at the meeting of American and Soviet forces. Dows was discharged in August 1945 as a technical sergeant. **(78, 83, 100, 104)**

O. I. Dudley. Biographical information not available. **(38)**

Alexander Edouart was born November 5, 1818, in London. He was educated in Edinburgh and studied art in Italy. He was living in New York City in 1848–50 and exhibited at the National Academy and the American Art Union. About 1852 he went to California, where he spent the rest

of his life except for a brief trip to Europe about 1859. Though he painted some California landscapes, he was best known as a photographer in San Francisco. About 1889 he moved to Los Angeles, where he died in 1892. **(10)**

E. W. Emerson. Biographical information not available. **(24)**

Brian Fairchild was educated in Pennsylvania and Maryland before being assigned to Illustration/Graphics Documentation, Lowry Air Force Base, Colorado. He was a staff sergeant assigned to the NCO Illustrators School at the time of his selection to Soldier-Artist Team 29. His assignment was to spend ninety days in Korea from February–May 1992. **(119, 128)**

Patrick Farrell graduated from Litchfield, Connecticut, High School and entered the Rhode Island School of Design. He received a bachelor of fine arts degree in 1984. He entered the Army in April 1985 as a motion picture documentation specialist. From 1985–87 he produced videotapes for the Training Support Center at Fort Lewis, Washington. He held the rank of specialist, fourth class, at the time of his selection to Soldier-Artist Team 22, which documented training at the National Training Center, Fort Irwin, California, August–October 1988. **(50)**

Gerald W. Ferguson. Biographical information not available. **(124)**

Gaylord Flory. Biographical information not available. **(34)**

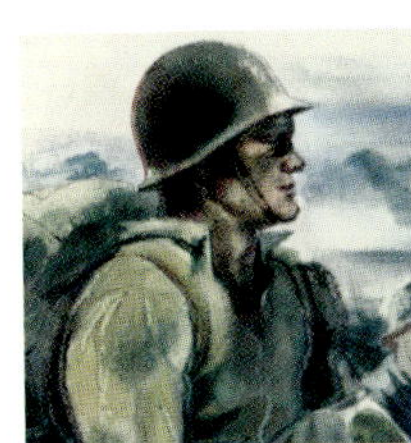

David Fredenthal was born April 27, 1914, in Detroit, Michigan. He studied at the Cranbrook Academy of Art, Bloomfield Hills, Michigan; the Wicker School of Art, Detroit; and the Colorado Springs, Colorado, Fine Arts Center with Boardman Robinson. Originally a civilian artist in the War Department Art Program, he became a *Life* magazine correspondent and continued his work begun with the South Pacific War Art Unit. Fredenthal died in 1958. **(83, 110, 119, 136)**

Albert Gold was born in Philadelphia on October 31, 1916, and studied at the Pennsylvania Museum School of Industrial Art. He was inducted into the Army in May 1942. In May 1943 he was selected by the War Art Advisory Committee to go overseas as a war artist. He was sent to England to make a pictorial record of the development of U.S. military concentrations. His work also appeared in the Continental edition of *Yank*. Gold was discharged December 1945 with the rank of technical sergeant. **(71)**

Elzie Golden studied at the School of Visual Arts in New York City and the University of Arizona. He was assigned to Training Support Activities, Eighth Army East–Korea, where he was an instructor in the computer graphics section and worked on animation techniques to enhance video capabilities while producing instructional videos for computer graphics operations. He was a sergeant in the U.S. Army when, as a member of Soldier-Artist Team 25 in 1990, he documented ROTC training at Fort Lewis, Washington. **(32)**

Robert MacDonald Graham, Jr., was born in New Rochelle, New York, November 1, 1919. He was the son of an Army officer and spent most of his early life moving from post to post. From 1937–41 he studied art at the Kansas City Art Institute with Thomas Hart Benton and John de Martelly. He was inducted into the Army in February 1942 at Fort Leavenworth, Kansas. He had various administrative assignments in the United States and overseas. Graham executed a large painting for the Far East Air Service Command while that headquarters was located at Hollandia, Netherlands East Indies. This led to his assignment in September 1945 to the Combat Art Section of General Headquarters, Office of the Chief Engineer, in Manila. Graham was discharged November 1946 with the rank of first lieutenant. **(129)**

David Grinstein was born in Spokane, Washington, April 18, 1944. He is a graduate of San Diego State College. As a member of Soldier-Artist Team 10, he was assigned to visit military installations north and south of Seoul, Korea, from March–June 1970. **(135)**

John Groth was born in 1908. In World War II he worked for the *Chicago Sun* as an artist-correspondent. In that role he was the first artist into Berlin the day it fell to the Allies. In 1946 he began teaching at the Art Students League, a position he maintained for most of his life. He also covered the Korean War with both sketchbook and camera. Groth died in New York City in 1988. **(115)**

John G. Hanlen was born in Winfield, Kansas, in 1922. He studied art at the Pennsylvania Academy of Fine Arts and in independent study with George Harding. Part of his military career was spent in China, where he completed a large collection of drawings and watercolors. Following the war he taught at Moore College of Art and at the Pennsylvania Academy of Fine Arts until his retirement in 1984. **(ix, 121)**

George Harding was born in Philadelphia, October 1, 1882. He studied with Howard Pyle and at the Philadelphia School of Art from 1889–1902. Harding was one of eight artists selected to serve with the American Expeditionary Forces, receiving his appointment in March 1918. He was present during the Marne, St. Mihiel, and Argonne campaigns as well as the Army occupation of Germany. He received six campaign bars on the AEF medal and General Staff Certificates of Commendation for his drawings. He accepted reappointment to the Officers' Reserve Corps on several occasions between World Wars I and II, finally being appointed captain in the Marine Corps Reserve in August 1942. He died in Philadelphia in 1959. **(69)**

Sieger Hartgers was born in Apeldoorn, Netherlands, in 1949. He studied at the Akademie Voor Beeldende Kunsten in Arnhem, Netherlands. He joined the U.S. Army in 1972 as an illustrator assigned to the Sergeants Major Academy. In 1979 he was selected for an Army artist team to document Army training in jungle and desert conditions. As an instructor/supervisor at Lowry Air Force Base, Colorado, in 1990, he was called upon to document DESERT SHIELD in the Persian Gulf. **(144)**

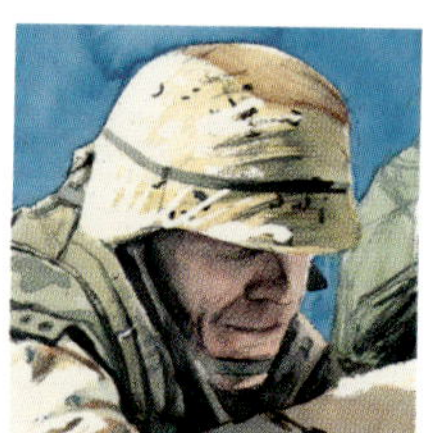

Richard Hasenauer attended Temple University's Tyler School of Fine Arts, Philadelphia, Pennsylvania. He joined the Army in 1974 and attended the DOD Mapping School at Fort Belvoir, Virginia. At the time of his selection to the Bicentennial artist team in 1976, he was a staff illustrator for *Army in Europe* magazine. The Bicentennial team documented the Army's participation in the festivities in the Washington, D.C., area from June–October 1976. **(30)**

Joseph S. Hindley is a native of New Jersey. He was assigned to the 121st Signal Battalion at Fort Riley, Kansas, when he was selected as a team member for Soldier-Artist Team 13 to document the REFORGER exercise in 1972. **(75)**

Joseph Hirsch was born April 25, 1920, in Philadelphia. He studied at the Pennsylvania Museum School of Industrial Art and with George Luks. He was commissioned by Abbott Laboratories to visit the European and Mediterranean Theaters of Operations to gather material for a series of paintings depicting the U.S. Army Medical Corps. He also went to the South Pacific, North Africa, and Italy as an artist-correspondent for the Navy. Hirsch died September 25, 1981, in New York City. **(viii, 99)**

Lester G. Hornby was born in 1882 in Lowell, Massachusetts. He studied at the Pape School of Art, Boston; Rhode Island School of Design, Providence; the Art Students League, New York City; and a number of European academies. In 1918 General John J. Pershing provided him with a pass to move freely through the American armies. He spent six months making sketches of frontline action, participating in the advances along the Marne and the Meuse. He died in 1956. **(64)**

Peter Hurd was born in 1904 in Roswell, New Mexico. He received his early education at the New Mexico Military Academy, followed by two years at the U.S. Military Academy. Then he turned his full attention to studying art at Haverford College in Philadelphia and at the Pennsylvania Academy of Art. During World War II he was attached to the Eighth Air Force and worked as an artist-correspondent for *Life* magazine. He died in New Mexico in 1984. **(26, 59, 72, 154, 159)**

Richard H. Jansen was born on July 25, 1919. He executed murals in the United States post offices in Lincolnton, North Carolina, and Reedsburg, Wisconsin, for the Section of Fine Arts of the Treasury Department. **(155, 167)**

Chester Jezerski attended high school in Clark's Summit, Pennsylvania, before studying at the Rhode Island School of Design. He served in the Army from 1966–70. He was assigned to Air Cavalry Troop, 6th Armored Cavalry Regiment, Fort Meade, Maryland, at the time of his selection for Soldier-Artist Team 10, February–June 1970, to document the Army in Korea. **(112)**

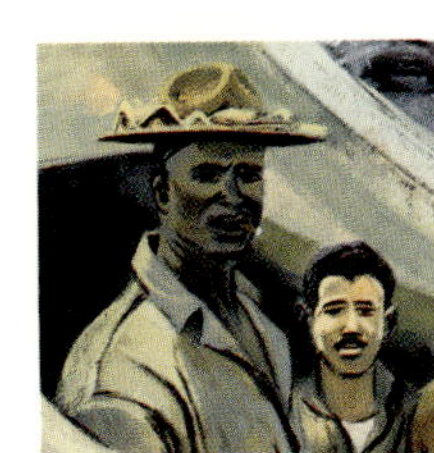

Joe Jones was born April 7, 1909, in St. Louis, Missouri. He was a self-taught artist, leaving school at the age of fourteen. By the age of twenty-three he was a recognized artist. In 1939, working for the Section of Fine Arts of the Treasury Department, he executed murals in five post offices, depicting the life of farm workers in the fields. As a private in the Army he was sent to Alaska to document the terrain as part of the War Art Unit. His work was picked up by *Life* magazine as part of its oversight of the program. **(13, 16)**

Steven R. Kidd was born in Chicago on June 11, 1911. He studied at the Art Students League in New York City with George R. Bridgman and attended classes in painting with Harvey Dunn at the Grand Central School of Art. His military career began in January 1943 when he was drafted into the Coast Artillery and given the assignment of acting camouflage sergeant. He also worked in Training Aids at Camp Crofton, Spartenburg, South Carolina. His next assignment was to the Psychological Warfare Branch on Leyte. There he received his assignment to the War Art Unit under Barse Miller. Miller assigned him to cover the occupation of Korea. **(139)**

F. Holroyd Lambert. Biographical information not available. **(51)**

Edward R. Laning was born April 16, 1906, in Petersburg, Illinois. He studied at the Art Institute of Chicago and at the Art Students League in New York with Max Weber, Boardman Robinson, John Sloan, and Kenneth H. Miller. In 1935 he began work on the Ellis Island Mural Project and installed the mural in 1937. Laning was selected for the War Art Unit for duty in Alaska, but he had accepted an assignment from *Life* magazine in February 1943. As a *Life* artist-correspondent he served in the Aleutians in 1943 and in Italy and North Africa in 1944. Laning was wounded by fragments of a German mortar shell and received a Purple Heart. He died May 6, 1981, in New York City. **(2, 37, 56, 76)**

Wayne D. Larabee was a first lieutenant when he was sent to China with the War Art Unit during World War II. He continued to paint and now lives in the Washington, D.C., area. **(111)**

Tom Lea was born in El Paso, Texas, in 1907. He studied at the Art Institute of Chicago with muralist John Norton. He was a *Life* artist-correspondent seeing action in the Pacific, where he participated in the Marine landing on Peleliu, and in the North Atlantic. **(15)**

Warren Leopold. Biographical information not available. **(18)**

Jonas Lie was born in Norway in 1880. He studied at the National Academy of Design and at the Art Students League in New York City. His series of paintings of the Panama Canal was presented in 1929 to the U.S. Military Academy as a memorial to Maj. Gen. George W. Goethals. **(29)**

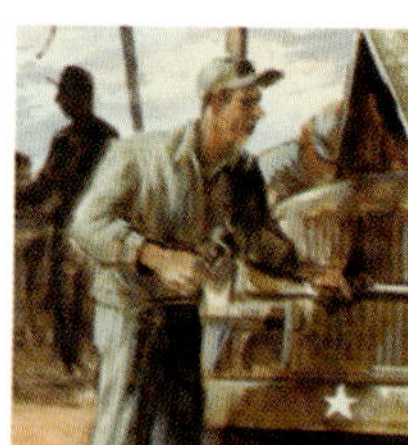

Carlos Lopez was born in 1908 in Havana, Cuba. He received his training at the Detroit Art Academy. Lopez was one of eight American artists commissioned by the War Department in 1942 to produce a series of paintings on American industry at war. In 1943 he was one of the civilian artists commissioned by the War Department to make a pictorial record of the war. He became a *Life* artist-correspondent in 1944. Lopez died in Ann Arbor, Michigan, in 1953. **(141, 145, 146, 149, 158, 170, 171)**

Dennis O. McGee was born May 1, 1940, in Chicago. He received his bachelor of arts degree in commercial art from San Jose State University in 1964. He was serving in Vietnam with the 34th Armored, a tank battalion near Long Binh, when he was selected to be a member of Soldier-Artist Team 3. **(135)**

Archie McLean. Biographical information not available. **(52)**

Ludwig Mactarian was born in New York City in 1908. He participated in the Works Progress Administration art programs, executing murals in the Agriculture Building and the United States post office in Dardenelle, Arkansas. As a sergeant with the 337th Engineers he served the Fifth Army in the European theater as an artist-correspondent. **(101)**

Hans Mangelsdorf was born in Leipzig, Germany, in 1903. He studied at the Industrial School of Ceramics in Bavaria and two years at the Academy of Fine Arts in Vienna. He was inducted into the Army September 9, 1942, and received his commission in the field in May 1945. Mangelsdorf received two commendations for his work as architect and assistant engineer officer for the Office of the Island Engineer on Saipan, Marianas. As chief of the Visual Documentary Section of the 2233d Engineer Construction Group he did drawings and paintings of engineer construction projects on the islands of the Western Pacific Base Command. In November 1945 Lieutenant Mangelsdorf joined the Combat Art Section of the Office of the Chief Engineer, General Headquarters, in Tokyo. Besides collecting Japanese war propaganda paintings, he covered activities of the occupation forces as well as of the people of Japan. **(129)**

Jeffrey T. Manuszak was born in Hammond, Indiana, on December 11, 1968. He studied in Chicago at Ray College of Design and continues independent studies at various schools. He enlisted in the Army in 1992 and holds the rank of specialist. **(172, 173)**

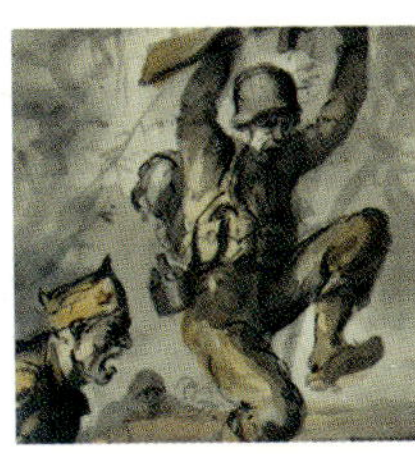

Reginald Marsh was born in Paris on March 14, 1898. He received his art education at Yale University and the Art Students League. He was a teacher at the Art Students League as well as a free-lance artist for many publications. He was an artist-correspondent for *Life* magazine in 1943. Marsh died in Dorst, Vermont, on July 3, 1954. **(17, 36)**

Fletcher Martin was born in Palisade, Colorado, in 1904. He was a self-taught artist. Martin served four years in the Navy from 1922–26. During World War II he was an artist-correspondent for *Life* magazine. He died in 1979. **(23, 151, 152, 163)**

Milton Marx was born in Chicago, January 11, 1898. He studied at the Art Institute of Chicago, the Chicago Academy of Fine Arts, the University of Illinois, the Art Students League, and Columbia University. Marx served with the Navy in World War I as an apprentice seaman. He enlisted in 1942 as a first lieutenant to do photo interpretation. He transferred to public relations with the Army Air Forces to illustrate the official history of the Ninth Air Force. **(150, 157, 164)**

Barse Miller was born January 24, 1904, in New York City. He studied at the National Academy of Design, New York City; the Pennsylvania Academy of Fine Arts, Philadelphia; and in Europe. He enlisted July 1, 1943, and was discharged April 10, 1946, with the rank of major. He served with the U.S. Army Corps of Engineers as the war art leader, Combat Art Section, for the Southwest Pacific Area. In September 1945 he received the Legion of Merit. Prior to his enlistment, he was commissioned by *Life* magazine to sketch the West Coast Defense Area in 1942. He died January 22, 1973. **(53, 125)**

Richard J. Peterson received his art training at St. Cloud State College, St. Cloud, Minnesota; Santa Monica City College, Santa Monica, California; San Fernando Valley State College, Northridge, California; and UCLA Extension, Los Angeles, California. Peterson entered the Army in September 1972 and was with the 76th Field Artillery in Europe at the time of his selection to participate in Soldier-Artist Team 14. He served with the team, documenting cold weather research, arctic test activities, and northern warfare training in Alaska from March 15 until his discharge September 15, 1974. Peterson died in June 1975. **(42)**

John Pike was born June 30, 1911, in Boston. He studied painting with Charles Hawthorn and portraiture with Richard Mill. In 1942 he received the American Watercolor Society Award. In the spring of 1943 he served as a civilian with psychological warfare organizations in Egypt, Corsica, southern France, and the Philippine Islands via India and China. On V–J Day he received the assignment from the combat engineers to head the Combat Art Section in Korea, the only civilian to head an art section. Pike died in 1979. **(132)**

Ogden Pleissner was born April 29, 1905, in Brooklyn, New York. He studied at the Art Students League, New York City, with F. J. Bost, George Bridgman, and Frank V. DuMond. He entered the Army Air Corps in January 1943 and was attached to the Eleventh Air Force in Alaska and the Aleutians. He depicted the activities of the Eleventh Air Force for *Life* magazine, which also sent him to Europe. He died in New York City in October 1983. **(40, 70)**

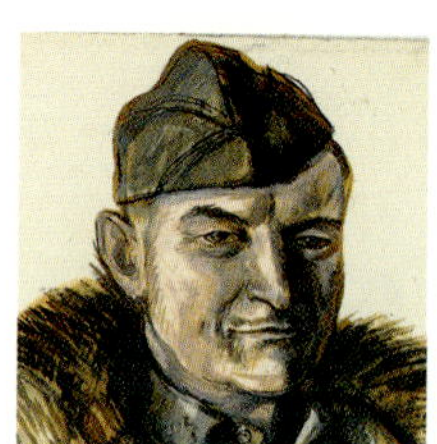

Henry Varnum Poor was born in 1888 in Chapman, Kansas. He studied art at Stanford University, California; Slade School, London; and the Julien Academie, Paris. He was an instructor at Stanford University and taught at the California School of Fine Arts. Under the Treasury's Section of Fine Arts, he executed twelve panels in fresco in the Department of Justice Building and fresco panels in the New Interior Building, Washington, D.C. He was drafted in 1918. During his service in France, he sketched continuously—his camp, his officers, his fellow soldiers. Poor was soon designated regimental artist and excused from all other duties. In World War II, he was a leader of a group of artists sent by the Army to Alaska and the Aleutians. He died December 8, 1970, in New York City. **(20, 55)**

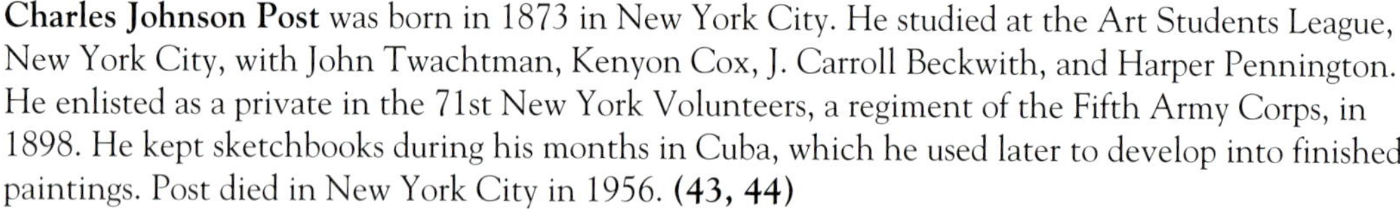

Charles Johnson Post was born in 1873 in New York City. He studied at the Art Students League, New York City, with John Twachtman, Kenyon Cox, J. Carroll Beckwith, and Harper Pennington. He enlisted as a private in the 71st New York Volunteers, a regiment of the Fifth Army Corps, in 1898. He kept sketchbooks during his months in Cuba, which he used later to develop into finished paintings. Post died in New York City in 1956. **(43, 44)**

William Pretyman. Biographical information not available. **(28)**

Roger W. Price graduated from high school in Reidsville, North Carolina, and immediately went into the Army where he continued art training with work in design, layout, illustration, and photography. He had achieved the rank of staff sergeant assigned to the Reprographics Section, U.S. Army Engineer Division, Europe, at the time of his selection to Soldier-Artist Team 25. For that assignment he documented the experiences of the 1st Armored Division in training in Germany and in celebration of the fiftieth anniversary of World War II, June–September 1990. **(86)**

Savo Radulovic was born January 27, 1911, in Niksich, Yugoslavia. He studied at Washington University, St. Louis, Missouri, and at Harvard University. He enlisted in July 1942 and was discharged November 1945 as a technical sergeant. He became a member of the Army Art Corps in 1943 and was sent to North Africa. Later he joined the 45th Infantry Division in Italy and participated in the battles for Cassino and Anzio. He received the Bronze Star and five Battle Stars for combat. **(78, 81)**

Allen C. Redwood was born on June 19, 1834, in Lancaster County, Virginia. He studied art at the Polytechnic Institute, Brooklyn, New York, while visiting with his father. In 1861 he joined the "Middlesex Southrons," which later became part of the 55th Virginia, and served through the war in the Army of Northern Virginia, achieving the rank of major. He was active in many major campaigns and participated in Maj. Gen. Jubal Early's attack on the defenses of Washington in 1864 as well as the Battle of Gettysburg. Redwood's own combat experience inspired him to portray the heroism of the Confederate soldier in his sketches and paintings. Redwood was injured three times and captured twice. After the war, he became a successful book and magazine illustrator, particularly known for his scenes of the war providing authentic documentation from the Southern side. He died at Asheville, North Carolina, on December 24, 1922. **(1)**

Edward A. Reep was born in Brooklyn, New York, in 1918. A graduate of the Art Center College of Design in Los Angeles, he enlisted in the Army in July 1942. He received a commission as a second lieutenant in 1942 and in 1943 accepted assignment in the Army Art Corps. He served in Africa and Italy, receiving two battlefield promotions, one for action on the Anzio beachhead. He served as a frontline artist throughout the Italian campaign, voluntarily participating in action as a combat soldier from time to time. For this he was awarded the Bronze Star. At the time of discharge, he was a captain. In 1971 Reep returned to Europe as a civilian artist for the Army Art Collection and documented his impressions of the Berlin Wall. **(68, 73, 92, 94, 96)**

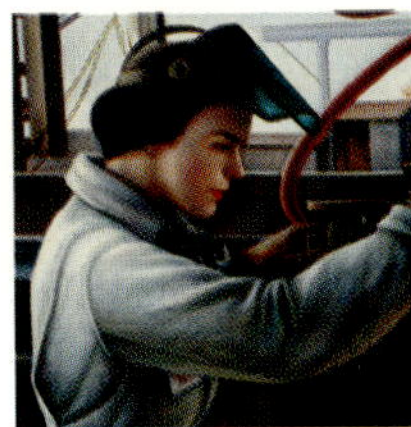

Edna Reindel was born in Detroit, Michigan, in 1900. She studied at the Pratt Institute in New York City. In 1943 she contacted Daniel Longwell about doing a series of paintings on the topic of women in war. Reindel visited the Lockheed and Vega plants in California which were building planes for the war effort. **(46, 47)**

Raymond R. Reuter is from New Jersey. He has a bachelor of arts degree in art education from Marshall University, Huntington, West Virginia. He was serving with the 101st Airborne Division when selected for Soldier-Artist Team 16 in 1975 to document the resettlement activities at the Vietnamese refugee camp at Fort Chaffee, Arkansas, and the U.S. Army in Japan. **(137)**

Paul Rickert was born in Philadelphia in 1947. He studied at the Los Angeles Art Center College of Design with his father, William H. Rickert, and with Nelson Shanks. A specialist, fourth class, Rickert was a member of the first soldier-artist team in Vietnam, from August–December 1966. **(130)**

John A. Ruge was born in Faribault, Minnesota, October 2, 1915. He attended the Art Students League of New York, studying under George Bridgman, Robert Brackman, and Frank V. DuMond. He had cartoons and illustrations accepted by the *New Yorker* and the *Saturday Evening Post* among other publications prior to his induction into the Army in September 1942. That civilian work experience was responsible for his transfer to the staff of *Yank* magazine. In 1944 *Yank* sent him to the Pacific theater where he was assigned to the battleship *Tennessee* before the invasion of Iwo Jima. He was on Okinawa until it was secured. Ruge was discharged on December 9, 1945, as a staff sergeant. He died in 1982. **(122)**

Edward A. Sallenback was born September 12, 1918, in Hood River, Oregon. He graduated from the Yale School of Fine Arts in 1942. He served in Headquarters Company, 390th Infantry, 98th Division, from November 1942–May 1945, when he joined the Visual Documentary Section of AFMIDPAC in Hawaii. Sallenback was discharged January 1946. He died in the late 1960s. **(127)**

Paul Sample was born September 14, 1896, in Louisville, Kentucky. He studied at Dartmouth College; the Greenleaf Art School, New York City; and the Otis Art Institute of Los Angeles. He also studied with Jonas Lie, F. Tolles Chamberlain, and Stanton MacDonald-Wright. In 1918–19 Sample took a leave of absence from Dartmouth College to serve in the U.S. Navy. In 1942 *Life* magazine commissioned him to portray the strength and beauty of the naval air war. He was accredited as a naval correspondent and for months lived on the job seeing firsthand how planes operate. He died February 26, 1974. **(134)**

Robert Sankner was born April 19, 1951, in Carteret, New Jersey. He received a bachelor of arts degree in fine arts from Newark State College in 1973 and a degree in fine arts from Niagara County Community College, Sanborn, New York, in 1980. Sankner enlisted in the Army in October 1975 and received his commission from Officer Candidate School in 1976. He held the rank of major in the U.S. Army Reserve when selected for Soldier-Artist Team 30 to document the Army in the Canal Zone, Panama, from August–November 1992. **(14, 39)**

Joseph Santoro graduated from the Vesper George School of Art. He received the Louis C. Tiffany grant and many other prizes and awards. As a civilian he spent time at Fort Sill, Oklahoma, documenting Army activities in 1970. **(7)**

Kenneth J. Scowcroft studied with the Famous Artist Commercial School and the Graphic Arts Facility at Fort Huachuca, Arizona, and received a degree from the University of Arizona. A specialist, sixth class, Scowcroft was a member of Soldier-Artist Team 3 which served in Vietnam from February–June 1967. **(131)**

Joseph Gary Sheahan was born July 14, 1893, in Winnetka, Illinois. He studied at the Chicago Art Institute; the Academy of Fine Arts, Chicago; and the AEF University, Beaune, Cote d'Or, France. Sheahan was the staff artist for the *Chicago Tribune* for thirty-two years. Many of his watercolors and drawings were printed in the *Tribune*. He died January 14, 1978, in Laguna Beach, California. **(74, 90)**

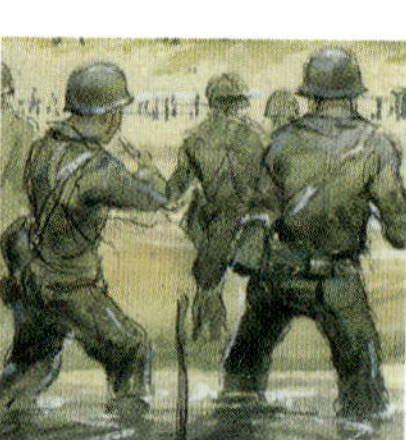

Stephen H. Sheldon was born April 19, 1943. He studied at the Art Center College of Design in Los Angeles. He held the rank of private when he served as a member of Soldier-Artist Team 3 in Vietnam from February–June 1967. **(128)**

Mitchell Siporin was born in New York City in 1910. He was a graduate of Crane Junior College and the Art Institute of Chicago. Under the Section of Fine Arts of the Treasury Department, he won two national open competitions. Together with Edward Willman he won the largest mural competition for the decoration in fresco of the public foyer in the new main St. Louis post office. Siporin was inducted December 4, 1942, and assigned to the North African theater in April 1943 to cover the Italian campaign as a member of the North African War Art Unit. He died June 11, 1976, in New York City. **(95, 105)**

M. W. Slaughter. Biographical information not available. **(33)**

Jules Andre Smith was born in Hong Kong in 1880. He received his art training in architecture from Cornell University. He was a first lieutenant in the Engineer Reserve Corps as a member of a camouflage unit before being selected for the AEF War Art Program. He was commissioned a captain and went to France in 1917 until the war's end. Smith died in 1959. **(79, 85)**

Lawrence Beall Smith was born in Washington, D.C., in 1909. He studied at the University of Chicago and the Art Institute of Chicago. He was an accredited war correspondent sent to the European Theater of Operations by Abbott Laboratories to gather material pertaining to the U.S. Army Medical Corps. The paintings were given to the Army for its permanent collection. **(102)**

Samuel D. Smith was born in Thorndale, Texas, on February 11, 1918. He is a self-taught artist. Smith was inducted in February 1941 and began his military career in New Mexico with the 45th Division. He was transferred to Camp Barkley, Texas, to paint murals for the Service Club and the Officers Club and to do a series of paintings on infantry weapons. He was selected by the War Art Advisory Committee to participate in the war art program. Smith was shipped to Accra, Gold Coast, where he was assigned to work with Carlos Lopez, a *Life* correspondent. He also covered the ground and air activities of the Army Transport Command in the Africa-India territory. **(166)**

Xanthus Smith. Biographical information not available. **(12)**

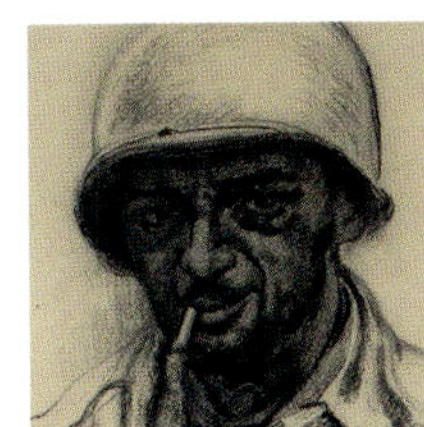

Harrison Standley was born July 11, 1916, in San Francisco, California. He studied at Stanford University, Pomona College, and the Art Center College of Design in Los Angeles. He was inducted in April 1941. He was assigned to the Army Historical Section and sent first to air bases in England. He hitchhiked to OMAHA Beach, Normandy, a week after D-Day, then was assigned to the First Army doing paintings and sketches of the invasion from Normandy to the Rhine River in Germany. Standley was discharged in September 1945 with the rank of technical sergeant. **(87, 93)**

William H. Steel graduated from Redwood High School, Larkspur, California, in 1964 and the California School of Arts and Design in Oakland, California, in 1968. He was a private, first class, assigned to Headquarters and Headquarters Company, lst Brigade, 5th Infantry Division (Mechanized). He was selected for Soldier-Artist Team 10, February–June 1970, to document U.S. Army activities in Korea. **(112, 120)**

Frank M. Thomas was born February 7, 1939, in La Habra, California. He studied art and education at Brigham Young University and the University of South Carolina. He is an art and history instructor in Utah and has his own studio. Colonel Thomas was called to six months' active duty to document DESERT STORM. **(156)**

Manuel Tolegian was born in Fresno, California, October 18, 1912. He graduated from Manual Arts High School in Los Angeles in 1930 and then completed four years at the Art Students League in New York City. John Sloan, Thomas Hart Benton, and John Steuart Curry were his professors. He completed a series of paintings on Army Nurse Corps training at Camp White, Oregon, under contract to Abbott Laboratories. **(49)**

James Barre Turnbull was born in St. Louis, Missouri, in 1909. He attended the University of Missouri and Washington University in St. Louis. He later studied at the St. Louis School of Fine Arts and at the Pennsylvania Academy of Art in Philadelphia. In 1938 he was director of the Works Progress Administration's art project in Missouri. Turnbull documented two areas of the war for *Life* magazine, training at the Caribbean Army Base and in the Pacific. He took part in the landing at Luzon's Lingayen Gulf. He died in Florida on December 10, 1976. **(31, 54, 57)**

Peter G. Varisano was born in Kane, Pennsylvania, in 1956. He received his bachelor of fine arts degree from Vermont College in 1994. He entered the Army in 1974. Sergeant Varisano was an instructor at the basic course and then at advanced courses at the NCO Illustrators School, Lowry Air Force Base, Colorado, from 1984–91. He participated in two art teams, the first in 1989 documenting training with the Wisconsin National Guard. In 1990 he was called upon to document DESERT SHIELD in the Persian Gulf. He also depicted Army activities in Florida following Hurricane Andrew and in Somalia in 1993. **(vi, 20, 21, 22, 143, 147, 161, 165)**

Frede Vidar was born June 6, 1911, in Asko, Denmark. He studied at the California School of Fine Arts, the University of California, and the Royal Academy of Denmark. He also studied with Diego Rivera. He enlisted in the Army August 5, 1942. He served three years' combat duty in the Pacific as official U.S. Army combat artist where he participated in the initial landing on and operations through New Guinea, New Britain, the Philippines, and Japan. He was discharged in January 1946 with the rank of major. Vidar died January 12, 1967, in Ann Arbor, Michigan. **(109, 114, 117)**

William F. Voiland was born in 1948 and educated at Washington State University, Pullman, Washington. While still in college he started his own design business, doing silkscreen posters, commissioned artwork, and portraits. He was drafted in 1971. At the time of his selection to Soldier-Artist Team 13, Voiland held the rank of specialist, fourth class, in the 4th Infantry Division. He documented activities of the U.S. Army in Germany from October–December 1972. **(85)**

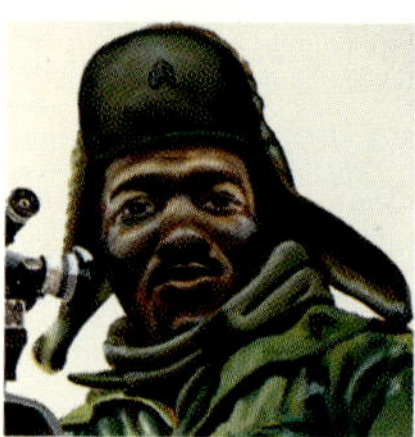

Rudolph C. Von Ripper was born January 29, 1905, in Klausenburg, Austria-Hungary. He studied at the Art Academy in Duesseldorf, Germany. As a free-lance artist he did four posters for the Office of War Information. He was inducted in September 1942 and discharged in May 1945 with the rank of captain. He went to North Africa as an artist-correspondent in May 1943. When the program was terminated, he transferred to the Military Intelligence Service. He served with the 34th Infantry Division in Italy. He was attached to the 168th Infantry in September 1943. He volunteered to lead patrols behind the lines and many times fought with the vanguard of the division. He was wounded twice and decorated for valor in action on the field of battle. **(169)**

James Walker was born June 8, 1818, in England. He was largely a self-taught artist. He was living in Mexico City in 1846 when the Mexican War began. Walker offered his services as interpreter to the staff of Brig. Gen. William J. Worth and was present at the Battles of Contreras, Churubusco, and Chapultepec and the capture of Mexico City. In 1864 he spent several months with the Army of the Cumberland and ultimately was commissioned by Maj. Gen. Joseph Hooker to paint the *Battle of Lookout Mountain*. Walker died in Watsonville, California, in 1889. **(25, 27)**

John Wheat was born in New York City in 1920. He studied at the Art Students League and the Yale School of Fine Arts. During World War II he was an artist with the Office of Strategic Services. He was a civilian artist for the U.S. Army in Vietnam, February 15–March 15, 1968. **(113)**

Robert A. Winter studied at Monterey Peninsula College before joining the Army in March 1971. He held the rank of specialist, fourth class, assigned to the 4th Infantry Division at the time of his selection for Soldier-Artist Team 13, which spent October–December 1972 documenting Army activities in Germany. **(103)**

A Brief History
of the Army Art Collection

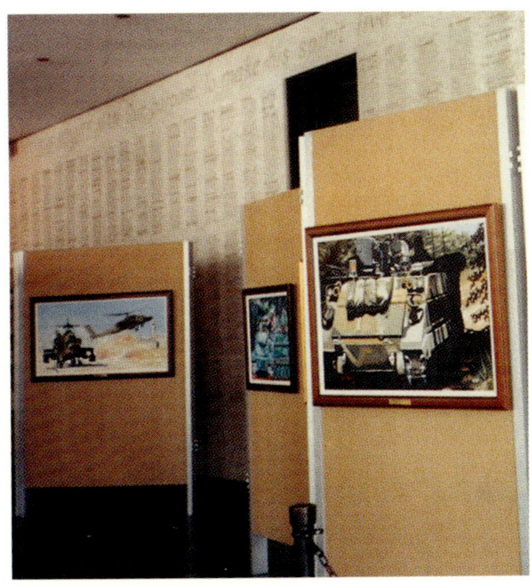

THE ARMY'S OFFICIAL INTEREST IN ART ORIGINATED IN World War I when eight artists were commissioned as captains in the Corps of Engineers and sent to Europe to record the activities of the American Expeditionary Forces. At the end of the war most of the team's artwork went to the Smithsonian Institution, which at that time was the custodian of Army historical property and art.

There was no Army program for acquiring art during the interwar years, but with the advent of World War II the Corps of Engineers, drawing on its World War I experience, established a War Art Unit in late 1942. The War Art Advisory Committee, a select group of civilian art experts, nominated military and civilian artists to serve in the unit. By the spring of 1943 the committee had selected 42 artists: 23 active duty military and 19 civilians. The first artists were sent to the Pacific theater, but in May 1943 Congress withdrew funding from the program and the War Art Unit was inactivated. The Army assigned the military artists to other units and released the civilians.

The effort to create a visual record of the American military experience in World War II was then taken up by the private sector in two different programs, one by *Life* magazine and one by Abbott Laboratories, a large medical supply company. When *Life* offered to employ civilian artists as war correspondents, the War Department agreed to provide them the same support already being given to print and film correspondents. Seventeen of the nineteen civilian artists who had been selected by the War Art Advisory Committee joined *Life* as war correspondents. Abbott, in coordination with the Army's Office of the Surgeon General, commissioned twelve artists to record the work of the Army Medical Corps. These two programs resulted in a wide range of work by distinguished artists who had the opportunity to observe the war firsthand.

In June 1944 Congress reconsidered its position on military art and authorized the Army to use soldier-artists. The Adjutant General reactivated the War Art Unit in the Pacific with headquarters in Manila. The soldier-artists assigned to the unit produced images of the war in the Philippines, China, Japan, and Korea until it was inactivated in 1946. Soldier-artists assigned to *Yank*, the Army weekly newspaper, and to Army historical units also created visual images of their impressions of the war. In addition, a number of other soldier-artists who worked on their own contributed much of their work to the Army during the course of the war.

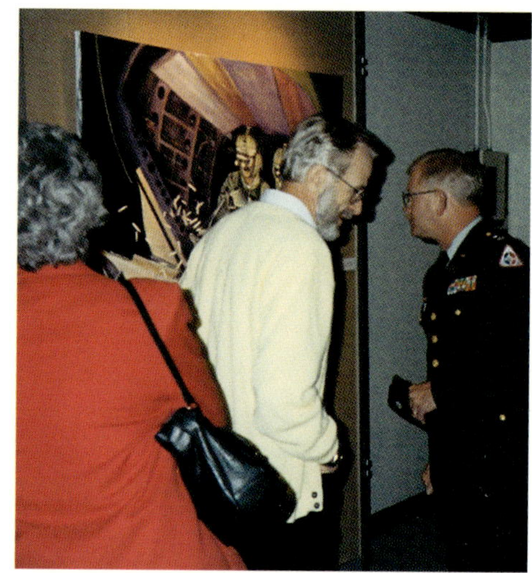

By the end of World War II the Army had acquired over 2,000 pieces of art. In June 1945 the Army established a Historical Properties Section to maintain and exhibit this collection, thus creating the nucleus of today's Army Art Collection. The *Life* and Abbott collections initially were not included, but the 240 Abbott medical paintings became part of the Army's collection in 1946, and in 1960 the *Time-Life* Corporation donated its 1,050 World War II paintings as well.

There was no organized effort by either the Army or the private sector to visually capture the Korean War, so the Army's collection has relatively few images of that war. The few pieces that do exist have come mainly from soldier-artists who recorded their impressions and later donated their artwork to the Army.

During the Vietnam conflict the Army renewed its interest in using artists to create a visual record of its activities. In 1966 the Chief of Military History, who had been given responsibility for the Army Art Collection in 1952, instituted an art program that used both military and civilian artists to record images of that war. Between 1966 and 1969 a total of forty-two soldier-artists served four- or five-month tours of duty in Vietnam producing paintings. In addition ten civilian artists, hosted by the Army, toured Vietnam for thirty-day periods where they gathered impressions of the war. They then turned these impressions into completed artwork in studios on their return home. The images which resulted from this program also joined the Army Art Collection.

Following the Vietnam War, the Army continued to use both soldier and civilian artists. They have covered such peacetime activities as summer training for Reserve Officers' Training Corps (ROTC) cadets, Army National Guard annual training, and tank gunnery training in Europe. The Army Art Collection has also acquired depictions of the Army's operations in Panama and Operations DESERT SHIELD and DESERT STORM.

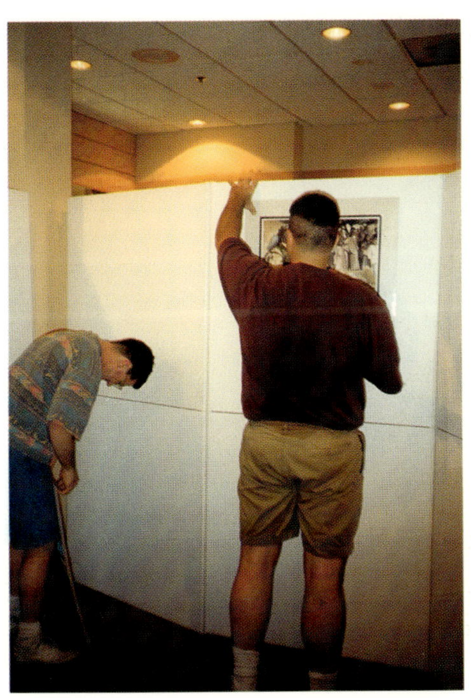

The Army Art Collection presently comprises over 10,000 pieces of art. Through donations and limited acquisitions the collection now includes artwork which depicts images from virtually every conflict in which the Army has fought, as well as its role in disaster relief, such as in the wake of Hurricane Andrew and in Somalia. The Army has no separate art gallery to display its holdings, but many of the paintings are on public display in Army museums, Army installations, and at the Pentagon. Pieces from the collection are also loaned to appropriate agencies for short periods of time, and, in addition, the Center of Military History sponsors several traveling exhibits throughout the Army. Finally, the Center also hosts special openings featuring recently acquired artwork. Permanent exhibits at the Pentagon include the official portraits of the Commanding Generals and Chiefs of Staff of the Army and the Secretaries of War and of the Army. A portion of the *Time-Life* collection is also on permanent display in the Pentagon.

Within the U.S. Army Center of Military History, the Art and Exhibits Branch maintains the Army Art Collection and creates exhibits drawn from it. It also responds to queries from within the Army and from veterans, researchers, and the general public and deals directly with individuals who wish to donate artwork to the collection. Such donations have greatly contributed to the continual growth of the collection over the years.

PIN : 073232-000